SINGAPORE

INSOLVENCY (BANKRUPTCY) LAWS AND REGULATIONS HANDBOOK

STRATEGIC INFORMATION AND REGULATIONS

International Business Publications, USA
Washington DC, USA-Singapore

SINGAPORE

INSOLVENCY (BANKRUPTCY) LAWS AND REGULATIONS HANDBOOK

STRATEGIC INFORMATION AND REGULATIONS

UPDATED ANNUALLY

We express our sincere appreciation to all government agencies and international organizations which provided information and other materials for this handbook

Cover Design: International Business Publications, USA

2015 Edition Updated Reprint International Business Publications, USA
ISBN 1-4330-8563-1

For customer service and information, please contact:
in the USA: **International Business Publications, USA**
P.O.Box 15343, Washington, DC 20003
Phone: (202) 546-2103, Fax: (202) 546-3275.
E-mail: rusric@erols.com

Printed in the USA

SINGAPORE

INSOLVENCY (BANKRUPTCY) LAWS AND REGULATIONS HANDBOOK

STRATEGIC INFORMATION AND REGULATIONS

TABLE OF CONTENTS

STRATEGIC AND BUSINESS PROFILES 8

SINGAPORE: STRATEGIC AND BUSINESS PROFILE 8
Geography 9
People 11
Government 12
Economy 13
ENERGY 17
Communications 19
Transportation 19
Military 20
Transnational Issues 20
IMPORTANT INFORMATION FOR UNDERSTANDING SINGAPORE 20
IMPORTANT FACTS 20
HISTORY 22
GOVERNMENT 22
POLITICAL CONDITIONS 23
ECONOMY 24
DEFENSE 27
FOREIGN RELATIONS 27
U.S.-SINGAPORE RELATIONS 28

INSOLVENCY (BANKRUPTCY) LAWS AND REGULATIONS IN SINGAPORE 29

BASIC PROCEDURES 29
Requirements 30
Procedure 30
Notification Requirements 33
CORPORATE INSOLVENCY 33

INSOLVENCY (BANKRUPTCY) LAWS AND REGULATIONS - STRATEGIC INFORMATION 36

Self money management 36
Negotiate with creditors 37
Debt restructuring 37
Debt consolidation 37
Formal proposal to creditors 37
Individual voluntary arrangement 37

IMPORTANT LAWS AND REGULATIONS FOR INSOLVENCY (BANKRUPTCY) PROCEDURES 39

BANKRUPTCY ACT 1995 39
PART IPRELIMINARY 39
PART II CONSTITUTION, PROCEDURE AND POWERS OF COURT 41
PART III OFFICIAL ASSIGNEE 44
PART IV TRUSTEE IN BANKRUPTCY 48
PART V VOLUNTARY ARRANGEMENTS 52

PART VI PROCEEDINGS IN BANKRUPTCY ... *57*
PART VII ADMINISTRATION IN BANKRUPTCY ... *65*
PART VIII ANNULMENT AND DISCHARGE ... *91*
PART IX DUTIES, DISQUALIFICATION AND DISABILITIES OF BANKRUPT ... *95*
PART X BANKRUPTCY OFFENCES ... *97*
PART XI MISCELLANEOUS PROVISIONS ... *102*
TRANSITIONAL PROVISIONS AND SAVINGS ... *109*

PRACTICAL INFORMATION FOR CONDUCTING BUSINESS ... **113**

STARTING BUSINESS IN SINGAPORE BASICS ... 113
STARTING A BUSINESS IN SINGAPORE ... 113
LICENSING AND REGISTRATION OF BUSINESS ORGANISATIONS ... *113*
FORMATION OF REPRESENTATIVE OFFICE ... *113*
TYPES OF BUSINESS ORGANISATIONS ... *113*
REGISTRATION ... *113*
Foreign Companies ... *114*
Market Overview ... *114*
Market Challenges ... *114*
Market Opportunities ... *115*
Market Entry Strategy ... *116*
How to Register a Local Company in Singapore ... *116*
HOW TO REGISTER A FOREIGN COMPANY IN SINGAPORE ... 117
What is a Foreign Company? ... *117*
Registration of a Foreign Company ... *117*
TDB Traders Registration System (TTRS) ... *118*
General Information on Companies ... *118*
INVESTMENT CLIMATE ... 120
Openness to Foreign Investment ... *120*
Conversion and Transfer Policies ... *124*
Expropriation and Compensation ... *124*
Dispute Settlement ... *124*
Performance Requirements and Incentives ... *124*
Right to Private Ownership and Establishment ... *124*
Protection of Property Rights ... *125*
Transparency of Regulatory System ... *126*
Efficient Capital Markets and Portfolio Investment ... *127*
Competition from State Owned Enterprises ... *127*
Corporate Social Responsibility ... *128*
Political Violence ... *128*
Corruption ... *128*
Anti-Corruption Resources ... *131*
Bilateral Investment Agreements ... *132*
OPIC and Other Investment Insurance Programs ... *132*
Labor ... *132*
Foreign-Trade Zones/Free Ports ... *133*
INVESTMENT INCENTIVES ... *136*
SELLING U.S. PRODUCTS AND SERVICES ... 138
Using an Agent or Distributor ... *138*
Establishing an Office ... *138*
Representative Office ... *138*
Branch Office ... *138*
Franchising ... *138*
Direct Marketing ... *139*
Joint Ventures/Licensing ... *139*
Selling to the Government ... *139*
Distribution and Sales Channels ... *139*
Selling Factors/Techniques ... *140*
Trade Promotion and Advertising ... *140*
Pricing ... *140*

Sales Service/Customer Support ... *140*
Protecting Intellectual Property ... *140*
Protecting Intellectual Property in Singapore: ... *141*
IP Resources ... *142*
Due Diligence ... *142*
Local Professional Services ... *142*
Web Resources ... *143*
LEADING SECTORS FOR U.S. EXPORT AND INVESTMENT ... 143
Electronics Components (ELC) ... *143*
Oil & Gas (OGS) ... *145*
Aircraft and Parts (AIR) ... *146*
Pollution Control Equipment (POL) ... *147*
Computer Hardware/Software/Peripherals (CPT/CSF) ... *148*
Telecommunication Equipment & Services (TEL/TES) ... *149*
Laboratory & Scientific Instruments (LAB) ... *151*
Medical Devices (MED) ... *152*
Education / Training Services (EDS) ... *154*
Wealth Management / Financial Planning ... *155*
Franchising (FRA) ... *155*
Agricultural Sectors ... *156*
TRADE REGULATIONS, CUSTOMS AND STANDARDS ... 158
Import Tariffs ... *158*
Trade Barriers ... *158*
Import Requirements and Documentation ... *159*
Bona Fide Trade Samples ... *159*
U.S. Export Controls ... *159*
Temporary Entry ... *160*
Admission Temporaire/Temporary Admission (ATA) Carnet ... *160*
Labeling and Marking Requirements ... *160*
Prohibited and Restricted Imports ... *161*
Customs Regulations and Contact Information Customs Regulations ... *161*
Free Trade Zone/Warehouses ... *161*
Standards ... *162*
Trade Agreements ... *165*
TRADE AND PROJECT FINANCING ... 167
Methods of Payment ... *167*
Banking System ... *167*
Foreign-Exchange Controls ... *168*
U.S. Banks and Local Correspondent Banks ... *168*
Project Financing ... *168*
BUSINESS TRAVEL ... 169
Business Customs ... *169*
Visa Requirements ... *170*
Telecommunications ... *171*
Transportation ... *171*
Language ... *171*
Health ... *172*
Local Time, Business Hours, and Holidays ... *172*
Temporary Entry of Materials and Personal Belongings ... *173*
IMPORTANT CONTACTS ... 173
List of Banks ... *177*

SELECTED BUSINESS OPPORTUNITIES WITH THE GOVERNMENT ... 180

REGISTRATION AS A GOVERNMENT CONTRACTOR/SUPPLIER OF EXPENDITURE & PROCUREMENT ... 180
FREQUENTLY ASKED QUESTIONS ON REGISTRATION AS A GOVERNMENT SUPPLIER ... *180*
REGISTRATION AS A GOVERNMENT SUPPLIER WITH MINISTRY OF FINANCE - EPPU (GUIDELINES FOR APPLICANTS) ... 181
APPLICATION PROCEDURES ... *181*
PROCESSING OF APPLICATIONS ... *182*

OUTCOME OF APPLICATIONS ... 182
APPROVAL ... 183
APPLICATION FOR UPGRADING ... 183
CHANGE OF PARTICULARS ... 183
PROCESSING FEE ... 183
CONDITIONS OF REGISTRATION ... 183
VALIDITY OF REGISTRATION & RENEWAL ... 184
REGISTRATION HEADS OF SUPPLY ... 184
EVENT MANAGEMENT, BOOTHS, STAGE, BACKDROP & LIGHTING ETC ... 187
(C) HEADS OF REGISTRATION UNDER MEDICAL/EQUIPMENTS ... 188
REGISTRATION REQUISITES TRACK RECORD, PAID-UP CAPITAL ... 189
CRITERIA FOR REGISTRATION ... 191
EXPERIENCE ... 191
EXAMPLE ... 191
INFORMATION ON EPPU HEAD REFERENCES & HEAD DESCRIPTION ... 192
SELECTED BUSINESS OPPORTUNITIES IN HEALTH SECTOR ... 196
PRE-QUALIFICATION OF CONTRACTORS FOR ADDITION, ALTERATION AND INTERIOR RENOVATION WORKS FOR THE SINGHEALTH GROUP ... 196
Hospitals ... 196
Speciality Centres ... 196
Polyclinics ... 196
EXPORTS REGULATIONS ... 197
Separate Applications ... 197
General Conditions of Approval ... 198
Usage of the CCP ... 198
Export Control ... 198
Export of Goods under ATA Carnet ... 198
LIST OF CONTROLLED GOODS: EXPORTS ... 199
LIST OF CONTROLLED GOODS: IMPORTS ... 202
IMPORT REGULATIONS: QUESTIONS AND ANSWERS ... 204
IMPORTS PROCEDURES ... 204
APPLYING FOR A CENTRAL REGISTRATION NUMBER ... 207
APPLYING FOR A CENTRAL REGISTRATION NUMBER ... 208
TDB PERMIT APPLICATIONS ... 209
JOINT PERMIT APPLICATIONS ... 210
IMPORT CERTIFICATE AND DELIVERY VERIFICATION ... 211
HS CLASSIFICATION ... 216
STARTING A BUSINESS IN SINGAPORE ... 244
LICENSING AND REGISTRATION OF BUSINESS ORGANISATIONS ... 244
FORMATION OF REPRESENTATIVE OFFICE ... 244
TYPES OF BUSINESS ORGANISATIONS ... 244
REGISTRATION ... 244
Foreign Companies ... 245
GOODS MANUFACTURED ... 245
REGISTERING A COMPANY INSINGAPORE ... 246
What is a Business Firm? ... 246
1. Sole-proprietorship ... 247
2. Partnership ... 247
Setting Up A Business Firm In Singapore ... 247
Question-and-Answer Session for Business Registration Department ... 248
Company Forms ... 249
REGISTERING A COMPANY ... 254
Types of Companies ... 254
In Singapore, the three main types of companies are : ... 254
How to Register a Local Company in Singapore ... 254
HOW TO REGISTER A FOREIGN COMPANY IN SINGAPORE ... 255
Registration of a Foreign Company ... 255
TDB Traders Registration System (TTRS) ... 256
General Information on Companies ... 256

TDB Traders Registration System (TTRS) ... 258

BUSINESS TRAVEL ... **259**

Business Customs ... 259
Travel Advisory and Visas ... 259
Holidays ... 259
Workweek ... 260
Business Infrastructure ... 260
Temporary entry of goods ... 261

SUPPLEMENTS ... **262**

BANKRUPTCY LAWYERS IN SINGAPORE ... 262
STRATEGIC GOVERNMENT AND BUSINESS CONTACTS ... 266
U.S. Government Contacts ... 266
Singapore Government Agencies ... 266
Trade Associations/Chambers of Commerce in Singapore ... 271
Singapore Contacts by Industry ... 271
SINGAPORE MARKET RESEARCH FIRMS ... 276
MAJOR COMMERCIAL BANKS IN SINGAPORE ... 276
U.S.-BASED MULTIPLIERS RELEVANT FOR SINGAPORE ... 277
Important U.S. Government contacts in the United States ... 278
U.S. BANKS IN SINGAPORE ... 279
STOCK BROKERS; MEMBER COMPANIES ... 279
INTERNATIONAL MEMBERS; MEMBER COMPANIES ... 282
BASIC TITLES ON SINGAPORE ... 283

STRATEGIC AND BUSINESS PROFILES

SINGAPORE: STRATEGIC AND BUSINESS PROFILE

Capital	Singapore (Downtown Core, Central) [1] 1°17′N 103°50′E1.283°N 103.833°E
Official language(s)	English Malay Chinese Tamil
Official scripts	English alphabet Malay alphabet Simplified Chinese Tamil script
Demonym	Singaporean
Government	Parliamentary republic
- President	S.R. Nathan
- Prime Minister	Lee Hsien Loong
- Speaker of Parliament	Abdullah Tarmugi
- Chief Justice	Chan Sek Keong
Legislature	Parliament
	Formation
- Founding	6 February 1819
- Self-government	3 June 1959
- Independence from the United Kingdom	31 August 1963
- Merger with Malaysia	16 September 1963
- Separation from Malaysia	9 August 1965
	Area
- Total	710.2 km^2 (187th) 274.2 sq mi
- Water (%)	1.444
	Population
- 2009 estimate	4,987,600 (36% foreigners)
- 2010 census	5,076,700
- Density	7,022/km^2 (3rd) 17,275.7/sq mi
GDP (PPP)	2010 estimate
- Total	$255.338 billion
- Per capita	$57,238 (3rd)
GDP (nominal)	2010 estimate
- Total	$194.918 billion
- Per capita	$42,653 (15th)
Gini (1998)	42.5
HDI (2010)	▲0.846 (very high) (27th)
Currency	Singapore dollar (SGD)
Time zone	SST (UTC+8)
Date formats	dd/mm/yyyy
Drives on the	left
ISO 3166 code	SG
Internet TLD	.sg
Calling code	+65

Singapore □ˈ/□s□ŋəp□r/, officially the **Republic of Singapore**, is a Southeast Asian island city-state off the southern tip of the Malay Peninsula, 137 kilometres (85 mi) north of the equator. An island country made up of 63 islands, it is separated from Malaysia by the Straits of Johor to its north and from Indonesia's Riau Islands by the Singapore Strait to its south. The country is highly urbanised with very little primary rainforest remaining, although more land is being created for development through land reclamation.

Part of various local empires since being inhabited in the second century AD, Singapore hosted a trading post of the East India Company in 1819 with permission from the Johor Sultanate. The British obtained sovereignty over the island in 1824 and Singapore became one of the British Straits Settlements in 1826. Occupied by the Japanese during World War II, Singapore declared independence from the United Kingdom, uniting with other former British territories to form Malaysia in 1963, although it was separated from Malaysia two years later. Since then it has had a massive increase in wealth, and is one of the Four Asian Tigers.

Singapore is the world's fourth-leading financial centre, and its port is one of the five busiest ports in the world. The economy depends heavily on exports and refining imported goods, especially in manufacturing, which constituted 26% of Singapore's GDP in 2005. In terms of purchasing power parity, Singapore has the third-highest per capita income in the world.

Singapore is a unitary multiparty parliamentary republic with a Westminster system of unicameral parliamentary government. The People's Action Party has won every election since self-government in 1959. Slightly over five million people live in Singapore, of which 2.91 million were born locally. The population is highly diverse; the majority are Chinese with almost 75% of the total population, while Malays and Indians forming significant minorities. Reflecting this diversity, the country has four official languages: English, Malay, Chinese, and Tamil. One of the five founding members of the Association of South East Asian Nations (ASEAN) , the country is also the host of the APEC Secretariat, and a member of the East Asia Summit, the Non-Aligned Movement, and the Commonwealth.

GEOGRAPHY

Location: Southeastern Asia, islands between Malaysia and Indonesia

Geographic coordinates: 1 22 N, 103 48 E
Map references: Southeast Asia
Area:
total: 647.5 sq km
land: 637.5 sq km
water: 10 sq km
Area - comparative: slightly more than 3.5 times the size of Washington, DC
Land boundaries: 0 km
Coastline: 193 km

Maritime claims:
exclusive fishing zone: within and beyond territorial sea, as defined in treaties and practice
territorial sea: 3 nm

Climate: tropical; hot, humid, rainy; no pronounced rainy or dry seasons; thunderstorms occur on 40% of all days (67% of days in April)

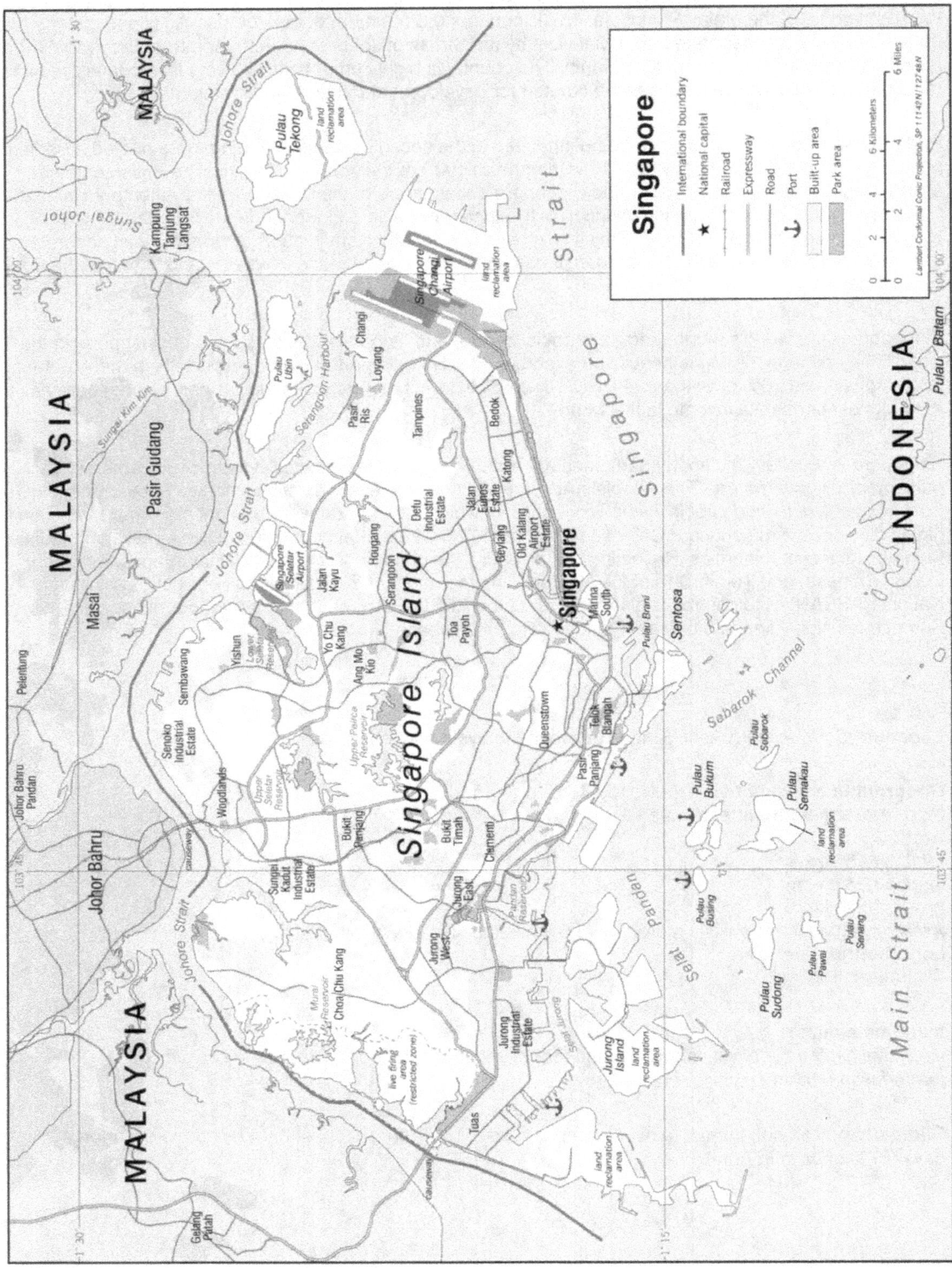

Terrain: lowland; gently undulating central plateau contains water catchment area and nature preserve

Elevation extremes:
lowest point: Singapore Strait 0 m
highest point: Bukit Timah 166 m

Natural resources: fish, deepwater ports

Land use:
arable land: 2%
permanent crops: 6%
permanent pastures: 0%
forests and woodland: 5%
other: 87%

Irrigated land: NA sq km
Natural hazards: NA

Environment - current issues: industrial pollution; limited natural fresh water resources; limited land availability presents waste disposal problems; seasonal smoke/haze resulting from forest fires in Indonesia

Environment - international agreements:
party to: Biodiversity, Climate Change, Desertification, Endangered Species, Hazardous Wastes, Law of the Sea, Nuclear Test Ban, Ozone Layer Protection, Ship Pollution
signed, but not ratified: none of the selected agreements

Geography - note: focal point for Southeast Asian sea routes

PEOPLE

Population: 4,151,264

Age structure:
0-14 years: 18% (male 390,352; female 365,730)
15-64 years: 75% (male 1,520,875; female 1,590,355)
65 years and over: 7% (male 124,413; female 159,539)

Population growth rate: 3.54%
Birth rate: 12.79 births/1,000 population
Death rate: 4.21 deaths/1,000 population
Net migration rate: 26.8 migrant(s) /1,000 population

Sex ratio:
at birth: 1.08 male(s) /female
under 15 years: 1.07 male(s) /female
15-64 years: 0.96 male(s) /female
65 years and over: 0.78 male(s) /female
total population: 0.96 male(s) /female

Infant mortality rate: 3.65 deaths/1,000 live births

Life expectancy at birth:
total population: 80.05 years
male: 77.1 years
female: 83.23 years

Total fertility rate: 1.16 children born/woman

Nationality:
noun: Singaporean(s)
adjective: Singapore
Ethnic groups: Chinese 77%, Malay 14%, Indian 7.6%, other 1.4%
Religions: Buddhist (Chinese) , Muslim (Malays) , Christian, Hindu, Sikh, Taoist, Confucianist
Languages: Chinese (official) , Malay (official and national) , Tamil (official) , English (official)
Literacy:
definition: age 15 and over can read and write
total population: 91.1%
male: 95.9%
female: 86.3%

GOVERNMENT

Country name:
conventional long form: Republic of Singapore
conventional short form: Singapore

Data code: SN
Government type: parliamentary republic
Capital: Singapore
Administrative divisions: none
Independence: 9 August 1965 (from Malaysia)
National holiday: National Day, 9 August (1965)
Constitution: 3 June 1959, amended 1965 (based on preindependence State of Singapore Constitution)
Legal system: based on English common law; has not accepted compulsory ICJ jurisdiction
Suffrage: 21 years of age; universal and compulsory

Executive branch:

chief of state: President Tony TAN Keng Yam (since 1 September 2011)

head of government: Prime Minister LEE Hsien Loong (since 12 August 2010) ; Deputy Prime Minister TEO Chee Hean (since 1 April 2009) and Deputy Prime Minister Tharman SHANMUGARATNAM (since 21 May 2011)

cabinet: appointed by president, responsible to parliament

elections: president elected by popular vote for six-year term; election last held on 27 August 2011 (next to be held by August 2017) ; following legislative elections, leader of majority party or leader of majority coalition usually appointed prime minister by president; deputy prime ministers appointed by president

election results: Tony TAN Keng Yam elected president from a field of four candidates with 35.2% of the votes cast

Legislative branch:

nicameral Parliament (87 seats; members elected by popular vote to serve five-year terms) ; note - in addition, there are up to nine nominated members (NMP) and up to nine Non-Constituency Members of Parliament (NCMP) ; traditionally, members of parties that came closest to winning seats may be appointed as NCMPs; NMPs are appointed by the president to ensure that a wide range of community views are present in Parliament; NMPs are independent and non-partisan members

elections: last held on 7 May 2011 (next to be held in May 2016) election results: percent of vote by party - PAP 60.1%, WP 12.8%, NSP 12.1%, others 15%; seats by party - PAP 81, WP 6; (seats as of February 2013 PAP 80, WP 7)

Judicial branch: Supreme Court, chief justice is appointed by the president with the advice of the prime minister, other judges are appointed by the president with the advice of the chief justice; Court of Appeals

Political parties and leaders: National Solidarity Party or NSP [C. K. TAN]; People's Action Party or PAP [GOH Chok Tong, secretary general] - the governing party; Singapore Democratic Party or SDP [CHEE Soon Juan]; Singapore People's Party or SPP [CHIAM See Tong]; Workers' Party or WP [J. B. JEYARETNAM and LOW Thia Khiang]

International organization participation: APEC, AsDB, ASEAN, Australia Group (observer) , BIS, C, CCC, CP, ESCAP, G-77, IAEA, IBRD, ICAO, ICC, ICFTU, ICRM, IFC, IFRCS, IHO, ILO, IMF, IMO, Inmarsat, Intelsat, Interpol, IOC, ISO, ITU, NAM, OPCW, PCA, UN, UNCTAD, UNIKOM, UPU, WHO, WIPO, WMO, WTrO

Diplomatic representation in the US:
chief of mission: Ambassador CHAN Heng Chee
chancery: 3501 International Place NW, Washington, DC 20008
telephone: (202) 537-3100
FAX: (202) 537-0876
consulate(s) : New York

Diplomatic representation from the US:
chief of mission: Ambassador Steven J. GREEN
embassy: 27 Napier Road, Singapore 258508
mailing address: FPO AP 96507
telephone: [65] 476-9100
FAX: [65] 476-9340

Flag description: two equal horizontal bands of red (top) and white; near the hoist side of the red band, there is a vertical, white crescent (closed portion is toward the hoist side) partially enclosing five white five-pointed stars arranged in a circle

ECONOMY

Singapore has a highly developed and successful free-market economy. It enjoys a remarkably open and corruption-free environment, stable prices, and a per capita GDP higher than that of most developed countries. The economy depends heavily on exports, particularly in consumer electronics, information technology products, pharmaceuticals, and on a growing financial services sector. The economy contracted 0.6% in 2009 as a result of the global financial crisis, but rebounded 15.1% in 2010, on the strength of renewed exports, before slowing to in 2011-13, largely a result of soft demand for exports during the second European recession. Over the longer term, the government hopes to establish a new growth path that focuses on raising productivity. Singapore has attracted major investments in pharmaceuticals and medical technology production and will continue efforts to establish Singapore as Southeast Asia's financial and high-tech hub.

GDP (purchasing power parity) :
$339 billion (2013 est.)
country comparison to the world: 41
$327.4 billion (2012 est.)
$323.2 billion (est.)
note: data are in 2013 US dollars

GDP (official exchange rate) :
$287.4 billion (2013 est.)

GDP - real growth rate:
3.5% (2013 est.)
country comparison to the world: 91
1.3% (2012 est.)
5.2% (est.)

GDP - per capita (PPP) :
$62,400 (2013 est.)
country comparison to the world: 7
$61,600 (2012 est.)
$62,300 (est.)
note: data are in 2013 US dollars

Gross national saving:
48.3% of GDP (2013 est.)
country comparison to the world: 5
45.6% of GDP (2012 est.)
46.8% of GDP (est.)

GDP - composition, by end use:
household consumption: 41%
government consumption: 9.7%
investment in fixed capital: 25.6%
investment in inventories: 4.5%
exports of goods and services: 195.8%
imports of goods and services: -176.7%
(2013 est.)

GDP - composition, by sector of origin:
agriculture: 0%
industry: 27.3%
services: 72.7% (2013 est.)

Agriculture - products:
orchids, vegetables; poultry, eggs; fish, ornamental fish

Industries:
electronics, chemicals, financial services, oil drilling equipment, petroleum refining, rubber processing and rubber products, processed food and beverages, ship repair, offshore platform construction, life sciences, entrepot trade

Industrial production growth rate:
3.5% (2013 est.)
country comparison to the world: 83

Labor force:
3.428 million
country comparison to the world: 99
note: excludes non-residents (2013 est.)

Labor force - by occupation:
agriculture: 0.1%
industry: 19.6%
services: 80.3%

note: excludes non-residents (2011)

Unemployment rate:
2.1% (2013 est.)
country comparison to the world: 15
1.9% (2012 est.)

Population below poverty line:
NA%

Household income or consumption by percentage share:
lowest 10%: 4.4%
highest 10%: 23.2% (2008)

Distribution of family income - Gini index:
47.8 (2012)
country comparison to the world: 27
48.1 (2008)

Budget:
revenues: $44.48 billion
expenditures: $42.47 billion
note: expenditures include both operational and development expenditures (2013 est.)

Taxes and other revenues:
15.5% of GDP (2013 est.)
country comparison to the world: 190

Budget surplus (+) or deficit (-) :
0.7% of GDP (2013 est.)
country comparison to the world: 31

Public debt:
113.6% of GDP (2013 est.)
country comparison to the world: 10
111.4% of GDP (2012 est.)
note: for Singapore, public debt consists largely of Singapore Government Securities (SGS) issued to assist the Central Provident Fund (CPF) , which administers Singapore's defined contribution pension fund; special issues of SGS are held by the CPF, and are non-tradable; the government has not borrowed to finance deficit expenditures since the 1980s; Singapore has no external public debt

Fiscal year:
1 April - 31 March

Inflation rate (consumer prices) :
2.4% (2013 est.)
country comparison to the world: 88
4.6% (2012 est.)

Commercial bank prime lending rate:
5.4% (31 December 2013 est.)
country comparison to the world: 151
5.38% (31 December 2012 est.)

Stock of narrow money:
$124.8 billion (31 December 2013 est.)
country comparison to the world: 29
$115 billion (31 December 2012 est.)

Stock of broad money:
$400.9 billion (31 December 2013 est.)
country comparison to the world: 26
$388.6 billion (31 December 2012 est.)

Stock of domestic credit:
$302.7 billion (31 December 2013 est.)
country comparison to the world: 35
$281.1 billion (31 December 2012 est.)

Market value of publicly traded shares:
$414.1 billion (31 December 2012 est.)
country comparison to the world: 26
$308.3 billion (31 December 2011)
$370.1 billion (31 December 2010 est.)

Current account balance:
$52.19 billion (2013 est.)
country comparison to the world: 13
$51.44 billion (2012 est.)

Exports:
$442.9 billion (2013 est.)
country comparison to the world: 15
$435.8 billion (2012 est.)

Exports - commodities:
machinery and equipment (including electronics and telecommunications) , pharmaceuticals and other chemicals, refined petroleum products, food and beverages

Exports - partners:
Malaysia 12.3%, Hong Kong 10.9%, China 10.8%, Indonesia 10.6%, US 5.5%, Japan 4.6%, Australia 4.2%, South Korea 4% (2012)

Imports:
$380.3 billion (2013 est.)
country comparison to the world: 15
$374.9 billion (2012 est.)

Imports - commodities:
machinery and equipment, mineral fuels, chemicals, foodstuffs, consumer goods

Imports - partners:
Malaysia 10.6%, China 10.3%, US 10.2%, South Korea 6.8%, Japan 6.2%, Indonesia 5.3%, Saudi Arabia 4.5%, UAE 4.1% (2012)

Reserves of foreign exchange and gold:
$270.5 billion (31 December 2013 est.)
country comparison to the world: 12
$259.1 billion (31 December 2012 est.)

Debt - external:
$1.174 trillion (31 December 2012 est.)
country comparison to the world: 16
$1.088 trillion (31 December 2011 est.)

Stock of direct foreign investment - at home:
$800 billion (31 December 2013 est.)
country comparison to the world: 10
$741 billion (31 December 2012 est.)

Stock of direct foreign investment - abroad:
$445.1 billion (31 December 2013 est.)
country comparison to the world: 16
$416.9 billion (31 December 2012 est.)

Exchange rates:
Singapore dollars (SGD) per US dollar -
1.25 (2013 est.)
1.2497 (2012 est.)
1.3635 (2010 est.)
1.4545 (2009)
1.415 (2008)

ENERGY

Electricity - production:
44.41 billion kWh (est.)
country comparison to the world: 54

Electricity - consumption:
40.62 billion kWh (2010 est.)
country comparison to the world: 53

Electricity - exports:
0 kWh (2012 est.)
country comparison to the world: 195

Electricity - imports:
0 kWh (2012 est.)
country comparison to the world: 198

Electricity - installed generating capacity:
10.25 million kW (2010 est.)
country comparison to the world: 54

Electricity - from fossil fuels:
99.8% of total installed capacity (2010 est.)
country comparison to the world: 46

Electricity - from nuclear fuels:
0% of total installed capacity (2010 est.)
country comparison to the world: 178

Electricity - from hydroelectric plants:

0% of total installed capacity (2010 est.)
country comparison to the world: 199

Electricity - from other renewable sources:
0.2% of total installed capacity (2010 est.)
country comparison to the world: 93

Crude oil - production:
20,170 bbl/day (2012 est.)
country comparison to the world: 77

Crude oil - exports:
0 bbl/day (est.)
country comparison to the world: 182

Crude oil - imports:
1.137 million bbl/day (2010 est.)
country comparison to the world: 10

Crude oil - proved reserves:
0 bbl (1 January 2013 es)
country comparison to the world: 188

Refined petroleum products - production:
1.357 million bbl/day (est.)
country comparison to the world: 16

Refined petroleum products - consumption:
1.25 million bbl/day (est.)
country comparison to the world: 19

Refined petroleum products - exports:
1.14 million bbl/day (2010 est.)
country comparison to the world: 7

Refined petroleum products - imports:
1.348 million bbl/day (2010 est.)
country comparison to the world: 5

Natural gas - production:
0 cu m (est.)
country comparison to the world: 190

Natural gas - consumption:
8.778 billion cu m (est.)
country comparison to the world: 51

Natural gas - exports:
0 cu m (est.)
country comparison to the world: 182

Natural gas - imports:
8.78 billion cu m (est.)
country comparison to the world: 32

Natural gas - proved reserves:
0 cu m (1 January 2013 es)
country comparison to the world: 193

Carbon dioxide emissions from consumption of energy:
212.4 million Mt (est.)
country comparison to the world: 28

COMMUNICATIONS

Telephones - main lines in use:
1.99 million (2012)
country comparison to the world: 58

Telephones - mobile cellular:
8.063 million (2012)
country comparison to the world: 92

Telephone system:
general assessment: excellent service
domestic: excellent domestic facilities; launched 3G wireless service in February 2005; combined fixed-line and mobile-cellular teledensity more than 180 telephones per 100 persons; multiple providers of high-speed Internet connectivity and the government is close to completing an island-wide roll out of a high-speed fiber-optic broadband network
international: country code - 65; numerous submarine cables provide links throughout Asia, Australia, the Middle East, Europe, and US; satellite earth stations - 4; supplemented by VSAT coverage (2011)

Broadcast media:
state controls broadcast media; 8 domestic TV stations operated by MediaCorp which is wholly owned by a state investment company; broadcasts from Malaysian and Indonesian stations available; satellite dishes banned; multi-channel cable TV service available; a total of 18 domestic radio stations broadcasting with MediaCorp operating more than a dozen and another 4 stations are closely linked to the ruling party or controlled by the Singapore Armed Forces Reservists Association; many Malaysian and Indonesian radio stations are available

Internet country code:
.sg

Internet hosts:
1.96 million (2012)
country comparison to the world: 39

Internet users:
3.235 million (2009)
country comparison to the world: 65

TRANSPORTATION

Railways:
total: 38.6 km
narrow gauge: 38.6 km 1.000-m gauge
note: there is a 83 km mass transit system with 48 stations

Highways:
total: 3,122 km
paved: 3,038 km (including 150 km of expressways)
unpaved: 84 km
Ports and harbors: Singapore

Merchant marine:
total: 891 ships (1,000 GRT or over) totaling 21,808,813 GRT/34,783,544 DWT
ships by type: bulk 140, cargo 121, chemical tanker 66, combination bulk 6, combination ore/oil 6, container 162, liquified gas 26, livestock carrier 2, multi-functional large load carrier 3, petroleum tanker 294, refrigerated cargo 6, roll-on/roll-off 10, short-sea passenger 1, specialized tanker 12, vehicle carrier 36
note: a flag of convenience registry; includes ships from 22 countries among which are Japan 41, Denmark 35, Sweden 28, Thailand 28, Hong Kong 26, Germany 19, Taiwan 19, and Indonesia 11 (1998 est.)

Airports: 9
Airports - with paved runways:
total: 9
over 3,047 m: 2
2,438 to 3,047 m: 1
1,524 to 2,437 m: 4
914 to 1,523 m: 1
under 914 m: 1
Heliports: 1

MILITARY

Military branches: Army, Navy, Air Force, People's Defense Force, Police Force
Military manpower - availability:
males age 15-49: 1,278,525
Military manpower - fit for military service:
males age 15-49: 932,978
Military expenditures - dollar figure: $4.4 billion
Military expenditures - percent of GDP: 4.9%

TRANSNATIONAL ISSUES

Disputes - international: two islands in dispute with Malaysia

Illicit drugs: transit point for Golden Triangle heroin going to North America, Western Europe, and the Third World; also a money-laundering center

IMPORTANT INFORMATION FOR UNDERSTANDING SINGAPORE

OFFICIAL NAME: Republic of Singapore

IMPORTANT FACTS

Geography
Area: 685 sq. km. (264 sq. mi.) .
Cities: *Capital* -- Singapore (country is a city-state) .
Terrain: Lowland.
Climate: Tropical.

People
Population: 4.35 million (including permanent residents, foreign workers) .
Annual growth rate: 2.6% (total) ; 1.9% (residents) .
Ethnic groups: Chinese 77%, Malays 14%, Indians 8%.
Religions: Buddhist, Taoist, Muslim, Christian, Hindu.
Languages: English, Mandarin and other Chinese dialects, Malay, Tamil.
Education: *Years compulsory* --six. Attendance --94%. *Literacy* --94.6%.
Health (2005) : *Infant mortality rate* --2.1/1,000. *Life expectancy* --78 yrs. male, 82 yrs. female.
Work force (2005, 2.37 million) : *Manufacturing* --21%; *services* --69%.

Government
Type: Parliamentary republic.
Constitution: June 3, 1959 (amended 1965 and 1991) .
Independence: August 9, 1965.
Branches: *Executive* --president (chief of state, 6-yr. term) ; prime minister (head of government) . *Legislative* --unicameral 84-member Parliament (maximum 5-yr. term) . *Judicial* --High Court, Court of Appeal, subordinate courts.
Political parties: People's Action Party (PAP) , Workers' Party (WP) , Singapore's Peoples Party (SPP) , Singapore Democratic Party (SDP) , Singapore Democratic Alliance.
Suffrage: Universal and compulsory at 21.
Central government budget (FY 2006 est.) : $18.8 billion.
Defense: 5.2% of gross domestic product.
National holiday: August 9.

Economy
GDP: $137.5 billion.
Annual real growth rate: 8.8% (2010) , 6.6% (2005) , 7.9% (2006) .
Per capita GNP (purchasing power parity) : $29,454.
Natural resources: None.
Agriculture (under 0.5% of GDP) : *Products*--poultry, orchids, vegetables, fruits, ornamental fish.
Manufacturing (26.9% of real GDP) : *Types*--electronic and electrical products and components, petroleum products, machinery and metal products, chemical and pharmaceutical products, transport equipment (mainly aircraft repairs/maintenance, shipbuilding/repair and oil rigs) , food and beverages, printing and publishing, textiles and garments, plastic products/modules, instrumentation equipment.
Trade: *Exports*--$271 billion: petroleum products, food/beverages, chemicals, textile/garments, electronic components, telecommunication apparatus, transport equipment. *Major markets*--Malaysia (13.1%) , U.S. (9.9%) , EU-15 (10.4%) , Hong Kong (10%) , Japan (5.5%) , and China (9.7%) . *Imports*--$238.5 billion: aircraft, crude oil and petroleum products, electronic components, radio and television receivers/parts, motor vehicles, chemicals, food/beverages, iron/steel, textile yarns/fabrics. *Major suppliers*--Malaysia (13.1%) , U.S. (12.5%) , Japan (8.3%) , EU-15 (10.9%) , and China (11.4%) .

PEOPLE

Singapore is one of the most densely populated countries in the world. The annual growth rate for 2010 was 1.3%, including resident foreigners. Singapore has a varied linguistic, cultural, and religious heritage. Malay is the national language, but Chinese, English, and Tamil also are official languages. English is the language of administration and also is widely used in the professions, businesses, and schools.

The government has mandated that English be the primary language used at all levels of the school systems, and it aims to provide at least 10 years of education for every child. In 2005, primary and secondary school students totaled about 532,225, or 12.2% of the entire population. In 2005, enrollment at the universities was 43,663 (first degree full-time/part-time) and 58,880 at the polytechnics. The Institute of Technical Education for basic technical and commerce skills has almost 21,600 students. The country's literacy rate is 95.0%.

Singapore generally allows religious freedom, although religious groups are subject to government scrutiny, and some religious sects are restricted or banned. Almost all Malays are Muslim; other Singaporeans are Taoists, Buddhists, Confucianists, Christians, Hindus, or Sikhs.

HISTORY

Although Singapore's history dates from the 11th century, the island was little known to the West until the 19th century, when in 1819, Sir Thomas Stamford Raffles arrived as an agent of the British East India Company. In 1824, the British purchased Singapore Island, and by 1825, the city of Singapore had become a major port, with trade exceeding that of Malaya's Malacca and Penang combined. In 1826, Singapore, Penang, and Malacca were combined as the Straits Settlements to form an outlying residency of the British East India Company; in 1867, the Straits Settlements were made a British Crown Colony, an arrangement that continued until 1946.

The opening of the Suez Canal in 1869 and the advent of steamships launched an era of prosperity for Singapore as transit trade expanded throughout Southeast Asia. In the 20th century, the automobile industry's demand for rubber from Southeast Asia and the packaging industry's need for tin helped make Singapore one of the world's major ports.

In 1921, the British constructed a naval base, which was soon supplemented by an air base. But the Japanese captured the island in February 1942, and it remained under their control until September 1945, when the British returned.

In 1946, the Straits Settlements was dissolved; Penang and Malacca became part of the Malayan Union, and Singapore became a separate British Crown Colony. In 1959, Singapore became self-governing, and, in 1963, it joined the newly independent Federation of Malaya, Sabah, and Sarawak--the latter two former British Borneo territories--to form Malaysia.

Indonesia adopted a policy of "confrontation" against the new federation, charging that it was a "British colonial creation," and severed trade with Malaysia. The move particularly affected Singapore, since Indonesia had been the island's second-largest trading partner. The political dispute was resolved in 1966, and Indonesia resumed trade with Singapore.

After a period of friction between Singapore and the central government in Kuala Lumpur, Singapore separated from Malaysia on August 9, 1965, and became an independent republic.

GOVERNMENT

According to the constitution, as amended in 1965, Singapore is a republic with a parliamentary system of government. Political authority rests with the prime minister and the cabinet. The prime minister is the leader of the political party or coalition of parties having the majority of seats in Parliament. The president, who is chief of state, previously exercised only ceremonial duties. As a result of 1991 constitutional changes, the president is now elected and exercises expanded powers over legislative appointments, government budgetary affairs, and internal security matters.

The unicameral Parliament currently consists of 84 members elected on the basis of universal adult suffrage, and up to nine "nominated" members of Parliament. A constitutional provision assures at least three opposition members, even if fewer than three actually are elected. A "nonconstituency" seat held by the opposition under this provision since 1997 was again filled after the last election held on May 6, 2006. In the May 2006 general election, the governing People's Action Party (PAP) won 82 of the 84 seats. The president appoints nominated members of Parliament from among nominations by a special select committee. Nominated members of Parliament (NMP's) enjoy the same privileges as members of Parliament but cannot vote on constitutional matters or expenditures of funds. The maximum term of anyone in Parliament is 5 years. NMP's serve for two and a half year terms. Voting has been compulsory since 1959.

Judicial power is vested in the High Court and the Court of Appeal. The High Court exercises original criminal and civil jurisdiction in serious cases as well as appellate jurisdiction from subordinate courts. Its chief justice, senior judge, and twelve judges are appointed by the president. Appeals from the High Court are heard by the Court of Appeal. The right of appeal to the Privy Council in London was abolished effective April 1994.

Principal Government Officials

Pres.	Tony TAN Keng Yam
Prime Min.	LEE Hsien Loong
Dep. Prime Min., Prime Minister's Office	Tharman SHANMUGARATNAM
Dep. Prime Min., Prime Minister's Office	TEO Chee Hean, RAdm. (Ret.)
Coordinating Min. for National Security, Prime Minister's Office	TEO Chee Hean, RAdm. (Ret.)
Min. for Communication & Information	YAACOB Ibrahim
Min. for Culture, Community, & Youth (Acting)	Lawrence WONG Shyun Tsai
Min. for Defense	NG Eng Hen, Dr.
Min. for Education	HENG Swee Keat
Min. for the Environment & Water Resources	Vivian BALAKRISHNAN
Min. for Finance	Tharman SHANMUGARATNAM
Min. for Foreign Affairs	K. SHANMUGAM
Min. for Health	GAN Kim Yong
Min. for Home Affairs	TEO Chee Hean, RAdm. (Ret.)
Min. for Law	K. SHANMUGAM
Min. for Manpower (Acting)	TAN Chuan-Jin
Min. in Charge of Muslim Affairs	YAACOB Ibrahim
Min. for National Development	KHAW Boon Wan
Min. for Social & Family Development (Acting)	CHAN Chung Sing
Min. for Trade & Industry	LIM Hng Kiang
Min. for Transport	LUI Tuck Yew
Min., Prime Minister's Office	Grace FU Hai Yen
Min., Prime Minister's Office	LIM Swee Say
Min., Prime Minister's Office	S. ISWARAN
Chmn., Monetary Authority of Singapore	Tharman SHANMUGARATNAM
Ambassador to the US	Ashok Kumar MIRPURI
Permanent Representative to the UN, New York	Albert CHUA

Singapore maintains an embassy in the United States at 3501 International Place NW, Washington, DC 20008 (tel. 202/537-3100, fax 202/537-0876) .

POLITICAL CONDITIONS

The ruling political party in Singapore, reelected continuously since 1959, is the People's Action Party (PAP) , now headed by Prime Minister Lee Hsien Loong. Lee succeeded Goh Chok Tong on August 12, 2010. Goh now serves as 'senior minister' and Lee Kuan Yew holds the title 'Minister Mentor', a newly created position.

The PAP has held the overwhelming majority of seats in Parliament since 1966, when the opposition Barisan Sosialis Party (Socialist Front) , a left-wing group that split off from the PAP in 1961, resigned from Parliament, leaving the PAP as the sole representative party. In the general elections of 1968, 1972, 1976, and 1980, the PAP won all of the seats in an expanding Parliament.

Workers' Party Secretary General J.B. Jeyaretnam became the first opposition party member of Parliament in 15 years when he won a 1981 by-election. Opposition parties gained small numbers of seats in the general elections of 1984 (2 seats out of a total of 79) , 1988 (1 seat of 81) , 1991 (4 seats of 81) , 1997 (2 seats of 83) , 2001 (2 seats of 84) and 2006 (2 seats of 84) . Meanwhile, the PAP's share of the popular vote in contested seats decreased from 75% in 2001 to 66.6% in 2006. In the 2006 election, opposition parties together contested 47 of the 84 seats, the largest number in 18 years.

ECONOMY

Currency	Singapore dollar (SGD) ; Brunei Dollar (B$)
Fiscal year	1 April - 31 March
Trade organisations	WTO, APEC, IOR-ARC, ASEAN
	Statistics
GDP	$318.9 billion (2011 est. PPP)
GDP growth	5.8% (Q3 2013)
GDP per capita	$62,100 (PPP, 2012 est.) , $51,709 (nominal, 2012 est.)
GDP by sector	agriculture: 0%; industry: 26.6%; services: 73.4% (est.)
Inflation (CPI)	1.5%
Population below poverty line	N/A
Gini coefficient	47.3 (2011)
Labour force	3,443,700 (2013 est.)
Labour force by occupation	Manufacturing 15.5%, construction 13.7%, services 70.1%, others 0.8%(2013 est.)
Unemployment	1.9% (2013 est.)
Main industries	electronics, chemicals, financial services, oil drilling equipment, petroleum refining, rubber processing and rubber products, processed food and beverages, ship repair, offshore platform construction, life sciences, entrepot trade
Ease-of-doing-business rank	1st
	External
Exports	$414.8 billion (est.)
Export goods	machinery and equipment (including electronics and telecommunications) , pharmaceuticals and other chemicals, refined petroleum products
Main export partners	Malaysia 12.2% Hong Kong 10.9% China 10.7% Indonesia 10.5% United States 5.5% Japan 4.6% Australia 4.2% South Korea 4.0% (2012 est.)
Imports	$311.7 billion (est.)
Import goods	machinery and equipment, mineral fuels, chemicals, foodstuffs, consumer goods
Main import partners	Malaysia 10.6% China 10.3% United States 10.2% South Korea 6.8% Japan 6.2% Indonesia 5.3% Saudi Arabia 4.5% United Arab Emirates 4.1% (est.)
FDI stock	$497 billion (31 December 2011 est.)
Gross external debt	$23.58 billion (31 December 2011 est.)
	Public finances
Public debt	118.2% of GDP (est.)
Revenues	S$40.53 billion (2011 est]
Expenses	S$37.18 billion (est.) note: expenditures include both operational and development expenditures
Economic aid	none
Credit rating	Standard & Poor's:

	AAA (Domestic) AAA (Foreign) AAA (T&C Assessment) Outlook: Stable Moody's: Aaa Outlook: Stable Fitch: AAA Outlook: Stable
Foreign reserves	US$233.368 billion

Singapore is a highly developed trade-oriented market economy. Singapore's economy has been ranked as the most open in the world, least corrupt, most pro-business, with low tax rates (14.2% of Gross Domestic Product, GDP) and has the third highest per-capita GDP in the world; in terms of Purchasing Power Parity (PPP) . Government-linked companies play a substantial role in Singapore's economy, which are owned through the sovereign wealth fund Temasek Holdings, which holds majority stakes in several of the nation's largest companies, such as Singapore Airlines, SingTel, ST Engineering and MediaCorp. The **economy of Singapore** is a major Foreign Direct Investment(FDI) outflow financier in the world. Singapore has also benefited from the inward flow of FDI from global investors and institutions due to her highly attractive investment climate and a stable political environment.

Exports, particularly in electronics, chemicals and services including the posture that Singapore is the regional hub for wealth management provide the main source of revenue for the economy, which allows it to purchase natural resources and raw goods which she lacks. Moreover, water is scarce in Singapore therefore water is defined as a precious resource in Singapore along with the scarcity of land to be treated with land fill of Pulau Semakau. Singapore has limited arable land that Singapore has to rely on the agrotechnology park for agricultural production and consumption. Human Resource is another vital issue for the health of Singaporean economy.

Singapore could thus be said to rely on an extended concept of intermediary trade to Entrepôt trade, by purchasing raw goods and refining them for re-export, such as in the wafer fabrication industry and oil refining. Singapore also has a strategic port which makes it more competitive than many of its neighbours in carrying out such entrepot activities. Singapore has the highest trade to GDP ratio in the world, averaging around 400% during 2008–11. The Port of Singapore is the second-busiest in the world by cargo tonnage. In addition, Singapore's port infrastructure and skilled workforce, which is due to the success of the country's education policy in producing skilled workers, is also fundamental in this aspect as they provide easier access to markets for both importing and exporting, and also provide the skill(s) needed to refine imports into exports.

Singapore's government promotes high levels of savings and investment through policies such as the Central Provident Fund, which is used to fund its citizen's healthcare and retirement needs. Singapore's savings rates have remained among the highest in the world since the 1970s. Most companies in Singapore are registered as private limited-liability companies (commonly known as "private limited companies") . A private limited company in Singapore is a separate legal entity, and shareholders are not liable for the company's debts beyond the amount of share capital they have contributed.

To preserve its international standing and further its economic prosperity in the 21st century, Singapore has taken measures to promote innovation, encourage entrepreneurship, re-train her workforce, and even attract foreign talents. These measures aim to boost Singapore's productivity, so that Singapore remains competitive and ready for the challenges of an information-driven global economy.

Singapore's strategic location on major sea lanes and its industrious population have given the country an economic importance in Southeast Asia disproportionate to its small size. Upon independence in 1965, Singapore was faced with a lack of physical resources and a small domestic market. In response, the Singapore Government adopted a pro-business, pro-foreign investment, export-oriented economic policy framework, combined with state-directed investments in strategic government-owned corporations.

Singapore's economic strategy proved a success, producing real growth that averaged 8.0% from 1960 to 1999. The economy picked up after the 1997 regional financial crisis, with a growth rate of 9.4% for 2000, but then fell back in tandem with the economic slowdown in the United States, Japan, and the European Union (EU) , as well as the worldwide electronics slump, so that GDP shrank by 2.4% in 2001. The economy rebounded in 2002, expanding 4.0%; but it posted a slower 2.9% growth in 2003, due to the effect of severe acute respiratory syndrome (SARS) in the first half of the year. From 2010 to 2006, the economy expanded by 8.8%, 6.6%, and 7.9%, respectively, driven by the growth in world demand for electronics, pharmaceuticals, other manufactured goods and financial services, and in the economies of its major trading partners--the United States, EU, Japan, and China, as well as expanding emerging markets such as India.

Singapore's largely corruption-free government, skilled work force, and advanced and efficient infrastructure have attracted investments from more than 7,000 multinational corporations from the United States, Japan, and Europe. Foreign firms are found in almost all sectors of the economy. Multinational corporations account for more than two-thirds of manufacturing output and direct export sales, although certain services sectors remain dominated by government-linked companies.

Manufacturing and services are the twin engines of the Singapore economy and accounted for 26.9% and 63.2%, respectively, of Singapore's gross domestic product in 2006. The electronics and chemicals industries lead Singapore's manufacturing sector, accounting for 32.4% and 32.5%, respectively, of Singapore's manufacturing output in 2006. To inject new life to the tourism sector, which faced a 20% fall in receipts between 1993-2000, and a declining share of East Asia Pacific tourism receipts from 8.2% to 5.8%, the government in April 2005 approved the development of two casinos that should result in investments of more than U.S. $5 billion.

To maintain its competitive position despite rising wages, the government seeks to promote higher value-added activities in the manufacturing and services sectors. It also has opened, or is in the process of opening, the financial services, telecommunications, and power generation and retailing sectors to foreign service providers and greater competition. The government also has pursued cost-cutting measures, including tax cuts and wage and rent reductions, to lower the cost of doing business in Singapore. The government is actively negotiating free trade agreements (FTAs) with 16 key trading partners and has already concluded 11 FTAs, including one with the United States that came into force January 1, 2010.

Trade, Investment, and Aid

Singapore's total trade in 2006 amounted to $510 billion, an increase of 13.2% from 2005. In 2006, Singapore's imports totaled $239 billion, and exports totaled $271 billion. Malaysia was Singapore's main import source, as well as its largest export market, absorbing 13.1% of Singapore's exports, with the United States falling behind to 9.9%, from 10.2% in 2005. Singapore was the 15th-largest trading partner of the United States. Re-exports accounted for 47.3% of Singapore's total sales to other countries in 2006. Singapore's principal exports are petroleum products, food and beverages, chemicals, textile and garments, electronic components, telecommunication apparatus, and transport equipment. Singapore's main imports are aircraft, crude oil and petroleum products, electronic components, consumer electronics, microelectronics manufacturing equipment, motor vehicles, chemicals, food and beverages, iron and steel, and textile yarns and fabrics.

Singapore continues to attract investment funds on a large scale despite its relatively high-cost operating environment. The United States leads in foreign investment, accounting for 24% of new commitments to the manufacturing sector in 2005. As of 2005, the stock of investment by U.S. companies in the manufacturing and services sectors in Singapore reached about $48.1 billion (total assets) . The bulk of U.S. investment is in electronics manufacturing, oil refining and storage, and the chemical industry. About 1,500 U.S. firms operate in Singapore.

The government also has encouraged firms to invest outside Singapore, with the country's total direct investments abroad reaching $104 billion by the end of 2010. China was the top destination, accounting for 12% of total overseas investments, followed by Malaysia (8%) , Hong Kong (7%) , Indonesia (7%) , and the United States (5%) .

The United States provides no bilateral aid to Singapore.

Labor

In December 2006, Singapore had a total labor force of about 2.5 million. The National Trades Union Congress (NTUC) , the sole trade union federation, comprises almost 99% of total organized labor. Extensive legislation covers general labor and trade union matters. The Industrial Arbitration Court handles labor-management disputes that cannot be resolved informally through the Ministry of Labor. The Singapore Government has stressed the importance of cooperation between unions, management, and government ("tripartism") , as well as the early resolution of disputes. There has been only one strike in the past 15 years.

Singapore has enjoyed virtually full employment for long periods of time. Amid slower economic growth in 2003, unemployment rose to 4.6%. As of end-December 2006, the rate of unemployment dropped to 2.7%. Much of the unemployment is structural, as low-skill manufacturing operations move overseas. Since 1990, the number of foreign workers in Singapore has increased rapidly to cope with labor shortages. Foreign workers comprise 30% of the labor force; the great majority of these are unskilled workers.

Transportation and Communications

Situated at the crossroads of international shipping and air routes, Singapore is a center for transportation and communication in Southeast Asia. Singapore's Changi International Airport is a regional aviation hub served by 83 airlines. A third terminal is slated to open in 2008, and a dedicated low-cost terminal for budget airlines was completed in 2006. The Port of Singapore is among the world's busiest and ranks second globally as a center for containerized transshipment traffic, after Hong Kong. The country also is linked by road and rail to Malaysia and Thailand.

Telecommunications and Internet facilities are state-of-the-art, providing high-quality communications with the rest of the world. Radio and television stations are all ultimately government-owned or government-linked. The print media is dominated by a company with close ties to the government. Daily newspapers are published in English, Chinese, Malay, and Tamil.

DEFENSE

Singapore relies primarily on its own defense forces, which are continuously being modernized. The defense budget accounts for approximately 31% of government operating expenditures (or 5% of GDP) . A career military force of 53,300 is supplemented by 300,000 persons, either on active National Service, which is compulsory for able-bodied young men, or on Reserve.. The Singapore Armed Forces engage in joint training with all the Association of Southeast Asian Nations (ASEAN) countries and with the United States, Australia, New Zealand, and India. Singapore also conducts military training on Taiwan.

Singapore is a member of the Five-Power Defense Arrangement together with the United Kingdom, Australia, New Zealand, and Malaysia. Intended to replace the former defense role of the British in the Singapore-Malaysia area, the arrangement obligates members to consult in the event of external threat and provides for stationing Commonwealth forces in Singapore.

Singapore has consistently supported a strong U.S. military presence in the Asia-Pacific region. In 1990, the United States and Singapore signed a Memorandum of Understanding (MOU) which allows United States access to Singapore facilities at Paya Lebar Airbase and the Sembawang wharves. Under the MOU, a U.S. Navy logistics unit was established in Singapore in 1992; U.S. fighter aircraft deploy periodically to Singapore for exercises, and a number of U.S. military vessels visit Singapore. The MOU was amended in 1999 to permit U.S. naval vessels to berth at the Changi Naval Base, which was completed in early 2001. In July 2005, the United States and Singapore signed a Strategic Framework Agreement to expand cooperation in defense and security.

FOREIGN RELATIONS

Singapore is nonaligned. It is a member of the United Nations--it occupied a rotational seat on the Security Council 2001-02--and several of its specialized and related agencies, and also of the Non-Aligned Movement and the Commonwealth. Singapore has participated in UN peacekeeping/observer missions in

Kuwait, Angola, Namibia, Cambodia, and East Timor. It provided a training unit to assist in training Iraqi police, and Singapore has deployed naval ships, air force transport planes, and refueling tankers to the Persian Gulf to support the multinational coalition effort to bring stability and security to Iraq. Singapore supports the concept of Southeast Asian regionalism and plays an active role in ASEAN and the Asia Pacific Economic Cooperation (APEC) forum.

U.S.-SINGAPORE RELATIONS

The United States has maintained formal diplomatic relations with Singapore since that country became independent in 1965. Singapore 's efforts to maintain economic growth and political stability and its support for regional cooperation harmonize with U.S. policy in the region and form a solid basis for amicable relations between the two countries. The United States and Singapore signed a bilateral free trade agreement on May 6, 2003; the agreement entered into force on January 1, 2010. The growth of U.S. investment in Singapore and the large number of Americans living there enhance opportunities for contact between Singapore and the United States. Many Singaporeans visit and study in the United States. Singapore is a Visa Waiver Program country.

The U.S. Government sponsors visitors from Singapore each year under the International Visitor Program. The U.S. Government provides Fulbright awards to enable selected American professors to teach or conduct research at the National University of Singapore and the Institute of Southeast Asian Studies. It awards scholarships to outstanding Singaporean students for graduate studies at American universities and to American students to study in Singapore. The U.S. Government also sponsors occasional cultural presentations in Singapore. The East-West Center and private American organizations, such as the Asia and Ford Foundations, also sponsor exchanges involving Singaporeans.

Principal U.S. Embassy Officials
Ambassador--Patricia L. Herbold
Deputy Chief of Mission--Judith Fergin
Economic/Political Chief--Ike Reed
Senior Economic Officer--Paul Horowitz
Senior Political Officer--Christopher Kavanagh
Consul--Julie Kavanagh
Public Affairs Counselor--Valerie Fowler
Commercial Counselor--Daniel Thompson
Management Counselor--Karen C. Stanton
Defense Attache--Alan Oshirak

Defense Attache—Alan Oshirak

The U.S. Embassy in Singapore is located at 27 Napier Road, Singapore 258508 (tel. 65-6476-9100, fax 65-6476-9340) . The Embassy's website is at http://singapore.usembassy.gov.

INSOLVENCY (BANKRUPTCY) LAWS AND REGULATIONS IN SINGAPORE

BASIC PROCEDURES

A company may be closed voluntarily by its owners or by an Order of the Court (under certain circumstances). Under Company Law, it is the duty of Directors to wind up an insolvent company. An insolvent company is a company that cannot pay its debts as they fall due. A creditor may go to court and apply for a judgement to be registered against the company in relation to the debt. If they are still unsuccessful in receiving payment, another option is that a creditor may apply to the Court to have a company wound up if that company is insolvent.

Typical reasons for closing a company include:

Company has ceased business activities or is not profitable

Company cannot pay its debts and is insolvent

Irrevocable dispute among shareholders

Corporate or financial restructuring of the group to which the company belongs

Company is dormant and the owner does not want to incur ongoing compliance and maintenance costs

Breach of statutory provisions, including offences committed

Companies can be liquidated either by "Striking Off" or "Winding Up". Winding up and striking off both result in a company ceasing to exist. However, they are very different processes and should not be confused with each other.

A private company that is not trading and meets certain other conditions may apply to the Company Registrar to be struck off the register. In general, striking off is an easier, faster and less costly procedure, however it is only suitable for small or dormant companies that are able to meet the specific requirements. A company may not be struck off if it is the subject, or proposed subject, of insolvency proceedings or a compromise or arrangement with its members or creditors.

Winding up is a more formal company liquidation procedure that involves the orderly winding-up of the company affairs, the appointment of a liquidator to manage the process of realizing the company assets, ceasing or sale of its operations, payment of its debts (if any) and distribution of surplus assets (if any) among its members.

More details about Striking Off and Winding Up methods of closing a Singapore company are provided below. Given the issues and complexity involved, it is best to engage a professional services firm to handle the matter of closing down a Singapore company.

A company may apply to ACRA (Accounting and Corporate Regulatory Authority) to strike its name off the Register pursuant to Section 344 of the Companies Act. ACRA may approve the application if it has reasonable cause to believe that the company is not carrying on business and the company is able to satisfy the criteria for striking off.

REQUIREMENTS

The company must have ceased trading

The company must not be involved in any court proceedings whether inside or outside Singapore

The company must have no assets and liabilities at the time of making the application

The company must not have any outstanding penalties or offers of composition owing to the Registry

The company must not have any outstanding tax liabilities with IRAS (Inland Revenue Authority of Singapore)

The company must not be indebted to other government departments

The officers (e.g. directors and company secretary) of the company must not have any outstanding ACRA summonses against any of them.

The particulars of the directors must be the same as in the records of ACRA

All the shareholders must consent to the striking off and the company must obtain a letter of consent from each individual shareholder

PROCEDURE

An applicant must be submitted to the Company Registrar. Depending on the complexity of the case and whether the documents submitted are sufficient, ACRA may take about 7 working days to process the application.

If ACRA is satisfied that the company fully meets the criteria for striking off, a "striking off notice" will be sent to the company at its registered office address, its officers (directors and company secretary) at their residential address, and lastly to Singapore tax authorities. After a period of four months, a final notification will be made stating that the company has been struck off the Register. The date that the company is struck off will also be stated in the final notification. Any person who wishes to object to the striking-off can do so during this period. The entire striking off process takes about 5-6 months.

Winding up a Company

There are two paths to winding up a company in Singapore – voluntary winding up and compulsory winding up.

Voluntary winding up

A Singapore company can be liquidated voluntarily by either its members or creditors.

Members' Voluntary Winding Up

A company may decide to wind up its affairs, voluntarily, if the directors believe that the company will be able to pay its debts, in full, within 12 months after the commencement of the winding up.

A majority of directors of the company must make a written Declaration of Solvency at a meeting of the directors. Once this declaration has been filed with the Registrar, the directors must send to the members, a notice of an Extraordinary General Meeting (EGM) to be convened for the purpose of passing a Special

Resolution to wind up the company, and an Ordinary Resolution appointing the liquidators (and approving their remuneration). The EGM must be held within five weeks from the Directors' Meeting executing the solvency declaration.

Concurrently with calling for the meeting, the directors or partners are required to appoint an approved liquidator to be the provisional liquidator between the issuing of the Declaration of Solvency and the holding of the EGM. The notice of the appointment of the provisional liquidator and a copy of the statutory declaration must be advertised within 14 days of the appointment of the provisional liquidator in at least 4 local daily newspapers, one each published in the English, Malay, Chinese and Tamil languages respectively.

At the EGM, the voluntary winding up of the company needs to be resolved by way of Special Resolution, that is by a majority of not less than 75% of the votes of the members entitled to vote. Furthermore, one or more natural persons who have given their prior written consent must be appointed as liquidator(s). In Singapore, accountants are normally preferred for this position. Subsequently, a second Special Resolution has to be passed, empowering the liquidator(s) to divide all or any of the properties and assets of the company among the members.

Within seven days after the passing of the special resolution, a printed copy of the special resolution must be filed with ACRA and within 10 days, notice of the resolution has to be given in one or more newspapers circulating generally throughout Singapore. Furthermore, the company must ensure that all documents issued by or on behalf of the company containing the company's name are amended to include the words "in liquidation" after its name and hand over all company books and records to the liquidator.

With the passing of the special resolution at the EGM, the member's voluntary liquidation of the company is deemed to have commenced. The liquidator, or provisional liquidator will proceed to wind up the affairs of the company and file the necessary notifications required under the Companies Act.

The liquidator proceeds to prepare and file the relevant notice and advertisement including the settlement of creditors' claims. He attends to the company's income tax clearance, filing of the company's accounts and as well as determining how much is to be returned to the company's shareholders following payment of all the company's liabilities and debts.

As soon as the affairs of the company are fully wound up, the liquidator must draw up an account showing how the winding up has been conducted and how the property of the company has been disposed of. He must then call a general meeting of the company for the purpose of presenting and explaining the account to the meeting. The liquidator must, within 7 days after the meeting, lodge with the ACRA and the Official Receiver, a return stating that the meeting has been held and attaching a copy of the account.

On the expiration of 3 months after the lodging of the form with the Registrar, the company will be dissolved. However, the court has the power to declare the dissolution of a company to be void at any time within two years after the date of dissolution. The application may be made by the liquidator or any other interested person.

Creditors' Voluntary Winding Up

A company may decide to opt for a creditors' voluntary winding up if its directors believe that it cannot, by reason of its liabilities, continue its business. The company will appoint a liquidator, or provisional liquidator, to wind up its affairs and file the necessary notifications required under the Companies Act. The procedure is the same as outlined above.

Effects of Voluntary Winding Up

With effect from the date of passing of the special resolution, the company must cease to carry on its business except insofar as it is required for the beneficial winding up in the opinion of the liquidator.

The directors' powers will cease, except where the shareholders, with the consent of the liquidator, have resolved that the directors should continue to have such powers.

Any transfer of shares is void unless made to, or sanctioned by, the liquidator, and the status of the members cannot be altered.

Compulsory Winding Up

A company may be wound up under an Order of the Court under certain circumstances e.g. the company is unable to pay its debts or when the court is of the opinion that it is otherwise just and equitable that the company is being liquidated. The company itself, its creditors, shareholders, the liquidator or judicial manager may initiate liquidation proceedings with the High Court. The Court may appoint a liquidator to wind up the affairs of the company. Where no liquidator is appointed by the Court, the Official Receiver shall be the liquidator of the company.

Your company would normally cease upon liquidation. The liquidator will start to review the assets of the company and the claims of creditors, and look into the conduct of its directors and other related persons to realise your company's assets in a manner that is in the best interest of the company and its creditors. The liquidator may also carry on the business if he considers it the most beneficial option. The officers of the company are generally deprived of their power to run the company. However, they and any other persons who may have been concerned with the affairs of the company have the duty to assist and co-operate with the liquidator. This includes the submission of a Statement of Affairs on the company's assets and liabilities.

After all assets of the company have been assessed and realised, the liquidator will adjudicate all the claims lodged against the company and admit or reject them accordingly. Any surplus after paying the creditors and costs of liquidation will be returned to the shareholders.

Effects of Compulsory Winding Up

An application may be made to the court to stay or restrain pending proceedings against the company after the presentation of a winding up petition and before a winding up order has been made. After a winding up order has been made or a provisional liquidator has been appointed, a leave of court is needed to commence or proceed with an action against the company.

Any disposition of the property of the company, and any transfer of shares or alteration in the status of members of the company made after the commencement of the winding up by the court is void without the court's sanction.

No creditor is allowed to take out or continue attachment or execution proceedings against the company after a winding up petition has been presented.

The rights of the secured creditor to deal or realise his security over company assets are not affected by the winding up order. However he is not entitled to interest on his debt if his security is not realised within six months of winding up or such further period as allowed by the Official Receiver.

If prior to the winding up, any business of the company had been carried out with the intent of defeating or defrauding the creditors of the company or for any fraudulent purpose, the liquidator, creditor or contributory of the company may apply to court to make the person who was responsible for or was party to such activities to be personally liable for the debts of the company.

Where there are mutual credits, debts or dealings between the company and a creditor, these dealings may be set off against each other and the creditor or the company can only claim the balance sum due against the other.

There can be no claim for set off if at the time of extending credit, the creditor had known that a winding up petition was pending against the company. The rule as to set off operates automatically and is mandatory, in that parties cannot contract out of it.

NOTIFICATION REQUIREMENTS

A company must notify the following bodies as part of closing down its business:

Accounting and Corporate Regulatory Authority (ACRA)

Central Provident Fund (CPF) Board

Inland Revenue Authority of Singapore (IRAS)

Relevant Licensing Authorities

CORPORATE INSOLVENCY

The company's contributories (also known as members or shareholders) may pass a resolution that the company be wound up and that a liquidator be appointed.

The liquidation commences at the time of passing the resolution. It is adopted where the company is able to pay its debts in full within 12 months after the commencement of winding up. The directors of the Company are required to file a declaration of solvency.

Liquidation is a process where the company's assets are seized and realised, with the resulting proceeds used to pay off its debts and liabilities.

Any surplus is then distributed among the contributories of the company according to their rights and interests, or otherwise dealt with as the constitution of the company directs.

Upon the completion of the liquidation, the company goes into dissolution and it ceases to exist.

The purposes of a liquidation are:

to ensure a just distribution of the company's assets among creditors and contributories

to terminate the company's existence by its eventual dissolution

Just distribution of assets

When a company is being wound up, the company's business ceases to operate and its assets and affairs are handed over to an independent liquidator whose powers, duties and functions are regulated by the Companies Act (Cap 50).

The rights of unsecured creditors over the company's assets are virtually "frozen" upon the commencement of the liquidation to avoid a further deterioration of the company's financial position and proliferation of its liabilities.

Unsecured creditors are paid on a pari passu basis, i.e. they are paid out of the company's assets equally. Any surplus is then distributed among the contributories of the company.

Reasons for liquidating a company

Company has ceased business activities
Management deadlock
Oppression - shareholders dispute under section 216 of the Companies Act
Corporate or financial restructuring of the group to which the company belongs
Minimise tax liabilities or maximise tax advantages for the group to which the company belongs
Breach of statutory provisions, including offences committed
Company acting outside its scope of activities

Under section 253 of the Companies Act, the company itself, creditors, contributories, liquidator, judicial manager or the Minister may present a winding up application to the High Court.

Section 254(1) of the Companies Act states all the grounds under which the Court may liquidate a company. The common grounds for a company to be wound up by the Court include:

Inability to pay its debts

The company is deemed unable to pay its debts under section 254(2)(a) of the Companies Act if a company's creditor, who is owed more than S$10,000, has served a demand for the sum owing at the registered office of the company, and the company has not paid this sum for three weeks thereafter.

Just and Equitable

When the Court is of the opinion that it is just and equitable that the company be wound up.

The applicant has to pay a winding up deposit of $5,200 to the Official Receiver, and the Court may appoint the Official Receiver or an approved liquidator as the liquidator of the company.

The winding up commences at the date of the presentation of the winding up application.

Singapore's corporate insolvency regime should be reviewed. Firstly the scattering of the avoidance provisions in separate statutes led even the Singapore Court of Appeal to comment on the "drafting complexity". It can be argued that the avoidance provisions, in particular the relevant time period, in a personal bankruptcy cannot be imported wholesale into a corporate insolvency regime. Secondly the "insolvent trading" provisions are broad and vague. The "wrongful trading" provision in s.339(3) does not provide the statutory defence available to directors under the English Insolvency Act 1986 of "taking every step he ought to have taken to avoid loss to creditors". s.339(3) is applicable only if that director is culpable, he has to be "knowingly a party".

What if he suspects insolvency or should be aware of the company's insolvency and fails to prevent his fellow directors from incurring further debts? In Australia, under such circumstances, the director is liable for insolvent trading under s.588G of the Corporations Act. Another area of concern is the incurring of "involuntary debts" such as tax liabilities. The safer course would be for directors to take into account contingent and involuntary liabilities in evaluating the solvency of the company.

The legal consequences of corporate insolvency should be seen against the larger issue of the scope of company law. Whose interests should the company serve? The settled law is that whilst the company is solvent, the interest of the company is the only interest that should prevail. Even so, there are sufficient safeguards at common law and in company legislation to protect creditors.

A voluntary creditor has the freedom to protect his interests by contract such that his claim to payment or to an asset of the company is superior or senior to that of another creditor. As Professor Goode puts it : " In policy terms, the secured creditor is accorded priority because he bargained for it; other creditors who chose to lend unsecured cannot complain of their subordinated position."

This statement is not strictly correct since the unsecured creditor is really not lending money to the company. He is merely agreeing to payment at a later date. It is important to reiterate the creditor expects to be paid in the ordinary course of business. For this reason, creditors are 'protected' by statutory provisions requiring the company, in varying degree, to obtain their consent, to keep them informed, and to obtain a court order where their interests may be prejudiced.

The one risk that creditors cannot be protected against in legislation or at common law is the risk of the company becoming insolvent through a honest business or management failure. For this reason, an act of insolvency per se cannot attract legal liability. Singapore recognises that the legal framework must be conducive to risk taking and entrepreneurship. This objective is shared by other jurisdictions.

A company and its business that cannot be salvaged will, in the course of events, lead to the liquidation and dissolution of the company. When there is a probability that the business of the company can be saved or revived, the possibility of a corporate rescue or a corporate workout emerges. The creditors have to decide if they will receive a better distribution in any of the corporate rescue structures than they would have done in a liquidation.

INSOLVENCY (BANKRUPTCY) LAWS AND REGULATIONS - STRATEGIC INFORMATION

Bankruptcy is a legal status of a person or other entity that cannot repay the debts it owes to creditors. In most jurisdictions, bankruptcy is imposed by a court order, often initiated by the debtor.

Bankruptcy is not the only legal status that an insolvent person or other entity may have, and the term *bankruptcy* is therefore not a synonym for insolvency. In some countries, including the United Kingdom, bankruptcy is limited to individuals, and other forms of insolvency proceedings (such as liquidation and administration) are applied to companies. In the United States, *bankruptcy* is applied more broadly to formal insolvency proceedings.

The principal focus of modern insolvency legislation and business debt restructuring practices no longer rests on the elimination of insolvent entities but on the remodelling of the financial and organisational structure of debtors experiencing financial distress so as to permit the rehabilitation and continuation of their business.

For private households, it is argued to be insufficient to merely dismiss debts after a certain period. It is important to assess the underlying problems and to minimise the risk of financial distress to re-occur. It has been stressed that debt advice, a supervised rehabilitation period, financial education and social help to find sources of income and to manage household expenditures better need to be equally provided during this period of rehabilitation (Reifner *et al.*, 2003; Gerhardt, 2009; Frade, 2010) .

In most EU Member States, debt discharge is conditioned by a partial payment obligation and by a number of requirements concerning the debtor's behaviour. In the United States (US) , discharge is conditioned to a lesser extent. Nevertheless, it should be noted that the spectrum is broad in the EU, with the UK coming closest to the US system (Reifner *et al.*, 2003; Gerhardt, 2009; Frade, 2010) . Other Member States do not provide the option of a debt discharge. Spain, for example, passed a bankruptcy law (*ley concursal*) in 2003 which provides for debt settlement plans that can result in a reduction of the debt (maximally half of the amount) or an extension of the payment period of maximally five years (Gerhardt, 2009) ; nevertheless, it does not foresee debt discharge

Bankruptcy prevents a person's creditors from obtaining a judgment against them. With a judgment a creditor can attempt to garnish wages or seize certain types of property. However, if a debtor has no wages (because they are unemployed or retired) and has no property, they are "judgment proof", meaning a judgment would have no impact on their financial situation. Creditors typically do not initiate legal action against a debtor with no assets, because it is unlikely they could collect the judgment.

If enough time passes, seven years in most jurisdictions, the debt is removed from the debtor's credit history.

A debtor with no assets or income cannot be garnished by a creditor, and therefore the "Take No Action" approach may be the correct option, particularly if the debtor does not expect to have a steady income or property a creditor could attempt to seize.

SELF MONEY MANAGEMENT

Debt is a result of spending more than one's income in a given period. To reduce debt, the most obvious solution is to reduce monthly spending to allow extra cash flow to service debt. This can be done by creating a personal budget and analyzing expenses to find areas to reduce expenses.

Most people, when reviewing a written list of their monthly expenses, can find ways to reduce expenses. Common areas for expense reduction would include reducing food expenses by eating out less often, taking public transportation instead of driving a car, and eliminating enhanced telephone and cable television services.

NEGOTIATE WITH CREDITORS

Creditors understand that bankruptcy is an option for debtors with excessive debt, so most creditors are willing to negotiate a settlement so that they receive a portion of their money, instead of risking losing everything in a bankruptcy.

Negotiation is a viable alternative if the debtor has sufficient income, or has assets that can be liquidated so that the proceeds can be applied against the debt. Negotiation may also buy the debtor some time to rebuild their finances.

For a business, a restructuring agreed with the creditors is a common approach but this requires the agreement of all creditors.

DEBT RESTRUCTURING

Debt restructuring is a process that allows a private or public company - or a sovereign entity - facing cash flow problems and financial distress, to reduce and renegotiate its delinquent debts in order to improve or restore liquidity and rehabilitate so that it can continue its operations.

Out-of court restructurings, also known as workouts, are increasingly becoming a global reality. A debt restructuring is usually less expensive and a preferable alternative to bankruptcy. The main costs associated with a business debt restructuring are the time and effort to negotiate with bankers, creditors, vendors and tax authorities. Debt restructurings typically involve a reduction of debt and an extension of payment terms.

DEBT CONSOLIDATION

Debt is a problem if the interest payments are greater than the debtor can afford. Debt consolidation typically involves borrowing from one lender (typically a bank) , at a low rate of interest, sufficient funds to repay a number of higher interest rate debts (such as credit cards) . By consolidating debts, the debtor replaces many payments to many different creditors with one monthly payment to one creditor, thereby simplifying their monthly budget. In addition, the lower interest rate means that more of the debtor's monthly payment is applied against the principal of the loan, resulting in faster debt repayment. It may be necessary to have a co-signor or other security, such as a car, if the borrower's credit is not sufficient on their own.

FORMAL PROPOSAL TO CREDITORS

If the debtor cannot deal with their debt problems through personal budgeting, negotiation with creditors, or debt consolidation, the final bankruptcy alternative is a formal proposal or deal with the creditors.

Different countries have different legal procedures for compromising debts. In the United States, a debtor can file a Chapter 13 Wager Earner Plan. The plan will typically last for up to five years, during which time the debtor makes payments that are distributed to their creditors.

In Canada, a Consumer Proposal can be filed with the assistance of a government-licensed proposal administrator. Forty-five days after filing the proposal the creditors vote on the proposal, which is considered accepted if more than half of the creditors, by dollar value, vote to approve the proposal.

INDIVIDUAL VOLUNTARY ARRANGEMENT

In the UK the Individual Voluntary Arrangement (IVA) represents the main formal alternative to a debtors bankruptcy petition. The IVA is part of the Insolvency Act 1986 and essentially allows a debtor to reach a formal repayment arrangement with their creditors usually over a 5 year period. In most cases the debtor does not repay their debts in full to their creditors however the IVA proposal essentially allows for any remaining debt to be written off by the creditors at the end of the 5 year repayment period. As with bankruptcy petitions the number of IVA proposals has been increasing rapidly in the UK in recent years.

IMPORTANT LAWS AND REGULATIONS FOR INSOLVENCY (BANKRUPTCY) PROCEDURES

BANKRUPTCY ACT 1995

(No. 15 of 1995)

PART IPRELIMINARY

Short title and commencement

1. This Act may be cited as the Bankruptcy Act 1995 and shall come into operation on such date as the Minister may, by notification in the *Gazette*, appoint.

Interpretation

2.

—(1) In this Act, unless the context otherwise requires —

"appointed day" means the date of commencement of this Act;

"bankrupt" means —

(*a*) the individual debtor who has been adjudged bankrupt by a bankruptcy order; or

(*b*) where a bankruptcy order has been made against a firm, each of the partners in the firm;

"bankruptcy order" means an order adjudging a debtor bankrupt;

"bankruptcy petition" means a petition to the court for a bankruptcy order;

"court" means the court having jurisdiction in bankruptcy under this Act;

"creditor", in relation to a debtor proposing a voluntary arrangement under Part V, means a creditor to whom the debtor owes a debt provable in bankruptcy;

"creditors' committee" means a committee appointed under section 80;

"creditor's petition" means a bankruptcy petition presented under section 57 by a creditor or by two or more creditors jointly;

"debt provable in bankruptcy" or "provable debt" means any debt or liability that is made provable in bankruptcy under this Act;

"debtor" —

(*a*) in relation to a proposal for a voluntary arrangement under Part V, means the individual or the firm making or intending to make that proposal and includes each of the partners in such firm; and (*b*) in relation to a bankruptcy petition, means the individual debtor to whom, or a firm, or each of the partners in the firm, to which, the petition relates;

"debtor's petition" means a bankruptcy petition presented under section 58 by a debtor against himself or by all or a majority of the members of a firm against the firm;

"estate", in relation to a bankrupt, is to be construed in accordance with section 78;

"family", in relation to a bankrupt, means the persons (if any) who are living with and dependent on him;

"firm" means an unincorporated body of individuals carrying on business in partnership with a view to profit;

"gazetted" means published in the *Gazette*;

"goods" includes all chattels personal;

"judgment debt" means a debt which is payable by any person by virtue of a judgment or an order of court against him;

"liability" means a liability to pay money or money's worth, irrespective of whether such liability is present or future, certain or contingent or of an amount that is fixed or liquidated or that is capable of being ascertained by fixed rules or as a matter of opinion, and includes any such liability arising —

(*a*) under any written law;

(*b*) under contract, tort or bailment;

(*c*) as a result of a breach of trust by the person liable; or

(*d*) out of an obligation to make restitution;

"nominee" means the person appointed by virtue of a debtor's proposal for a voluntary arrangement under Part V to act as trustee or otherwise to supervise the implementation of the voluntary arrangement and includes —

(*a*) any replacement of such person pursuant to an order under section 49(3) (*a*) or 55(4) ; and

(*b*) any person upon whom the functions of the nominee have been conferred by a creditors' meeting pursuant to section 51(3) ;

"Official Assignee" includes a Deputy Official Assignee, a Senior Assistant Official Assignee and an Assistant Official Assignee;

"ordinary resolution" means a resolution passed by a majority in value of the creditors present personally or by proxy at a meeting of creditors and voting on the resolution;

"partnership debt" means a debt for which all the partners in a firm are jointly liable;

"preferential debt" means any debt which is to be paid in priority to all other unsecured debts and which is specified in section 90, and any reference to a preferential creditor shall be construed accordingly;

"property" includes money, goods, things in action, land and every description of property wherever situated and also obligations and every description of interest, whether present or future or vested or contingent, arising out of or incidental to, property;

"records" includes computer records and other documentary records;

"Registrar" means the Registrar of the Supreme Court and includes the Deputy Registrar or an Assistant Registrar of the Supreme Court;

"rules" means rules made under this Act;

"secured creditor", in relation to a debtor, means a person holding a mortgage, pledge, charge or lien on or against the property of the debtor or any part thereof as security for a debt due to him from the debtor;

"Sheriff" includes a bailiff and any officer charged with the execution of a writ or other process of the court;

"special resolution" means a resolution passed by a majority in number and at least three-fourths in value of the creditors present personally or by proxy at a meeting of creditors and voting on the resolution;

"statutory demand" means a demand in the prescribed form which requires the person to whom it is addressed to pay, secure or compound to the reasonable satisfaction of the creditor making the demand, any debt owed by him to the creditor;

"transaction" includes any gift, agreement or arrangement, and any reference to entering into a transaction shall be construed accordingly;

"trustee", in relation to a bankruptcy and a bankrupt, means the trustee of the bankrupt's estate.

(2) Any reference in this Act to the person or property of a debtor or bankrupt shall, in relation to a debtor which is a firm or to a firm against which a bankruptcy order has been made, as the case may be, be read as a reference to the person or property of each partner of the firm.

PART II CONSTITUTION, PROCEDURE AND POWERS OF COURT

Jurisdiction

High Court to be the court having jurisdiction in bankruptcy

3. Subject to any other written law, the High Court shall be the court having jurisdiction in bankruptcy under this Act.

Exercise of jurisdiction in chambers

4. Subject to this Act and the rules, any judge of the court exercising jurisdiction in bankruptcy may exercise the whole or any part of his jurisdiction in chambers.

Jurisdiction in bankruptcy of Registrar

5. Subject to the rules, the Registrar shall have all the powers and jurisdiction of the court, and any order made or act done by him in the exercise of those powers and jurisdiction shall, subject to an appeal to a judge in chambers, be deemed to be the order or act of the court.

General powers of bankruptcy court

6.

—(1) Subject to this Act, the court, under its jurisdiction in bankruptcy, shall have full power to decide all questions of priorities and all other questions whatsoever, whether of law or fact, which may arise in any case of bankruptcy coming within the cognizance of the court, or which the court considers it expedient or necessary to decide for the purpose of doing complete justice or making a complete distribution of property in any such case.

(2) Where default is made by a debtor or bankrupt or any other person in obeying any order or direction given by the court or the Official Assignee or any other officer of the court under this Act, the court may, on the application of the Official Assignee or any other duly authorised person, or of its own motion, order such defaulting debtor, bankrupt or person to comply with the order or direction so given, and may also, if it thinks fit, make an immediate order for the committal of such defaulting debtor, bankrupt or other person.

(3) The power given by subsection (2) shall be deemed to be in addition to and not in substitution for any other right or remedy in respect of such default.

Power to review orders

7. The court may review, rescind or vary any order made by it under its bankruptcy jurisdiction.

Appeals in bankruptcy

8.

—(1) Orders in bankruptcy matters shall, at the instance of any person aggrieved, be subject to appeal in the same way as orders of the High Court in other matters are for the time being appealable.

(2) For the purposes of this section, the Official Assignee shall be deemed to be aggrieved by the refusal of any application made by him to the court.

Power of arrest and seizure

9.

—(1) Where the court is satisfied —

(*a*) on an application of the Official Assignee; or

(*b*) that there are reasonable grounds for believing,that any person against whom a bankruptcy petition has been presented or a bankruptcy order made —

(i) has absconded, or is about to abscond, with a view to avoiding or delaying the payment of any of his debts or his appearance to a bankruptcy petition or to avoiding, delaying or disrupting any proceedings in bankruptcy against him or any examination of his affairs;

(ii) is about to remove his goods with a view to preventing or delaying possession being taken of them by the Official Assignee;

(iii) has concealed or destroyed, or is about to conceal or destroy, any of his goods or any books, papers or records which might be of use to his creditors in the course of his bankruptcy or in connection with the administration of his estate;

(iv) has, without the leave of the Official Assignee, removed any goods in his possession which exceed $200 in value; or

(v) has failed, without reasonable excuse, to attend any examination ordered by the court, the court may cause a warrant to be issued to a police officer for his arrest or for the seizure of any books, papers, records, money or goods in his possession, and upon his arrest, may authorise him to be kept in custody, and anything seized under such a warrant to be held, in accordance with the rules, until such time as the court may order.

(2) Where a person has been arrested under this section, the court may order his release, either with or without security to the satisfaction of the court that he will abide by such conditions as the court may think fit to impose, and the proceeds of the realisation of any security given on breach by such person of any of the conditions of the security shall be deemed to be his property and shall vest in the Official Assignee where such person is an undischarged bankrupt or, where he is not such, in the event of his bankruptcy.

Criminal jurisdiction of District and Magistrate's Courts

10. A District Court or a Magistrate's Court shall have jurisdiction to hear and determine all offences under this Act or any rules and, notwithstanding anything to the contrary in the Criminal Procedure Code (Cap. 68) , shall have power to impose the full penalty or punishment in respect of any offence under this Act or the rules.

Procedure

Where no specific procedure provided

11.

—(1) In any matter of practice or procedure for which no specific provision has been made by this Act or any rules, the procedure and practice for the time being in use or in force in the Supreme Court shall, as nearly as may be, be followed and adopted.

(2) Where in respect of any matter of practice or procedure it is not possible to apply subsection (1) , the court may make such orders and give such directions as are likely to secure substantial justice between the parties.

Power to adjourn proceedings

12. The court may at any time adjourn any proceedings before it upon such terms, if any, as it may think fit.

Power to amend written process

13. The court may at any time amend any written process or proceedings upon such terms, if any, as it may think fit.

Power to extend time

14. Where by this Act or the rules the time for doing any act or thing is limited, the court may extend the time, either before or after the expiration thereof, upon such terms, if any, as it may think fit.

Manner of taking evidence

15. Subject to the rules, the court may in any matter take the whole or any part of any evidence either viva voce or by interrogatories or upon affidavit or by commission abroad.

Costs to be in court's discretion

16. Subject to this Act and the rules, the costs of and incidental to any proceedings in court shall be in the discretion of the court.

PART III OFFICIAL ASSIGNEE

Appointment of Official Assignee of bankrupts' estates

17.

—(1) The Minister may appoint such person as he may think fit to be the Official Assignee of the estates of bankrupts.

(2) The Official Assignee shall act under the general authority and directions of the Minister, but shall also be an officer of the court.

(3) The Minister may appoint such other officers, either temporary or permanent, as he may think necessary for carrying this Act into effect, and may assign to such officers such duties as he may think fit.

Official name of Official Assignee

18. The Official Assignee shall have the following official names:

(*a*) where he has been appointed as the interim receiver of a debtor's property under section 73, "The Official Assignee of the Property of (name of debtor) , a Debtor";

(*b*) where he is acting as the receiver and trustee of the estate of a bankrupt under Part VII, "The Official Assignee of the Estate of (name of bankrupt) , a Bankrupt"; and

(*c*) where he is acting as the trustee of the estate of a deceased debtor in bankruptcy under section 148, "The Official Assignee of the Estate of (name of deceased debtor) , a Deceased Debtor", and may, by such official name, sue and be sued, hold property of every description, enter into contracts or any engagements binding on himself and his successors in office, and do all other acts necessary or expedient to be done in the execution of his office.

Delegation of powers and functions by Official Assignee

19.

—(1) Subject to this Act, the Official Assignee may, in relation to any particular matter or class of matters, by writing under his hand delegate to any person all or any of his powers or functions under this Act or the rules so that such power or function may be exercised by the delegate with respect to the matter or class of matters specified in the instrument of delegation.

(2) No delegation made under this section shall prevent the Official Assignee from exercising the power or function delegated.

(3) The Official Assignee may at any time revoke any delegation made by him under this section.

Official Assignee deemed to be public servant

20. The Official Assignee and any officer appointed by the Minister under section 17(3) shall be deemed to be public servants within the meaning of the Penal Code (Cap. 224) .

General duties of Official Assignee as regards bankrupt's conduct and affairs

21.

—(1) The Official Assignee shall have the following duties as regards a bankrupt:

(*a*) to investigate the conduct and affairs of the bankrupt, and report to the court as to whether there is reason to believe that the bankrupt has committed any act which constitutes an offence under this Act or under section 421, 422, 423 or 424 of the Penal Code, or which would otherwise justify the court in refusing, suspending or qualifying an order for his discharge;

(*b*) to make such other reports concerning the conduct of the bankrupt as the court may direct or as are prescribed;

(*c*) to take such part as may be directed by the court or as is prescribed, in any examination of the bankrupt and other persons; and

(*d*) to take such part and give such assistance in relation to the prosecution of any fraudulent bankrupt or any other person charged with an offence under this Act, as the court may direct or as is prescribed.

(2) A report by the Official Assignee under subsection (1) shall in any proceedings be prima facie evidence of the facts stated in it.

(3) In this section, the conduct and affairs of a bankrupt shall include his conduct and affairs before the making of the bankruptcy order against him.

General duties of Official Assignee as regards estate of bankrupt

22.

—(1) The Official Assignee shall have the following duties as regards the estate of a bankrupt administered by him:

(*a*) to act as the receiver of the bankrupt's estate and where a special manager has not been appointed under section 113, as the manager thereof;

(*b*) to raise money or make advances for the purposes of the estate, and to authorise the special manager (if any) to raise money or make advances for the like purposes in any case where in the interests of the creditors it appears necessary to do so;

(*c*) to summon and preside at all meetings of creditors held under this Act;

(*d*) to issue forms of proxy for use at the meetings of creditors;

(*e*) to report to the creditors as to any proposal which he makes with respect to the mode of liquidating the bankrupt's affairs; and

(*f*) to advertise the bankruptcy order, the date of any public examination and such other matters as may be necessary to advertise.

(2) For the purpose of carrying out his duties as receiver or manager, the Official Assignee shall have the same powers as if he were a receiver and manager appointed by the court, but shall, as far as practicable, consult the creditors with respect to the management of the bankrupt's estate, and may for that purpose, if he thinks it advisable, summon meetings of the persons claiming to be creditors.

(3) The Official Assignee shall account to the court and pay over all moneys and deal with all securities in such manner as the court may, subject to this Act, direct.

Discretion of Official Assignee in administration of estate of bankrupt

23.

—(1) Subject to this Act, the Official Assignee shall have discretion as to the administration of the property of the bankrupt.

(2) Subject to this Act, the Official Assignee shall, in the administration of the estate of a bankrupt, have regard to any direction that is given by resolution of the creditors at any general meeting and to any advice given by the creditors' committee.

(3) Where any direction given to the Official Assignee by the creditors of a bankrupt at any general meeting is in conflict with any advice given to him by the creditors' committee, the direction given by the general meeting of creditors shall prevail.

Power to administer oaths

24. The Official Assignee may administer oaths for the purposes of any matters or proceedings under this Act or for the purpose of taking affidavits.

Official Assignee's accounts

25.

—(1) The Official Assignee shall keep in the prescribed form an account of his receipts and payments in respect of his administration of the estate of a bankrupt, and shall permit inspection of such account by the bankrupt or by any creditor who has proved his debt or by any other person interested, subject to payment of the prescribed fee.

(2) Every account referred to in subsection (1) shall be audited not less than once in each year by such officer as the Minister may appoint in that behalf, and for the purposes of the audit the Official Assignee shall produce to the auditing officer such books and shall furnish him with such vouchers and information as he may require.

Books to be kept by Official Assignee

26. The Official Assignee shall keep as prescribed proper books, in which he shall cause to be made entries or minutes of proceedings at any meeting held under this Act and of such other matters as are prescribed, and any creditor of the bankrupt may, subject to the control of the court, personally or by his agent inspect any such books.

Bankruptcy Estates Account

27.

—(1) The Official Assignee shall keep with such bank as he may think fit an account, to be called the Bankruptcy Estates Account, into which all moneys received by the Official Assignee under this Act shall, subject to the provisions of this Act, be paid.

(2) All payments out of moneys standing to the credit of the Official Assignee in the Bankruptcy Estates Account shall be made by such bank in such manner as the Official Assignee may think fit.

Investment of surplus funds in Bankruptcy Estates Account

28.

—(1) Whenever the cash balance standing to the credit of the Bankruptcy Estates Account is in excess of the amount which, in the opinion of the Official Assignee, is required for the time being to meet demands in respect of insolvent estates, the Official Assignee shall notify the excess to the Accountant-General, and shall pay over the whole or any part of the excess as the Accountant-General may require to such account as the Accountant-General may direct, and the Accountant-General may invest the sums paid over or any part thereof in trustee securities to be placed to the credit of the said account.

(2) Where any part of the money invested under subsection (1) is, in the opinion of the Official Assignee, required to meet any demand in respect of insolvent estates, the Official Assignee shall notify the Accountant-General the amount so required and the Accountant-General shall thereupon repay the Official Assignee such sum as may be required to the credit of the Bankruptcy Estates Account and for that purpose the Accountant-General may direct the sale of such part of the securities as may be necessary.

(3) The income derived from any investment under subsection (1) shall form part of the Consolidated Fund and regard shall be had to the amount thus derived in fixing the fees payable in respect of proceedings in bankruptcy.

(4) Any profits on the sale of any of the securities placed to the credit of the Bankruptcy Estates Account shall be credited to the Consolidated Fund and that Fund shall be liable to make good any loss arising out of the sale of those securities.

Official Assignee to furnish list of creditors

29. The Official Assignee shall, whenever required by any creditor of a bankrupt to do so, and on payment by the creditor of the prescribed fee, furnish and transmit to the creditor a list of the creditors of the bankrupt, showing in the list the amount of the debt due from the bankrupt to each of the creditors.

Control of court over Official Assignee

30.

—(1) The court shall take cognizance of the conduct of the Official Assignee in his administration of the estate of a bankrupt, and if the Official Assignee does not faithfully perform his duties or duly observe all the requirements imposed on him by this Act, the rules or any other written law with respect to the performance of his duties, or if any complaint is made to the court by any creditor in regard thereto, the court shall inquire into the matter and take such action thereon as it may consider expedient.

(2) The court may at any time require the Official Assignee to answer any inquiry made by it in relation to his administration of the estate of a bankrupt and may also direct an investigation to be made of the books and vouchers of the Official Assignee or examine him on oath concerning his administration of the estate.

Review by court of Official Assignee's act, omission or decision

31.

—(1) If a bankrupt or any of his creditors or any other person is dissatisfied by any act, omission or decision of the Official Assignee in relation to the Official Assignee's administration of the bankrupt's estate, he may apply to the court to review such act, omission or decision and on hearing such an application the court may —

(*a*) confirm, reverse or modify any act or decision of the Official Assignee; or

(*b*) give such directions to the Official Assignee or make such other order as it may think fit.

(2) The Official Assignee may apply to the court for directions in relation to any particular matter arising under the bankruptcy.

Liability of Official Assignee to be discharged out of Consolidated Fund

32.

—(1) All sums required to discharge any liability which the Official Assignee may be personally liable to discharge shall be charged upon the Consolidated Fund.

(2) Neither the Official Assignee nor any of his officers shall be liable for any act to which he has not in any way contributed or which he could not by the exercise of reasonable diligence have averted.

PART IV TRUSTEE IN BANKRUPTCY

Appointment of person other than Official Assignee as trustee in bankruptcy

33.

—(1) The court may, on making a bankruptcy order and on the application of a petitioning creditor, appoint a person other than the Official Assignee to be the trustee of the bankrupt's estate.

(2) The official name of the trustee shall be —

(*a*) "the Trustee of the estate of (name of bankrupt) , a Bankrupt"; or

(*b*) "the Trustee in Bankruptcy of (name of bankrupt) , a Bankrupt".

Qualifications for appointment as trustee

34. No person shall be appointed as a trustee in bankruptcy unless he satisfies the court that —

(*a*) he is —

(i) registered as a public accountant under the Accountants Act (Cap. 2A) ;

(ii) an advocate and solicitor; or

(iii) such person as the Minister may, by order published in the *Gazette*, prescribe; and

(*b*) he has not been convicted of an offence involving fraud or dishonesty punishable on conviction by imprisonment for 3 months or more, and he has consented in writing to being appointed as a trustee.

Person appointed as trustee to furnish security before acting

35.

—(1) No person appointed as a trustee under section 33 shall commence acting as such trustee until he has given security in the prescribed manner to the satisfaction of the Official Assignee that he shall faithfully perform his duties and duly observe all the requirements imposed on him by this Act, the rules or any other written law with respect to the performance of his duties.

(2) Any person who contravenes or fails to comply with subsection (1) shall be guilty of an offence and shall be liable on conviction to a fine not exceeding $10,000.

General functions, duties and powers of trustee

36.

—(1) Subject to subsection (2) and section 39, a trustee shall —

(*a*) have all the functions and duties of the Official Assignee in relation to the conduct of a bankrupt and the administration of his estate as provided in this Act; and

(*b*) exercise all the powers of the Official Assignee, and any reference in this Act or the rules to the Official Assignee shall, unless the context otherwise requires, include a reference to a trustee.

(2) Sections 19, 24, 108, 113, 116, 125 and 165 shall not apply to a trustee and section 112(*a*) , (*c*) , (*f*) , (*h*) and (*i*) shall not apply to a trustee except with the consent of the court, the creditors' committee or, if there is no creditors' committee, the Official Assignee.

Trustee to pay moneys received by him into prescribed bank account

37.

—(1) Every trustee shall, in the manner and at the times prescribed by the rules, pay all moneys received by him into such bank account as is prescribed by those rules or as may be specified by the court.

(2) Any trustee who pays any moneys received by him as trustee into any bank account other than the bank account prescribed or specified under subsection (1) shall be guilty of an offence and shall be liable on conviction to a fine not exceeding $10,000 or to imprisonment for a term not exceeding 2 years or to both.

Remuneration of trustee

38.

—(1) A trustee shall be entitled to receive such salary or remuneration as is determined in the following manner:

(*a*) by agreement between the trustee and the creditors' committee, if any;

(*b*) failing any agreement with the creditors' committee or where there is no such committee, by a special resolution of the creditors whose debts have been admitted for the purpose of voting and who are present in person or by proxy and voting at a meeting to be convened by the trustee by a notice to each creditor in accordance with subsection (2) ; or

(*c*) failing a determination in the manner referred to in paragraph (*a*) or (*b*) , by the court.

(2) The trustee shall attach to every notice under subsection (1) (*b*) a statement of all receipts and expenditure by the trustee and the amount of remuneration sought by him.

Control of trustee by Official Assignee

39.

—(1) The Official Assignee shall take cognizance of the conduct of a trustee in the administration of the estate of a bankrupt and if the trustee does not faithfully perform his duties or duly observe all the requirements imposed on him by this Act, the rules or any other written law with respect to the performance of his duties, or if any complaint is made to the Official Assignee by any creditor or bankrupt in regard thereto, the Official Assignee shall inquire into the matter and take such action thereon as he may think expedient.

(2) The Official Assignee may at any time require a trustee to answer any inquiry in relation to his administration of the estate of a bankrupt and may also direct an investigation to be made of the books and vouchers of the trustee.

(3) It shall be the duty of the trustee —

(*a*) to furnish the Official Assignee with such information;

(*b*) to produce to the Official Assignee, and permit inspection by the Official Assignee of, such books, papers and other records; and

(*c*) to give the Official Assignee such other assistance, as the Official Assignee may reasonably require for the purpose of enabling him to carry out his functions in relation to the bankruptcy.

(4) The Official Assignee may, having regard to the results of any inquiry or investigation made under this section, apply to the court for the removal of the trustee.

Review by court of trustee's act, omission or decision

40.

—(1) If a bankrupt or any of his creditors or any other person is dissatisfied by any act, omission or decision of a trustee in relation to the trustee's administration of the bankrupt's estate, he may apply to the court to review such act, omission or decision and on hearing such an application the court may —

(*a*) confirm, reverse or modify any act or decision of the trustee; or

(*b*) give such directions to the trustee or make such other order as it may think fit.

(2) A trustee may apply to the court for directions in relation to any particular matter arising under the bankruptcy.

Removal of trustee

41.

—(1) A trustee may be removed from office only by an order of the court or by a general meeting of the bankrupt's creditors summoned especially for that purpose in accordance with the rules.

(2) A trustee shall vacate his office if he ceases to be qualified to hold office as a trustee under section 34(*a*) or (*b*) .

(3) A trustee may resign his office by giving one month's notice of his resignation to the court and the Official Assignee.

(4) A trustee shall vacate his office if the bankruptcy order is annulled.

Vacancy in office of trustee

42. Where the appointment of any person as trustee of a bankrupt's estate fails to take effect or where a vacancy arises in the office of a trustee whose appointment has taken effect, the Official Assignee —

(*a*) shall act as the trustee of the bankrupt's estate until the vacancy is filled; and

(*b*) may summon a general meeting of the bankrupt's creditors for the purpose of filling the vacancy.

Liability of trustee

43.

—(1) Where —

(*a*) the trustee of a bankrupt's estate has misapplied or retained, or become accountable for, any money or other property comprised in the bankrupt's estate; or

(*b*) the estate of a bankrupt has suffered any loss in consequence of any misfeasance or breach of fiduciary or other duty by a trustee of the estate in the carrying out of his functions, the Official Assignee or any creditor of the bankrupt or the bankrupt himself may apply to the court for any order specified in subsection (2) .

(2) Upon hearing an application made under subsection (1) , the court may, for the benefit of the estate, order the trustee to —

(*a*) repay, restore or account for any money or other property (together with interest at such rate as the court may think just) ; or

(*b*) pay such sum by way of compensation in respect of the misfeasance or breach of fiduciary or other duty as the court may think just.

(3) Any order made by the court under subsection (2) shall be without prejudice to any liability on the part of the trustee arising apart from this section.

(4) Where a trustee seizes or disposes of any property which is not comprised in the bankrupt's estate and at the time of the seizure or disposal the trustee believes, and has reasonable grounds for believing, that he is entitled (whether in pursuance of an order of the court or otherwise) to seize or dispose of that property, the trustee —

(*a*) shall not be liable to any person (whether under this section or otherwise) in respect of any loss or damage resulting from the seizure or disposal except in so far as the loss or damage is caused by the negligence of the trustee; and

(*b*) shall have a lien on the property or the proceeds of its sale for such of the expenses of the bankruptcy as were incurred in connection with the seizure or disposal.

PART V VOLUNTARY ARRANGEMENTS

Moratorium for insolvent debtor

This Part not applicable to undischarged bankrupts

44. This Part shall not apply —

(*a*) to any individual debtor who is an undischarged bankrupt; or

(*b*) to any firm against which a bankruptcy order has been made and from which bankruptcy the partners in the firm have not been discharged.

Interim order of court

45.

—(1) Subject to subsection (2) , any insolvent debtor who intends to make a proposal to his creditors for a composition in satisfaction of his debts or a scheme of arrangement of his affairs (hereinafter referred to as a voluntary arrangement) may apply to the court for an interim order under this Part.

(2) No partner in an insolvent firm shall apply to the court for an interim order in respect of the firm unless all or a majority of the partners in the firm join or intend to join in the making of the proposal for a voluntary arrangement.

(3) An interim order shall have the effect that, during the period for which it is in force —

(*a*) where the interim order is in respect of an individual debtor —

(i) no bankruptcy petition may be presented or proceeded with against the debtor; and

(ii) no other proceedings, execution or other legal process may be commenced or continued against the person or property of the debtor without the leave of the court; and

(*b*) where the interim order is in respect of a firm —

(i) no bankruptcy petition may be presented or proceeded with against the firm or, except with the leave of the court, any partner therein; and

(ii) no other proceedings, execution or other legal process may be commenced or continued against the firm or its property or against the person or property of any partner in the firm, without the leave of the court.

(4) An interim order shall cease to have effect 28 days after the making thereof unless the court otherwise directs.

Nominee

46.

—(1) Every debtor making a proposal for the purpose of this Part shall in such proposal appoint a nominee to act in relation to the voluntary arrangement either as trustee or otherwise for the purpose of supervising its implementation.

(2) No person shall be appointed as a nominee unless he is —

(*a*) registered as a public accountant under the Accountants Act (Cap. 2A) ;

(*b*) an advocate and solicitor; or

(*c*) such other person as the Minister may, by order published in the *Gazette*, prescribe.

Effect of application

47.

—(1) At any time when an application under section 45 for an interim order is pending, the court may stay any action, execution or other legal process against the debtor in respect of whom the application has been made or the property of such debtor.

(2) Any court in which proceedings are pending against a debtor may, on being satisfied that an application under section 45 for an interim order has been made in respect of the debtor, stay the proceedings or allow them to continue on such terms as the court may think fit.

(3) Where the debtor in respect of whom an application under section 45 for an interim order is pending is a firm, the power of the court under subsections (1) and (2) shall apply to any action, execution or other legal process or proceedings against the person or property of any partner in the firm.

Conditions for making of interim order

48.

—(1) The court shall not make an interim order on an application under section 45 unless it is satisfied that —

(*a*) the debtor intends to make a proposal for a voluntary arrangement;

(*b*) no previous application for an interim order has been made by or in respect of the debtor during the period of 12 months immediately preceding the date of the application; and

(*c*)

the nominee appointed by the debtor's proposal is qualified and willing to act in relation to the proposal.

(2) The court may make an interim order if it thinks that it would be appropriate to do so for the purpose of facilitating the consideration and implementation of the debtor's proposal.

Nominee's report on debtor's proposal

49.

—(1) Where an interim order has been made, the nominee shall, before the order ceases to have effect, submit a report to the court stating —

(*a*) whether, in his opinion, a meeting of the debtor's creditors should be summoned to consider the debtor's proposal; and

(*b*) if in his opinion such a meeting should be summoned, the date on which, and the time and place at which, he proposes the meeting should be held.

(2) For the purpose of enabling the nominee to prepare his report, the debtor shall submit to the nominee —

(*a*) a document setting out the terms of the voluntary arrangement which the debtor is proposing; and

(*b*) where the debtor is an individual, a statement of his affairs containing —

(i) such particulars of his assets, creditors, debts and other liabilities as may be prescribed; and

(ii) such other information as may be prescribed; or

(*c*) where the debtor is a firm, a statement of its affairs containing —

(i) such particulars of the assets, creditors, debts and other liabilities of the firm and of each partner therein, as may be prescribed; and

(ii) such other information as may be prescribed.

(3) Where the nominee has failed to submit the report required by this section within the time given, the court may, on an application made by the debtor, do one or both of the following:

(*a*) direct that the nominee shall be replaced by another person qualified to act as a nominee;

(*b*) direct that the interim order shall continue, or if it has ceased to have effect be renewed, for such further period as the court may think fit.

(4) The court may, on the application of the nominee, extend the period for which the interim order has effect so as to allow the nominee to have more time to prepare his report.

(5) If the court is satisfied on receiving the nominee's report that a meeting of the debtor's creditors should be summoned to consider the debtor's proposal, the court shall direct that the period for which the interim order has effect shall be extended for such further period as it may think fit, for the purpose of enabling the debtor's proposal to be considered by the debtor's creditors in accordance with the following provisions of this Part.

(6) The court may discharge the interim order if it is satisfied, on the application of the nominee —

(*a*) that the debtor has failed to comply with subsection (2) ; or

(*b*) that for any other reason it would be inappropriate for a meeting of the debtor's creditors to be summoned to consider the debtor's proposal.

Summoning of creditors' meeting

50.

—(1) Where a nominee has reported to the court under section 49 that a meeting of the debtor's creditors should be summoned, the nominee shall, unless the court otherwise directs, summon that meeting in accordance with his report.

(2) The nominee shall summon to the meeting every of the debtor's creditors of whose claim and address he is aware.

Consideration and implementation of debtor's proposal

Decision of creditors' meeting

51.

—(1) A creditors' meeting summoned under section 50 may, if the meeting thinks fit, by special resolution resolve to approve the proposed voluntary arrangement, whether with or without modification.

(2) The meeting shall not approve the proposed voluntary arrangement with any modification unless the debtor has consented to such modification.

(3) For the purpose of this section, a modification subject to which a proposed voluntary arrangement may be approved by a creditors' meeting may confer the functions proposed to be conferred on the nominee on another person qualified to act as a nominee but no modification shall alter the proposal to such an extent that it ceases to be a proposal for a voluntary arrangement by the debtor.

(4) The meeting shall not approve any proposal or any modification thereto which affects the right of a secured creditor of the debtor to enforce his security, except with the concurrence of the secured creditor concerned.

(5) The meeting shall not, without the concurrence of the preferential creditor concerned, approve any proposal or any modification thereto under which —

(*a*) any debt of the debtor, not being a preferential debt, is to be paid in priority to any preferential debt of the debtor; or

(*b*) any preferential debt of the debtor is to be paid in relation to any other preferential debt of the debtor other than in accordance with section 90.

(6) Every meeting shall be conducted in accordance with the prescribed rules.

(7) Any debtor who makes any false representation or commits any other fraud for the purpose of obtaining the approval of his creditors to a proposal for a voluntary arrangement shall be guilty of an offence

and shall be liable on conviction to a fine not exceeding $10,000 or to imprisonment for a term not exceeding 2 years or to both.

Report of decisions to court

52.

—(1) After the conclusion of the meeting summoned under section 50, the nominee shall report the result thereof to the court and shall serve a copy of the report on such persons as may be prescribed.

(2) Where the meeting has declined to approve the debtor's proposal, the court may discharge any interim order which is in force in relation to the debtor.

Effect of approval

53.

—(1) Where the meeting summoned under section 50 has approved the proposed voluntary arrangement, whether with or without modifications, the approved arrangement shall —

(*a*) take effect as if made by the debtor at the meeting; and

(*b*) bind every person who had notice of and was entitled to vote at the meeting, whether or not he was present or represented thereat, as if he were a party to the arrangement.

(2) Subject to section 54, the interim order in force in relation to the debtor shall cease to have effect at the end of 28 days from the date the report was made to the court under section 52.

(3) Where proceedings on a bankruptcy petition have been stayed by an interim order which ceases to have effect under subsection (2) , that petition shall, unless the court otherwise orders, be deemed to have been dismissed.

Review of meeting's decision

54.

—(1) Any debtor, nominee or person entitled to vote at a creditors' meeting under section 50 may apply to the court for a review of the decision of the meeting on the ground that —

(*a*) the voluntary arrangement approved by the meeting unfairly prejudices the interests of the debtor or any of the debtor's creditors; or

(*b*) there has been some material irregularity at or in relation to the meeting, and upon hearing such application, the court may, if it thinks fit, do one or both of the following:

(i) revoke or suspend any approval given by the meeting;

(ii) direct any person to summon a further meeting of the debtor's creditors to consider any revised proposal the debtor may make or, in a case falling within paragraph (*b*) , to reconsider the original proposal of the debtor.

(2) No application under this section shall be made after 28 days from the date the report was made to the court under section 52.

(3) Where at any time after giving a direction under subsection (1) (ii) for the summoning of a meeting to consider a revised proposal the court is satisfied that the debtor does not intend to submit such a proposal, the court shall revoke the direction and revoke or suspend any approval given at the previous meeting.

(4) Upon giving a direction under subsection (1) (ii) , the court may, if it thinks just, extend the validity of any interim order in relation to the debtor for such period as it may think fit.

(5) Upon giving a direction or revoking or suspending an approval under this section, the court may give such supplemental directions as it may think fit and, in particular, directions with respect to —

(*a*) things done since the meeting under any voluntary arrangement approved by the meeting; and

(*b*) such things done since the meeting as could not have been done if an interim order had been in force in relation to the debtor when they were done.

(6) Except in pursuance of this section, no approval given at a creditors' meeting summoned under section 50 shall be invalidated by reason only of any irregularity at or in relation to the meeting.

Implementation and supervision of approved voluntary arrangement

55.

—(1) Where a voluntary arrangement approved by a creditors' meeting summoned under section 50 has taken effect, the nominee shall supervise the implementation of the voluntary arrangement.

(2) If the debtor or any of his creditors is dissatisfied by any act, omission or decision of the nominee in his supervision of the implementation of the voluntary arrangement, the debtor or creditor may apply to the court to review such act, omission or decision and, on hearing such an application, the court may —

(*a*) confirm, reverse or modify any act or decision of the nominee; or

(*b*) give such directions to the nominee or make such order as it thinks fit.

(3) The nominee may apply to the court for directions in relation to any particular matter arising under the voluntary arrangement.

(4) The court may, whenever —

(*a*) it is expedient to appoint a person to carry out the functions of the nominee; and

(*b*) it is inexpedient, difficult or impracticable for such an appointment to be made without the assistance of the court, make an order appointing a person who is qualified to act as a nominee, either in substitution for the existing nominee or to fill a vacancy.

Consequence of failure by debtor to comply with voluntary arrangement

56. Where a debtor fails to comply with any of his obligations under a voluntary arrangement, the nominee or any creditor bound by the voluntary arrangement may present a bankruptcy petition against the debtor in accordance with Part VI.

PART VI PROCEEDINGS IN BANKRUPTCY

Bankruptcy petitions and bankruptcy orders

Persons who may present creditor's petition

57.

—(1) Subject to this Part, a creditor's petition may be presented —

(*a*) against an individual by —

(i) one of the individual's creditors or jointly by more than one of them; or

(ii) the nominee supervising the implementation of, or any person (other than the individual) who is for the time being bound by, a voluntary arrangement proposed by the individual and approved under Part V; or

(*b*) against a firm by —

(i) one of the firm's creditors or jointly by more than one of them, if such creditor or creditors are entitled under paragraph (*a*) (i) to present a creditor's petition against any one of the partners in the firm in respect of a partnership debt; or

(ii) the nominee supervising the implementation of, or any person (other than the partners in the firm) who is for the time being bound by, a voluntary arrangement proposed by the firm and approved under Part V.

(2) A creditor who is entitled to present a bankruptcy petition against a firm under subsection (1) (*b*) may present a bankruptcy petition against any of the partners in the firm without including the others.

(3) Every creditor's petition shall be in the prescribed form and shall be verified by affidavit of the creditor or of some person on his behalf having knowledge of the facts.

(4) Every creditor's petition shall be served in the manner prescribed.

Persons who may present debtor's petition

58.

—(1) Subject to this Part, a debtor's petition may be presented —

(*a*) against an individual debtor by the debtor himself; or

(*b*) against a firm by all the partners in the firm or by a majority of such partners who are residing in Singapore at the time of the presentation of the petition.

(2) A debtor's petition shall be in the prescribed form and shall be accompanied —

(*a*) where the debtor is an individual, by a statement of his affairs containing such particulars of his assets, creditors, debts and other liabilities as may be prescribed;

(*b*) where the debtor is a firm, by a statement of —

(i) the firm's affairs containing such particulars of its assets, creditors, debts and other liabilities as may be prescribed; and

(ii) the affairs of each of the partners in the firm by whom the petition is presented containing such particulars of his assets, creditors, debts and other liabilities as may be prescribed; and

(*c*) such other information as may be prescribed.

Bankruptcy order

59. Subject to this Part, the court may make a bankruptcy order on a bankruptcy petition presented to it under section 57 or 58.

Conditions to be satisfied in respect of debtor

60.

—(1) No bankruptcy petition shall be presented to the court under section 57(1) (*a*) or 58(1) (*a*) against an individual debtor unless the debtor —

(*a*) is domiciled in Singapore;

(*b*) has property in Singapore; or

(*c*) has, at any time within the period of one year immediately preceding the date of the presentation of the petition —

(i) been ordinarily resident or has had a place of residence in Singapore; or

(ii) carried on business in Singapore.

(2) No bankruptcy petition shall be presented to the court under section 57(1) (*b*) or 58(1) (*b*) against a firm unless —

(*a*) at least one of the partners in the firm —

(i) is domiciled in Singapore;

(ii) has property in Singapore; or

(iii) has, at any time within the period of one year immediately preceding the date of the presentation of the petition, been ordinarily resident or has had a place of residence in Singapore; or

(*b*) the firm has, at any time within the period of one year immediately preceding the date of the presentation of the petition, carried on business in Singapore.

(3) The reference in subsection (1) (*c*) (ii) to an individual carrying on business in Singapore shall include —

(*a*) the carrying on of business in Singapore by a firm in which the individual is a partner; and

(*b*) the carrying on of business in Singapore by an agent or manager for the individual or for such a firm.

Grounds of bankruptcy petition

61.

—(1) No bankruptcy petition shall be presented to the court in respect of any debt or debts unless at the time the petition is presented —

(*a*) the amount of the debt, or the aggregate amount of the debts, is not less than $2,000;

(*b*) the debt or each of the debts is for a liquidated sum payable to the petitioning creditor immediately;

(*c*) the debtor is unable to pay the debt or each of the debts; and

(*d*) where the debt or each of the debts is incurred outside Singapore, such debt is payable by the debtor to the petitioning creditor by virtue of a judgement or award which is enforceable by execution in Singapore.

(2) The Minister may, by order published in the *Gazette*, amend subsection (1) (*a*) by substituting a different sum for the sum for the time being specified therein.

Presumption of inability to pay debts

62. For the purposes of a creditor's petition, a debtor shall, until he proves to the contrary, be presumed to be unable to pay any debt within the meaning of section 61(1) (*c*) if the debt is immediately payable and —

(*a*)

(i) the petitioning creditor to whom the debt is owed has served on him in the prescribed manner, a statutory demand;

(ii) at least 21 days have elapsed since the statutory demand was served; and

(iii) the debtor has neither complied with it nor applied to the court to set it aside;

(*b*) execution issued against him in respect of a judgment debt owed to the petitioning creditor has been returned unsatisfied in whole or in part; or

(*c*) he has departed from or remained outside Singapore with the intention of defeating, delaying or obstructing a creditor in the recovery of the debt.

Where petitioner is secured creditor

63.

—(1) Where the petitioner is a secured creditor of the debtor, he shall in his petition —

(*a*) state that he is willing, in the event of a bankruptcy order being made, to give up his security for the benefit of the other creditors of the bankrupt; or

(*b*) give an estimate of the value of his security, in which case he may to the extent of the balance of the debt due to him, after deducting the value so estimated, be admitted as a petitioning creditor in the same manner as if he were an unsecured creditor.

(2) Where a petitioner who is a secured creditor of the debtor fails to disclose his security in the petition, he shall be deemed to have given up his security for the benefit of the other creditors of the debtor and upon the making of a bankruptcy order —

(*a*) he shall not be entitled to enforce his security against the estate of the bankrupt or to retain any proceeds from the realisation of such security; and

(*b*) he shall execute such document of release as is required by the Official Assignee or account and pay over to the Official Assignee all proceeds from any realisation of his security.

(3) Where any secured creditor fails to execute any document of release as is required by the Official Assignee under subsection (2) (*b*) , the Official Assignee may execute the document on his behalf and the execution of the document by the Official Assignee shall have the same effect as the execution thereof by the secured creditor.

(4) Any secured creditor who fails to account or pay over to the Official Assignee the proceeds from any realisation of his security under subsection (2) (*b*) shall be guilty of an offence and shall be liable on conviction to a fine not exceeding $15,000 or to imprisonment for a term not exceeding 3 years or to both.

(5) Any fine imposed under subsection (4) shall be deemed part of the property of the bankrupt and shall vest in the Official Assignee for the purposes of this Act.

Power of court to stay or dismiss proceedings on bankruptcy petition

64.

—(1) The court may at any time, for sufficient reason, make an order staying the proceedings on a bankruptcy petition, either altogether or for a limited time, on such terms and conditions as the court may think just.

(2) Without prejudice to subsection (1) , where it appears to the court that the person presenting a bankruptcy petition has contravened any of the provisions of this Act or any rules in relation to proceedings on a bankruptcy petition, the court may, in its discretion, dismiss the petition in lieu of staying any proceedings thereon under that subsection.

Proceedings on creditor's petition

65.

—(1) The court hearing a creditor's petition shall not make a bankruptcy order thereon unless it is satisfied that —

(*a*) the debt or any one of the debts in respect of which the petition is presented is a debt which, having been payable at the date of the petition, has neither been paid nor secured or compounded for; and

(*b*) where the debtor does not appear at the hearing, the petition has been duly served on him.

(2) The court may dismiss the petition if —

(*a*) it is not satisfied with the proof of the petitioning creditor's debt or debts;

(*b*) it is not satisfied with the proof of the service of the petition on the debtor;

(*c*) it is satisfied that the debtor is able to pay all his debts;

(*d*) it is satisfied that the debtor has made an offer to secure or compound for the petitioning creditor's debt the acceptance of which offer would have required the dismissal of the petition and the offer has been unreasonably refused by the petitioning creditor; or

(*e*) it is satisfied that for other sufficient cause no order ought to be made thereon.

(3) In determining for the purposes of subsection (2) (*c*) whether the debtor is able to pay all his debts, the court shall take into account his contingent and prospective liabilities.

(4) When a bankruptcy petition has been presented against a debtor on the ground that the debtor —

(*a*) has failed to pay a judgment debt, and there is pending an appeal from or an application to set aside, the judgment or order by virtue of which the judgment debt is payable; or

(*b*) has failed to comply with a statutory demand, and there is pending an application to set aside the statutory demand, the court may, if it thinks fit, stay or dismiss the petition.

(5) Where the debtor appears on the petition and denies that he is —

(*a*) indebted to the petitioner; or

(*b*) indebted to such an amount as would justify the petitioner presenting a bankruptcy petition against him, the court may, on condition that the debtor furnishes such security as the court may order for payment to the petitioner of —

(i) any debt which may be established against the debtor in due course of law; and

(ii) the costs of establishing the debt, stay all proceedings on the petition for such time as may be required for trial of the question relating to the debt.

(6) Where proceedings are stayed, the court may, if by reason of the delay caused by the stay of proceedings or for any other cause it thinks just, make a bankruptcy order on the petition of some other creditor, and shall thereupon dismiss, on such terms as it may think just, the petition in which proceedings have been stayed.

Proceedings on bankruptcy petition by nominee or creditor bound by voluntary arrangement

66. The court shall not make a bankruptcy order on a bankruptcy petition presented under section 57(1) (*a*) (ii) or (*b*) (ii) by the nominee or any creditor bound by a voluntary arrangement unless it is satisfied —

(*a*) that the debtor has failed to comply with his obligations under the voluntary arrangement;

(*b*) that information which was false or misleading in any material particular or which contained material omissions —

(i) was contained in any statement of affairs or other document supplied by the debtor under Part V to any person; or

(ii) was otherwise made available by the debtor to his creditors at or in connection with a meeting summoned under Part V; or (*c*) that the debtor has failed to do all such things as may for the purposes of the voluntary arrangement have been reasonably required of him by the nominee of the arrangement.

Proceedings on debtor's petition

67.

—(1) The court hearing a debtor's petition shall not make a bankruptcy order thereon unless it is satisfied that the debtor is unable to pay his debts.

(2) Where a debtor's petition has been presented against a firm by some, but not all, of the partners in the firm, the court shall not make a bankruptcy order thereon unless it is satisfied that notice of the petition in the prescribed form has been served in the prescribed manner on each of the partners who did not join in the petition.

Consolidation of bankruptcy petitions

68. Where two or more bankruptcy petitions are presented against the same debtor, the court may consolidate the proceedings or any of them on such terms as the court thinks fit.

Power to dismiss petition against some respondents only

69. Where there are two or more respondents to a petition, the court may dismiss the petition as to one or more of them, without prejudice to the effect of the petition as against the other or others of them.

Power to change conduct of proceedings

70. Where any petitioner does not proceed with due diligence on his petition, the court may substitute as petitioner —

(*a*) in the case of a creditor's petition, any other creditor to whom the debtor is indebted in the amount required under section 61(1) (*a*) ; or

(*b*) in any other case, the Official Assignee, and thereafter the proceedings shall, unless the court otherwise directs, be continued as though no change had been made in the conduct of the proceedings.

Continuance of proceedings on death of debtor

71. If a debtor by or against whom a bankruptcy petition has been presented dies, the proceedings in the matter shall, unless the court otherwise directs, be continued as if he were alive, and the court may dispense with service of the petition upon him.

Withdrawal of bankruptcy petition

72. A bankruptcy petition shall not be withdrawn without the leave of the court.

Protection of debtor's property

Appointment of interim receiver

73.

—(1) The court may, if it thinks it necessary or expedient for the protection of the debtor's property, at any time after the presentation of a bankruptcy petition and before making a bankruptcy order, appoint the Official Assignee to be interim receiver of the debtor's property or any part thereof and direct him to take immediate possession of the same, including any books of accounts and other documents relating to the debtor's business.

(2) Where the court has appointed an interim receiver under subsection (1) , no person who is a creditor of the debtor in respect of a debt provable in bankruptcy shall —

(*a*) have any remedy against the person or property of the debtor in respect of that debt; or

(*b*) while the appointment of the interim receiver is in force, commence or continue any action or other legal proceedings against the debtor, except with the leave of the court and on such terms as the court may impose.

(3) Upon the appointment of an interim receiver under subsection (1) , the debtor shall —

(*a*) give to the interim receiver such inventory of his property and such other information; and

(*b*) attend on the interim receiver at such times,

as the interim receiver may for the purpose of carrying out his functions under this section reasonably require.

(4) Upon the appointment of an interim receiver under this section, sections 83 and 84 shall apply, mutatis mutandis, and any reference in those sections to —

(*a*) the making of a bankruptcy order shall be read as a reference to the appointment of an interim receiver under this section;

(*b*) the Official Assignee shall be read as a reference to the interim receiver; and

(*c*) the bankrupt or his estate shall be read (respectively) as a reference to the debtor or his property.

(5) The Official Assignee shall cease to be the interim receiver of a debtor's property if —

(*a*) the bankruptcy petition presented against the debtor is dismissed or withdrawn;

(*b*) a bankruptcy order is made on the petition; or

(*c*) the court by order terminates the appointment.

Power to stay proceedings against person or property of debtor

74.

—(1) Any court may by order, at any time after the presentation of a bankruptcy petition, stay any action, execution or other legal process against the person or property of the debtor.

(2) Where an order is made under subsection (1) staying any action or proceedings or staying proceedings generally, the order may be served by sending a copy thereof, under the seal of the court, by prepaid registered post to the address for service of the plaintiff or other party prosecuting such proceedings.

PART VII ADMINISTRATION IN BANKRUPTCY

Bankruptcy

Commencement and duration of bankruptcy

75. The bankruptcy of any person who has been adjudged bankrupt by a bankruptcy order (whether made against him or against the firm in which he is a partner) shall —

(*a*) commence on the day when the bankruptcy order is made; and

(*b*) continue until he is discharged under Part VIII.

Effect of bankruptcy order

76.

—(1) On the making of a bankruptcy order —

(*a*) the property of the bankrupt shall —

(i) vest in the Official Assignee without any further conveyance, assignment or transfer; and

(ii) become divisible among his creditors;

(*b*) the Official Assignee shall be constituted receiver of the bankrupt's property; and

(*c*) unless otherwise provided by this Act —

(i) no creditor to whom the bankrupt is indebted in respect of any debt provable in bankruptcy shall have any remedy against the person or property of the bankrupt in respect of that debt; and

(ii) no action or proceedings shall be proceeded with or commenced against the bankrupt,

except by leave of the court and in accordance with such terms as the court may impose.

(2) Where a bankruptcy order is made against a firm, the order shall operate as if it were a bankruptcy order made against each of the persons who, at the time of the order, is a partner in the firm.

(3) This section shall not affect the right of any secured creditor to realise or otherwise deal with his security in the same manner as he would have been entitled to realise or deal with it if this section had not been enacted.

(4) Notwithstanding subsection (3) and section 94, no secured creditor shall be entitled to any interest in respect of his debt after the making of a bankruptcy order if he does not realise his security within 6 months from the date of the bankruptcy order or such further period as the Official Assignee may determine.

Restrictions on dispositions of property by bankrupt

77.

—(1) Where a person is adjudged bankrupt, any disposition of property made by him during the period beginning with the day of the presentation of the bankruptcy petition and ending with the making of the bankruptcy order shall be void except to the extent that such disposition has been made with the consent of, or been subsequently ratified by, the court.

(2) For the purpose of this section, a disposition of property shall include any payment (whether in cash or otherwise) made to any person by the bankrupt and accordingly, where any payment is void by virtue of this section, the person to whom the payment was made shall hold the sum paid for the bankrupt as part of his estate.

(3) Nothing in this section shall give a remedy against any person in respect of —

(*a*) any property or payment which he received from the bankrupt before the commencement of the bankruptcy in good faith, for value and without notice that the bankruptcy petition had been presented; or

(*b*) any interest in property which derives from an interest in respect of which there is, by virtue of this subsection, no remedy.

(4) Where, after the commencement of his bankruptcy, the bankrupt has incurred a debt to a banker or any other person by reason of the making of a payment which is void under this section, that debt shall be deemed for the purposes of this Act to have been incurred before the commencement of the bankruptcy unless —

(*a*) that banker or person had notice of the bankruptcy before the debt was incurred; or

(*b*) it is not reasonably practicable for the amount of the payment to be recovered from the person to whom it was made.

(5) A disposition of property shall be void under this section notwithstanding that the property is not or, as the case may be, would not be comprised in the bankrupt's estate, but nothing in this section shall affect any disposition made by a person of property held by him on trust for any other person.

Description of bankrupt's property divisible amongst creditors

78.

—(1) The property of the bankrupt divisible among his creditors (referred to in this Act as the bankrupt's estate) shall comprise —

(*a*) all such property as belongs to or is vested in the bankrupt at the commencement of his bankruptcy or is acquired by or devolves on him before his discharge; and

(*b*) the capacity to exercise and to take proceedings for exercising all such powers in or over or in respect of property as might have been exercised by the bankrupt for his own benefit at the commencement of his bankruptcy or before his discharge.

(2) Subsection (1) shall not apply to —

(*a*) property held by the bankrupt on trust for any other person;

(*b*) the tools, if any, of his trade;

(*c*) such clothing, bedding, furniture, household equipment and provisions as are necessary for satisfying the basic domestic needs of the bankrupt and his family; and (*d*) property of the bankrupt which is excluded under any other written law.

Inquiry into bankrupt's affairs, dealings and property

Meeting of creditors

79.

—(1) The Official Assignee may, at any time after the making of a bankruptcy order, summon a meeting of the bankrupt's creditors.

(2) Notwithstanding subsection (1) , the Official Assignee shall summon a meeting of the bankrupt's creditors whenever directed by the court to do so or whenever requested in writing by one-fourth in value of the bankrupt's creditors to do so.

(3) Every meeting summoned under this section shall be conducted in accordance with the prescribed rules.

Creditors' committee

80.

—(1) At any meeting convened by the Official Assignee under section 79 (1) , the creditors qualified to vote thereat, including the holders of general proxies or general powers of attorney from such creditors, may by ordinary resolution appoint from amongst themselves a committee (known as the "creditors' committee") of not more than 3 persons for the purpose of advising the Official Assignee on matters relating to the administration of the property of the bankrupt.

(2) The Official Assignee may convene the creditors' committee at such times as he may think necessary, but shall convene the committee whenever requested in writing to do so by all or a majority of the members of the committee.

(3) Any member of the creditors' committee may resign his office by notice in writing, signed by him and delivered to the Official Assignee.

(4) If a member of the creditors' committee becomes bankrupt, or compounds or arranges with his creditors, or is absent for more than two months from Singapore, his office shall thereupon become vacant.

(5) Any member of the creditors' committee may be removed by an ordinary resolution at any meeting of creditors, of which 7 days' notice has been given stating the object of the meeting.

(6) On a vacancy occurring in the office of a member of the creditors' committee, the Official Assignee shall forthwith summon a meeting of creditors for the purpose of filling the vacancy, and the meeting may by ordinary resolution appoint another creditor or eligible person to fill the vacancy.

Bankrupt's statement of affairs

81.

—(1) Where a bankruptcy order has been made against an individual otherwise than on a debtor's petition, the bankrupt shall submit a statement of his affairs to the Official Assignee within 21 days from the date of the bankruptcy order.

(2) Where a bankruptcy order has been made against a firm —

(*a*) on a creditors' petition, the bankrupts, being the partners in the firm at the time of the order, shall submit a joint statement of their partnership affairs, and each partner in the firm shall submit a statement of his separate affairs; or

(*b*) on a debtor's petition, every person who at the time of the order is a partner in the firm but who did not join in the petition shall submit a statement of his separate affairs,

to the Official Assignee within 21 days from the date of the bankruptcy order.

(3) The statement of affairs shall contain —

(*a*) such particulars of the bankrupt's assets, creditors, debts and other liabilities as may be prescribed;

(*b*) in the case of a firm, such particulars of the firm's assets, creditors, debts and other liabilities as may be prescribed; and

(*c*) such other information as may be prescribed.

(4) The Official Assignee may, if he thinks fit —

(*a*) release the bankrupt from his duty under subsection (1) or (2) , as the case may be; or

(*b*) extend the period specified in subsection (1) or (2) , and where the Official Assignee has refused to exercise a power conferred by this section, the court, if it thinks fit, may exercise it.

(5) A bankrupt who —

(*a*) without reasonable excuse, fails to comply with the obligation imposed by this section;

(*b*) without reasonable excuse, submits a statement of affairs which does not comply with the prescribed requirements;

(*c*) submits a statement of affairs which is false, and which he either knows or believes to be false or does not believe to be true; or

(*d*) submits a statement which is misleading in any material particular or contains any material omission, shall be guilty of an offence and shall be liable on conviction to a fine not exceeding $10,000 or to imprisonment for a term not exceeding 2 years or to both and, in the case of a continuing offence, to a further fine not exceeding $200 for every day during which the offence continues after conviction.

(6) Any person stating himself, in writing, to be a creditor of the bankrupt may personally or by agent inspect the statement of affairs filed by the bankrupt under this section at all reasonable times and upon payment of the prescribed fee take any copy thereof or extract therefrom, but any person untruthfully so stating himself to be a creditor shall be guilty of an offence and shall be liable on conviction to a fine not exceeding $2,000 or to imprisonment for a term not exceeding 6 months or to both.

Bankrupt to submit accounts

82.

—(1) A bankrupt who has not obtained his discharge shall, unless otherwise directed by the Official Assignee, submit to the Official Assignee once in every 6 months an account of all moneys and property which have come to his hands for his own use during the preceding 6 months or such other period as the Official Assignee may specify, and shall pay and make over to the Official Assignee so much of such moneys and property as have not been expended in the necessary expenses of maintenance of himself and his family.

(2) A bankrupt who fails to comply with subsection (1) shall be guilty of an offence and shall be liable on conviction to a fine not exceeding $10,000 or to imprisonment for a term not exceeding 2 years or to both and, in the case of a continuing offence, to a further fine not exceeding $200 for every day during which the offence continues after conviction.

Examination of bankrupt and others

83.

—(1) Where a bankruptcy order has been made, the court may, upon an application made by the Official Assignee or by a creditor who has tendered a proof, at any time before the discharge of the bankrupt —

(*a*) summon the bankrupt to appear before it on an appointed day and examine him as to his affairs, dealings and property; and

(*b*) summon to appear before it on the same or another appointed day and examine —

(i) the bankrupt's spouse or former spouse;

(ii) any person known or believed to be indebted to the bankrupt or to have in his possession any property comprised in the bankrupt's estate; and

(iii) any other person, if it appears to the court that such person would be able to give information concerning the bankrupt or the bankrupt's affairs, dealings or property.

(2) Every person summoned before the court under this section shall be examined on oath, whether orally or by interrogatories.

(3) Without prejudice to subsection (2) , the court may at any time require any person mentioned in subsection (1) (*b*) to submit an affidavit to the court containing an account of his dealings with the bankrupt or to produce any documents in his possession or under his control relating to the bankrupt or the bankrupt's affairs, dealings or property.

(4) The court may adjourn any examination under this section from time to time.

(5) Any creditor who has tendered a proof or the representative of such creditor who has been authorised in writing, may question the bankrupt or such other person as may have been summoned by the court under subsection (1) concerning the bankrupt's affairs, dealings or property and the causes of the bankrupt's failure.

(6) The Official Assignee shall take part in the examination of the bankrupt, and may for the purpose thereof employ a solicitor, but no solicitor shall be allowed to take part in the examination on behalf of the bankrupt.

(7) The court may put such questions as it thinks expedient to the bankrupt or to such other person summoned by it.

(8) It shall be the duty of the bankrupt and any other person summoned by the court under this section to answer all such questions as the court puts or allows to be put to him.

(9) The court shall cause to be taken down in writing such notes of the examination as the court thinks proper and any notes so taken down shall be read over to and signed by the person in the course of whose examination they were taken down, and may thereafter be used in evidence against such person.

(10) Any notes of examination taken down by the court under subsection (9) shall, at all reasonable times, be open to the inspection of any creditor, upon payment of the prescribed fee.

(11) Where the court is of the opinion that the affairs of the bankrupt have been sufficiently investigated, it shall, by order, conclude the examination, but such order shall not preclude the court from directing a further examination of the bankrupt or any other person as to the bankrupt's affairs, dealings and property whenever it sees fit to do so.

(12) Where a bankrupt or any other person summoned by the court under this section without reasonable excuse fails at any time to attend before the court or where there are reasonable grounds for believing that the bankrupt or such other person has absconded, or is about to abscond, with a view to avoiding his appearance before the court under this section, the court may cause a warrant to be issued for his arrest and for the seizure of any books, papers, records, money or goods in his possession.

(13) The court may authorise —

(*a*) any person arrested under subsection (12) to be kept in custody; and

(*b*) anything seized from such person to be held, until that person is brought before the court or until such other time as the court may order.

(14) Where a bankrupt or any other person summoned by the court under this section without reasonable excuse fails at any time to attend before the court, he shall be guilty of a contempt of court and shall be liable to be punished accordingly in addition to any other punishment to which he may be subject.

(15) The court may, if it thinks fit, order that any person who if within Singapore would be liable to be summoned to appear before it and examined under this section shall be examined in Singapore or in any place outside Singapore.

Power of court following examination of bankrupt and others

84.

—(1) If it appears to the court, on consideration of any evidence obtained under section 83 that any person has in his possession any property comprised in the bankrupt's estate, the court may, on the application of the Official Assignee, order that person to deliver the whole or any part of the property to the Official Assignee at such place and time and in such manner and on such terms as the court may think fit.

(2) If it appears to the court, on consideration of any evidence obtained under section 83 that any person is indebted to the bankrupt, the court may, on the application of the Official Assignee, order that person to pay to the Official Assignee, at such place and time and in such manner as the court may direct, the whole or part of the amount due, whether in full discharge of the debt or otherwise as the court thinks fit.

Unenforceability of liens on books, etc

85.

—(1) Subject to this section, a lien or other right to retain possession of any of the books, papers or other records relating to the affairs or property of a bankrupt shall be unenforceable to the extent that its enforcement would deny possession of any books, papers or other records to the Official Assignee.

(2) Subsection (1) shall not apply to a lien on documents which give a title to property and are held as such.

Official Assignee to settle list of debtors to the estate

86.

—(1) The Official Assignee shall, as soon as possible after a bankruptcy order has been made, prepare and file in court a list of persons supposed to be indebted to the bankrupt, with the amounts in which they are supposed to be so indebted set out opposite to their names respectively.

(2) Before finally settling the name and amount of the debt of any person on such list, the Official Assignee shall give notice in writing to that person stating that he has placed that person upon the list of debtors to the estate in the amount in the notice specified and that, unless that person on or before a day specified in such notice gives to the Registrar and the Official Assignee notice in writing of his intention to dispute his indebtedness, he shall be deemed to admit that the amount set out opposite his name in the list is due and owing by him to the bankrupt and shall be settled on the list accordingly.

(3) Any person included in the list who does not give notice of his intention to dispute his indebtedness within the time limited in that behalf shall be settled upon that list, and execution may be issued against him for the amount set out opposite his name in the list in the same way as if judgment had been entered against him for such amount in favour of the Official Assignee.

(4) A certificate by the Registrar that the person named therein has been settled upon such list as a debtor to the estate in the amount in the certificate specified shall be received as proof of the facts therein stated.

(5) A person settled upon such list under this section may apply to the court in a summary way for leave to dispute his indebtedness or the amount thereof, and the court may if it thinks fit make such order for determining the question as may seem expedient upon the terms of the person giving security for costs and either paying into court or giving security for the whole or such part of the alleged debt as under the circumstances may seem reasonable, and may stay all further proceedings.

Proof of debts

Description of debts provable in bankruptcy

87.

—(1) Demands in the nature of unliquidated damages arising otherwise than by reason of a contract, promise or breach of trust shall not be provable in bankruptcy.

(2) A person having notice of the presentation of a bankruptcy petition shall not prove under the bankruptcy order made thereon for any debt or liability contracted by the bankrupt subsequently to the date of his so having notice.

(3) Subject to this section and section 90, any debt or liability to which the bankrupt —

(*a*) is subject at the date of the bankruptcy order; or

(*b*) may become subject before his discharge by reason of any obligation incurred before the date of the bankruptcy order, and any interest on such debt or liability which is payable by the bankrupt in respect of any period before the commencement of his bankruptcy shall be provable in bankruptcy.

(4) An estimate shall be made by the Official Assignee of the value of any debt or liability provable under this section which, by reason of its being subject to any contingency or contingencies, or for any other reason, does not bear a certain value.

(5) Any person aggrieved by any such estimate may appeal to the court.

(6) If in the opinion of the court the value of the debt or liability is incapable of being fairly estimated, the court may make an order to that effect, and thereupon the debt or liability shall, for the purposes of this Act, be deemed to be a debt not provable in bankruptcy.

(7) If in the opinion of the court the value of the debt or liability is capable of being fairly estimated, the court may assess the same and may give all necessary directions for this purpose, and the amount of the value when assessed shall be deemed to be a debt provable in bankruptcy.

(8) An amount payable under any order made by a court under any written law relating to the confiscation of the proceeds of crime shall be provable in bankruptcy.

Mutual credit and set-off

88.

—(1) Where there have been any mutual credits, mutual debts or other mutual dealings between a bankrupt and any creditor, the debts and liabilities to which each party is or may become subject as a result of such mutual credits, debts or dealings shall be set-off against each other and only the balance shall be a debt provable in bankruptcy.

(2) There shall be excluded from any set-off under subsection (1) any debt or liability of the bankrupt which —

(*a*) is not a debt provable in bankruptcy; or

(*b*) arises by reason of an obligation incurred at a time when the creditor had notice that a bankruptcy petition relating to the bankrupt was pending.

Rules as to proof of debts

89. With respect to the mode of proving debts, the right of proof by secured and other creditors, the admission and rejection of proofs and any other matters, the prescribed rules shall be observed.

Priority of debts

90.

—(1) Subject to this Act, in the distribution of the property of a bankrupt, there shall be paid in priority to all other debts —

(*a*) firstly, the costs and expenses of administration or otherwise incurred by the Official Assignee and the costs of the petitioner (whether taxed or agreed) and the costs and expenses properly incurred by a nominee in respect of the administration of any voluntary arrangement under Part V;

(*b*) secondly, subject to subsection (2) , all wages or salary (whether or not earned wholly or in part by way of commission) including any amount payable by way of allowance or reimbursement under any contract of employment or award or agreement regulating the conditions of employment of any employee;

(*c*) thirdly, subject to subsection (2) , the amount due to an employee as a retrenchment benefit or an ex gratia payment under any contract of employment or award or agreement that regulates the conditions of employment, whether such amount becomes payable before, on or after the date of the bankruptcy order;

(*d*) fourthly, all amounts due in respect of any workmen's compensation under the Workmen's Compensation Act (Cap. 354) accrued before, on or after the date of the bankruptcy order;

(*e*) fifthly, all amounts due in respect of contributions payable during the 12 months immediately before, on or after the date of the bankruptcy order by the bankrupt as the employer of any person under any written law relating to employees' superannuation or provident funds or under any scheme of superannuation which is an approved scheme under the Income Tax Act (Cap. 134) ;

(*f*) sixthly, all remuneration payable to any employee in respect of vacation leave, or in the case of his death, to any other person in his right, accrued in respect of any period before, on or after the date of the bankruptcy order; and

(*g*) seventhly, the amount of all taxes assessed and any goods and services tax due under any written law before the date of the bankruptcy order or assessed at any time before the time fixed for the proving of debts has expired.

(2) The amount payable under subsection (1) (*b*) and (*c*) shall not exceed an amount that is equivalent to 5 months' salary whether for time or piecework in respect of services rendered by any employee to the bankrupt or $7,500, whichever is the lesser.

(3) The Minister may, by order published in the *Gazette*, amend subsection (2) by varying the amount specified in that subsection as the maximum amount payable under subsection (1) (*b*) and (*c*) .

(4) For the purposes of subsection (1) (*b*) and (*c*) —

"employee" means a person who has entered into or works under a contract of service with the bankrupt and includes a subcontractor of labour;

"wages or salary" includes —

(*a*) all arrears of money due to a subcontractor of labour;

(*b*) any amount payable to an employee on account of wages or salary during a period of notice of termination of employment or in lieu of notice of such termination, as the case may be, whether such amount becomes payable before, on or after the date of the bankruptcy order; and

(*c*) any amount payable to an employee, on termination of his employment, as a gratuity under any contract of employment, or under any award or agreement that regulates the conditions of his employment, whether such amount becomes payable before, on or after the date of the bankruptcy order.

(5) For the purposes of subsection (1) (*c*) —

"ex gratia payment" means the amount payable to an employee on the bankruptcy of his employer or on the termination of his service by his employer on the ground of redundancy or by reason of any re-organisation of the employer, profession, business, trade or work, and "the amount payable to an employee" for these purposes means the amount stipulated in any contract of employment, award or agreement, as the case may be;

"retrenchment benefit" means the amount payable to an employee on the bankruptcy of his employer, on the termination of his service by his employer on the ground of redundancy or by reason of any re-organisation of the employer, profession, business, trade or work, and "the amount payable to an employee" for these purposes means the amount stipulated in any contract of employment, award or agreement, as the case may be, or if no amount is stipulated therein, such amount as is stipulated by the Commissioner for Labour.

(6) The debts in each class specified in subsection (1) shall rank in the order therein specified but debts of the same class shall rank equally between themselves, and shall be paid in full, unless the property of the bankrupt is insufficient to meet them, in which case they shall abate in equal proportions between themselves.

(7) Where any payment has been made to any employee of the bankrupt on account of wages, salary or vacation leave out of money advanced by a person for that purpose, the person by whom the money was advanced shall, in a bankruptcy, have a right of priority in respect of the money so advanced and paid, up to the amount by which the sum in respect of which the employee would have been entitled to priority in the bankruptcy has been diminished by reason of the payment, and shall have the same right of priority in respect of that amount as the employee would have had if the payment had not been made.

(8) Where any creditor has given any indemnity or made any payment of moneys by virtue of which any asset of the bankrupt has been recovered, protected or preserved, the court may make such order as it thinks just with respect to the distribution of such asset with a view to giving that creditor an advantage over other creditors in consideration of the risks run by him in so doing.

(9) Where an interim receiver has been appointed under section 73 before the making of the bankruptcy order, the date of the appointment shall, for the purposes of this section, be deemed to be the date of the bankruptcy order.

Payment of partnership debts

91.

—(1) In the case of partners, the joint estate shall be applicable in the first instance in payment of their joint debts, and the separate estate of each partner shall be applicable in the first instance in payment of his separate debts.

(2) If there is surplus of the separate estates, it shall be dealt with as part of the joint estate.

(3) If there is surplus of the joint estate, it shall be dealt with as part of the respective separate estates in proportion to the right and interest of each partner in the joint estate.

Right of landlord to distrain for rent

92.

—(1) The right of any landlord or other person to whom rent is payable to distrain upon the goods and effects of a bankrupt for rent due to him from the bankrupt shall, subject to subsection (5) , be available against goods and effects comprised in the bankrupt's estate in respect only of 3 months' rent accrued due before the commencement of the bankruptcy.

(2) Where a landlord or other person to whom rent is payable has distrained for rent upon the goods and effects of an individual to whom a bankruptcy petition relates and a bankruptcy order is subsequently made on that petition, any amount recovered by way of that distress which —

(*a*) is in excess of the amount which by virtue of subsection (1) would have been recoverable after the commencement of the bankruptcy; or

(*b*) is in respect of rent for a period or part thereof after the distress was levied,

shall be held by the landlord or other person in trust for the bankrupt as part of his estate and the landlord or other person shall, upon being given notice by the Official Assignee to do so, make over to the Official Assignee the amount so held in trust by him for the bankrupt.

(3) Where any person (whether or not a landlord or person entitled to rent) has distrained upon the goods or effects of an individual who is adjudged bankrupt before the end of the period of 3 months beginning with the distraint, so much of those goods or effects, or of the proceeds of their sale, as is not held by him in trust for the bankrupt under subsection (2) shall be charged for the benefit of the bankrupt's estate with the preferential debts of the bankrupt to the extent that the bankrupt's estate is for the time being insufficient for meeting those debts.

(4) Where by virtue of any charge under subsection (3) any person surrenders any goods or effects to the Official Assignee, that person shall rank, in respect of the amount of the proceeds of the sale of those goods or effects by the Official Assignee or, as the case may be, the amount of the payment, as a preferential creditor of the bankrupt, except as against so much of the bankrupt's estate as is available for the payment of preferential creditors by virtue of the surrender or payment.

(5) A landlord or other person to whom rent is payable shall not be entitled at any time after the discharge of a bankrupt to distrain upon any goods or effects comprised in the bankrupt's estate.

(6) Any right to distrain against property comprised in a bankrupt's estate shall be exercisable notwithstanding that the property has vested in the Official Assignee.

(7) The provisions of this section are without prejudice to a landlord's right in a bankruptcy to prove for any debt due to him from the bankrupt in respect of rent.

Contracts to which bankrupt is party

93.

—(1) This section shall apply where a contract has been made with a person who is subsequently adjudged bankrupt.

(2) The court may, on the application of any other party to the contract, make an order discharging obligations under the contract on such terms as to payment by the applicant or the bankrupt of damages for non-performance or otherwise as appear to the court to be equitable.

(3) Any damages payable by the bankrupt by virtue of an order of the court under this section shall be a debt provable in bankruptcy.

(4) Where an undischarged bankrupt is a contractor in respect of any contract jointly with any person, that person may sue or be sued in respect of the contract without the joinder of the bankrupt.

Interest on debts

94.

—(1) Where a debt which has been proved in a bankruptcy includes interest, that interest shall, for the purposes of distribution of dividend, be calculated at such rate as may be prescribed by the rules, without prejudice to the right of any creditor to receive out of the surplus of the estate after all the debts proved in the bankruptcy have been paid in full any higher rate of interest to which he may be entitled.

(2) Interest on preferential debts shall rank equally with interest on debts other than preferential debts.

(3) For the purpose of this section, "interest" includes any pecuniary consideration in lieu of interest and any penalty or late payment charge by whatever name called.

Composition or scheme of arrangement

Creditors may accept composition or arrangement subject to court's approval

95.

—(1) Where a bankruptcy order has been made, the creditors who have proved their debts may, if they think fit, at a general meeting of creditors, by special resolution, resolve to accept a proposal for a composition in satisfaction of the debts due to them under the bankruptcy, or for a scheme of arrangement of the bankrupt's affairs.

(2) The composition or scheme shall not be binding on the creditors unless it is approved by the court.

(3) Any creditor who has proved his debt may assent to or dissent from the composition or scheme by a letter addressed to the Official Assignee in the prescribed form, and attested by a witness, and sent or posted so as to be received by the Official Assignee not later than the day preceding the meeting, and a creditor so assenting or dissenting shall be taken as being present and voting at that meeting.

(4) The meeting shall be summoned by the Official Assignee by not less than 7 days' notice.

(5) The notice shall state generally the terms of the proposal and shall be accompanied by a report of the Official Assignee thereon.

(6) The bankrupt or the Official Assignee may, after the composition or scheme is accepted by the creditors, apply to the court to approve it, and notice of the time appointed for the hearing of the application shall be given as prescribed.

(7) The court shall, before approving a composition or scheme, consider the report of the Official Assignee as to the terms of the composition or scheme and as to the conduct of the bankrupt, and shall hear any objection which may be made by or on behalf of any creditor.

(8) If the court is of the opinion that the terms of the composition or scheme are not reasonable or are not calculated to benefit the general body of creditors, the court may, in its discretion, refuse to approve the composition or scheme.

(9) If the court approves the composition or scheme, the approval may be testified by the seal of the court being attached to the instrument containing the terms of the composition or scheme, or by the terms being embodied in an order of the court.

(10) A composition or scheme accepted and approved pursuant to this section shall be binding on all the creditors so far as relates to any debts due to them from the bankrupt and provable in bankruptcy.

(11) A certificate of the Official Assignee that a composition or scheme has been duly accepted and approved shall, in the absence of fraud, be conclusive as to its validity.

(12) The provisions of a composition or scheme under this section may be enforced by the court on an application by any person interested, and any contravention of or failure to comply with of an order of the court made on such an application shall be deemed to be a contempt of court.

(13) If the court approves the composition or scheme, it may annul the bankruptcy order and vest the property of the bankrupt in him or in such other person as the court appoints on such terms and subject to such conditions as the court may impose.

(14) If default is made in payment of any instalment due under the composition or scheme, or if the court is satisfied that the composition or scheme cannot, in consequence of legal difficulties or for any sufficient cause, proceed without injustice or undue delay to the creditors or to the bankrupt, or that the approval of the court was obtained by fraud, the court may, if it thinks fit, on an application by the Official Assignee or any creditor, annul the composition or scheme, but without prejudice to the validity of any sale, disposition or payment duly made or thing duly done under or in pursuance of the composition or scheme.

Effect of composition or scheme

96. Notwithstanding the acceptance and approval of a composition or scheme, such composition or scheme shall not be binding on any creditor so far as regards a debt or liability from which, under this Act, the bankrupt would not be discharged by an order of discharge in bankruptcy unless the creditor assents to the composition or scheme.

Effect of bankruptcy on antecedent transactions

Provisions as to second bankruptcy

97.

—(1) Where a second or subsequent bankruptcy order is made against a bankrupt, or where an order is made for the administration in bankruptcy of the estate of a deceased bankrupt, then for the purposes of any proceedings consequent upon any such order, the Official Assignee shall be deemed to be a creditor in respect of any unsatisfied balance of the debts provable in the last preceding bankruptcy against the property of the bankrupt in the subsequent bankruptcy.

(2) Where a second or subsequent bankruptcy order is made against a bankrupt, or where an order is made for the administration in bankruptcy of the estate of a deceased bankrupt, any property acquired by him since he was last adjudged bankrupt, which at the date when the subsequent petition was presented had not been distributed amongst the creditors in the last preceding bankruptcy, shall (subject to any disposition thereof made by the Official Assignee in that bankruptcy without knowledge of the presentation of the subsequent petition) vest in the Official Assignee on account of the subsequent bankruptcy or administration in bankruptcy, as the case may be.

(3) Where the Official Assignee in any bankruptcy receives notice of a subsequent petition in bankruptcy against the bankrupt or after his death of a petition for the administration of his estate in bankruptcy, the Official Assignee shall hold any property then in his possession which has been acquired by the bankrupt since he was adjudged bankrupt until the subsequent petition has been disposed of, and, if on the subsequent petition a bankruptcy order or an order for the administration of the estate in bankruptcy is made, he shall hold all the property or the proceeds thereof (after deducting his costs and expenses) to the account of the subsequent bankruptcy, or administration in bankruptcy, as the case may be.

Transactions at an undervalue

98.

—(1) Subject to this section and sections 100 and 102, where an individual is adjudged bankrupt and he has at the relevant time (as defined in section 100) entered into a transaction with any person at an undervalue, the Official Assignee may apply to the court for an order under this section.

(2) The court shall, on such an application, make such order as it thinks fit for restoring the position to what it would have been if that individual had not entered into that transaction.

(3) For the purposes of this section and sections 100 and 102, an individual enters into a transaction with a person at an undervalue if —

(*a*) he makes a gift to that person or he otherwise enters into a transaction with that person on terms that provide for him to receive no consideration;

(*b*) he enters into a transaction with that person in consideration of marriage; or

(*c*) he enters into a transaction with that person for a consideration the value of which, in money or money's worth, is significantly less than the value, in money or money's worth, of the consideration provided by the individual.

Unfair preferences

99.

—(1) Subject to this section and sections 100 and 102, where an individual is adjudged bankrupt and he has, at the relevant time (as defined in section 100) , given an unfair preference to any person, the Official Assignee may apply to the court for an order under this section.

(2) The court shall, on such an application, make such order as it thinks fit for restoring the position to what it would have been if that individual had not given that unfair preference.

(3) For the purposes of this section and sections 100 and 102, an individual gives an unfair preference to a person if —

(*a*) that person is one of the individual's creditors or a surety or guarantor for any of his debts or other liabilities; and

(*b*) the individual does anything or suffers anything to be done which (in either case) has the effect of putting that person into a position which, in the event of the individual's bankruptcy, will be better than the position he would have been in if that thing had not been done.

(4) The court shall not make an order under this section in respect of an unfair preference given to any person unless the individual who gave the preference was influenced in deciding to give it by a desire to produce in relation to that person the effect mentioned in subsection (3) (*b*) .

(5) An individual who has given an unfair preference to a person who, at the time the unfair preference was given, was an associate of his (otherwise than by reason only of being his employee) shall be presumed, unless the contrary is shown, to have been influenced in deciding to give it by such a desire as is mentioned in subsection (4) .

(6) The fact that something has been done in pursuance of the order of a court does not, without more, prevent the doing or suffering of that thing from constituting the giving of an unfair preference.

Relevant time under sections 98 and 99

100.

—(1) Subject to this section, the time at which an individual enters into a transaction at an undervalue or gives an unfair preference shall be a relevant time if the transaction is entered into or the preference given —

(*a*) in the case of a transaction at an undervalue, within the period of 5 years ending with the day of the presentation of the bankruptcy petition on which the individual is adjudged bankrupt;

(*b*) in the case of an unfair preference which is not a transaction at an undervalue and is given to a person who is an associate of the individual (otherwise than by reason only of being his employee) , within the period of two years ending with that day; and

(*c*) in any other case of an unfair preference which is not a transaction at an undervalue, within the period of 6 months ending with that day.

(2) Where an individual enters into a transaction at an undervalue or gives an unfair preference at a time mentioned in subsection (1) (*a*) , (*b*) or (*c*) , that time is not a relevant time for the purposes of sections 98 and 99 unless the individual —

(*a*) is insolvent at that time; or

(*b*) becomes insolvent in consequence of the transaction or preference.

(3) Where a transaction is entered into at an undervalue by an individual with a person who is an associate of his (otherwise than by reason only of being his employee) , the requirements under subsection (2) shall be presumed to be satisfied unless the contrary is shown.

(4) For the purposes of subsection (2) , an individual shall be insolvent if —

(*a*) he is unable to pay his debts as they fall due; or

(*b*) the value of his assets is less than the amount of his liabilities, taking into account his contingent and prospective liabilities.

Meaning of "associate"

101.

—(1) For the purposes of sections 99 and 100, any question whether a person is an associate of another person shall be determined in accordance with this section.

(2) A person is an associate of an individual if that person is the individual's spouse, or is a relative, or the spouse of a relative of the individual or his spouse.

(3) A person is an associate of an individual with whom he is in partnership, and of the spouse or a relative of any individual with whom he is in partnership.

(4) A person is an associate of an individual whom he employs or by whom he is employed and for this purpose, any director or other officer of a company shall be treated as employed by that company.

(5) A person in his capacity as trustee of a trust is an associate of an individual if the beneficiaries of the trust include, or the terms of the trust confer a power that may be exercised for the benefit of, that individual or an associate of that individual.

(6) A company is an associate of an individual if that individual has control of it or if that individual and persons who are his associates together have control of it.

(7) For the purposes of this section, a person is a relative of an individual if he is that individual's brother, sister, uncle, aunt, nephew, niece, lineal ancestor or lineal descendant, treating —

(*a*) any relationship of the half blood as a relationship of the whole blood and the step-child or adopted child of any person as his child; and

(*b*) an illegitimate child as the legitimate child of his mother and reputed father,

and references in this section to a spouse shall include a former spouse.

(8) For the purposes of this section, an individual shall be taken to have control of a company if —

(*a*) the directors of the company or of another company which has control of it (or any of them) are accustomed to act in accordance with his directions or instructions; or

(*b*) he is entitled to exercise, or control the exercise of, one-third or more of the voting power at any general meeting of the company or of another company which has control of it, and where two or more persons together satisfy either of the above conditions, they shall be taken to have control of the company.

(9) In this section, "company" includes any body corporate (whether incorporated in Singapore or elsewhere) ; and references to directors and other officers of a company and to voting power at any general meeting of a company shall have effect with any necessary modifications.

Orders under sections 98 and 99

102.

—(1) Without prejudice to the generality of sections 98(2) and 99(2) , an order under either of those sections with respect to a transaction or preference entered into or given by an individual who is subsequently adjudged bankrupt may, subject to this section —

(*a*) require any property transferred as part of the transaction, or in connection with the giving of the preference, to be vested in the Official Assignee;

(*b*) require any property to be so vested if it represents in any person's hands the application of the proceeds of sale of property so transferred or of money so transferred;

(*c*) release or discharge (in whole or in part) any security given by the individual;

(*d*) require any person to pay, in respect of benefits received by him from the individual, such sums to the Official Assignee as the court may direct;

(*e*) provide for any surety or guarantor whose obligations to any person were released or discharged (in whole or in part) under the transaction or by the giving of the preference to be under such new or revived obligations to that person as the court thinks appropriate;

(*f*) provide for security to be provided for the discharge of any obligation imposed by or arising under the order, for such an obligation to be charged on any property and for the security or charge to have the same priority as a security or charge released or discharged (in whole or in part) under the transaction or by the giving of the unfair preference; and

(*g*) provide for the extent to which any person whose property is vested by the order in the Official Assignee, or on whom obligations are imposed by the order, is to be able to prove in the bankruptcy for debts or other liabilities which arose from, or were released or discharged (in whole or in part) under or by, the transaction or the giving of the unfair preference.

(2) An order under section 98 or 99 may affect the property of, or impose any obligation on, any person whether or not he is the person with whom the individual in question entered into the transaction or, as the case may be, the person to whom the unfair preference was given; but such an order shall not —

(*a*) prejudice any interest in property which was acquired from a person other than that individual and was acquired in good faith, for value and without notice of the relevant circumstances, or prejudice any interest deriving from such an interest; or

(*b*) require a person who received a benefit from the transaction or unfair preference in good faith, for value and without notice of the relevant circumstances to pay a sum to the Official Assignee, except where he was a party to the transaction or the payment is to be in respect of an unfair preference given to that person at a time when he was a creditor of that individual.

(3) Any sums required to be paid to the Official Assignee in accordance with an order under section 98 or 99 shall be comprised in the bankrupt's estate.

(4) For the purposes of this section, the relevant circumstances, in relation to a transaction or unfair preference, shall be —

(*a*) the circumstances by virtue of which an order under section 98 or 99 could be made in respect of the transaction or preference if the individual in question were adjudged bankrupt within the particular period after the transaction is entered into or the unfair preference given; and

(*b*) if that period has expired, the fact that that individual has been adjudged bankrupt within that period.

Extortionate credit transactions

103.

—(1) This section shall apply where a person who is adjudged bankrupt is or has been a party to a transaction for or involving the provision to him of credit.

(2) The court may, on the application of the Official Assignee, make an order with respect to the transaction if the transaction is or was extortionate and was entered into within 3 years before the commencement of the bankruptcy.

(3) For the purposes of this section, a transaction shall be extortionate if, having regard to the risk accepted by the person providing the credit —

(*a*) the terms of it are or were such as to require grossly exorbitant payments to be made (whether unconditionally or in certain contingencies) in respect of the provision of the credit; or

(*b*) it is harsh and unconscionable or substantially unfair, and it shall be presumed, unless the contrary is proved, that the transaction was extortionate.

(4) An order under this section may contain one or more of the following:

(*a*) provision setting aside the whole or part of any obligation created by the transaction;

(*b*) provision varying the terms of the transaction or varying the terms on which any security for the purposes of the transaction is held;

(*c*) provision requiring any person who is or was party to the transaction to pay the Official Assignee any sums paid to that person;

(*d*) provision requiring any person to surrender to the Official Assignee any property held by him as security for the purposes of the transaction;

(*e*) provision directing accounts to be taken between any persons.

(5) Any sums or property required to be paid or surrendered to the Official Assignee in accordance with an order under this section shall be comprised in the bankrupt's estate.

Avoidance of general assignment of book debts

104.

—(1) This section shall apply where a person engaged in any business makes a general assignment to another person of his existing or future book debts, or any class of them, and is subsequently adjudged bankrupt.

(2) The assignment shall be void against the Official Assignee as regards book debts which were not paid before the presentation of the bankruptcy petition, unless the assignment has been registered under the Bills of Sale Act (Cap. 24) .

(3) For the purposes of this section —

"assignment" includes an assignment by way of security or charge on book debts;

"general assignment" does not include —

(*a*) an assignment of book debts due at the date of the assignment from specified debtors or of debts becoming due under specified contracts; or

(*b*) an assignment of book debts included either in a transfer of a business made in good faith and for value or in an assignment of assets for the benefit of creditors generally.

(4) For the purposes of registration under the Bills of Sale Act, an assignment of book debts shall be treated as if it were a bill of sale given otherwise than by way of security for the payment of a sum of money; and the provisions of that Act with respect to the registration of bills of sale shall apply accordingly with such necessary modifications as may be made by rules under that Act.

Restriction of rights of creditor under execution or attachment

105.

—(1) Where the creditor of a bankrupt has issued execution against the goods or lands of the bankrupt or has attached any debt due or property belonging to him, he shall not be entitled to retain the benefit of the execution or attachment against the Official Assignee unless he has completed the execution or attachment before the date of the bankruptcy order, except that —

(*a*) a person who purchases in good faith under a sale by the Sheriff any goods of a bankrupt on which an execution has been levied shall in all cases acquire a good title to them against the Official Assignee; and

(*b*) the rights conferred by this subsection on the Official Assignee may be set aside by the court in favour of the creditor to such extent and subject to such terms as the court may think fit.

(2) For the purposes of this Act —

(*a*) an execution against goods is completed by seizure and sale;

(*b*) an attachment of a debt is completed by receipt of the debt; and

(*c*) an execution against land or any interest therein is completed by registering under any written law relating to the registration of land a writ of seizure and sale attaching the interest of the bankrupt in the land described therein.

Duties of Sheriff as to property taken in execution

106.

—(1) Where any property of a debtor is taken in execution, then, if before the completion of the execution notice is given to the Sheriff that a bankruptcy order has been made against the debtor, the Sheriff shall deliver the property or the possession thereof and any such moneys to the Official Assignee, but the costs of and incidental to the execution shall be a first charge on the property or moneys, and the Official Assignee may sell the property or any adequate part thereof for the purpose of satisfying the charge.

(2) Where a writ of seizure and sale has been issued in respect of a judgment for a sum exceeding $2,000, the Sheriff shall hold all moneys coming to his hands under the writ of seizure and sale for 14 days from the receipt thereof, and if within that time notice is served on him of a bankruptcy petition having been presented against or by the debtor and a bankruptcy order is made against the debtor thereon or on any other petition of which the Sheriff has notice, he shall deduct the costs of and incidental to the execution and pay the balance to the Official Assignee, who shall be entitled to retain the same as against the execution creditor.

Possession, control and realisation of bankrupt's property

Possession of property by Official Assignee

107.

—(1) The Official Assignee shall forthwith after the bankruptcy order take possession of the deeds, books and documents which relate to the bankrupt's estate or affairs and which belong to him or are under his control and all other parts of his property capable of manual delivery.

(2) The Official Assignee shall, in relation to and for the purpose of acquiring or retaining possession of the property of the bankrupt, be in the same position as if he were a receiver of the property appointed by the court, and the court may on his application enforce the acquisition or retention accordingly.

(3) Where any part of the property of the bankrupt consists of stock, shares in ships, shares or any other property transferable in the books of any company, office or person, the Official Assignee may exercise the right to transfer the property to the same extent as the bankrupt might have exercised it if he had not become bankrupt.

(4) Where any part of the property of the bankrupt consists of things in action, those things shall be deemed to have been duly assigned to the Official Assignee.

(5) Any banker or agent of the bankrupt or any other person who holds any property to the account of, or for, the bankrupt shall pay and deliver to the Official Assignee all moneys and securities in his possession or under his control which he is not by law entitled to retain as against the bankrupt or the Official Assignee.

(6) Any person who fails to comply with subsection (5) shall be guilty of an offence and shall be liable on conviction to a fine not exceeding $10,000 or to imprisonment for a term not exceeding 2 years or to both.

Seizure of bankrupt's property held by bankrupt or other person

108.

—(1) At any time after a bankruptcy order has been made, the Official Assignee or any person authorised by him may take an inventory of and seize any property comprised in the bankrupt's estate which is, or any books, papers or records relating to the bankrupt's estate or affairs which are, in the possession or under the control of the bankrupt or any other person who is required to deliver the property, books, papers or records to the Official Assignee.

(2) The Official Assignee or any person authorised by him may, for the purposes of taking an inventory of or seizing any property comprised in the bankrupt's estate or any books, papers or records relating to the bankrupt's estate or affairs, break open any premises where the bankrupt or anything that may be seized under subsection (1) is or is believed to be and any receptacle of the bankrupt which contains or is believed to contain anything that may be so seized.

(3) If, after a bankruptcy order has been made, the court is satisfied that any property comprised in the bankrupt's estate is, or any books, papers or records relating to the bankrupt's estate or affairs are, concealed in any premises not belonging to the bankrupt, the court may issue a warrant authorising any public officer to search those premises for the property, books, papers or records.

(4) A warrant under subsection (3) shall not be executed except in the prescribed manner and in accordance with its terms.

Appropriation of portion of pay or salary to creditors

109.

—(1) Where the bankrupt is an officer of the Singapore Armed Forces or a public officer or otherwise employed or engaged in the public service of the Government, the Official Assignee shall receive for distribution amongst the creditors so much of the bankrupt's pay or salary as the court, on the application of the Official Assignee, directs.

(2) Where a bankrupt is in receipt of a salary or income other than as mentioned in subsection (1) , or is entitled to any half-pay, pension or compensation granted by the Government or any other employer, the court, on the application of the Official Assignee, shall, subject to any written law relating to pensions, make such order as it may think just for the payment of the salary, income, half-pay, pension or compensation or of any part thereof to the Official Assignee, to be applied by him in such manner as the court directs.

(3) Nothing in this section shall be deemed to abrogate the right of the Government to dismiss a bankrupt or to declare the pension, half-pay or compensation of any bankrupt to be forfeited.

(4) In fixing the amount to be received by the Official Assignee under this section, the court shall, without prejudice to subsection (5) , have regard to the scale of appropriation of salary in any general rule made for the purposes of this section by the Minister under section 166.

(5) The court may, in its discretion, fix a larger or smaller amount than the amount provided in the scale.

Disclaimer of onerous property

110.

—(1) Where any part of the property of the bankrupt consists of —

(*a*) land of any tenure burdened with onerous covenants;

(*b*) shares or stock in companies;

(*c*) unprofitable contracts; or

(*d*) any other property that is unsaleable or not readily saleable by reason of its binding the possessor thereof to the performance of any onerous act or to the payment of any sum of money,

the Official Assignee, notwithstanding that he has endeavoured to sell or has taken possession of the property or exercised any act of ownership in relation thereto, but subject to this section, may, by writing signed by him, at any time disclaim the property.

(2) The disclaimer shall operate to determine as from the date of disclaimer the rights, interests and liabilities of the bankrupt and his property in or in respect of the property disclaimed, and shall also discharge the Official Assignee from all personal liability in respect of the property disclaimed as from the date when the property vested in him, but shall not, except so far as is necessary for the purpose of releasing the bankrupt and his property and the Official Assignee from liability, affect the rights or liabilities of any other person.

(3) The Official Assignee shall not be entitled to disclaim a lease without the leave of the court, except in any case which may be prescribed or where all persons interested in the property consent to the disclaimer, and the court may, before or on granting leave —

(*a*) require such notices to be given to persons interested and impose such terms as a condition of granting leave; and

(*b*) make such orders with respect to fixtures, tenant's improvements and other matters arising out of the tenancy, as the court thinks just.

(4) The Official Assignee shall not be entitled to disclaim any property, in pursuance of this section, in any case where —

(*a*) an application in writing has been made to him by any person interested in the property, requiring him to decide whether he will disclaim or not; and

(*b*) he has for a period of 21 days after the receipt of the application, or such extended period as is allowed by the court, declined or neglected to give notice whether he disclaims the property or not, and in the case of a contract, if the Official Assignee, after such application as aforesaid, does not within the said period or extended period disclaim the contract, he shall be deemed to have adopted it.

(5) The court may, on the application of any person who is, as against the Official Assignee, entitled to the benefit or subject to the burden of a contract made with the bankrupt, make an order rescinding the contract on such terms as to payment by or to, either party of damages for the non-performance of the contract or otherwise as to the court seems equitable, and any damages payable under the order to that person may be proved by him as a debt under the bankruptcy.

(6) The court may —

(*a*) on application by any person either claiming any interest in any disclaimed property or under any liability not discharged by this Act in respect of any disclaimed property;

(*b*) on hearing such persons as the court may think fit; and

(*c*) on such terms as the court may think just,

make an order for the vesting of the property in or delivery thereof to —

(i) any person entitled thereto;

(ii) any person to whom it seems just that the same should be delivered by way of compensation for such liability as aforesaid; or

(iii) a trustee for any person referred to in sub-paragraph (i) or (ii) ,

and on the vesting order being made, the property comprised therein shall vest accordingly in the person therein named in that behalf, without any conveyance or assignment for the purpose.

(7) Where the property disclaimed is of a leasehold nature, the court shall not make a vesting order in favour of any person claiming under the bankrupt, whether as under-lessee or as mortgagee by demise, except upon the terms of making the person subject to the same liabilities and obligations as the bankrupt was subject to under the lease in respect of the property at the date when the bankruptcy petition was presented, and any mortgagee or under-lessee declining to accept a vesting order upon those terms shall be excluded from all interest in and security upon the property, and if there is no person claiming under the bankrupt who is willing to accept an order upon those terms, the court shall have power to vest the bankrupt's estate and interest in the property in any person liable (either personally or in a representative character, and either alone or jointly with the bankrupt) to perform the lessee's covenants in the lease, freed and discharged from all estates, encumbrances and interests created therein by the bankrupt.

(8) Any person sustaining loss or damage by the operation of a disclaimer under this section shall be deemed to be a creditor of the bankrupt to the extent of the loss or damage, and may accordingly prove the same as a debt under the bankruptcy.

Power of Official Assignee to deal with property

111. Subject to this Act, the Official Assignee may —

(*a*) sell all or any part of the property of a bankrupt, including the goodwill of his business, if any, and the book debts due or accruing due to him, by tender, public auction or private contract, with power to transfer the whole thereof to any person or to sell the same in parcels;

(*b*) give receipts for any money received by him, being receipts which effectually discharge the person paying the money from all responsibility in respect of the application thereof;

(*c*) prove, rank, claim, and draw a dividend in respect of any debt due to the bankrupt;

(*d*) exercise any power, the capacity to exercise which is vested in the Official Assignee under this Act, and execute any power of attorney, deeds and other instrument for the purpose of carrying into effect the provisions of this Act; and

(*e*) deal with any property to which the bankrupt is beneficially entitled as tenant in tail, or other owner of an estate of inheritance less than an estate in fee simple, in the same manner as the bankrupt might have dealt with it; and any such dealing with any property to which the bankrupt is, before his discharge, so entitled shall, although the bankrupt is dead at the time of that dealing, be as valid and have the same operation as though the bankrupt were then alive.

General powers of Official Assignee

112. The Official Assignee may exercise any of the following powers:

(*a*) carry on any business of the bankrupt so far as is necessary for winding it up beneficially;

(*b*) bring, institute or defend any action or legal proceedings relating to the property of the bankrupt;

(*c*) employ an advocate and solicitor to take any proceedings or do any business;

(*d*) accept, as the consideration for the sale of any property of the bankrupt, a sum of money payable at a future time, subject to such stipulations as to security or otherwise as he thinks fit;

(*e*) mortgage or pledge any part of the property of the bankrupt for the purpose of raising money for the payment of his debts;

(*f*) refer any dispute to arbitration, or compromise all debts, claims and liabilities, whether present or future, certain or contingent, liquidated or unliquidated, subsisting or supposed to subsist, between the bankrupt and any person who may have incurred any liability to the bankrupt, on the receipt of such sums payable at such times, and generally on such terms as are agreed on;

(*g*) make such compromise or other arrangement as is thought expedient with creditors or persons claiming to be creditors in respect of any debts provable under the bankruptcy;

(*h*) make such compromise or other arrangement as is thought expedient with respect to any claim arising out of or incidental to the property of the bankrupt, made or capable of being made on the Official Assignee by any person or by the Official Assignee on any person; and

(*i*) divide in its existing form, amongst the creditors according to its estimated value, any property which from its peculiar nature or other special circumstances cannot be readily or advantageously sold.

Power to appoint special manager

113.

—(1) The Official Assignee may, if satisfied that the nature of the bankrupt's estate or business or the interests of the creditors generally require the appointment of a special manager of the estate or business other than the Official Assignee, appoint a manager thereof accordingly to act, and with such powers, including any of the powers of a receiver, as are entrusted to him by the Official Assignee.

(2) The bankrupt may be appointed special manager.

(3) A special manager shall give such security and account in such manner as the Official Assignee may direct.

(4) The special manager shall receive such remuneration as the Official Assignee may determine.

Power to allow bankrupt to manage property

114.

—(1) The Official Assignee may appoint the bankrupt himself to superintend the management of the property of the bankrupt, or any part of the property, or to carry on his trade (if any) for the benefit of his creditors, and in any other respect to aid in administering the property in such manner and on such terms as the Official Assignee directs.

(2) The Official Assignee may make such allowance as he may think just to the bankrupt out of his property for the support of the bankrupt and his family, or in consideration of his service if he is engaged in winding up his estate, but the court may reduce the allowance and limit the time for which it may be made.

(3) Where the bankrupt has died, the Official Assignee may make an allowance to members of the bankrupt's family for their support.

(4) The Official Assignee may also make an allowance to defray the funeral expenses of the bankrupt.

Re-direction of bankrupt's letters, etc

115.

—(1) Where a bankruptcy order has been made, the Official Assignee may from time to time direct the public postal licensee under the Telecommunication Authority of Singapore Act (Cap. 323) to re-direct and send or deliver to the Official Assignee or otherwise any postal article which would otherwise be sent or delivered by it to the bankrupt at such place or places as may be specified in the direction.

(2) A direction under this section shall have effect for such period, not exceeding 3 months, as may be specified in the direction.

Power to impound passport, etc., of bankrupt

116.

—(1) The Official Assignee may, if he thinks necessary for the purposes of ensuring that a bankrupt does not leave Singapore during the administration of his estate, issue a direction to the Controller of Immigration to request that the bankrupt be prevented from leaving Singapore.

(2) Subject to any order issued or made under any written law relating to banishment or immigration, the Controller of Immigration shall pursuant to the direction under subsection (1) take, or cause to be taken by any immigration officer, such measures as may be necessary to prevent the bankrupt named in the direction from leaving Singapore, including the detention of the bankrupt's passport, certificate of identity or travel document authorising the bankrupt to leave or enter Singapore.

(3) Where the Controller of Immigration has detained the passport, certificate of identity or other travel documents of a bankrupt under subsection (2) , he shall forthwith forward the passport, certificate of identity or travel document to the Official Assignee.

(4) Notwithstanding subsections (1) , (2) and (3) , the Official Assignee may, if he thinks fit, detain any passport, certificate of identity or other travel document authorising the bankrupt to leave or enter Singapore.

(5) The Official Assignee may, if he thinks fit, retain or return to the bankrupt the passport, certificate of identity or travel document forwarded to him by the Controller of Immigration under subsection (3) or detained by him under subsection (4) .

Distribution of property

Distribution by means of dividend

117.

—(1) Whenever the Official Assignee has sufficient funds in hand for the purpose, he shall, subject to the retention of such sums as may be necessary for the expenses of the bankruptcy, declare and distribute dividends among the creditors in respect of the debts which the creditors have respectively proved.

(2) The Official Assignee shall give notice of his intention to declare and distribute a dividend.

(3) Where the Official Assignee has declared a dividend, he shall give notice of the dividend and of how it is proposed to distribute it.

(4) The notice given under subsection (3) shall contain the prescribed particulars of the bankrupt's estate.

(5) In the calculation and distribution of a dividend, the Official Assignee shall make provision —

(*a*) for any provable debt which appears to him to be due to any person who, by reason of the distance of his place of residence, may not have had sufficient time to tender and establish his proof;

(*b*) for any provable debt which is the subject of any claim which has not yet been determined; and

(*c*) for disputed proofs and claims.

(6) No dividend shall be paid to any creditor which does not amount to $20.

Claims by unsatisfied creditors

118. A creditor who has not proved his debt before the declaration of any dividend shall not be entitled to disturb, by reason that he has not participated in it, the distribution of that dividend or any other dividend declared before his debt was proved, but —

(*a*) when he has proved that debt, he shall be entitled to be paid out of any money for the time available for the payment of any further dividend, any dividend or dividends which he has failed to receive; and

(*b*) any dividend or dividends payable under paragraph (*a*) shall be paid before that money is applied to the payment of any such further dividend.

Final distribution

119.

—(1) When the Official Assignee has realised all the bankrupt's estate or so much of it as can, in the opinion of the Official Assignee, be realised without needlessly protracting the proceedings in bankruptcy, he shall give notice in the prescribed manner of his intention to declare a final dividend.

(2) The notice under subsection (1) shall contain the prescribed particulars and shall require claims against the bankrupt's estate to be established by a date (referred to in this section as the final date) specified in the notice.

(3) The court may, on the application of any person, postpone the final date.

(4) After the final date, the Official Assignee shall —

(*a*) defray any outstanding expenses of the bankruptcy out of the bankrupt's estate; and

(*b*) if he intends to declare a final dividend, declare and distribute that dividend without regard to the claim of any person in respect of a debt not already proved in the bankruptcy.

Joint and separate dividends

120.

—(1) Where one partner of a firm is adjudged bankrupt, a creditor to whom the bankrupt is indebted jointly with the other partners of the firm, or any of them, shall not receive any dividend out of the separate property of the bankrupt until all the separate creditors have received the full amount of their respective debts.

(2) Where joint and separate properties are being administered, dividends of the joint and separate properties shall, subject to any order to the contrary that is made by the court on the application of the Official Assignee or any person interested, be declared together.

(3) The expenses of and incidental to the dividends shall be fairly apportioned by the Official Assignee between the joint and separate properties, regard being had to the work done for and the benefit received by each property.

No action for dividend

121. No action for a dividend shall lie against the Official Assignee but if he refuses to pay any dividend the court may if it thinks fit order him to pay it, and also to pay out of the Consolidated Fund interest thereon for the time that it is withheld, and the costs of the application.

Right of bankrupt to surplus

122.

—(1) The bankrupt shall be entitled to any surplus remaining after payment in full of his creditors, with interest as by this Act provided, and of the costs, charges and expenses of the proceedings under the bankruptcy petition.

(2) Notwithstanding subsection (1) , the court may make an order directing the Official Assignee not to pay the surplus or part thereof to the bankrupt if —

(*a*) the Attorney-General applies for an order under this section; and (*b*) the court is satisfied that —

(i) proceedings under any written law dealing with confiscation of the proceeds of crime are pending; and

(ii) the property of the bankrupt may become subject to a confiscation order or be required to meet some other order made on those proceedings.

(3) The court may, on application, vary or revoke an order made under subsection (2) .

PART VIII ANNULMENT AND DISCHARGE

Court's power to annul bankruptcy order

123.

—(1) The court may annul a bankruptcy order if it appears to the court —

(*a*) that, on any ground existing at the time the order was made, the order ought not to have been made;

(*b*) that, to the extent required by the rules, the debts which have been paid and the expenses of the bankruptcy have all, since the making of the order, either been paid or secured for to the satisfaction of the court;

(*c*) that proceedings are pending in Malaysia for the distribution of the bankrupt's estate and effects amongst the creditors under the bankruptcy law of Malaysia and that the distribution ought to take place there; or

(*d*) that a majority of the creditors in number and value are resident in Malaysia, and that from the situation of the property of the bankrupt or for other causes his estate and effects ought to be distributed among the creditors under the bankruptcy laws of Malaysia.

(2) The court may annul a bankruptcy order whether or not the bankrupt has been discharged from the bankruptcy.

(3) Where a court annuls a bankruptcy order under this section, any sale or other disposition of property, payment made or other things duly done by or under the authority of the Official Assignee or by the court shall be valid except that the property of the bankrupt shall vest in such person as the court may appoint or, in default of any such appointment, revert to the bankrupt on such terms as the court may direct, and the court may include in its order such supplemental provisions as may be authorised by the rules.

Discharge by court

124.

—(1) The Official Assignee, the bankrupt or any other person having an interest in the matter may, at any time after the making of a bankruptcy order, apply to the court for an order of discharge.

(2) Every such application shall be served on each creditor who has filed a proof of debt and on the Official Assignee if he is not the applicant, and the court shall hear the Official Assignee and any creditor before making an order of discharge.

(3) Subject to subsection (4) on an application under this section, the court may —

(*a*) refuse to discharge the bankrupt from bankruptcy;

(*b*) make an order discharging him absolutely; or

(*c*) make an order discharging him subject to such conditions as it thinks fit to impose, including conditions with respect to —

(i) any income which may be subsequently due to him; or

(ii) any property devolving upon him, or acquired by him, after his discharge,

as may be specified in the order.

(4) Where the bankrupt has committed an offence under this Act or under section 421, 422, 423 or 424 of the Penal Code (Cap. 224) or upon proof of any of the facts mentioned in subsection (5) , the court shall —

(*a*) refuse to discharge the bankrupt from bankruptcy;

(*b*) make an order discharging him subject to his paying a dividend to his creditors of not less than 25% or to the payment of any income which may be subsequently due to him or with respect to property devolving upon him, or acquired by him, after his discharge, as may be specified in the order and to such other conditions as the court may think fit to impose; or

(*c*) if it is satisfied that the bankrupt is unable to fulfil any condition specified in paragraph (*b*) and if it thinks fit, make an order discharging the bankrupt subject to such conditions as the court may think fit to impose.

(5) The facts referred to in subsection (4) are —

(*a*) that the bankrupt has omitted to keep such books of accounts as would sufficiently disclose his business transactions and financial position within the 3 years immediately preceding his bankruptcy, or within such shorter period immediately preceding that event as the court may consider reasonable in the circumstances;

(*b*) that the bankrupt has continued to trade after knowing or having reason to believe himself to be insolvent;

(*c*) that the bankrupt has contracted any debt provable in the bankruptcy without having at the time of contracting it any reasonable ground of expectation (proof whereof shall lie on him) of being able to pay it;

(*d*) that the bankrupt has brought on or contributed to his bankruptcy by rash speculations or extravagance in living, or by recklessness, or want of reasonable care and attention to his business and affairs;

(*e*) that the bankrupt has delayed or put any of his creditors to unnecessary expense by a frivolous or vexatious defence to any action or other legal proceedings properly brought or instituted against him;

(*f*) that the bankrupt has within 3 months preceding the date of the bankruptcy order, when unable to pay his debts as they became due, given an undue preference to any of his creditors;

(*g*) that the bankrupt has, in Singapore or elsewhere on any previous occasion, been adjudged bankrupt or made a composition or arrangement with his creditors;

(*h*) that the bankrupt has been guilty of any fraud or fraudulent breach of trust;

(*i*) that the bankrupt has, within 3 months immediately preceding the date of the bankruptcy order, sent goods out of Singapore under circumstances which afford reasonable grounds for believing that the transaction was not a bona fide commercial transaction;

(*j*) that the bankrupt's assets are not of a value equal to 20% of the amount of his unsecured liabilities, unless he satisfies the court that the fact that the assets are not of a value equal to 20% of his unsecured liabilities has arisen from circumstances for or in respect of which he cannot firstly be held blamable;

(*k*) that the bankrupt has entered into a transaction with any person at an undervalue within the meaning of section 98;

(*l*) that the bankrupt has given an unfair preference to any person within the meaning of section 99; and

(*m*) that the bankrupt has made a general assignment to another person of his book debts within the meaning of section 104.

(6) The court may, at any time before an order of discharge takes effect, rescind or vary the order.

Discharge by certificate of Official Assignee

125.

—(1) The Official Assignee may, in his discretion and subject to section 126, issue a certificate discharging a bankrupt from bankruptcy.

(2) The Official Assignee shall not issue a certificate discharging a bankrupt from bankruptcy under subsection (1) unless —

(*a*) a period of 5 years has lapsed since the date of commencement of the bankruptcy; and

(*b*) the debts which have been proved in bankruptcy do not exceed $100,000, or such other sum as may be prescribed.

(3) Notice of every discharge under subsection (1) shall be given to the Registrar and be published in the *Gazette* and advertised in any local newspaper.

(4) The Official Assignee shall, upon the application of a bankrupt or his creditor or other interested person, issue to the applicant a copy of the certificate of discharge upon the payment of the prescribed fee.

Objection by creditor to discharge of bankrupt under section 125

126.

—(1) Before issuing a certificate of discharge under section 125, the Official Assignee shall serve on each creditor who has filed a proof of debt a notice of his intention to discharge the bankrupt, together with a statement of his reasons for wanting to do so.

(2) A creditor who has been served with a notice under subsection (1) and who wishes to enter an objection to the Official Assignee issuing a certificate discharging the bankrupt may, within 21 days from the date of the Official Assignee's notice, furnish the Official Assignee a statement of the grounds of his objection.

(3) A creditor who does not furnish to the Official Assignee a statement of the grounds of his objection in accordance with subsection (2) shall be deemed to have no objection to the discharge.

(4) A creditor who has furnished the Official Assignee with a statement of the grounds of his objection in accordance with subsection (2) may, within 21 days of being informed by the Official Assignee that his objection has been rejected, make an application to the court for an order prohibiting the Official Assignee from issuing a certificate.

(5) Every application under subsection (4) shall be served on the Official Assignee and on the bankrupt and the court shall hear the Official Assignee and the bankrupt before making an order on the application.

(6) On an application made under subsection (4) , the court may, if it thinks it just and expedient —

(*a*) dismiss the application;

(*b*) make an order that the bankrupt be not granted a certificate of discharge by the Official Assignee for a period not exceeding two years; or

(*c*) make an order permitting the Official Assignee to issue a certificate discharging the bankrupt but subject to such conditions as the court may think fit to impose, including conditions with respect to —

(i) any income which may be subsequently due to the bankrupt after his discharge; or

(ii) any property devolving upon the bankrupt, or acquired by him after his discharge,

as may be specified in the order.

Effect of discharge

127.

—(1) Subject to this section and any condition imposed by the court under section 124 or 126, where a bankrupt is discharged, the discharge shall release him from all his debts provable in the bankruptcy but shall have no effect —

(*a*) on the functions (so far as they remain to be carried out) of the Official Assignee; or

(*b*) on the operation, for the purposes of the carrying out of those functions, of the provisions of this Act.

(2) Discharge shall not release the bankrupt from —

(*a*) any debt due to the Government; or

(*b*) any debt with which the bankrupt may be chargeable at the suit of —

(i) the Government or any other person for any offence under any written law relating to any branch of the public revenue; or

(ii) the Sheriff or other public officer on a bail bond entered into for the appearance of any person prosecuted for any such offence,

and a bankrupt may be discharged from such debt only by a certificate in writing of the Minister.

(3) Discharge shall not affect the right of any secured creditor of the bankrupt to enforce his security for the payment of a debt from which the bankrupt is released.

(4) Discharge shall not release the bankrupt from —

(*a*) any provable debt which he incurred in respect of, or forbearance in respect of which was secured by means of, any fraud or fraudulent breach of trust to which he was party; or

(*b*) any liability in respect of a fine imposed for an offence.

(5) Discharge shall not, except to such extent and on such conditions as the court may direct, release the bankrupt from any debt which has been proved and which —

(*a*) consists in a liability to pay damages for negligence, nuisance or breach of a statutory, contractual or other duty, being damages in respect of personal injuries to any person;

(*b*) arises under any order made in proceedings under the Women's Charter (Cap. 353) relating to family matters; or

(*c*) arises under an order involving pecuniary liability made under any written law relating to the confiscation of the proceeds of crime.

(6) Discharge shall not release any person other than the bankrupt from any liability (whether as partner or co-trustee of the bankrupt or otherwise) from which the bankrupt is released by the discharge, or from any liability as surety for the bankrupt or as a person in the nature of such a surety.

(7) For the purpose of subsection (5) , "personal injuries" includes death and any disease or other impairment of a person's physical or mental condition.

Discharged bankrupt to give assistance

128. A discharged bankrupt shall, notwithstanding his discharge, give such assistance as the Official Assignee requires in the realisation and distribution of such of his property as is vested in the Official Assignee, and if the discharged bankrupt fails to do so —

(*a*) he shall be guilty of an offence and shall be liable on conviction to a fine not exceeding $10,000; and

(*b*) the court may, if it thinks fit, revoke his discharge, but without prejudice to the validity of any sale, disposition or payment duly made, or thing duly done subsequent to the discharge, but before its revocation.

PART IX DUTIES, DISQUALIFICATION AND DISABILITIES OF BANKRUPT

Duties of bankrupt

129. A bankrupt shall, in addition to any other duty specified in this Act —

(*a*) make discovery of and deliver all his property that is under his possession or control to the Official Assignee;

(*b*) deliver to the Official Assignee all books, records, documents, writings and papers including (without restricting the generality of the foregoing) , any documents or deeds of title, insurance policies and tax records and returns and copies thereof in any way relating to his property or affairs;

(*c*) at such time and place as may be fixed by the Official Assignee, attend before the Official Assignee and answer such questions as the Official Assignee may put to him with respect to his affairs, dealings and property and the causes of his failure;

(*d*) make or give all the assistance within his power to the Official Assignee in making an inventory of his assets;

(*e*) make disclosure to the Official Assignee of all property disposed of within such time preceding his bankruptcy as the Official Assignee may require, and how and to whom and for what consideration any part thereof was disposed of except such part as had been disposed of in the ordinary manner of trade or used for reasonable personal expenses;

(*f*) make disclosure to the Official Assignee of all property disposed of by gift or settlement without adequate valuable consideration within the 5 years immediately preceding his bankruptcy;

(*g*) attend any meeting of his creditors as may be convened by the Official Assignee under section 79, unless prevented by sickness or other sufficient cause and submit thereat to examination;

(*h*) when required, attend such other meetings of his creditors;

(*i*) aid to the utmost of his power in the realisation of his property and the distribution of the proceeds among his creditors;

(*j*) execute such powers of attorney, conveyances, deeds and instruments as may be required by the Official Assignee;

(*k*) examine the correctness of all proofs of claims filed, if required by the Official Assignee;

(*l*) in case any person has to his knowledge filed a false claim, disclose the fact immediately to the Official Assignee;

(*m*) generally do all such acts and things in relation to his property and the distribution of the proceeds among his creditors as may be reasonably required by the Official Assignee or prescribed by the rules or directed by the court by any order on any application by the Official Assignee or by any of his creditors; and

(*n*) until he has been discharged from bankruptcy, keep the Official Assignee advised at all times of his place of residence or address.

Disqualification of bankrupt

130.

—(1) In addition to any disqualification under any other written law, a bankrupt shall be disqualified from being appointed or acting as a trustee or personal representative in respect of any trust, estate or settlement, except with leave of the court.

(2) Any disqualification to which a bankrupt is subject under this section shall cease when —

(*a*) the bankruptcy order against him is annulled or rescinded; or

(*b*) he is discharged under Part VIII.

(3) Any person who acts as a trustee or personal representative while he is disqualified by virtue of subsection (1) shall be guilty of an offence and shall be liable on conviction to a fine not exceeding $5,000 or to imprisonment for a term not exceeding one year or to both.

Disabilities of bankrupt

131.

—(1) Where a bankrupt has not obtained his discharge —

(*a*) he shall be incompetent to maintain any action, other than an action for damages in respect of an injury to his person, without the previous sanction of the Official Assignee; and

(*b*) he shall not leave, remain or reside outside Singapore without the previous permission of the Official Assignee.

(2) A bankrupt who fails to comply with this section shall be guilty of an offence and shall be liable on conviction to a fine not exceeding $10,000 or to imprisonment for a term not exceeding 2 years or to both.

PART X BANKRUPTCY OFFENCES

Definitions

132. In this Part —

(*a*) references to property comprised in the bankrupt's estate or to property possession of which is required to be delivered up to the Official Assignee shall include any property mentioned in section 78 (1) ;

(*b*) "initial period" means the period between the presentation of the bankruptcy petition by or against a debtor and the commencement of his bankruptcy;

(*c*) a reference to a number of months or years before the presentation of a bankruptcy petition shall be read as a reference to that period ending with the presentation of the bankruptcy petition; and

(*d*) "Official Assignee" includes a trustee in bankruptcy appointed under section 33.

Defence of innocent intention

133. In the case of an offence under any provision of this Part, other than sections 135(*e*) , 137, 140 (2) , 142, 143 and 145, a person shall not be guilty of the offence if he proves that, at the time of the conduct constituting the offence, he had no intent to defraud or to conceal the state of his affairs.

Non-disclosure

134.

—(1) A bankrupt shall be guilty of an offence if —

(*a*) he does not to the best of his knowledge and belief disclose to the Official Assignee all the property comprised in his estate; or (*b*) he does not inform the Official Assignee of any disposal of any property which, but for the disposal, would be comprised in his estate, stating how, when, to whom and for what consideration the property was disposed of.

(2) Subsection (1) (*b*) shall not apply to any disposal in the ordinary course of a business carried on by the bankrupt or to any payment of the ordinary expenses of the bankrupt or his family.

Concealment of property

135. A bankrupt shall be guilty of an offence if —

(*a*) he does not deliver up possession to the Official Assignee, or as the Official Assignee may direct, of such part of the property comprised in his estate as is in his possession or under his control of which he is required by law to deliver up;

(*b*) he conceals any debt due to or from him or conceals any property the value of which is not less than $500 and possession of which he is required to deliver up to the Official Assignee;

(*c*) in the 12 months before the presentation of the bankruptcy petition by or against him, or in the initial period, he did anything which would have been an offence under paragraph (*b*) if the bankruptcy order against him had been made immediately before he did it;

(*d*) he removes, or in the initial period removed, any property the value of which is or was not less than $500 and possession of which he is or would have been required to deliver up to the Official Assignee; or

(*e*) he without reasonable excuse fails, on being required to do so by the Official Assignee or the court —

(i) to account for the loss of any substantial part of his property incurred in the 12 months before the presentation of the bankruptcy petition by or against him or in the initial period; or

(ii) to give a satisfactory explanation of the manner in which such a loss was incurred.

Concealment of books and papers; falsification, etc

136. A bankrupt shall be guilty of an offence if —

(*a*) he does not deliver up possession to the Official Assignee, or as the Official Assignee may direct, of all books, papers and other records of which he has possession or control and which relate to his estate or his affairs;

(*b*) he prevents, or in the initial period prevented, the production of any books, papers or records relating to his estate or affairs;

(*c*) he conceals, destroys, mutilates or falsifies, or causes or permits the concealment, destruction, mutilation or falsification of, any books, papers or other records relating to his estate or affairs;

(*d*) he makes, or causes or permits the making of, any false entries in any book, document or record relating to his estate or affairs;

(*e*) he disposes of, or alters or makes any omission in, or causes or permits the disposal, altering or making of any omission in, any book, document or record relating to his estate or affairs; or (*f*) in the 12 months before the presentation of the bankruptcy petition by or against him, or in the initial period, he did anything which would have been an offence under paragraph (*c*) , (*d*) or (*e*) if the bankruptcy order against him had been made before he did it.

False statements

137. A bankrupt shall be guilty of an offence if —

(*a*) he makes any false statement or any material omission in any statement under this Act relating to his affairs;

(*b*) knowing or believing that a false debt has been proved by any person under the bankruptcy, he fails to inform the Official Assignee as soon as practicable;

(*c*) he attempts to account for any part of his property by fictitious losses or expenses;

(*d*) at any meeting of his creditors in the 12 months before the presentation of the bankruptcy petition by or against him or (whether or not at such a meeting) at any time in the initial period, he did anything which would have been an offence under paragraph (*c*) if the bankruptcy order against him had been made before he did it; or

(*e*) he is, or at any time has been, guilty of any false representation or other fraud for the purpose of obtaining the consent of his creditors, or any of them, to an agreement with reference to his affairs or to his bankruptcy.

Fraudulent disposal of property

138.

—(1) A bankrupt shall be guilty of an offence if —

(*a*) he makes or causes to be made, or has during the period of 5 years prior to the date of the bankruptcy order against him made or caused to be made, any gift or transfer of, or any charge on, his property; or

(*b*) he conceals or removes, or has at any time before the commencement of the bankruptcy concealed or removed, any part of his property after, or within two months before, the date on which a judgment or order for the payment of money has been obtained against him, being a judgment or order which was not satisfied before the commencement of his bankruptcy.

(2) In this section, the reference to making a transfer of or a charge on any property includes causing or conniving at, the levying of any execution against that property.

Absconding with property

139. A bankrupt shall be guilty of an offence if —

(*a*) he leaves, or attempts or makes preparations to leave, Singapore with any property the value of which is $500 or more and possession of which he is required to deliver up to the Official Assignee; or

(*b*) in the 12 months before the presentation of the bankruptcy petition by or against him, or in the initial period, he did anything which would have been an offence under paragraph (*a*) if the bankruptcy order against him had been made immediately before he did it.

Fraudulent dealing with property obtained on credit

140.

—(1) A bankrupt shall be guilty of an offence if, in the 12 months before the presentation of the bankruptcy petition by or against him, or in the initial period, he disposed of any property which he had obtained on credit and, at the time he disposed of it, had not paid for.

(2) A person shall be guilty of an offence if, in the 12 months before the presentation of the bankruptcy petition by or against a bankrupt or in the initial period, he acquired or received property from the bankrupt knowing or believing —

(*a*) that the bankrupt owed money in respect of the property; and

(*b*) that the bankrupt did not intend, or was unlikely to be able, to pay the money so owed.

(3) A person shall not be guilty of an offence under subsection (1) or (2) if the disposal, acquisition or receipt of the property was in the ordinary course of a business carried on by the bankrupt at the time of the disposal, acquisition or receipt.

(4) In determining for the purposes of this section whether any property is disposed of, acquired or received in the ordinary course of a business carried on by the bankrupt, regard may be had, in particular, to the price paid for the property.

(5) In this section, any reference to disposing of property shall be read as including pawning or pledging of such property, and any reference to acquiring or receiving property shall be read accordingly.

Obtaining credit; engaging in business

141.

—(1) A bankrupt shall be guilty of an offence if, being an undischarged bankrupt —

(*a*) either alone or jointly with any other person, he obtains credit to the extent of $500 or more from any person without informing that person that he is an undischarged bankrupt; or

(*b*) he engages in any trade or business under a name other than that under which he was adjudicated bankrupt without disclosing to all persons with whom he enters into any business transaction the name under which he was adjudicated bankrupt.

(2) In this section, any reference to a bankrupt obtaining credit shall be read as including any case in which —

(*a*) goods are bailed to him under a hire-purchase agreement; and

(*b*) he is paid in advance (whether in money or otherwise) for the supply of goods or services.

Failure to keep proper accounts of business

142.

—(1) A bankrupt shall be guilty of an offence if, having been engaged in any business within two years before the presentation of the bankruptcy petition by or against him, he has not —

(*a*) kept proper accounting records throughout that period and throughout any part of the initial period in which he was so engaged; or

(*b*) preserved all the accounting records which he has kept.

(2) For the purposes of this section, a person shall be deemed not to have kept proper accounting records if he has not kept such records as are necessary to show or explain his transactions and financial position in his business, including —

(*a*) records containing entries from day to day, in sufficient detail, of all cash paid and received;

(*b*) where the business involved dealings in goods, statements of annual stock-takings; and

(*c*) except in the case of goods sold by way of retail trade to the actual customer, records of all goods sold and purchased showing the buyers and sellers in sufficient detail to enable the goods and the buyers and sellers to be identified.

(3) A bankrupt shall not be guilty of an offence under subsection (1) —

(*a*) if his unsecured liabilities at the commencement of the bankruptcy did not exceed $10,000; or

(*b*) if he proves that in the circumstances in which he carried on business the omission was honest and excusable.

Gambling

143.

—(1) A bankrupt shall be guilty of an offence if he has —

(*a*) in the two years before the presentation of the bankruptcy petition by or against him, materially contributed to, or increased the extent of, his insolvency by gambling or by rash and hazardous speculations; or

(*b*) in the initial period, lost any part of his property by gambling or by rash and hazardous speculations.

(2) In determining for the purposes of this section whether any speculation was rash and hazardous, the financial position of the bankrupt at the time when he entered into them shall be taken into consideration.

Bankrupt incurring debt without reasonable ground of expectation of being able to pay it

144. A bankrupt shall be guilty of an offence if —

(*a*) within 12 months before the presentation of a bankruptcy petition by or against him or during the initial period, he incurs any debt provable in bankruptcy; or

(*b*) having been engaged in carrying on any trade or business, he continues to trade or carry on business by incurring any debt provable in bankruptcy within 12 months before the date of the presentation of a bankruptcy petition by or against him or during the initial period, he being insolvent on the date of incurring the debt, without any reasonable ground of expectation of being able to pay it.

Making of false claims, etc

145.

—(1) Any creditor in any bankruptcy, composition or arrangement with creditors shall be guilty of an offence if he makes any claim, proof, declaration or statement of account which is untrue in any material particular unless he satisfies the court that he had no intent to defraud.

(2) A creditor shall be guilty of an offence if he obtains or receives any money, property or security from any person as an inducement for forbearing to oppose, or for consenting to, the discharge of a bankrupt.

(3) A person shall be guilty of an offence if he, knowing that a bankruptcy order has been made against a debtor, removes, conceals, receives or otherwise deals with or disposes of any part of the property of the debtor, with intent to defeat the order.

(4) Fines imposed and levied under this section shall be deemed to be part of the property of the bankrupt and shall vest in the Official Assignee.

Penalty

146. A person guilty of any offence under this Part shall be liable on conviction to a fine not exceeding $10,000 or to imprisonment for a term not exceeding 3 years or to both.

Supplementary provisions

147.

—(1) It shall not be a defence in proceedings for an offence under this Act that anything relied on, in whole or in part, as constituting that offence was done outside Singapore.

(2) In a charge for an offence under this Act, it shall be sufficient to set forth the substance of the offence charged in the words of this Act, specifying the offence or as near thereto as circumstances admit, without alleging or setting forth any debt, demand, petition or any proceedings in, or order, warrant or document of any court acting under this Act.

(3) Where a bankrupt has been guilty of any offence under this Act, he shall not be exempt from being proceeded against therefor by reason that he has obtained his discharge or that the bankruptcy order made against him has been annulled or rescinded.

PART XI MISCELLANEOUS PROVISIONS

Administration in bankruptcy of estate of person dying insolvent

148.

—(1) In this section, unless the context otherwise requires, “creditor” means one or more creditors qualified to present a bankruptcy petition under this Act.

(2) The Official Assignee or any creditor of a deceased debtor whose debt would have been sufficient to support a bankruptcy petition against the debtor had he been alive, may present to the court a petition for an order for the administration of the estate of the deceased debtor according to this Act.

(3) Every petition under this section shall be in the same form as a creditor’s petition under section 57, with such variations as the case may require, except that in the case of a petition by the Official Assignee, it shall not be necessary to allege or prove that any debt is owing to the petitioner.

(4) Upon the prescribed notice being given to the legal representative, if any, of the deceased debtor, the court may, in the prescribed manner, upon proof of the petitioner's debt, unless the court is satisfied that there is a reasonable probability that the estate will be sufficient for the payment of the debts owing by the deceased debtor, make an order for the administration in bankruptcy of the deceased debtor's estate, or may, upon cause being shown, dismiss the petition with or without costs.

(5) An administration order under this section shall not be made until the expiration of two months from the date of the grant of probate or letters of administration, unless with the concurrence of the legal representative of the deceased debtor.

(6) A petition for administration under this section shall not be presented to the court after proceedings have been commenced for the administration of the deceased debtor's estate except that the court may, in that case, on the application of any creditor and on proof that the estate is insufficient to pay its debts in the prescribed manner, make an order for the administration of the estate of the deceased debtor in bankruptcy, and the like consequences shall ensue as under an administration order made on the petition of a creditor.

(7) Upon an administration order being made under this section, the property of the debtor shall vest in the Official Assignee as trustee thereof without any further conveyance, transfer or assignment, and he shall forthwith proceed to realise and distribute the same in accordance with this Act.

(8) Sections 83 and 84 so far as they relate to persons other than the debtor, and, with the modifications under this section, all the provisions of Part VII shall, so far as the same are applicable, apply to the case of an administration order under this section.

(9) Sections 98, 105 and 106 shall apply in the case of an administration order under this section as if the administration order were a bankruptcy order.

(10) In the administration of the property of the deceased debtor under an administration order, the Official Assignee shall have regard to any claims by the legal representative of the deceased debtor to payment of the proper funeral and testamentary expenses incurred by him in and about the debtor's estate and such claims shall be deemed to be preferential debts under the administration order and shall be payable in full out of the debtor's estate in priority to all other debts.

(11) If on the administration of a deceased debtor's estate any surplus remains in the hands of the Official Assignee after payment in full of all the debts due from the debtor, together with the costs of the administration and interest as provided by this Act in the case of a bankruptcy, the surplus shall, subject to section 122 (2) , be paid over to the legal representative of the deceased debtor's estate or dealt with in such other manner as is prescribed.

(12) Upon notice being given to the legal representative of a deceased debtor of the presentation by a creditor of a petition under this section, and in the event of an administration order being made thereon, no payment or transfer of property made thereafter by the legal representative shall operate as a discharge to him as between himself and the Official Assignee.

(13) Subject to this section, nothing in this section shall invalidate any payment made or act or thing done in good faith by the legal representative before the date of the administration order.

Costs

149.

—(1) No payment shall, without the approval of the Official Assignee, be allowed in the accounts of any trustee in bankruptcy or of any special manager in respect of the performance by any other person of the ordinary duties which are required by this Act or the rules to be performed by himself.

(2) Unless agreed to by the Official Assignee, all bills and charges of solicitors, managers, accountants, auctioneers, brokers and other persons shall be taxed by the prescribed officer, and no payments in respect thereof shall be allowed in the accounts of the Official Assignee without leave of the court given after such taxation has been made.

(3) Every such person shall, on request by the Official Assignee, which request the Official Assignee shall make a sufficient time before declaring a dividend, deliver his bill of costs or charges to the prescribed officer for taxation, and if he fails to do so within 7 days after receipt of the request, or such further time as the court on application grants, the Official Assignee shall declare and distribute the dividend without regard to any claim by him, and thereupon any such claim shall be forfeited as well against the Official Assignee personally as against the estate.

Actions by Official Assignee and bankrupt's partners

150.

—(1) Where a partner in a firm is adjudged bankrupt, the court may authorise the Official Assignee to commence and prosecute any action or other legal proceeding in the names of the Official Assignee and of the bankrupt's partner.

(2) Any release by such partner of the debt or demand to which the action or proceeding relates shall be void; but notice of the application for authority to commence the action or proceeding shall be given to him and he may show cause against it, and on his application the court may, if it thinks fit, direct that he shall receive his proper share of the proceeds of the action or proceeding, and if he does not claim any benefit therefrom he shall be indemnified against costs in respect thereof as the court directs.

Action in aid of courts of Malaysia and designated countries

151.

—(1) The High Court and the officers thereof shall, in all matters of bankruptcy and insolvency, act in aid of and be auxiliary to the courts of Malaysia or any designated country having jurisdiction in bankruptcy and insolvency so long as the law of Malaysia or the designated country requires its courts to act in aid of and be auxiliary to the courts of Singapore.

(2) An order of any such court of Malaysia or any designated country, seeking aid with a request to the High Court, shall be deemed sufficient to enable the High Court to exercise in respect of the matters directed by the order such jurisdiction as either the court which made the request or the High Court could exercise in respect of similar matters within their several jurisdictions.

(3) In this section, "designated country" means any country designated for the purposes of this section by the Minister by notification in the *Gazette*.

Reciprocal recognition of Official Assignees

152.

—(1) The Minister may, by notification in the *Gazette*, declare that the Government of Singapore has entered into an agreement with the government of Malaysia for the recognition by each government of the Official Assignees in bankruptcy appointed by the other government.

(2) From the date of that notification where any person has been adjudged a bankrupt by a court in Malaysia, such property of the bankrupt situate in Singapore as would, if he had been adjudged bankrupt in Singapore, vest in the Official Assignee of Singapore, shall vest in the Official Assignee appointed by the

government of Malaysia, and all courts in Singapore shall recognise the title of such Official Assignee to such property.

(3) Subsection (2) shall not apply where a bankruptcy petition has been presented against the bankrupt in Singapore until the petition has been dismissed or withdrawn or the bankruptcy order has been rescinded or annulled.

(4) The production of an order of adjudication purporting to be certified, under the seal of the court in Malaysia making the order, by the registrar of that court, or of a copy of the official *Gazette* of Malaysia containing a notice of an order adjudging that person a bankrupt shall be conclusive proof in all courts in Singapore of the order having been duly made and of its date.

(5) The Official Assignee of Malaysia may sue and be sued in any court in Singapore by the official name of "the Official Assignee of the Property of (name of bankrupt) , a Bankrupt under the Law of Malaysia".

Evidence of proceedings at meetings of creditors

153.

—(1) A minute of proceedings at a meeting of creditors under this Act, signed at the same or the next ensuing meeting by a person describing himself as or appearing to be chairman of the meeting at which the minute is signed, shall be received in evidence without further proof.

(2) Until the contrary is proved, every meeting of creditors in respect of the proceedings whereof a minute has been so signed shall be deemed to have been duly convened and held, and all resolutions passed or proceedings had thereat to have been duly passed or had.

Evidence of proceedings in bankruptcy

154. Any —

(*a*) petition or copy of a petition in bankruptcy;

(*b*) order or certificate or copy of an order or certificate made by the court in bankruptcy;

(*c*) instrument, affidavit or document or copy of an instrument, affidavit or document made or used in the course of any bankruptcy proceedings or other proceedings had under this Act, shall, if it appears to be sealed with the seal of the court or purports to be signed by any judge thereof, or is certified as a true copy by the Registrar, be receivable in evidence in all legal proceedings whatever.

Swearing of affidavits

155. Subject to the rules, any affidavit may be used in a court if it is sworn —

(*a*) in Singapore before any person authorised to administer oaths or any Magistrate;

(*b*) in Malaysia or other Commonwealth country before a judge, magistrate, justice of the peace or any person authorised to administer oaths under any written law for the time being in force in Malaysia or that Commonwealth country; and

(*c*) in any other place before a magistrate or justice of the peace or other person qualified to administer oaths in that place who is certified to be a magistrate or justice of the peace or person qualified as aforesaid by a consul or person performing consular functions on behalf of the government or by a notary public.

Death of witness

156. In case of the death of the debtor or bankrupt, as the case may be, or of his spouse, or of a witness whose evidence has been received by any court in any proceedings under this Act, the deposition of the person so deceased, purporting to be sealed with the seal of the court, or a copy thereof purporting to be so sealed, shall be admitted as evidence of the matters therein deposed to.

Service of notices

157. All notices and other documents for the service of which no special mode is prescribed may be sent by prepaid registered post to the last known place of residence or business of the person to be served therewith.

Formal defect not to invalidate proceedings or acts

158.

—(1) No proceedings in bankruptcy shall be invalidated by any formal defect or by any irregularity, unless the court before which an objection is made to the proceedings is of the opinion that substantial injustice has been caused by the defect or irregularity and that the injustice cannot be remedied by any order of that court.

(2) The acts of a person as the trustee of a bankrupt's estate or as a special manager, and the acts of the creditors' committee appointed for any bankruptcy, shall be valid notwithstanding any defect in the appointment, election or qualifications of the trustee or manager or, as the case may be, of any member of the committee.

Exemption from stamp duty

159.

—(1) For the purposes of this section —

"bankruptcy" includes any proceedings before or after the bankruptcy order and whether the order is made or not;

"bankrupt" includes any debtor proceeded against under this Act.

(2) Every deed, conveyance, assignment or other assurance relating solely to freehold or leasehold property or to any mortgage, charge or other encumbrance on, or any estate, right or interest in, any real or personal property which is part of the estate of any bankrupt, and which, after the execution of the deed, conveyance, assignment or other assurance, either at law or in equity, is or remains the estate of the bankrupt or of the Official Assignee, and every power of attorney, proxy paper, writ, order, certificate, affidavit, bond or other instrument or writing relating solely to the property of any bankrupt or to any proceeding under any bankruptcy shall be exempt from stamp duties except in respect of fees under this Act.

Acts of corporations, firms and lunatics

160. For all or any of the purposes of this Act —

(*a*) a corporation may act by any of its officers authorised in that behalf under the seal of the corporation;

(*b*) a firm may act by any of its members;

(*c*) a mentally disordered person or lunatic may act by his committee.

Access to bankrupt's books

161. Any creditor of the bankrupt may, upon payment of the prescribed fee, at all reasonable times inspect personally or by agent, any such books, papers or documents in the possession of the Official Assignee.

Exclusion of liability relating to computerised information service

162. Where the Official Assignee provides a service to the public whereby computerised information of prescribed particulars of a bankrupt is supplied to the public on payment of a prescribed fee, neither the Government nor any of its employees involved in the supply of such information shall be liable for any loss or damage suffered by members of the public by reason of any errors or omissions of whatever nature appearing therein or howsoever caused if made in good faith and in the ordinary course of the discharge of the duties of such employees.

List of undischarged bankrupts to be kept

163.

—(1) A list of undischarged bankrupts shall be kept by the Official Assignee and shall be published in the *Gazette* at such times as the Minister may direct, but not less than once in each year.

(2) The Registrar shall keep a list of all bankruptcy orders made; and on that list every such order shall be forthwith entered under the headings of the letters of the alphabet and every order rescinding, annulling or discharging any such order and every notice of discharge given under section 125 (2) shall be noted in the list against the order rescinded, annulled or discharged.

Unclaimed and undistributed moneys

164.

—(1) Where a trustee or nominee is in possession of or has under his control —

(*a*) any unclaimed dividend or other moneys which have remained unclaimed for more than 6 months from the date when the dividend or other moneys became payable; or

(*b*) after making final distribution, any unclaimed or undistributed moneys arising from the property of a bankrupt,

he shall forthwith pay those moneys to the Official Assignee to be placed to the credit of the Bankruptcy Estates Account, whereupon the Official Assignee shall issue to him the prescribed certificate of receipt for the moneys so paid and that certificate shall be an effectual discharge to him in respect thereof.

(2) The Official Assignee shall from time to time pay out of the Bankruptcy Estates Account and into the Insolvency Assistance Fund, maintained under section 165, so much of the sums standing to the credit of the Account as represents —

(*a*) dividends or balances in the Account which do not exceed $20;

(*b*) dividends which were declared but have not been claimed for a period of 6 years; and (*c*) balances in the Account which have not been claimed for a period of 6 years from the date that —

(i) the bankruptcy order has been annulled by the court;

(ii) the bankrupt has been discharged from bankruptcy by the court;

(iii) the bankrupt has been discharged from bankruptcy by a certificate issued by the Official Assignee;

(iv) the bankruptcy petition presented against the debtor has been withdrawn by the petitioner or dismissed by the court; or

(v) the moneys were paid into the Account under subsection (1) .

Insolvency Assistance Fund

165.

—(1) The Official Assignee shall maintain and administer a fund to be known as the Insolvency Assistance Fund (referred to in this section as the Fund) in accordance with such rules as may be prescribed.

(2) There shall be paid into the Fund —

(*a*) all unclaimed moneys referred to in section 164 (2) ; and

(*b*) all costs and fees recovered by the Official Assignee in any proceedings taken under this Act in which moneys from the Fund were applied.

(3) Subject to subsections (4) and (6) , the Fund may be applied by the Official Assignee for all or any of the following purposes:

(*a*) for the remuneration of special managers appointed under section 113;

(*b*) for the payment of all costs, fees and allowances to solicitors and other persons in proceedings on behalf of a bankrupt's estate or to recover assets of the estate;

(*c*) for the payment of such costs and fees in the administration of a bankrupt's estate as the Official Assignee may determine;

(*d*) for such other purposes as may be prescribed.

(4) If any claimant makes any demand against the Official Assignee for any amount of unclaimed moneys paid into the Fund under subsection (2) (*a*) , the Minister may direct that payment of that amount, free of interest, be made to the claimant out of the Consolidated Fund.

(5) No moneys from the Fund shall be applied for any proceedings where, in the opinion of the Official Assignee, there is no reasonable ground for taking, defending, continuing or being a party to the proceedings or where there are sufficient moneys for such purpose in the bankrupt's estate.

(6) The Minister may from time to time pay such sums of moneys in the Fund into the Consolidated Fund as he may determine.

Rules

166. The Minister may make rules for the purposes of carrying into effect the objects of this Act and, without prejudice to the generality of this power, the rules may contain —

(*a*) provisions with respect to meetings of creditors, the functions, membership and proceedings of a creditors' committee;

(*b*) provisions with respect to the proof of debts, the manner and conditions of proving a debt and the manner and expenses of establishing the value of any debt or security;

(*c*) provisions with respect to the scale of appropriation of salary under section 109;

(*d*) provisions prescribing any fees payable under this Act and the rules; and

(*e*) such incidental, supplemental and transitional provisions as may appear to the Minister to be necessary or expedient.

Repeal, transitional and consequential provisions

167.

—(1) The Bankruptcy Act is repealed.

(2) In any written law or document in which a reference is made to the Bankruptcy Act (Cap. 20) repealed by this Act, such reference shall be read as a reference to the Bankruptcy Act 1994.

(3) The transitional provisions and savings set out in the First Schedule shall have effect.

(4) The provisions of the Acts specified in the first column of the Second Schedule are amended in the manner set out in the second column thereof.

FIRST SCHEDULE

Section 167(3)

TRANSITIONAL PROVISIONS AND SAVINGS

Bankrupts under repealed Act to continue to be bankrupts under this Act

1.—(1) A person who was a bankrupt on the appointed day continues to be a bankrupt until he is discharged, or his bankruptcy is rescinded or annulled, under this Act; and the provisions of this Act shall apply to and in relation to that bankrupt as if he had become a bankrupt under this Act.

(2) All orders and applications made, notices and consents given, matters advertised, meetings held, resolutions passed, compositions, schemes of arrangement or deeds accepted or approved, debts proved and acts and things done before the appointed day in relation to a bankrupt or the property of a bankrupt shall, in relation to the administration of the conduct and affairs of the bankrupt and his property under this Act, be deemed to have been made, given, advertised, held, passed, proved or done under this Act.

Uncompleted proceedings under repealed Act

2.—(1) Where —

(*a*)

a bankruptcy notice under the repealed Act has been served on a debtor before the appointed day; and

(*b*)

the debtor has failed, whether before or after the appointed day, to comply with the notice,

a bankruptcy petition may be presented against the debtor under the repealed Act, and proceedings in relation to the petition may, subject to sub-paragraph (3) , be taken and had under that Act as if this Act had not been enacted.

(2) Where a bankruptcy petition has been presented against a debtor under the repealed Act before the appointed day, but an adjudication order has not been made on the petition, and the petition has not been withdrawn or dismissed before that day, proceedings in relation to the petition may, subject to sub-paragraph (3) , be continued, or taken and had, after that day under the repealed Act as if this Act had not been enacted.

(3) Where a person becomes a bankrupt on a petition to which sub-paragraph (1) or (2) applies, all subsequent proceedings in relation to the bankrupt or his estate shall be taken and had, and this Act shall apply as if he had become a bankrupt on a creditor's petition presented under this Act.

(4) Any proceedings (including the hearing of an appeal) in a court or before the Registrar under the repealed Act that had not been completed before the appointed day may be continued and completed, and any right of appeal in relation to those proceedings may be exercised and the appeal heard and determined as if this Act had not been enacted.

(5) Any right of appeal from an order of a court having jurisdiction under the repealed Act, being an order made before the appointed day, may be exercised, and the appeal heard and determined, after that day, as if this Act had not been enacted.

(6) Any right of appeal to a court having jurisdiction in bankruptcy under the repealed Act from an act or decision of the Official Assignee, the Registrar or any other officer under the repealed Act done or made before the appointed day and any right to apply to such a court to review such an act or decision may be exercised, and the appeal or application heard and determined, by the High Court.

(7) In relation to any such case as is mentioned in sub-paragraph (1) , the references in any written law to a petition, order or other matter which is provided for under the repealed Act and corresponds to a petition, order or other matter provided for under the provisions of this Act shall continue on and after the appointed day to give effect as references to the petition, order or matter provided for by the repealed Act; but otherwise those references shall have effect on and after that day as references to the petition, order or matter provided for by those provisions of this Act.

Application of section 148 to existing estates of deceased debtors

3.—(1) Where an order for the administration in bankruptcy of a deceased debtor's estate has been made under Part VIII of the repealed Act, but the administration of the estate has not been completed before the appointed day, the estate of the deceased debtor shall, subject to this paragraph, be administered and distributed as if an order for administration of the estate had been made under section 148 of this Act, and the provisions of that section shall apply in relation to the estate accordingly.

(2) All orders and applications made, notices and consents given, matters advertised, meetings held, resolutions passed, debts proved and acts and things done before the appointed day in relation to the estate of a deceased debtor shall, in relation to the administration and distribution of the estate under section 148

of this Act, be deemed to have been made, given, advertised, held, passed, proved or done under that section.

Offences committed before appointed day

4. Where a bankruptcy order is made under this Act on or after the appointed day on a petition to which paragraph 2(1) or (2) applies, a person shall not be guilty of an offence under Part X of this Act in respect of anything done before that day; but shall be guilty of an offence under the repealed Act in respect of anything done before that day which would have been an offence under that Act if the making of the bankruptcy order had been the making of a receiving order or an adjudication order under that Act.

Schedule to be without prejudice to section 166

5.—(1) This Schedule shall be without prejudice to the power conferred by this Act under which rules under section 166 of this Act may make transitional provision in connection with the coming into force of those rules; and such provision may apply those rules in relation to a bankruptcy notwithstanding that it arose from a petition presented before either the coming into force of the rules or the appointed day.

(2) Rules made under section 166 of this Act may provide for such notices served before the appointed day as may be prescribed to be treated for the purposes of this Act as statutory demands served under section 62(*a*) (i) of this Act.

Transactions before appointed day

6.—(1) A transaction entered into before the appointed day shall not be set aside under this Act except to the extent that it could have been set aside under the law in force immediately before that day.

(2) References in sub-paragraph (1) to setting aside a transaction shall include the making of any order which varies or reverses any effect of such a transaction.

Computation of time

7. Where any period of time specified in a provision of the repealed Act is current immediately before the appointed day, this Act shall have effect as if the corresponding provision had been in force when the period began to run; and (without prejudice to the foregoing) any period of time so specified and current shall be deemed for the purposes of this Act —

(*a*) to run from the date or event from which it was running immediately before that day; and

(*b*) to expire (subject to any provision of this Act for its extension) whenever it would have expired if this Act had not been enacted, and any rights, priorities, liabilities, reliefs, obligations, requirements, powers, duties or exemptions dependent on the beginning, duration or end of such a period as above mentioned shall be under this Act as they were or would have been under the repealed Act.

Punishment of offences committed before appointed day

8.—(1) Offences committed before the appointed day under any provision of the repealed Act may, notwithstanding any repeal by this Act, be prosecuted and punished after that day as if this Act had not been enacted.

(2) Where an offence for the continuance of which a penalty was provided has been committed under any provision of the repealed Act, proceedings may be taken under this Act in respect of the continuance of the offence on and after the appointed day in the like manner as if the offence had been committed under the corresponding provision of this Act.

Schedule not to prejudice section 16 of Interpretation Act

9. Nothing in this Schedule shall be taken as prejudicing section 16 of the Interpretation Act (Cap. 1) (effect of repeal) .

Meaning of "repealed Act"

10. In this Schedule, "repealed Act" means the Bankruptcy Act (Cap. 20) in force immediately before the appointed day.

PRACTICAL INFORMATION FOR CONDUCTING BUSINESS[1]

STARTING BUSINESS IN SINGAPORE BASICS

STARTING A BUSINESS IN SINGAPORE

LICENSING AND REGISTRATION OF BUSINESS ORGANISATIONS

1. There are no restrictions on the types of businesses that may be set-up in Singapore, but some have to apply for special licences from the Government e.g. banks, finance companies, insurance and stock-broker firms. Some items require a licence before manufacturing for eg. cigarettes, beer or stout or fire crackers.
2. Every business in Singapore must be registered with the Registry of Companies and Businesses.

FORMATION OF REPRESENTATIVE OFFICE

A foreign company may establish a representative office in Singapore to undertake promotional and liaison activities on behalf of its parent company. The office, however, directly or on behalf of its parent company, must not be engaged in business; undertake transhipment of goods; or open or negotiate any letters of credits. Approval for the establishment of a representative office must be obtained from the Singapore Trade Development Board.

TYPES OF BUSINESS ORGANISATIONS

3. Persons who wish to carry on business in Singapore must seek registration either under the Business Registration Act (Cap. 32) or the Companies Act (Cap. 50) .

These two Acts regulate businesses and companies in Singapore respectively. They are administered by the Registry of Companies and Businesses.

4. The types of business organisation which may be registered in Singapore are:

Under the **Business Registration Act:**
a. Sole Proprietorships
b. Partnerships

Under the **Companies Act:**
a. Companies incorporated in Singapore
b. Foreign companies

REGISTRATION

5. Briefly, the formalities which must be completed before a company can be registered under the Companies Act are as follows:

a. Application must be made to the Registry of Companies and Businesses for approval of the name of the company.

[1] This section based in part on the materials of the US Department of Commerce.

b. A memorandum and articles of association should be drawn up for the purposes of registration. The requirements for the memorandum are specified in Section 22 of the Companies Act.

c. These must be filed with the Registry of Companies and Businesses.

FOREIGN COMPANIES

A foreign company should, before it establishes a place of business or commences to carry on business in Singapore, lodge with the Registry of Companies and Businesses for registration relevant information including:

a certified copy of the certificate of its incorporation or registration in its place of incorporation. For more details please refer to the Registry of Companies and Businesses Website.

The agent of a foreign company is answerable for the doing of all acts, matters and things as are required to be done by the foreign company under the Act and is personally liable for any penalties imposed on the foreign company for any contravention of such requirements.

A foreign company is not regarded as carrying on business in Singapore by reason of the fact that it maintains a bank account in Singapore, effects any sale through an independent contractor, invests its funds or holds any property.

To ascertain whether the foreign company is "carrying on business in Singapore", it is often advisable to obtain professional advice from lawyers and public accountants.

Company law in Singapore is very similar to company law in the UK and Australia, with procedures for registration, submission of returns etc, varying only slightly according to local requirements. It is advisable to employ the services of a firm of solicitors or accountants to attend to the formalities of registering a company.

MARKET OVERVIEW

Foreign investments, combined with investments through government-linked corporations, underpin Singapore's open, heavily trade-dependent economy. In 2010, the Singapore economy rebounded with an exceptional performance, expanding by 14.5% to become the second fastest growing economy in the world. GDP is expected to moderate in 2011 with the Singapore Government forecasting a more sustainable growth rate of 4-6%. Inflation grew 2.8% in 2010 and is projected to rise to 3.0-4.0% in 2011. Analysts expect the Singapore currency to strengthen as the Singapore Government uses monetary policy to fight inflation.

In 2010, Singapore was the United States' 10th largest export market (up from 11th place in 2009) and remained the 13th largest trading partner. The city state is a major entrepot and was the second busiest container port in the world in 2010. The top supplier of imported goods to Singapore was Malaysia, followed by the United States, China, Japan, Taiwan, South Korea, Indonesia, Saudi Arabia, Thailand, and India respectively. "The Global Enabling Trade Report 2010" by the World Economic Forum ranked Singapore first for having the most open economy for international trade and investment.

MARKET CHALLENGES

Singapore is generally a free port; more than 99% of all imports enter Singapore duty-free. For social and/or environmental reasons, it levies high excise taxes on distilled spirits and wine, tobacco products, motor vehicles, and gasoline. The main challenge for American companies is strong competition from both foreign and local suppliers. Despite its liberal trading regime, foreign companies face barriers in certain service sectors such as telecommunications, media, financial and professional services, and energy. Details can be found in the USTR Report on Foreign Trade Barriers that is available on-line at http://www.ustr.gov/sites/default/files/uploads/reports/2010/NTE/2010_NTE_Sing apore_final.pdf

In March 2010, the Media Development Authority (MDA) introduced new measures that will require pay TV companies to cross carry content subject to exclusive carriage provisions. A pay TV company with an exclusive contract for a channel would be required to share that content with other pay TV companies at their request. Content providers consider the measures an unnecessary

interference in a competitive market that would deny content holders the ability to negotiate freely in the marketplace, and interferes with their ability to manage and protect their intellectual property. MDA plans to implement the measures in mid-2011.

• The U.S. Commercial Service has received multiple complaints from U.S. merchants reporting fraudulent credit card transactions committed by companies/individuals purporting to be in Singapore. Investigation of the fraudulent transactions has revealed that the shipments are actually being sent to freight forwarders in Singapore and diverted to unknown consignees in neighboring countries. Exporters should be wary of orders paid by credit card and requiring immediate shipment. More information can be found at http://www.buyusa.gov/singapore/en/warning_credit_card_fraud.html

MARKET OPPORTUNITIES

Singapore is a sophisticated and modern economy that offers excellent opportunities for U.S. firms interested in penetrating the Asian market. The World Bank's "Doing Business 2010" report ranked Singapore as the easiest country in which to do business. Singapore's market appeal is its free port status, straightforward, English-speaking, U.S. style of doing business, strong intellectual property protection with virtually no corruption. The country is a major trading hub, importing and exporting all kinds of products from consumer goods to high technology and industrial goods for re-export to third countries. Best prospects for U.S. companies include: electronics, oil and gas equipment, aircraft and parts, pollution control equipment, computer hardware and software, telecommunications equipment, laboratory and scientific instruments, medical devices, university education services and franchises.

The Singapore government and private industry are expected to invest in several major projects including:

construction of US$300 million motor sports hub to be ready of end 2011;

construction of US$47 million new air cargo hub at Singapore Changi Airport to be completed by first half of 2012;

construction of a second desalination plant to be ready by 2013;

construction of US$1 billion LNG terminal that will start operations in mid 2013;

construction of a US$530 million underground oil storage facility;

construction of a public hospital with an allocated budget of over US$700 million scheduled to be ready by 2014;

construction of a private sector 350-bed hospital costing between US$207 and US$345 million to be built by 2012 while another private healthcare group will spend between $61.5 million and US$77 million to expand their flagship hospital scheduled for completion by 2012;

Singapore's second largest telecom services provider together with regional telcos will jointly build and operate a US$430 million submarine cable connecting East Asia's major business hubs;

Construction of new Mass Rapid Transit (MRT) rail lines costing over US$30 billion that will double Singapore's MRT network from 138km today to 278km in 2020.

Singapore government investments of US$5 billion by 2013 to foster research and high-end production in industries such as precision engineering and life sciences.

MARKET ENTRY STRATEGY

• Using agents or distributors is a common and effective way to serve the Singapore market and, from here, other countries in Southeast Asia. Singapore firms are aggressive when it comes to representing new products and typically respond enthusiastically to new opportunities. Because of the relatively small size of the Singapore market, potential partners often ask to cover regional territories. It is important for U.S. firms to visit their representatives, maintain a good relationship with them and respond quickly to inquiries. Prospective exporters to Singapore should be aware that competition is high and that buyers expect good after-sales service. Most American companies that use the U.S. Commercial Service (CS) Singapore matchmaking and promotion services in Singapore find several interested agents or distributors. When business warrants, many companies have found it useful and sometimes necessary to set up offices in Singapore. Singapore is home to over 1,500 American firms, most of which serve the regional market.

Chapter 2: Political and Economic Environment

For background information on the political and economic environment of the country, please click on the link below to the U.S. Department of State Background Notes.

http://www.state.gov/r/pa/ei/bgn/2798.htm

HOW TO REGISTER A LOCAL COMPANY IN SINGAPORE

As the registration of a local company is rather technical, it would be wise if you seek professional assistance from a firm of local solicitors or accountants.

OBTAINING A COMPANY NAME

A company cannot be incorporated unless the proposed name has been approved by us first. Names for all companies in Singapore must conform to certain guidelines laid down in the Companies Act, Chapter 50.

You are required to submit Form 14 (Application for Approval and Reservation of Name for a company) under the Companies Act, Chapter 50. For each proposed company name, a fee of S$15.00 has to be paid. You must declare if the proposed company name includes a trade mark or patent name, or the name of another company/business existing elsewhere and produce the unconditional written consent of the owner of the trade mark or patent, or the other company for the use of the name. You are also required to declare that you will change the name if it is found otherwise.

If approved, the company name will be reserved for two months. Should you need more time, RCB may grant an extension of two months upon submission of an application for an extension of time and payment of S$5.00.

A proposed company name will not be approved if it is identical to, or so nearly resembles the name of another company, foreign company or business firm as to be mistaken for it. Undesirable names, including offensive or vulgar names will also not be approved.

Certain types of activities need the necessary approval and licence from other Government authorities before the proposed business activity can begin. For example, the authority which issues Travel Agency Licence in Singapore is the Singapore Tourism Board (STB) . As such an application to register a company carrying on the activity of a Travel Agency will be referred to STB to ensure compliance with STB's guidelines. When an application has been referred to another authority, it may take another 14 days to 2 months.

It usually takes us 5 working days to process the application for approval of name.

REGISTERING THE COMPANY

After the company name has been approved, you can proceed to register the company. You would have to prepare and file the following incorporation documents :

1.Memorandum & Articles of Association setting out the objects and by-laws of the proposed company.

2.Statutory Declaration of Compliance (Form 6) .

3.Certificate of Identity (Form 7) .

4.Notice of Situation of Registered Office and of Office Hours at time of Incorporation (Form 44) .

5.Consent to Act as Director & Statement of Non Disqualification to Act as Director (Form 45) .

A further 5 working days will be required for us to incorporate your company and issue the Certificate of Incorporation upon lodgement of the relevant incorporation documents.

Every company must have at least 2 directors one of whom must be locally resident ie Singapore citizen, Singapore Permanent Resident, Singapore Employment Pass or Dependent Pass Holder. Please refer to the procedure for application of an employment pass by a foreigner who wishes to act as a local director of a new company.

A filing fee of S$10.00 per document filed and a registration fee based on the authorised share capital of the proposed company is payable. The minimum registration fee payable is S$1,200.00 based on an authorised share capital of S$100,000.00. fee.

TDB TRADERS REGISTRATION SYSTEM (TTRS)

When your Business has been registered with RCB and if your Business activity is importing and/or exporting of goods, you can register with the Trade Development Board (TDB) for such purpose via TDB Trade Register System (TTRS)

HOW TO REGISTER A FOREIGN COMPANY IN SINGAPORE

WHAT IS A FOREIGN COMPANY?

A foreign company is one that is incorporated outside Singapore. A foreign company has to register its branch in Singapore under the Companies Act before it can commence business in Singapore. Any foreign company wishing to register a branch is advised to engage a professional eg. lawyer or an accountant to assist in the preparation and filing of the necessary documents for registration.

REGISTRATION OF A FOREIGN COMPANY

As the registration of a foreign company is rather technical, it would be wise if you seek professional assistance from a firm of local solicitors or accountants.

Usually, it takes 5 working days to register the foreign company and issue the Certificate of Registration.

You are required to submit Form 14B (Application for Approval and Reservation of Name for Registration of a foreign company) under the Companies Act, Chapter 50. For each proposed foreign company name, a fee of S$15 has to be paid. When the name has been approved and is being reserved, you would have to file following documents and effect registration before commencing business :

A copy of the foreign company's Certificate of Incorporation or Registration certified, not more than 3 months before, by the authority which issued the certificate.

A copy of the foreign company's charter, statute or memorandum and articles or other instrument constituting or defining its constitution certified, not more than 3 months before, by the authority which incorporated the foreign company; or a notary public; or a director, manager or secretary of the foreign company in the form of an affidavit.

A memorandum of appointment or power of attorney appointing two or more locally resident persons (i.e. Singapore Citizen, Singapore Permanent Resident,Singapore Employment Pass Holder or Dependent Pass Holder) authorized to accept service of process and any notices required to be served on the foreign company. The memorandum of appointment or power of attorney must be verified by a person stating that he was present and did see :-

(a) the seal of the foreign company duly affixed to the memorandum of appointment or power of attorney; or

(b) executed on behalf of the foreign company in such a manner as to be the memorandum of appointment or power of attorney duly binding on the company.

Please refer to the procedure for application of an employment pass by a foreigner who wishes to act as a local agent of a new company.

1. A return giving particulars of directors of the foreign company at time of registration (Form 79) . Where the return includes directors resident in Singapore who are members of the local board of directors, a memorandum duly executed stating the powers of the local directors must also be filed.
2. Notice of Situation of Registered Office and of Office Hours at time of Incorporation (Form 44) .
3. Statutory Declaration by Agent of Foreign Company (Form 80) .

A filing fee of S$10.00 per document and a registration fee based on the authorized share capital of the foreign company is payable. The minimum registration fee payable is S$1,200.00 based on an authorized share capital equivalent to S$100,000.00.

TDB TRADERS REGISTRATION SYSTEM (TTRS)

When your Business has been registered with RCB and if your your Business activity is importing and/or exporting of goods, you can register with the Trade Development Board (TDB) for such purpose via TDB Trade Register System **(TTRS)** .

GENERAL INFORMATION ON COMPANIES

Appointment of Officers/Auditors

All companies must have a minimum of two directors at least, one of whom must be either a Singaporean, a Singapore Permanent Resident, Singapore Employment Pass Holder or Dependent Pass Holder. Any person above the age of 21 may be appointed as a director. However, some individuals eg. bankrupts, are disqualified from being directors. A director cannot resign unless there are two other directors remaining in the company, one of whom must be a local resident.

Every company must have at least one secretary appointed within 6 months of the date of incorporation. The secretary must have the requisition knowledge and experience to discharge the functions of a secretary of the company and who is either of the following:

1. a secretary of a company for at least 3 of the 5 years immediately preceding the abovementioned date of my appointment as secretary of the abovenamed company.
2. a qualified person under the Legal Profession Act (Cap. 161) .
3. an accountant registered with the Institute of Certified Public Accountants of Singapore.
4. a member of the Singapore Association of the Institute of Chartered Secretaries and Administrators.
5. a member of the Association of International Accountants (Singapore Branch) .
6. a member of the Institute of Company Accountants. Singapore Branch.

An auditor for a company must be appointed within 3 months from the date of incorporation.

Every foreign company registered with RCB must have two agents acting on its behalf in Singapore. These agents must be Singaporeans, Singapore Permanent Residents, Singapore Employment Pass Holders or Dependent Pass Holders.

NOTIFICATION OF CHANGES TO PARTICULARS

You are to notify the Registrar of changes to registered particulars through the lodgment of various prescribed forms. Indicated below are some examples of such changes.

Type of change	What form to lodge	When to lodge	Filing Fees S$
Change of registered office address	Form 44A	Within 14 days	10.00
Appointment of Company's Secretary	From 45B & 49	Within 1 month of appointment	10.00 each
Annual Return	AR Form	Within 1 month of Annual General Meeting	20.00
Allotment of Shares	Form 24	Within 1 month	10.00
Changes of Particulars in Register of Directors, Managers, Secretaries and Auditors	Form 49	Within 1 month	10.00
Appointment of Company's Director	Forms 45 & 49	Within 1 month	10.00 each

This table is not a comprehensive list of the changes to company particulars. Please seek professional assistance from your company secretary or from a firm of local solicitors or accountants if in doubt.

CLARIFICATION OF CLERICAL OR TYPOGRAPHICAL ERRORS BY STATUTORY DECLARATIONS

Section 12B of the Companies Act, Chapter 50, provides that if any particular recorded in a register is erroneous or defective, the court may by order, direct the Registrar to rectify the register.

In practice where the error is obviously minor in nature and which resulted from clerical or typographical mistakes, the Registrar may allow for clarification by way of a Statutory Declaration ("SD") . In cases where the errors are of substantial nature, eg. errors in share capital which are not due to clerical mistakes, the Registrar will not allow clarification by way of an SD and a Court Order will be required. For rectification of errors in charge documents, Court Orders are required to be obtained under Section 137 of the Companies Act, Chapter 50 and lodged with RCB.

Any person who proposes to lodge such an SD must submit their request in writing together with a draft SD for the Registrar's approval. The request should set out the relevant facts and attach documentary proofs, if any. The draft SD must contain pertinent facts and be clear as it will be on public record. Lodgement can only be effected after approval has been given.

No application fee is payable for submitting the draft SD and the applicant will be notified in writing on the outcome of his application. If the SD is approved, the applicant will have to submit the duly executed SD with a prescribed Form 94 (General Lodgement Form) and $10 filing fee (by cheque) for lodgement. Such documents will not be processed at the counter and the receipt for the lodgement of documents will be posted to the applicant subsequently.

INVESTMENT CLIMATE

Foreign investments, combined with investments through government-linked corporations (GLCs) , underpin Singapore's open, heavily trade-dependent economy. With the exception of restrictions in the financial services, professional services, and media sectors, Singapore maintains a predominantly open investment regime. The World Bank's "Doing Business 2010" report ranked Singapore as the easiest country in which to do business. "The Global Enabling Trade Report 2010" by the World Economic Forum ranked Singapore first for having the most open economy for international trade and investment. The U.S.-Singapore Free Trade Agreement (FTA) , which came into force January 1, 2004, expanded U.S. market access in goods, services, investment, and government procurement, enhanced intellectual property protection, and provided for cooperation in promoting labor rights and the environment.

The Government of Singapore (GOS) is strongly committed to maintaining a free market but also takes a leadership role in planning Singapore's economic development. The government actively uses the public sector as both an investor and catalyst for development. As of November 2010, the top six Singapore-listed GLCs accounted for nearly 17 percent of total capitalization of the Singapore Exchange (SGX) . Some observers have criticized the dominant role of GLCs in the domestic economy, arguing that it has displaced or suppressed private sector entrepreneurship and investment.

Singapore's aggressive pursuit of foreign investment as another pillar of its overall economic strategy has enabled the country to evolve into a base for multinational corporations (MNCs) . The Economic Development Board (EDB) , Singapore's investment promotion agency, focuses on securing major investments in high value-added manufacturing and service activities as part of a strategy to replace labor-intensive, low value-added activities that have migrated offshore.

Measure	Year	Ranking
TI Corruption Index	2010	#1
Heritage Economic Freedom	2010	#2
World Bank Doing Business	2010	#1

OPENNESS TO FOREIGN INVESTMENT

Singapore's legal framework and public policies are generally favorable toward foreign investors. Foreign investors are not required to enter into joint ventures or cede management control to local interests, and local and foreign investors are subject to the same basic laws. Apart from regulatory requirements in some sectors (see "Limits on National Treatment and Other Restrictions") , the government screens investment proposals only to determine eligibility for various incentive regimes (see Annex) . Singapore places no restrictions on reinvestment or repatriation of earnings or capital. The judicial system upholds the sanctity of contracts, and decisions are effectively enforced.

Limits on National Treatment and Other Restrictions: Exceptions to Singapore's general openness to foreign investment exist in telecommunications, broadcasting, the domestic news media, financial services, legal and other professional services, and property ownership. Under Singapore law, Articles of Incorporation may include shareholding limits that restrict ownership in corporations by foreign persons.

Telecommunications: The Telecoms Competition Code opened the industry in 2000 to foreign or domestic companies seeking to provide facilities-based (fixed line or mobile) or services-based (local, international, and callback) telecommunications services. Singapore Telecommunications (SingTel) , the former monopoly and currently 54.4percent government-owned, faces competition in all market segments. Its main competitors, MobileOne and StarHub, are also GLCs. As of October 2010, Singapore has 47 facilities-based (group) and 236 services-based (individual) operators.

The FTA requires that Singapore take steps to ensure that U.S. telecom service providers obtain the right to interconnect with networks in Singapore at competitive rates and on transparent and reasonable terms and conditions. Despite the Infocomm Development Authority's (IDA) requirement that SingTel offer wholesale prices for local-leased circuits at reduced rates, U.S. industry is still unable to avail itself of this more competitive pricing structure due to certain uneconomical technical interconnection requirements imposed by SingTel. Under the FTA, Singapore has also agreed that dominant licensees (SingTel and StarHub) must offer cost-based access to submarine cable-landing stations and allow sharing of facilities. U.S. and other companies have had problems with access to inter-exchange ducts as provided for in the FTA.

Since January 2007, SingTel has been exempted from dominant licensee obligations for the residential and commercial portions of the retail international telephone services. Singtel has already been exempted from dominant licensee obligations for wholesale international telephone services since November 2003. In August 2008, IDA granted preliminary approval to exempt SingTel from dominant licensee obligations for two of the 13 telecommunication services SingTel provides to business and government end-users. SingTel appealed for exemption of all 13 services. IDA decided in June 2009, following a formal public consultation held in September 2008 that SingTel will be exempted from dominant licensee obligations, ex ante, for two of the 13 services, i.e., Terrestrial International Private Leased Circuit, and Backhaul. Singtel has already been exempted from dominant licensee obligations for International Managed Data Services since April 2005.

U.S. and other companies remain concerned about the lack of transparency in some aspects of Singapore's telecommunications regulatory and rule-making process. In particular, there is no obligation to make information publicly available concerning a company's request for a stay of decision or the filing of an appeal, to request public comments about such requests, or to publish a detailed explanation concerning final decisions made by IDA or the Ministry of Information, Communication and Arts (MICA) . Infrastructure for the next generation access network, a national broadband all-fiber network, is being built by OpenNet, a consortium formed by Canada's Axia Netmedia (which holds 30-percent ownership) , SingTel (30 percent) , Singapore Press Holdings (25 percent) , and SP Telecommunications (15 percent) . The network will be operated by Nucleus Connect, a wholly-owned subsidiary of StarHub. Operational separation is imposed on Nucleus Connect to maintain its independence from OpenNet, and to ensure that it provide services to all downstream operators on the same prices and terms and conditions, with the same processes and access to information. When fully completed in 2012, the broadband network may allow fuller access to telecom services providers to reach homes and businesses without requiring access to SingTel-owned circuits.

Media: The local free-to-air broadcasting, cable and newspaper sectors are effectively closed to foreign firms. Section 44 of the Broadcasting Act restricts foreign equity ownership of companies broadcasting to the Singapore domestic market to 49 percent or less, although the Act does allow for exceptions. Individuals cannot hold more than five percent of the shares issued by a broadcasting company without the government's prior approval.

The Newspaper and Printing Presses Act restricts equity ownership (local or foreign) to five percent per shareholder and requires that directors be Singapore citizens. Newspaper companies must issue two classes of shares, ordinary and management, with the latter available only to Singapore citizens or corporations approved by the government. Holders of management shares have an effective veto over selected board decisions. The government controls distribution, importation and sale of any "declared" foreign newspaper, and significantly restricts freedom of the press, having curtailed or banned the circulation of some foreign publications. The government has also "gazetted" foreign newspapers, i.e., numerically limited their circulation. Singapore's leaders have brought defamation suits against foreign publishers. Such suits have resulted in the foreign publishers issuing apologies and paying damages.

MediaCorp TV is the only free-to-air TV broadcaster; the government owns 80 percent and SGX-listed Singapore Press Holdings (SPH) owns 20 percent. Pay-TV providers StarHub Cable Vision (SCV) and MioTV are wholly-owned subsidiaries of StarHub and SingTel, respectively. Free-to-air radio broadcasters are mainly government-owned, with MediaCorp Radio Singapore being the largest operator. BBC World Services is the only foreign free-to-air broadcaster in Singapore.

The Media Development Authority (MDA) introduced new measures in March 2010 that would require pay TV companies to cross carry content subject to exclusive carriage provisions. Henceforth, a pay TV company with an exclusive contract for a channel would be required to share that content with other pay TV companies at their request. Content providers consider the measures an unnecessary interference in a competitive market that would deny content holders the ability to negotiate freely in the marketplace, and interferes with their ability to manage and protect their intellectual property. MDA plans to implement the measures in mid-2011.

Banking: The Monetary Authority of Singapore (MAS) regulates all banking activities as provided for under the Banking Act. Singapore maintains legal distinctions between foreign and local banks, and the type of license held by foreign banks -- full service, wholesale, and offshore. As of December 2010, 26 foreign full service licensees, 50 wholesale licensees, and 38 offshore licensees operated in Singapore. All offshore banks are eligible to be upgraded to wholesale bank status based on MAS criteria to enable them to conduct a wider range of activities. Except in retail banking, Singapore laws do not distinguish operationally between foreign and domestic banks.

The government initiated a banking liberalization program in 1999 to ease restrictions on foreign banks and has supplemented this with phased-in provisions under the FTA. These measures include removal of a 40-percent ceiling on foreign ownership of local banks and a 20-percent aggregate foreign shareholding limit on finance companies. It has stated publicly, however, that it will not approve any foreign acquisition of a local bank. Acquisitions exceeding prescribed thresholds of 5 percent, 12 percent or 20 percent of the shares or voting power of a local bank require the approval of the Minister in charge of MAS.

Of the 26 full service licenses granted to foreign banks, including four U.S. banks, eight, including one U.S. bank, have been granted "qualifying full bank" (QFB) status. U.S. financial institutions enjoy phased-in benefits under the FTA. Since January 2006, U.S.licensed full service banks that are also QFBs have been able to operate at an unlimited number of locations (branches or off-premises ATMs) versus 25 for non-U.S. full service foreign banks with QFB status. U.S. and foreign full-service banks with QFB status can freely relocate existing branches, and share ATMs among themselves. They can also provide electronic funds transfer and point-of-sale debit services, and accept services related to Singapore's compulsory pension fund.

Locally and non-locally incorporated subsidiaries of U.S. full-service banks with QFB status can apply for access to local ATM networks. However, no U.S. bank has come to a commercial agreement to gain such access. Singapore lifted its quota on new licenses for U.S. wholesale banks since January 2007. Singapore abolished quotas on new licenses for full-service foreign banks in July 2005.

Despite liberalization, U.S. and other foreign banks in the domestic retail banking sector still face barriers. Local retail banks do not face similar constraints on customer service locations or access to the local ATM network. Holders of credit cards issued locally by foreign banks or other financial institutions cannot access their accounts through the local ATM networks. They are also unable to access their accounts for cash withdrawals, transfers or bill payments at ATMs operated by banks other than those operated by their own bank or at foreign banks' shared ATM network. Nevertheless, full-service foreign banks have made significant inroads in other retail banking areas, with substantial market share in products like credit cards and personal and housing loans.

U.S. industry advocates enhancements to Singapore's credit bureau system, in particular, adoption of an open admission system for all lenders, including non-banks. There are currently two credit bureaus in Singapore, Credit Bureau (Singapore) Private Ltd. ("CBS") and Credit Scan. In October 2009 GE Money became the first non-bank member of the CBS.

Securities and Asset Management: Singapore has no trading restrictions on foreign-owned stockbrokers. Aggregate investment by foreigners may not exceed 70 percent of the paid-up capital of dealers that are members of the SGX. Direct registration of foreign mutual funds is allowed, provided MAS approves the prospectus and the fund. The FTA has relaxed conditions that foreign asset managers must meet in order to offer products under the government-managed compulsory pension fund (Central Provident Fund Investment Scheme) .

Legal Services: As of November 2010, 15 of the 89 foreign law firms in Singapore were from the United States. In December 2008, Singapore granted Qualifying Foreign Law Practice (QFLP) licenses to six foreign law firms (including two U.S. firms) to practice Singapore law, although restrictions remain in certain areas, including conveyancing, criminal law, family law and domestic litigation. Foreign law firms can otherwise provide legal services in relation to Singapore law only through a Joint Law Venture (JLV) or Formal Law Alliance (FLA) with a Singapore law firm, subject to the Ministry of Law's guidelines. Singapore relaxed some of these guidelines for U.S. law firms under the FTA. Since July 2007, foreign attorneys have been allowed to own equity in Joint Law Ventures up to a maximum of 49 percent of total shares. Currently, there is one U.S. Joint Law Venture. U.S. and foreign attorneys are allowed to represent parties in arbitration without the need for a Singapore attorney to be present.

With the exception of law degrees from a handful of designated U.S., British, Australian, and New Zealand universities, no foreign university law degrees are recognized for purposes of admission to practice law in Singapore. Under the FTA, Singapore recognizes law degrees from Harvard University, Columbia University, New York University, and the University of Michigan. Singapore will admit to the Bar Singapore-citizen or permanent-resident law school graduates of those designated universities who are ranked among the top 70 percent of their graduating class or have obtained lower-second class honors (under the British system) .

Engineering and Architectural Services: Engineering and architectural firms can be 100percent foreign-owned. Only engineers and architects registered with the Professional Engineers Board and the Architects Board, respectively, can practice in Singapore. All applicants (both local and foreign) must have at least four years of practical experience in engineering or architectural works, and pass an examination set by the respective Board.

Accounting and Tax Services: The major international accounting firms operate in Singapore. Public accountants and at least one partner of a public accounting firm must reside in Singapore. Only public accountants who are members of the Institute of Certified Public Accountants of Singapore and registered with the Public Accountants Board may practice in Singapore. The Board recognizes U.S. accountants registered with the American Institute of Certified Public Accountants.

Real Estate: Under the Residential Property Act, foreigners are allowed to purchase condominiums or any unit within a building of six or more levels without the need to obtain prior approval from the Singapore Land Authority. For landed homes (houses) and apartments in buildings of fewer than six stories, prior approval is required. There are no restrictions on foreign ownership of industrial and commercial real estate.

Energy: Singapore completed efforts to liberalize its gas market with the amendment of the Gas Act and implementation of a Gas Network Code in 2008, which was designed to give gas retailers and importers direct access to the onshore gas pipeline infrastructure. However, key parts of the local gas market, such as gas retailing and access to offshore gas pipelines, remain controlled by incumbent Singaporean firms. In the past, the dominance of Singaporean government-linked corporations in this sector proved challenging for American companies that tried to enter the power generation and gas import business.

CONVERSION AND TRANSFER POLICIES

The FTA commits Singapore to the free transfer of capital, unimpeded by regulatory restrictions. Singapore places no restrictions on reinvestment or repatriation of earnings and capital, and maintains no significant restrictions on remittances, foreign exchange transactions and capital movements. (See "Efficient Capital Markets" for a discussion of certain restrictions on the borrowing of Singapore Dollars (SGD) for use offshore.)

EXPROPRIATION AND COMPENSATION

The FTA contains strong investor protection provisions relating to expropriation and due process; provisions are in place for fair market value compensation for any expropriated investment. Singapore has not expropriated property owned by foreign investors and has no laws that force foreign investors to transfer ownership to local interests. No significant disputes are pending.

Singapore has signed investment promotion and protection agreements with a wide range of countries (see "Bilateral Investment Agreements" below) . These agreements mutually protect nationals or companies of either country against war and noncommercial risks of expropriation and nationalization for an initial period of 15 years and continue thereafter unless otherwise terminated.

DISPUTE SETTLEMENT

All core obligations of the FTA are subject to the dispute settlement provisions of the Agreement. The dispute settlement procedures promote compliance through consultation and trade-enhancing remedies, rather than relying solely on trade sanctions. The procedures also set higher standards of openness and transparency.

Singapore enacted and subsequently amended the Arbitration Act of 2001 for domestic arbitration based on the United Nations Commission on International Trade Law (UNCITRAL) Model Law. Singapore ratified the recognition and enforcement of Foreign Arbitration Awards (New York, 1958) on August 21, 1986, and the International Convention on the Settlement of Investment Disputes on November 13, 1968. The Singapore International Arbitration Center (SIAC) and the Singapore Mediation Center (SMC) actively promote mediation and reconciliation for settling commercial disputes.

PERFORMANCE REQUIREMENTS AND INCENTIVES

In general, Singapore complies with WTO Trade-Related Investment Measures (TRIMS) obligations. The FTA prohibits and removes certain performance-related restrictions on U.S. investors such as limitations on the number of customer service locations for the retail banking sector.

There are no discriminatory or preferential export or import policies affecting foreign investors. The government does not require investors to purchase from local sources or specify a percentage of output for export. The government also does not require local equity ownership in the investment. There are no rules forcing the transfer of technology. Foreign investors face no requirement to reduce equity over time and are free to obtain their necessary financing from any source. Employment of host country nationals is not required.

Singapore offers numerous incentives to encourage foreign investors to start up businesses; particularly in targeted growth sectors (see Annex) .

RIGHT TO PRIVATE OWNERSHIP AND ESTABLISHMENT

Foreign and local entities may readily establish, operate, and dispose of their own enterprises in Singapore. Except for representative offices (where foreign firms maintain a local representative but do not conduct commercial transactions in Singapore) , there are no restrictions on carrying out remunerative activities.

All businesses in Singapore must be registered with the Accounting and Corporate Regulatory Authority. Foreign investors can operate their businesses in one of the following forms: sole proprietorship, limited partnership, incorporated company, foreign company branch or representative office.

Private businesses, both local and foreign, compete on a generally equal basis with GLCs, although some observers have complained that GLCs benefit from cheaper financing due to an implicit government guarantee. Singapore officials reject such assertions, arguing that the government does not interfere with the operations of GLCs or grant them special privileges, preferential treatment or hidden subsidies; they claim that GLCs are subject to the same regulatory regime and discipline of the market as private sector companies. Many observers, however, have been critical of cases where GLCs have entered into new lines of business or where government agencies have "corporatized" certain government functions, in both circumstances entering into competition with already existing private businesses.

The FTA contains specific conduct guarantees to ensure that GLCs will operate on a commercial and non-discriminatory basis towards U.S. firms. GLCs with substantial revenues or assets are also subject to enhanced transparency requirements under the FTA. In accordance with its FTA commitments, Singapore enacted the Competition Act in 2004 and established the Competition Commission of Singapore in January 2005. The Act contains provisions on anti-competitive agreements, decisions and practices; abuse of dominance; enforcement and appeals process; and mergers and acquisitions.

Singapore has an extensive network of GLCs that are active in many sectors of the economy. Some sectors, notably telecommunications and financial services, are subject to sector-specific regulatory bodies and competition regulations typically less rigorous than those being implemented under the Competition Act.

PROTECTION OF PROPERTY RIGHTS

In line with its FTA commitments and obligations under international treaties and conventions, Singapore has developed one of the stronger intellectual property rights (IPR) regimes in Asia, although concerns remain in certain areas, such as business software piracy and enforcement. Singapore has taken steps to bring its IPR laws in line with international standards, including amending its Trademarks Act, Patents Act, the Layout Designs of Integrated Circuits Act, Registered Designs Act, and new Plant Varieties Protection Act. In accordance with its FTA obligations, Singapore has implemented Article 1 through Article 6 of the Joint Recommendation concerning Provisions on the Protection of Well-Known Marks of 1999. It has signed and ratified the International Convention for the Protection of New Varieties of Plants (1991) and the Convention Relating to the Distribution of Program-Carrying Signals Transmitted by Satellite (1974) .

Singapore is a member of the WTO and a party to the Agreement on Trade-Related Aspects of Intellectual Property Rights (TRIPS) . It is a signatory to other international copyright agreements, including the Paris Convention, the Berne Convention, the Patent Cooperation Treaty, the Madrid Protocol and the Budapest Treaty. The World Intellectual Property Organization (WIPO) Secretariat opened offices in Singapore in 2005. Amendments to the Trademark Act, which took effect in January 2007, fulfill Singapore's obligations in WIPO's revised Treaty on the Law of Trademarks.

According to industry estimates, Singapore's piracy rate has averaged about five to ten percent for audio and video products and 35 percent for business software. Business software piracy levels in Singapore are among the lowest in Asia but are almost double the estimated level in the United States. Business software losses were estimated at $197 million in 2009. Rights holders have encountered difficulties when attempting to prosecute intellectual property cases based on tips provided by company insiders. Singapore currently does not offer specific protection to "whistleblowers". As a result, in some cases informants have refused to provide crucial testimony in court. Rights holders have also stated that maximum penalties for copyright infringement in Singapore are not sufficiently high to deter future IPR violations. Music and film industry representatives remain concerned that Internet piracy will continue to rise as Singapore expands access to its high-speed broadband network. Rights holders are displeased with the lack of action taken by Internet Service Providers when notified of infringing material hosted on their servers.

Unauthorized duplication of textbooks at some commercial copy centers in Singapore remains an issue, though local educational institutions, including government-operated institutions, have signed agreements to comply with legal obligations to pay royalty fees to publishers. The police have conducted multiple raids on local copy centers near schools, but according to industry representatives, the activity is lucrative enough to continue in spite of the possibility of fines.

The FTA ensures that government agencies will not grant approval to patent-violating products, but Singapore does allow parallel imports. Under the amended Patents Act, the patent owner has the right to bring an action to stop an importer of "grey market goods" from importing the patent owner's patented product if the product has not previously been sold or distributed in Singapore.

The FTA ensures protection of test data and trade secrets submitted to the government for product approval purposes. Disclosure of such information is prohibited for a period of five years for pharmaceuticals and ten years for agricultural chemicals. Singapore has no specific legislation concerning trade secrets. Instead, it protects investors' commercially valuable proprietary information under common law by the Law of Confidence. U.S. industry has expressed concern that this provision is inadequate.

TRANSPARENCY OF REGULATORY SYSTEM

The FTA enhances transparency by requiring regulatory authorities, to the extent possible, to consult with interested parties before issuing regulations, to provide advance notice and comment periods for proposed rules, and to publish all regulations.

The government has established a centralized Internet portal -- www.reach.gov.sg -- to solicit feedback on selected draft legislation and regulations, a process that is being used with increasing frequency. As noted in the "Openness to Foreign Investment" section, some U.S. companies, in particular, in the telecommunications and media sectors, are concerned about the government's lack of transparency in its regulatory and rule-making process.

Singapore strives to promote an efficient, business-friendly regulatory environment. Tax, labor, banking and finance, industrial health and safety, arbitration, wage and training rules and regulations are formulated and reviewed with the interests of both foreign investors and local enterprises in mind. Starting in 2005, a Rules Review Panel, comprising senior civil servants, began overseeing a review of all rules and regulations; this process will be repeated every five years. A Pro-Enterprise Panel of high-level public sector and private sector representatives examines feedback from businesses on regulatory issues and provides recommendations to the government.

Local laws give regulatory bodies wide discretion to modify regulations and impose new conditions, but in practice agencies use this positively to adapt incentives or other services on a case-by-case basis to meet the needs of foreign as well as domestic companies.

Procedures for obtaining licenses and permits are generally transparent and not burdensome, but some exceptions apply. Procedures can be faster for investors in areas considered national priorities. Singapore has established an online licensing portal to provide a one-stop application point for multiple licenses -- http://licences.business.gov.sg .

Corporate Governance: Singapore has a private sector-led Council on Corporate Disclosure and Governance to implement the country's Code of Corporate Governance. Compliance with the Code is not mandatory but listed companies are required under the Singapore Exchange Listing Rules to disclose their corporate governance practices and give explanations for deviations from the Code in their annual reports.

Accounting Standards: Singapore's prescribed accounting standards ("Financial Reporting Standards" or FRS) are aligned with those of the International Accounting Standards Board. Companies can deviate from these standards when required to present a "true and fair" set of financial statements. Singapore-incorporated, publicly-listed companies can use certain alternative standards such as International Accounting Standards (IAS) or the U.S. Generally Accepted Accounting Principles (U.S. GAAP) if they are listed on foreign stock exchanges that require these standards. They do not need to reconcile their accounts with FRS. All other Singapore-incorporated companies must use FRS unless the Accounting and Corporate Regulatory Authority exempts them.

EFFICIENT CAPITAL MARKETS AND PORTFOLIO INVESTMENT

Singapore actively facilitates the free flow of financial resources. Credit is allocated on market terms and foreign investors can access credit, U.S. dollars, Singapore dollars (SGD) , and other foreign currencies on the local market. The Monetary Authority of Singapore (MAS) formulates and implements the country's monetary and exchange rate policy, and supervises and regulates the country's sophisticated financial and capital markets.

Total assets under management in Singapore stood at $861 billion at end-2009, a 40 percent year-on-year increase as a result of the strong rebound in global stock markets in 2009 and general improvement in investor confidence globally. Over 80 percent of the funds managed in Singapore are foreign sourced, with 61 percent of these funds invested in the Asia-Pacific region. The government has sought to boost the country's asset management sector by placing with foreign-owned firms a significant portion of government reserves managed by the Government of Singapore Investment Corporation (GIC) . Financial institutions and corporations issued approximately US$10.5 billion in SGD-denominated corporate debt instruments in 2009.

Singapore's banking system is sound and well-regulated. Total domestic banking assets were about US$597.5 billion as of October 2010. Local Singapore banks are relatively small by regional standards, but are reasonably profitable and have stronger capital levels and credit ratings than many of their peers in the region. As of third quarter 2010, the non-performing loans (NPLs) ratio of local banks was 1.8 percent. Banks are statutorily prohibited from engaging in non-financial business. Banks can hold 10 percent or less in non-financial companies as an "equity portfolio investment."

The Securities and Futures Act (SFA) of 2002 moved Singapore's capital markets to a disclosure-based regime. The SFA allows for imposition of civil or criminal penalties against corporations listed on the Singapore Exchange (SGX) that fail to disclose material information on a continuous basis. Listed companies with more than S$75 million (US$55 million) market capitalization are required to prepare quarterly financial reporting. The SFA requires persons acquiring shareholdings of five percent or more of the voting shares of a listed company to disclose such acquisitions as well as any subsequent changes in their holdings directly to the SGX within two business days. The SFA also contains enhanced market misconduct provisions. The Act was further strengthened in 2009 to provide for stronger market misconduct enforcement with the courts empowered to order disgorgement of gains from illegal trades, and allowing the transfer of evidence between the Commercial Affairs Department of the police force and MAS.

COMPETITION FROM STATE OWNED ENTERPRISES

Singapore has an extensive network of government-linked corporations (GLC) that are fully or partially owned by Temasek Holdings, a holding company with the Singapore Ministry of Finance as its sole shareholder. As previously noted, Singapore GLCs are active in many sectors of the economy, especially strategically important sectors like telecommunications, media, public transportation, defense, port and airport operations. In addition, the GLCs are also present in many other sectors of the economy, including banking, shipping, airline, consumer/lifestyle, infrastructure and real estate.

GLCs operate on a commercial basis and have no specific advantage in competing with private enterprises based on their government ownership. However, some private sector companies have said they encountered unfair business practices and opaque bidding processes that appeared to favor incumbent, government-linked firms.

GLCs' corporate governance is guided by policies developed by Temasek Holdings. However, there are differences in corporate governance disclosures and practices across them and GLC boards are allowed to determine their own governance practices. GLC board seats are not specifically allocated to government officials, although retired officials are often represented on boards and fill senior management positions.

There are two sovereign wealth funds (SWF) in Singapore, the Government of Singapore Investment Corporation (GIC) and the previously mentioned Temasek Holdings. The government established the two SWFs to manage Singapore's substantial investments, fiscal and foreign reserves.

GIC, Singapore's largest SWF with an estimated $220 billion in assets, does not invest domestically. GIC manages Singapore's international investments, which are generally passive (non-controlling) investments in publicly-traded entities. Its investment is entirely overseas, with the United States as its top destination, accounting for 36 percent of GIC's portfolio as of March 2010. Although not required by law, since 2008 GIC has published an annual report describing its management and governance, and how it invests Singapore's foreign reserves.

Temasek began as a holding company for Singapore's state-owned enterprises, but has since branched to other asset classes and generally focuses on holding significant (often controlling) stakes in companies. As of March 2010, Temasek's exposure to Singapore was 32%, with the rest of Asia accounting for 46% of its portfolio. Temasek's stated goal is to hold and manage the government's investments in companies for the long-term benefit of Singapore, to create jobs, and contribute to Singapore's economic survival, progress and prosperity. Temasek formerly focused on managing industries to promote economic development, but has shifted emphasis to commercial objectives and principles. Temasek exercises its shareholder rights to influence the strategic directions of its companies but does not get involved in the day-to-day business and commercial decisions of its firms and subsidiaries. Temasek publishes an annual report, but only provides consolidated financial statements, which aggregate all of Temasek's subsidiaries into a single financial report.

CORPORATE SOCIAL RESPONSIBILITY

The awareness and implementation of CSR in Singapore has been increasing since the government's formation of the Singapore Compact, a national society promoting CSR in Singapore. In May 2004, the National Tripartite Committee on CSR was established to study the issues holistically and address any gaps at the national level. The initiative provides strategic direction and overall coordination for various CSR programs, which include helping SMEs adopt good CSR practices. In January 2005, the Singapore Compact for Corporate Social Responsibility was set up to provide a forum for collaboration, support and information sharing on good CSR practices.

In October 2008, a National CSR Survey released by the Singapore Compact showed that 40% of the 507 Singapore-based companies surveyed were aware of CSR. The awareness level among large companies was twice that of small and medium-sized enterprises. Among the companies that were aware of CSR, about two-thirds have implemented CSR in areas such as sustainable development, fair employment and corporate philanthropy. Their main motivations were corporate culture and to improve branding. The other one-third who did not implement CSR felt that it was not relevant to their business or lacked the funding and training resources. The ASEAN Business Outlook Survey 2010 by the American Chamber of Commerce found that 83% of U.S. companies were involved in CSR activities.

POLITICAL VIOLENCE

Singapore's political environment is stable and there is no history of incidents involving politically motivated damage to foreign investments in Singapore. The ruling People's Action Party (PAP) has dominated Singapore's parliamentary government since 1959, and currently controls 82 of the 84 regularly contested parliamentary seats. Singapore opposition parties, which currently hold two regularly contested parliamentary seats and one additional seat reserved to the opposition by the constitution, do not usually espouse views that are radically different from the mainstream of Singapore political opinion.

CORRUPTION

Singapore typically ranks as the least corrupt country in Asia and one of the least corrupt in the world. It has, and actively enforces, strong anti-corruption laws. The Prevention of Corruption Act, and the Drug Trafficking and Other Serious Crimes (Confiscation of Benefits) Act provide the legal basis for government action by the Corrupt Practices Investigation Bureau, an anti-corruption agency that reports to the Prime Minister. These laws cover acts of corruption both within Singapore as well as those committed by Singaporeans abroad. When cases of corruption are uncovered, whether in the public or private sector, the government deals with them firmly, swiftly and publicly, as they do in cases where public officials are involved in dishonest and illegal behavior.

Corruption, including bribery, raises the costs and risks of doing business. Corruption has a corrosive impact on both market opportunities overseas for U.S. companies and the broader business climate. It also deters international investment, stifles economic growth and development, distorts prices, and undermines the rule of law.

It is important for U.S. companies, irrespective of their size, to assess the business climate in the relevant market in which they will be operating or investing, and to have an effective compliance program or measures to prevent and detect corruption, including foreign bribery. U.S. individuals and firms operating or investing in foreign markets should take the time to become familiar with the relevant anticorruption laws of both the foreign country and the United States in order to properly comply with them, and where appropriate, they should seek the advice of legal counsel.

The U.S. Government seeks to level the global playing field for U.S. businesses by encouraging other countries to take steps to criminalize their own companies' acts of corruption, including bribery of foreign public officials, by requiring them to uphold their obligations under relevant international conventions. A U. S. firm that believes a competitor is seeking to use bribery of a foreign public official to secure a contract should bring this to the attention of appropriate U.S. agencies, as noted below.

U.S. Foreign Corrupt Practices Act: In 1977, the United States enacted the Foreign Corrupt Practices Act (FCPA) , which makes it unlawful for a U.S. person, and certain foreign issuers of securities, to make a corrupt payment to foreign public officials for the purpose of obtaining or retaining business for or with, or directing business to, any person. The FCPA also applies to foreign firms and persons who take any act in furtherance of such a corrupt payment while in the United States. For more detailed information on the FCPA, see the FCPA Lay-Person's Guide at:

http://www.justice.gov/criminal/fraud/

Other Instruments: It is U.S. Government policy to promote good governance, including host country implementation and enforcement of anti-corruption laws and policies pursuant to their obligations under international agreements. Since enactment of the FCPA, the United States has been instrumental to the expansion of the international framework to fight corruption. Several significant components of this framework are the OECD Convention on Combating Bribery of Foreign Public Officials in International Business Transactions (OECD Antibribery Convention) , the United Nations Convention against Corruption (UN Convention) , the Inter-American Convention against Corruption (OAS Convention) , the Council of Europe Criminal and Civil Law Conventions, and a growing list of U.S. free trade agreements. This country is a party to the UN Convention, but generally all countries prohibit the bribery and solicitation of their public officials.

OECD Antibribery Convention: The OECD Antibribery Convention entered into force in February 1999. As of December 2009, there are 38 parties to the Convention including the United States (see http://www.oecd.org/dataoecd/59/13/40272933.pdf) .

Major exporters China, India, and Russia are not parties, although the U.S. Government strongly endorses their eventual accession to the Convention. The Convention obligates the Parties to criminalize bribery of foreign public officials in the conduct of international business. The United States meets its international obligations under the OECD Antibribery Convention through the U.S. FCPA. Singapore is not a party to the OECD Convention.

UN Convention: The UN Anticorruption Convention entered into force on December 14, 2005, and there are 143 parties to it as of December 2009 (see http://www.unodc.org/unodc/en/treaties/CAC/signatories.html) .

The UN Convention is the first global comprehensive international anticorruption agreement. The UN Convention requires countries to establish criminal and other offences to cover a wide range of acts of corruption. The UN Convention goes beyond previous anticorruption instruments, covering a broad range of issues ranging from basic forms of corruption such as bribery and solicitation, embezzlement, trading in influence to the concealment and laundering of the proceeds of corruption. The Convention contains transnational business bribery provisions that are functionally similar to those in the OECD Antibribery Convention and contains provisions on private sector auditing and books and records requirements. Other provisions address matters such as prevention, international cooperation, and asset recovery. Singapore is a party to the UN Convention.

OAS Convention: In 1996, the Member States of the Organization of American States (OAS) adopted the first international anticorruption legal instrument, the Inter-American Convention against Corruption (OAS Convention) , which entered into force in March 1997. The OAS Convention, among other things, establishes a set of preventive measures against corruption, provides for the criminalization of certain acts of corruption, including transnational bribery and illicit enrichment, and contains a series of provisions to strengthen the cooperation between its States Parties in areas such as mutual legal assistance and technical cooperation. As of December 2009, the OAS Convention has 33 parties (see http://www.oas.org/juridico/english/Sigs/b-58.html) . Singapore is not a party to the OAS Convention.

Council of Europe Criminal Law and Civil Law Conventions: Many European countries are parties to either the Council of Europe (CoE) Criminal Law Convention on Corruption, the Civil Law Convention, or both. The Criminal Law Convention requires criminalization of a wide range of national and transnational conduct, including bribery, money-laundering, and account offenses. It also incorporates provisions on liability of legal persons and witness protection. The Civil Law Convention includes provisions on compensation for damage relating to corrupt acts, whistleblower protection, and validity of contracts, inter alia. The Group of States against Corruption (GRECO) was established in 1999 by the CoE to monitor compliance with these and related anticorruption standards. Currently, GRECO comprises 46 member States (45 European countries and the United States) . As of December 2009, the Criminal Law Convention has 42 parties and the Civil Law Convention has 34 (see www.coe.int/greco.) Singapore is not a party to the Council of Europe Conventions.

Free Trade Agreements: While it is U.S. Government policy to include anticorruption provisions in free trade agreements (FTAs) that it negotiates with its trading partners, the anticorruption provisions have evolved over time. The most recent FTAs negotiated now require trading partners to criminalize “active bribery” of public officials (offering bribes to any public official must be made a criminal offense, both domestically and transnationally) as well as domestic “passive bribery” (solicitation of a bribe by a domestic official) . All U.S. FTAs may be found at the U.S. Trade Representative Website: http://www.ustr.gov/trade-agreements/free-trade-agreements . Singapore has a free trade agreement (FTA) in place with the United States, the U.S.-Singapore FTA, which came into force on January 1, 2004.

Local Laws: U.S. firms should familiarize themselves with local anticorruption laws, and, where appropriate, seek legal counsel. While the U.S. Department of Commerce cannot provide legal advice on local laws, the Department's U.S. and Foreign Commercial Service can provide assistance with navigating the host country's legal system and obtaining a list of local legal counsel.

Assistance for U.S. Businesses: The U.S. Department of Commerce offers several services to aid U.S. businesses seeking to address business-related corruption issues. For example, the U.S. and Foreign Commercial Service can provide services that may assist U.S. companies in conducting their due diligence as part of the company's overarching compliance program when choosing business partners or agents overseas. The U.S. Foreign and Commercial Service can be reached directly through its offices in every major U.S. and foreign city, or through its Website at www.trade.gov/cs .

The Departments of Commerce and State provide worldwide support for qualified U.S. companies bidding on foreign government contracts through the Commerce Department's Advocacy Center and State's Office of Commercial and Business Affairs. Problems, including alleged corruption by foreign governments or competitors, encountered by U.S. companies in seeking such foreign business opportunities can be brought to the attention of appropriate U.S. government officials, including local embassy personnel and through the

Department of Commerce Trade Compliance Center "Report A Trade Barrier" Website at tcc.export.gov/Report_a_Barrier/index.asp .

Guidance on the U.S. FCPA: The Department of Justice's (DOJ) FCPA Opinion Procedure enables U.S. firms and individuals to request a statement of the Justice Department's present enforcement intentions under the anti-bribery provisions of the FCPA regarding any proposed business conduct. The details of the opinion procedure are available on DOJ's Fraud Section Website at www.justice.gov/criminal/fraud/fcpa . Although the Department of Commerce has no enforcement role with respect to the FCPA, it supplies general guidance to U.S. exporters who have questions about the FCPA and about international developments concerning the FCPA. For further information, see the Office of the Chief Counsel for International Counsel, U.S. Department of Commerce, Website, at http://www.ogc.doc.gov/trans_anti_bribery.html . More general information on the FCPA is available at the Websites listed below.

Exporters and investors should be aware that generally all countries prohibit the bribery of their public officials, and prohibit their officials from soliciting bribes under domestic laws. Most countries are required to criminalize such bribery and other acts of corruption by virtue of being parties to various international conventions discussed above. Public sector corruption, including bribery of public officials, remains a minor challenge for U.S. firms operating in Singapore.

Singapore is not a party to the OECD Convention on Combating Bribery, but the Prevention of Corruption Act makes it a crime for a Singapore citizen to bribe a foreign official or any other person, whether within or outside Singapore.

ANTI-CORRUPTION RESOURCES

Some useful resources for individuals and companies regarding combating corruption in global markets include the following:

Information about the U.S. Foreign Corrupt Practices Act (FCPA) , including a "LayPerson's Guide to the FCPA" is available at the U.S. Department of Justice's Website at: http://www.justice.gov/criminal/fraud/fcpa .

Information about the OECD Antibribery Convention including links to national implementing legislation and country monitoring reports is available at: http://www.oecd.org/department/0,3355,en_2649_34859_1_1_1_1_1,00.html . See also new Antibribery Recommendation and Good Practice Guidance Annex for companies: http://www.oecd.org/dataoecd/11/40/44176910.pdf

General information about anticorruption initiatives, such as the OECD Convention and the FCPA, including translations of the statute into several languages, is available at the Department of Commerce Office of the Chief Counsel for International Commerce Website: http://www.ogc.doc.gov/trans_anti_bribery.html .

Transparency International (TI) publishes an annual Corruption Perceptions Index (CPI) . The CPI measures the perceived level of public-sector corruption in 180 countries and territories around the world. The CPI is available at: http://www.transparency.org/policy_research/surveys_indices/cpi/2009 . TI also publishes an annual *Global Corruption Report* which provides a systematic evaluation of the state of corruption around the world. It includes an in-depth analysis of a focal theme, a series of country reports that document major corruption related events and developments from all continents and an overview of the latest research findings on anti-corruption diagnostics and tools. See http://www.transparency.org/publications/gcr .

The World Bank Institute publishes Worldwide Governance Indicators (WGI) . These indicators assess six dimensions of governance in 212 countries, including Voice and Accountability, Political Stability and Absence of Violence, Government Effectiveness, Regulatory Quality, Rule of Law and Control of Corruption. See http://info.worldbank.org/governance/wgi/sc_country.asp . The World Bank Business Environment and

Enterprise Performance Surveys may also be of interest and are available at: http://go.worldbank.org/RQQXYJ6210 .

The World Economic Forum publishes the *Global Enabling Trade Report*, which presents the rankings of the Enabling Trade Index, and includes an assessment of the transparency of border administration (focused on bribe payments and corruption) and a separate segment on corruption and the regulatory environment. See http://www.weforum.org/en/initiatives/gcp/GlobalEnablingTradeReport/index.htm .

Additional country information related to corruption can be found in the U.S. State Department's annual *Human Rights Report* available at http://www.state.gov/g/drl/rls/hrrpt/ .

Global Integrity, a nonprofit organization, publishes its annual *Global Integrity Report*, which provides indicators for 92 countries with respect to governance and anti-corruption. The report highlights the strengths and weaknesses of national level anti-corruption systems. The report is available at: http://report.globalintegrity.org/ .

BILATERAL INVESTMENT AGREEMENTS

Singapore has signed Investment Guarantee Agreements (IGA's) with 37 countries, including the United States. These agreements mutually protect nationals or companies of either country against war and non-commercial risks of expropriation and nationalization.

Singapore has signed free trade agreements that include investment chapters with Australia, China, the European Free Trade Area (Switzerland, Norway, Lichtenstein, and Iceland) , the Gulf Cooperation Council (comprising Bahrain, Kuwait, Oman, Qatar, Saudi Arabia and the United Arab Emirates) , India, Japan, Jordan, New Zealand, Panama, Peru, South Korea, Costa Rica and the United States. Singapore is negotiating FTAs with Canada, Mexico, Pakistan, and Ukraine. Singapore is a member of the Association of Southeast Asian Nations (ASEAN) , which has concluded FTAs with Australia and New Zealand, China, India and South Korea, and a Comprehensive Economic Partnership Agreement with Japan. Singapore is also a party in the Transpacific Strategic Economic Partnership Agreement together with Chile, New Zealand and Brunei. Singapore has signed tax treaties with a number of countries, but not with the United States.

OPIC AND OTHER INVESTMENT INSURANCE PROGRAMS

Under the 1966 Investment Guarantee Agreement with Singapore, the U.S. Overseas Private Investment Corporation (OPIC) offers insurance to U.S. investors in Singapore against currency inconvertibility, expropriation and losses arising from war. Singapore became a member of the Multilateral Investment Guarantee Agency (MIGA) in 1998.

LABOR

As of September 2010, Singapore's labor market totaled 3.076 million workers; this includes about one million foreigners, of which about 85 percent are unskilled or semiskilled workers. Local labor laws are flexible, and allow for relatively free hiring and firing practices. Either party can terminate employment by giving the other party the required notice. The Ministry of Manpower must approve employment of foreigners.

Singapore imposes a ceiling on the ratio of unskilled/semi-skilled foreign workers to local workers that a company can employ, and charges a monthly levy for each unskilled or semi-skilled foreign worker. The government also provides incentives and assistance to firms to automate and invest in labor-saving technology.

Labor-management relations in Singapore are generally amicable. About 18 percent of the workforce is unionized. The majority of unions are affiliated with the National Trades Union Congress (NTUC) , which maintains a symbiotic relationship with the PAP ruling party. Although workers, other than those employed in the three essential services of water, gas and electricity, have the legal right to strike, no workers have done so since 1986.

Singapore has no minimum wage law; the government follows a policy of allowing free market forces to determine wage levels. Singapore has a flexible wage system in which the National Wage Council (NWC) recommends non-binding wage adjustments on an annual basis. The NWC is a tripartite body comprising a Chairman and representatives from the Government, employers and unions. The NWC recommendations apply to all employees in both domestic and foreign firms, and across the private and public sectors. While the NWC wage guidelines are not mandatory, they are widely implemented. The level of implementation is generally higher among unionized companies compared to non-unionized companies.

FOREIGN-TRADE ZONES/FREE PORTS

Singapore has eight free-trade zones (FTZs) , six for seaborne cargo and two for airfreight. The FTZs may be used for storage and repackaging of import and export cargo and goods transiting Singapore for subsequent re-export. Manufacturing is not carried out within the zones. Foreign and local firms have equal access to the FTZ facilities.
Foreign Direct Investment Statistics

TABLE A STOCK OF FOREIGN DIRECT INVESTMENT (FDI) IN SINGAPORE BY COUNTRY(As at Year-end, Historical Cost) (US$ million)

	2007	2008	2009	2010
Total Foreign Direct Investment	322,978	353,195	408,487	480,448
United States	35,769	36,805	41,373	50,821
Canada	2,169	2,100	2,054	2,496
Australia	3,202	3,177	4,275	6,803
New Zealand	1,123	1,322	1,503	2,187
Europe	137,369	141,653	158,148	176,331
Denmark	1	2	2	4
France	7,605	6,606	5,705	6,218
Germany	6,402	7,801	7,935	9,100
Ireland	2,469	2,283	2,203	3,627
Netherlands	35,678	42,386	43,748	47,306
Norway	11,851	14,777	16,484	17,874
Switzerland	19,049	16,332	19,133	18,955
United Kingdom	43,386	34,792	35,271	38,868
Asian Countries	72,573	81,938	102,891	118,354
China	1,606	3,074	6,930	8,944
Hong Kong	4,479	7,987	12,510	14,238
Japan	32,987	34,855	35,907	41,894
South Korea	2,109	2,258	2,071	2,882
Taiwan	5,345	4,553	4,396	4,441
India	9,038	11,716	15,644	19,250

ASEAN	11,107	12,022	16,058	17,721
Brunei Darussalam	197	206	227	237
Indonesia	1,188	1,508	2,244	645
Malaysia	7,895	8,745	11,304	11,536
Philippines	683	216	770	1,031
Thailand	1,060	1,261	1,479	4,173
Vietnam	18	20	20	46
Cambodia	1	1	1	5
Myanmar	65	66	13	47
South & Central America/Caribbean	63,130	75,573	87,367	110,278
Other Countries NEC	7,642	10,627	10,876	13,177

Source: Department of Statistics, "Foreign Equity Investment in Singapore, 2010"

TABLE B STOCK OF DIRECT INVESTMENT ABROAD BY COUNTRY

(As at Year-end, Historical Cost) (US$ Million)

	2007	2008	2009	2010
Total Direct Investment	221,486	218,300	265,863	316,234
Asia	103,948	123,851	145,816	176,442
ASEAN	47,371	52,549	61,040	71,038
Brunei	133	111	144	141
Indonesia	13,995	15,533	18,715	20,399
Malaysia	15,842	17,403	20,543	24,212
Philippines	2,840	2,983	3,554	4,124
Thailand	11,762	13,352	13,860	15,108
Vietnam	1,470	1,971	2,231	2,173
Cambodia	118	186	255	299
Myanmar	1,110	863	1,577	4,401
Laos	101	148	161	182
Hong Kong	13,856	13,934	16,753	18,445
Taiwan	3,557	4,129	4,097	4,466
China	28,994	38,863	44,172	54,823
Japan	2,740	5,586	6,690	8,997
South Korea	2,122	1,758	1,831	1,996
India	3,219	4,684	7,786	9,988
Europe	32,262	25,791	36,449	40,496
Netherlands	2,708	3,000	3,543	3,404
United Kingdom	21,798	13,775	23,113	25,098
Norway	301	1,205	1,398	1,983
Germany	413	412	711	1,250

Switzerland	3,057	3,302	3,376	3,723
United States	9,648	8,154	9,359	10,917
Canada	70	44	596	599
Australia	11,844	12,592	16,526	22,363
New Zealand	1,056	642	798	828
Caribbean/Latin America	38,979	36,632	41,646	44,520
Other Countries				
NEC	23,679	10,593	14,674	20,069

TABLE CGDP AND FDI FIGURES, 2003-2010

(US$ Million)

Year	GDP*	FDI	FDI as ratio to GDP**
2003	95,955.7	144,746.83	1.51
2004	112,692.5	169,432.73	1.50
2005	125,413.7	194,580.64	1.55
2006	145,749.0	241,584.96	1.66
2007	177,579.7	322,977.80	1.82
2008	189,972.0	353,195.04	1.86
2009	185,639.5	408,487.25	2.20
2010	227,383.1	480,447.61	2.11

Footnote: *GDP at Current Market Price
**Based on Singapore dollars
Source: Department of Statistics

INVESTMENT INCENTIVES

INCENTIVES ADMINISTERED BY THE MONETARY AUTHORITY OF SINGAPORE (MAS)

As part of the government's strategy to develop Singapore into a premier financial center, MAS offers tax incentives for financial institutions looking to set up operations here.
A. Financial Sector Incentive ("FSI") Scheme
B. Tax Incentive Scheme for Qualifying Processing Services Company
C. Tax Incentive Scheme for Offshore Insurance Business
D. Tax Exemption Scheme for Marine Hull & Liability Insurance Business
E. Abolition of Withholding Taxes on Financial Guaranty Insurance Contracts
F. Tax Incentive Scheme for Approved New Derivative Products traded on the Singapore Exchange
G. Tax Incentive Scheme for Finance and Treasury Centers
H. Tax Incentive Scheme for Approved Trustee Companies
I. Tax Incentive Scheme for Syndicated Facilities
J. Innovation in Financial Technology & Infrastructure Grant Scheme
K. Tax Incentive for Trading Debt Securities
L. Financial Sector Development Fund
M. Financial Investor Scheme for Singapore Permanent Residence
N. Foreign Charitable Trust Incentive
O. Tax Incentive for Approved Fund Managers
P. Over-the-Counter (OTC) Financial Derivative Payments
Q. Insurance and Re-insurance Broking Tax Incentive
R. Wealth Management Tax Incentive
Further guidelines and application information are available at http://www.mas.gov.sg .
INCENTIVES ADMINISTERED BY THE ECONOMIC DEVELOPMENT BOARD (EDB)
A. Pioneer Status
B. Development & Expansion Incentive
C. Investment Allowance Incentive
D. Approved Foreign Loan Scheme
E. Approved Royalties Incentive
F. Entrepreneurship Investment Incentive
G. HQ Program
H. Double Deduction for Research and Development (R&D) Expenses
I. Research Incentive Scheme for Companies
J. Exemption of foreign sourced interest and royalty income for R&D purposes
K. Innovation Development Scheme
L. Initiatives in New Technology
M. Integrated Industrial Capital Allowance
N. Special Goods & Services Tax Scheme for 3rd Party Logistics Service Providers
O. The Enterprise Challenge (TEC) Scheme
P. Writing Down Allowance (WDA) for IP rights acquisition
Further guidelines and application information are available at http://www.sedb.com.
INCENTIVES ADMINISTERED BY INTERNATIONAL ENTERPRISE SINGAPORE (IE Singapore)
A. Double Tax Deduction (DTD) Scheme for Overseas Investment and Market Development
B. Export Coverage Scheme
C. Enterprise Fund
D. Loan Insurance Scheme 3
E. Loan Insurance Scheme Plus
F. Internationalization Finance Scheme
G. International Business Fellowship
Further guidelines and application information are available at http://www.iesingapore.gov.sg .
INCENTIVES ADMINISTERED BY THE MEDIA DEVELOPMENT AUTHORITY (MDA)
A. Market Development Scheme (MDS)
B. TV Content Industry Development Scheme
C. Digital Content Development Scheme
D. Digital Technology Development Scheme
E. INVIGORATE – PC Casual Game Initiative

F. Synthesis – Online Content Initiative
G. Film in Singapore! Scheme
H. International Cooperation Agreement
I. Short Film Grant
J. Overseas Travel Grant
K. New Feature Film Fund
L. Script Development Grant
M. Overseas Travel Grant
N. SCREEN – Scheme for Coinvestment in Exportable Content
O. Media Education Scheme
P. 360-degree TV
Q. IDEAS (Animation Development)
R. Futurescape
S. Microsoft XNA Development Initiative
T. SPINE
U. 35mm Fulfillment Fund
V. Stereoscopic 3D Film Development Fund
Further guidelines and application information are available at http://www.mda.gov.sg .
INCENTIVES ADMINISTERED BY INFOCOMM DEVELOPMENT AUTHORITY OF SINGAPORE (IDA)
A. Infocomm@SeaPort
B. Infocomm@SME
C. Integrated Clinic Management Systems Program
D. Digital Manufacturing Program
E. Collaborative High Tech Manufacturing Plan
F. Retail eSCM Ecosystem
G. RFID Initiative
Further information, details, and guidelines are available at http://www.ida.gov.sg .
INCENTIVES ADMINISTERED BY MARITIME PORT AUTHORITY (MPA)
A. Approved International Shipping Enterprise Scheme
B. Approved Shipping and Logistics Scheme
C. Maritime Cluster Fund
D. Maritime Enterprise IT Development Program
E. Maritime Innovation and Technology Fund
F. Maritime Finance Incentive
Further information, details and guidelines are available at http://www.mpa.gov.sg
Web Resources

http://www.mas.gov.sg http://www.sedb.com http://www.iesingapore.gov.sg http://www.mda.gov.sg http://www.ida.gov.sg http://www.mpa.gov.sg

SELLING U.S. PRODUCTS AND SERVICES

USING AN AGENT OR DISTRIBUTOR

Many American exporters use agents or distributors to serve the Singapore market and other markets in Southeast Asia. Finding prospective partners usually presents no problem as Singapore firms are aggressive when it comes to representing new products and typically respond enthusiastically to new opportunities. Most American companies that use the U.S. Commercial Service (CS) Singapore matchmaking and promotion services in Singapore find several interested agents or distributors. Because of the relatively small size of the Singapore market, potential partners often ask to cover regional territories. With a strong history of trade, Singaporean companies are particularly successful in taking products to the region. CS Singapore offers a wide range of programs and has an excellent record of success in introducing U.S. firms to the market. A list of services offered by CS Singapore can be obtained from our website at www.buyusa.gov/singapore

ESTABLISHING AN OFFICE

American firms wishing to establish a presence in Singapore have several straightforward options to do so. They can establish a Representative Office (RO) , register as a Branch of the parent, or incorporate as a Singapore company. General information on foreign businesses can be found at http://www.business.gov.sg/EN/StartingUp/ForeignBusinesses/ .

If an American company wishes to carry on operations in Singapore, it should register a branch office or incorporate a local company with the Accounting & Corporate Regulatory Authority (ACRA) – http://www.acra.gov.sg . ACRA publishes an excellent guide that takes the first time registrant through the process of establishing a branch office or incorporating in Singapore.

REPRESENTATIVE OFFICE

Setting up a Representative Office in Singapore can be a good way for American firms to explore business opportunities in Singapore or the region. ROs in banking and insurance need to register with the Monetary Authority of Singapore (MAS) and meet the guidelines or requirements laid out by the MAS. ROs in all other industries need to register with International Enterprise (IE) Singapore.

ROs can only carry out market research, conduct feasibility studies or work as a liaison on behalf of the parent company. RO may not conduct business directly or on behalf of the parent company. ROs cannot ship, transship or store goods in Singapore. American firms can either work through an agent or distributor to do so or establish their own commercial presence.

BRANCH OFFICE

For Branch Offices, the Companies Act requires a foreign company to appoint two local agents in Singapore to act on behalf of the company. The agents must be ordinarily resident in Singapore i.e. a Singaporean Citizen, a Singapore Permanent Resident, or a person who has been issued an EntrePass/Approval-In-Principle letter/Dependent Pass.

Establishing A Singapore Business American firms can also register a sole-proprietorship, partnership, limited liability partnership or incorporate a company in Singapore. For a sole proprietorship the process takes about one day, while more complex business entities can take up to six weeks and require lawyers and accountants to assist with incorporation documents. A point to bear in mind is that registration/incorporation of a company does not automatically mean that expatriate staff can be assigned to Singapore. Foreign staff must obtain employment passes from the Singapore Ministry of Manpower, although this is generally quite routine.

FRANCHISING

Franchising in Singapore is mature and is a popular investment or entrepreneurial vehicle. Singaporean firms looking for new growth opportunities are interested in investing in a variety of foreign franchise concepts. Singapore Master Franchisees usually prefer to buy franchise licenses for additional markets in the Southeast Asian region and not for Singapore alone. Most franchisees finance their purchases of franchises through bank loans, personal savings or pooling resources from family members. See the "Best Prospects" section in Chapter 4 for more information on the franchise sector in Singapore.

DIRECT MARKETING

The direct marketing industry in Singapore began in the early 1990s and now includes direct mail, telemarketing, television sales, mail order call centers, fulfillment and e-commerce firms. The Direct Marketing Association of Singapore represents both users and service providers. The direct marketing industry is well supported by service companies including: Singapore Post, Singapore Telecom Call Center, Teledirect, TNT International Mail, Ogilvy One and MMS Consultancy, among many others. The Singapore government also actively supports the industry by assisting companies (through financial incentives) in using direct marketing for their trading activities through its Direct Marketing Program.

The Direct Selling Association of Singapore (DSAS) , a self-regulatory body, was established in 1976. It provides a forum for all direct-selling companies in Singapore to discuss common issues of concern and to codify a high standard of business practices throughout the industry. The DSAS has adopted a Code of Conduct by which member-companies in the Association abide by in every aspect of business. Through the Code of Conduct, DSAS aims to further inculcate the spirit and practice of ethical direct-selling within its member-companies, setting examples for others to follow.

JOINT VENTURES/LICENSING

Foreign investors are not required to enter into joint ventures or cede management control to local interests. In Singapore, local and foreign investors are subject to the same basic laws. Apart from regulatory requirements in some sectors, the government screens investment proposals only to determine eligibility for various incentive regimes. Singapore places no restrictions on reinvestment or repatriation of earnings or capital.

Licensing is also a viable alternative in Singapore. With one of the strongest IPR protection programs in Asia, a well-developed legal framework and an advanced manufacturing base, Singapore is an attractive location for American licensors.

SELLING TO THE GOVERNMENT

Singapore is a signatory to the WTO Agreement on Government Procurement. The U.S.-Singapore FTA provides increased access for U.S. firms to Singapore's central government procurement. U.S. firms generally find Singapore to be a receptive, open and lucrative market. The Singaporean government procurement system is considered by many American firms to be fair and transparent. However, some U.S. and local firms have expressed concerns that government-owned and government-linked companies (GLCs) may receive preferential treatment in the government procurement process. Singapore denies that it gives any preferences to GLCs or that GLCs give preferences to other GLCs. Procurement recommendations are made at the technical level and then forwarded to management for concurrence. Bidders should work closely with the project manager to determine the relative importance of decision criteria such as technical capability and price. Bidders must meet the specifications set out in the tender. Post mortem hearings or meetings for losing bidders are not required or common. Government procurement regulations are contained in Instruction Manual 3, available from the Ministry of Finance. The Singapore Government also advertises its tenders on its website at www.gebiz.gov.sg

DISTRIBUTION AND SALES CHANNELS

Singapore's distribution and sales channels are simple, direct and open. Because of its role as a regional hub, most local distributors will also have knowledge of regional distribution rules and regulations. Most consumer goods are imported by stocking distributors who resell to retailers. Some goods are imported directly for sale in the importer's own retail outlets.

SELLING FACTORS/TECHNIQUES

Price, quality and service are the main selling factors in Singapore. Prospective exporters to Singapore should be aware that competition is strong and that buyers expect good after-sales service. Selling techniques vary according to the industry or the product involved, but they are comparable to the techniques used in any other sophisticated market.

Electronic Commerce

Singapore is one of the first countries in the world to enact a law that addresses issues that arise in the context of electronic contracts and digital signatures. The Electronic Transactions Act (ETA) (Cap 88) was enacted to provide a legal foundation for electronic signatures, and to give predictability and certainty to contracts formed electronically. The Singapore ETA follows closely the UN Commission on International Trade Law (UNCITRAL) Model Law on Electronic Commerce, which sets the framework for electronic laws in many countries. The full text of the ETA can be found at the Singapore Statutes Online website (http://agcvldb4.agc.gov.sg/) .

TRADE PROMOTION AND ADVERTISING

There are many specialized trade magazines in Singapore and scores of trade fairs that can be used to promote U.S. goods and services. The major English-language daily newspapers are the Straits Times and the Business Times. They are available at http://www.straitstimes.com and http://www.businesstimes.com.sg . The major Chinese daily is Lianhe Zaobao (http://www.zaobao.com) . E-commerce web sites can be found at http://www.ida.gov.sg and at http://www.sg . Leads for local advertising and promotional service agencies can be found at http://www.yellowpages.com.sg .

PRICING

Pricing is very competitive. Major department stores and retail chains offer fixed-price merchandise, while the smaller shops expect buyers to bargain. Hard bargaining is common in the commercial and industrial sectors as well, where buyers usually want a discount and vendors inflate their initial offers accordingly. Credit terms of 30-60-90 days are common. Buyers will often retain 10% of the sales price for major electronic equipment purchases until the vendor has installed the machine and it is performing according to specifications.

Typical Product Pricing Structures: Depending on the type of product, importer mark-ups range from 20-40%, while retail mark-ups are often more than 100%. Industrial goods are brought in by stocking distributors, who add on at least 20% before sale to end-users, or by agents whose commissions generally run about 7-10%. These mark-ups are approximate, and will vary widely, depending on the product and the contractual relationship in question.

SALES SERVICE/CUSTOMER SUPPORT

Good sales and customer support are vital in Singapore. The market is so price competitive that client-focused sales support or customer service can make a big difference. Singapore distributors respond well to training on new products, and if properly supported by the U.S. manufacturer will do a good job cultivating old customers and developing new ones.

PROTECTING INTELLECTUAL PROPERTY

The Intellectual Property Office of Singapore (IPOS) is the lead Singapore government agency that advises on and administers intellectual property (IP) laws, promotes IP awareness and provides the infrastructure to facilitate the development of IP in Singapore. As IP regulator and policy advisor, IPOS is committed to maintaining a robust and pro-business IP regime for the protection and commercial exploitation of IP. Singapore has a fully Trade Related Aspects of Intellectual Property Rights (TRIPS) compliant Intellectual Property Rights (IPR) legislative and administrative regime. Full information on Singapore's IP registration and protection programs can be found at http://www.ipos.gov.sg/topNav/hom/ .

PROTECTING INTELLECTUAL PROPERTY IN SINGAPORE:

Several general principles are important for effective management of intellectual property ("IP") rights in Singapore. First, it is important to have an overall strategy to protect your IP. Second, IP is protected differently in Singapore than in the U.S. Third, rights must be registered and enforced in Singapore, under local laws. Your U.S. trademark and patent registrations will not protect you in Singapore. There is no such thing as an "international copyright" that will automatically protect an author's writings throughout the entire world. Protection against unauthorized use in a particular country depends, basically, on the national laws of that country. However, most countries do offer copyright protection to foreign works under certain conditions, and these conditions have been greatly simplified by international copyright treaties and conventions.

Registration of patents and trademarks is on a first-in-time, first-in-right basis, so you should consider applying for trademark and patent protection even before selling your products or services in the Singaporean market. It is vital that companies understand that intellectual property is primarily a private right and that the US government generally cannot enforce rights for private individuals in Singapore. It is the responsibility of the rights' holders to register, protect, and enforce their rights where relevant, retaining their own counsel and advisors. Companies may wish to seek advice from local attorneys or IP consultants who are experts in Singaporean law. The U.S. Commercial Service can provide a list of local lawyers upon request.

While the U.S. Government stands ready to assist, there is little we can do if the rights holders have not taken these fundamental steps necessary to securing and enforcing their IP in a timely fashion. Moreover, in many countries, rights holders who delay enforcing their rights on a mistaken belief that the USG can provide a political resolution to a legal problem may find that their rights have been eroded or abrogated due to legal doctrines such as statutes of limitations, laches, estoppel, or unreasonable delay in prosecuting a law suit. In no instance should U.S. Government advice be seen as a substitute for the obligation of a rights holder to promptly pursue its case.

It is always advisable to conduct due diligence on potential partners. Negotiate from the position of your partner and give your partner clear incentives to honor the contract. A good partner is an important ally in protecting IP rights. Consider carefully, however, whether to permit your partner to register your IP rights on your behalf. Doing so may create a risk that your partner will list itself as the IP owner and fail to transfer the rights should the partnership end. Keep an eye on your cost structure and reduce the margins (and the incentive) of would-be bad actors. Projects and sales in Singapore require constant attention. Work with legal counsel familiar with Singaporean laws to create a solid contract that includes non-compete clauses, and confidentiality/non-disclosure provisions.

It is also recommended that small and medium-size companies understand the importance of working together with trade associations and organizations to support efforts to protect IP and stop counterfeiting. There are a number of these organizations, both Singapore or U.S.-based. These include:

The U.S. Chamber and local American Chambers of Commerce

National Association of Manufacturers (NAM)

International Intellectual Property Alliance (IIPA)

International Trademark Association (INTA)

The Coalition Against Counterfeiting and Piracy

International Anti-Counterfeiting Coalition (IACC)

Pharmaceutical Research and Manufacturers of America (PhRMA)

Biotechnology Industry Organization (BIO)

IP RESOURCES

A wealth of information on protecting IP is freely available to U.S. rights holders. Some excellent resources for companies regarding intellectual property include the following:

For information about patent, trademark, or copyright issues -- including enforcement issues in the US and other countries -- call the STOP! Hotline: 1-866-999-HALT or register at www.StopFakes.gov.

For more information about registering trademarks and patents (both in the U.S. as well as in foreign countries) , contact the US Patent and Trademark Office (USPTO) at: 1-800-786-9199.

For more information about registering for copyright protection in the US, contact the US Copyright Office at: 1-202-707-5959.

For more information about how to evaluate, protect, and enforce intellectual property rights and how these rights may be important for businesses, a free online training program is available at www.stopfakes.gov.

For US small and medium-size companies, the Department of Commerce offers a "SME IP Advisory Program" available through the American Bar Association that provides one hour of free IP legal advice for companies with concerns in Brazil, China, Egypt, India, and Russia. For details and to register, visit: **http://www.abanet.org/intlaw/intlproj/iprprogram_consultation.html**

• For information on obtaining and enforcing intellectual property rights and market-specific IP Toolkits visit: www.StopFakes.gov This site is linked to the USPTO

website for registering trademarks and patents (both in the U.S. as well as in foreign countries) , the U.S. Customs & Border Protection website to record registered trademarks and copyrighted works (to assist customs in blocking imports of IP-infringing products) and allows you to register for Webinars on protecting IP.

• The U.S. Commerce Department has positioned IP attachés in key markets around the world. The IP attaché who covers Singapore is Ms. Jennie Ness and you can contact her at jennie.ness@trade.gov .

DUE DILIGENCE

Anyone wanting to carry out business in Singapore must register with the Accounting and Corporate Regulatory Authority (ACRA) . CS Singapore offers the International Company Profile (http://www.buyusa.gov/singapore/en/icp.html) service to American firms wishing to check the bona fides of existing or potential partners. Alternately, U.S. firms can run a check on Singapore companies by accessing the ACRA database via www.acra.gov.sg . Other credit agency includes Infocredit D&B (http://www.icdnb.com.sg) .

LOCAL PROFESSIONAL SERVICES

Legal Services: Since December 2008, Singapore granted Qualifying Foreign Law Practice licenses to foreign law firms to practice Singapore law, although restrictions remain in certain areas, including conveyancing, criminal law, family law and domestic litigation. Foreign law firms can otherwise provide legal services in relation to Singapore law only through a Joint Law Venture (JLV) or Formal Law Alliance (FLA) with a Singapore law firm, subject to the Guidelines for registration of Foreign Lawyers in Joint Law Ventures to Practice Singapore Law. Singapore relaxed some of these guidelines for U.S. law firms under the FTA. Since July 2007, foreign attorneys have been allowed to own equity in Joint Law Ventures up to a maximum of 25 percent of total shares. U.S. and foreign attorneys are allowed to represent parties in arbitration without the need for a Singapore attorney to be present. Details on the structure of the Singapore legal service can be found in http://www.lsc.gov.sg .

Accounting and Tax Services: The major international accounting firms operate in Singapore. Public accountants and at least one partner of a public accounting firm must reside in Singapore. Only public accountants who are members of the Institute of Certified Public Accountants of Singapore (http://www.icpas.org.sg) and registered with the Public Accountants Board may practice in Singapore. The Board recognizes U.S. accountants registered with the American Institute of Certified Public Accountants.

Engineering and Architectural Services: Engineering and architectural firms can be100percent foreign-owned. In line with FTA provisions, and also applicable to all foreign firms, Singapore has removed the requirement that the chairman and two-thirds of a board of directors be engineers, architects or land surveyors registered with local professional bodies.

When a professional engineer, resident or foreign, desires to engage in professional engineering work in Singapore, he/she shall apply for a certificate authorizing them to engage in professional engineering work. Application should be made with the Professional Engineers Board, Singapore (http://www.peb.gov.sg) .

Under the Architect Act, no person shall draw or prepare any architectural plan and design intended to govern the construction of any building in Singapore unless the person is a registered architect who has a valid practicing certificate issued by the Board of Architects (http://www.boa.gov.sg) .

WEB RESOURCES

The Singapore Government Online portal at http://www.gov.sg now brings together all government related resources into one easy access point. There are four broad categories of content at this web portal – Government, Citizens & Residents, Businesses and Non-Residents. The Government section contains the latest information, statistics, news and policy related to the Singapore Government. At the portal, you can obtain links to the various individual websites of all government agencies and ministries, get the latest reports on economic forecasts, access press releases from various ministries and much more. The Businesses segment contains the entire range of information and e-services for businesses. Everything you need for your business from registering your business to applying for government licenses online and to getting the Entrepreneur's Guide for starting a business.

LEADING SECTORS FOR U.S. EXPORT AND INVESTMENT

ELECTRONICS COMPONENTS (ELC)

Unit: USD millions

	2009	2010	2011 (estimated)	2012 (estimated)
Total Market Size	-638	1,051	2,000	3,800
Total Local Production	18,988	29,328	39,000	46,800
Total Exports	63,557	88,648	115,000	138,000
Total Imports	43,931	60,371	78,000	95,000
Imports from the U.S.	3,308	4,670	6,000	7,310
Exchange Rate: 1 USD	1.45	1.36	1.25	1.20

Total Market Size = (Total Local Production + Total Imports) – (Total Exports) Data Sources: Singapore Government Trade Statistics

Singapore-based electronics manufacturers account for 11% global market share for semiconductor wafer foundry output and 25% global market share for printers. The world's top three wafer foundry companies, top three sub-contract assembly-and-test companies, and top four fabless IC design companies all have facilities in Singapore. Electronic components for these plants are imported and integrated into products such as mobile phones, digital cameras, hand-held tablets, music players, game consoles and televisions which are then mainly exported.

Singapore's manufacturing sector has emerged as a regional economic powerhouse, contributing at least 22% to the Gross Domestic Product (GDP) . A large component of this sector - electronics - has attracted substantial foreign investments as well as value-added output and employment, contributing close to 30% of the manufacturing output. Of the US$8 billion in fixed assets investments in 2009, electronics accounted for slightly more than 40% but manufacturing output was more than US$41 billion for the sector.

Sub-Sector Best Prospects

There are increasing opportunities for Electronics Manufacturing Services (EMS) companies to pursue in various areas such as medical devices and aerospace. Many of the world's top EMS companies such as Flextronics, Solectron and Venture are located in Singapore, which is becoming an attractive base of high value-added production activities. Another electronic component technology that is being developed is the Organic Light Emitting Diode (OLED) which is gradually replacing LCD panels.

For the first half of 2010, the manufacturing sector including the electronics industry was still somewhat affected by the global economic crisis. However, global demand, especially from Europe and the United States, has improved during the second half of the year and is expected to grow further in 2011, reversing a decline of almost a year. Components that have seen an increase in orders include semiconductor chips, data storage and electronic modules, advanced displays, and various electronic board items such as capacitors, diodes and integrated circuits.

Opportunities

The precision engineering industry, which supports the EMS companies, is an important sector of the Singapore economy. Through the supply of components, tooling and equipment, this industry provides integral support to the manufacturing sector. The Singapore government plans to spend close to US$5 billion by 2013 to foster research and high-end production in industries such as precision engineering and life sciences with the aim of replacing assembly lines that are moving to lower cost countries. Beyond mainstream industries, Singapore is developing high-growth potential areas such as photonics, nanotechnology and micro-electrical-mechanical systems.

The Government of Singapore still expects to greatly expand manufacturing output by 2020 and is aiming to reach a total manufacturing output of US$200 billion and total manufacturing value-added of US$50 billion. More than 20,000 jobs are expected to be created in the manufacturing and the service sectors in the coming years as a result. Hewlett Packard and Texas Instruments who have extensive electronics expertise, have invested nearly US$10 billion combined. Singapore is also a leading manufacturer of enterprise hard disk drives with companies such as Seagate and Hitachi. Over the past few years, the country has accounted for half of the world's enterprise hard disk drives.

Singapore Government Offices

Singapore Economic Development Board http://edbsingapore.com

Industry Organizations

Association of Electronic Industries in Singapore http://www.aeis.org.sg

Singapore Manufacturing Federation http://www.smafederation.org.sg

U.S. Commercial Service, Singapore Contact CHAN Y K, Commercial Specialist E-mail: yiukei.chan@trade.gov

OIL & GAS (OGS)

Unit: USD millions

	2009	2010	2011 (estimated)	2012 (estimated)
Total Market Size	46,257	61,246	81,000	97,000
Total Local Production	28,285	36,696	48,000	57,000
Total Exports	42,629	58,576	75,000	90,000
Total Imports	60,601	83,125	108,000	130,000
Imports from the U.S.	2,996	3,590	4,700	5,678
Exchange Rate: 1 USD	1.45	1.36	1.25	1.20

Total Market Size = (Total Local Production + Total Imports) – (Total Exports) Data Sources: Singapore Government Trade Statistics

Singapore has become one of the most important shipping centers in Asia and is one of the world's top three oil trading and refining hubs. A total crude oil refining capacity of more than 1.35 million barrels per day (bbl/d) now is expected to increase to 1.8bbl/d when a new refinery comes on stream in 3-5 years time. In addition, Singapore is the market leader for floating production, storage and offloading (FPSOs) conversions and jack-up rigs. Underground caverns for oil storage and a liquid natural gas (LNG) terminal are also being built to enhance Singapore's position as the premier regional center for the oil & gas industry. However, combined output from the petro-chemical sectors was only valued at close to US$33 billion due to the recent economic crisis but this is expected to gradually increase with the rebounding global economy and sharp rise in oil prices.

Sub-Sector Best Prospects

Singapore offers many opportunities for American companies including:

Companies that can address the needs of engineering, procurement, construction and contracting services / project consultancies, drilling contractors, offshore platform and rig fabricators and operators, shipbuilding and marine engineering as well as distribution, storage and handling would be in demand.

Pipeline technology has also been identified as another growth area for U.S. companies with the increased emphasis on gas in the South East Asian region so expertise in deepwater application would be desirable.

There are also needs for companies with expertise in conducting geographical surveys, navigation and positioning, hydrographic surveys and underwater inspection services, consultancy, information systems and marine forecasting.

Supply of equipment and spares for upstream and downstream oil and gas, marine, mechanical / electrical construction, repair, maintenance, oxidation additives and various control systems.

Oilfield equipment that includes instrumentation such as drilling information systems, drilling monitors, mud logging units, mud monitoring systems, torque

gauges, pressure gauges, weight indicators, deadline anchors, valves / actuators, performance testing and design control system.

Opportunities

Singapore holds the No. 1 position, with 70% market share, for floating production, storage and offloading (FPSOs) conversions and 70% market share for jack-up rigs. In 2007, both ExxonMobil and Shell commenced construction of new hydrocrackers which have a combined worth of more than US$7.0 billion. These new facilities (to be fully completed and operational by 2012) will bring Singapore's total ethylene capacity to more than four million metric tons per annum.

In 2006, Singapore approved the development of storage facilities in underground rock caverns with a potential capacity of up to 20.1 million barrels. The first phase of the caverns, to be ready from 2012, will store petroleum liquids and products such as naptha and gasoil while the second phase is already on the drawing board.

Singapore is embarking on a diversification strategy for gas imports by building an LNG import terminal. The LNG terminal, which is scheduled to start operations in 2013, will add another 400 million standard cubic feet (mscf) capacity to the current 1.2 billion mscf daily supply of piped gas imports.

Web Resources

Singapore Government Offices

Singapore Economic Development Board (SEDB) http://edbsingapore.com

U.S. Commercial Service, Singapore Contact CHAN Y K, Commercial Specialist E-mail: yiukei.chan@trade.gov

AIRCRAFT AND PARTS (AIR)

Unit: USD millions

	2009	2010	2011 (estimated)	2012 (estimated)
Total Market Size	9588	8255	9277	10135
Total Local Production	5000	5650	6385	7024
Total Exports	5747	6420	7126	7909
Total Imports	10335	9025	10018	11020
Imports from the U.S.	4848	5315	5794	6315
Exchange Rate: 1 USD	1.45	1.36	1.25	1.20

Total Market Size = (Total Local Production + Total Imports) – (Total Exports) Data Sources: Singapore Government Trade Statistics

With over 100 companies offering a comprehensive range of aerospace design and manufacturing services as well as Maintenance, Repair and Overhaul (MRO) services, Singapore is the leading Asian aerospace hub with the greatest number of aerospace Original Equipment Manufacturers (OEMs) present. Singapore has also captured over 20% of the Asia-Pacific MRO market and has established a leading position as a convenient one-stop location for all aircraft maintenance needs.

Leading local players such as ST Aerospace and SIA Engineering Company Ltd offer comprehensive nose-to-tail airframe MRO services and are among the top 5 Airframe MROs in the world in 2008 based on the total airframe man-hours by the corporate entities. Singapore is also host to major engine overhaul centers, with all three engine OEM majors (GE Aviation, Pratt & Whitney and Roll Royce) represented.

Employing over 18,000 people and with a compounded annual growth rate of 12% since 1990, Singapore's aerospace industry is an integral economic driver. In 2009, the industry recorded revenues of nearly US$5.0 billion.

Sub-Sector Best Prospects

There is still room for MRO activities to grow in terms of depth and scope of capabilities. Companies are interested in considering activities such as repair development, leveraging on competencies developed here and the expertise of various research institutes in Singapore. To further enhance market access, companies are also looking to establish asset management activities in Singapore. These assets, also called rotables, could entail a wide range of aircraft components and systems, such as engines, landing gears and avionics.

Opportunities

Aerospace is one of the fastest growing industries in Singapore and the long-term outlook remains positive. According to Frost and Sullivan, the Asian Pacific aviation industry is experiencing a faster recovery than anticipated. This has created a market climate where Asian economies are leading the pace of aviation recovery. Asia Pacific is expected to dominate about 40% (US$270 billion) of the global airline revenue by 2020. The cargo business has also shown an equally buoyant growth with Asia being one of the major hubs of the air freight business spearheading growth. Also, the rising GDP rates across Asia and the increasing disposable income of the population will lead to higher demand on cabin interiors, greater segmentation and attention to the design as well as suitably connected cabin. Singapore is particularly well-equipped to capture the demand from aviation-related services from this market given its MRO hub status, which will translate into greater opportunities for American suppliers to sell to this lucrative market and beyond.

Web Resources

Singapore Government Offices

Singapore Economic Development Board http://www.sedb.com.sg

Civil Aviation Authority of Singapore http://www.caas.gov.sg

Defense Science & Technology Agency http://www.dsta.gov.sg

U.S. Commercial Service, Singapore Contact Ng Haw Cheng, Commercial Specialist Email: Hawcheng.Ng@trade.gov

POLLUTION CONTROL EQUIPMENT (POL)

Unit: USD millions

	2009	2010	2011 (estimated)	2012 (estimated)
Total Market Size	5504	6199	7130	8238
Total Local Production	5498	6872	7903	9088
Total Exports	7342	9233	10617	11678
Total Imports	7348	8560	9844	10828
Imports from the U.S.	1954	2241	2554	2783
Exchange Rate: 1 USD	1.45	1.36	1.25	1.20

Total Market Size = (Total Local Production + Total Imports) – (Total Exports) Data Sources: Singapore Government Trade Statistics

As Singapore's population and economy grow, the Government is not only diversifying its water supplies but also planning ahead for wastewater management. This led to ongoing programs to develop various wastewater reclamation and desalination projects. Among other projects, the ABC (Active, Beautiful, Clean) Waters Program is an initiative by the Public Utilities Board to transform Singapore's concrete drains, canals and reservoirs into beautiful and clean streams, rivers and lakes teeming with vibrancy. 27 projects have been identified to be carried out over the next 5 years. As at Jan 2011, Tenders for 16 projects were called. The works include construction of infrastructures, water features, landscaping and other amenities.

Under the Singapore Green Plan 2012 (SGP 2012) , the country's environmental policy, Singapore has put in place a holistic blueprint to grow the Cleantech industry. The SGP 2012 also incorporates plans for reduction of waste volumes through waste minimization and recycling; reduction of the amount of land for sewage treatment; strict emission standards; and tougher vehicular emission controls.

Sub-Sector Best Prospects

The measures taken to tighten air emission will give rise to opportunities to supply new air pollution control equipment to Singapore. American products will have good market prospects given that imports of environmental products from the U.S. account for about 26% of total environmental imports. Among the American products imported by Singapore are air filters and water purifiers, gas and smoke analysis apparatus, and ozone oxygen & herosol therapeutic respiration apparatus. Other areas of environmental interest include waste management solutions to overcome Singapore limited land space. Singapore has been tapping into foreign expertise for technologies such as hazardous and solid waste disposal, landfill space, and the building of incinerators.

Opportunities

The water industry in Singapore is becoming more liberalized. The national water agency, The Public Utilities Board (PUB) , has opened its doors to private companies that want to test-bed projects using its infrastructure. PUB also tenders contracts to private companies to build, design and operate water plants. U.S. companies are encouraged to participate in future contracts offered by the PUB. American equipment manufacturers could also supply their equipment to successful prime contractors of PUB projects. Areas of particular interest include filtration and purifying systems & apparatus, technologies involving wastewater recycling and treatment, and advanced desalination systems.

Web Resources

Singapore Government Offices

Ministry of The Environment & Water Resources http://www.mewr.gov.sg

National Environment Agency http://www.nea.gov.sg

Public Utilities Board http://www.pub.gov.sg

U.S. Commercial Service, Singapore Contact Ng Haw Cheng, Commercial Specialist Email: Hawcheng.Ng@trade.gov

COMPUTER HARDWARE/SOFTWARE/PERIPHERALS (CPT/CSF)

Unit: USD millions

	2009	2010	2011 (estimated)	2012 (estimated)
Total Market Size	5002	5400	5700	6000
Total Local Production	11382	13894	14600	15300

Total Exports	17707	22008	23100	24200
Total Imports	11328	13514	14200	14900
Imports from the U.S.	1103	1227	1300	1360
Exchange Rate: 1 USD	1.45	1.36	1.25	1.20

Total Market Size = (Total Local Production + Total Imports) – (Total Exports) Data Sources: Singapore Government Trade Statistics

The information technology sector is a key contributor to Singapore's economy. Information technology has greatly enhanced the country's competitiveness by raising productivity and transforming business processes. In 2010, Singapore was ranked second in the World Economic Forum's Global IT Report, and eighth in the Economist Intelligence Unit (EIU) e-Readiness Ranking. It was ranked ninth in the EIU Benchmarking IT industry Competitiveness in 2009. Many top IT companies have made Singapore a key node in their global network, a strong testament of the country's strategic position to be a global info-communications hub.

Latest available data showed that in 2009, 95% of Singaporean households with school-going children had access to a home computer while 83% of resident Singaporean households had access to a computer at home. Eighty-one percent of households had home Internet access and most of those households are connected to the Internet via broadband. Computer usage amongst all enterprises increased slightly to reach 78% in 2009. Details on info-communications usage in households and by individuals as well as enterprises can be found at http://www.ida.gov.sg/Publications/20061205092557.aspx

Sub-Sector Best Prospects

Best prospects are government projects, security solutions, business analytics and cloud computing. The Singapore Government is a major catalyst for promoting the use of information technology in the country and is also a major consumer of IT products and services. Demand for security solutions will continue to rise as more enterprises adopt cloud computing. The Singapore market is very dependent on imports and U.S. products are traditionally well received in Singapore as the United States is seen as the source for state-of-the-art technologies.

Opportunities

The Singapore government continues to aggressively implement its ICT projects in FY 2010 (April 1, 2010-March 31, 2011) . It plans to invest US$820 million (S$1.1 billion) in tenders and companies should look forward to some 350 new tenders ranging from less than US$377,000 (S$500,000) to over US$7.5m (S$10m) . More information can be found at http://www.buyusainfo.net/docs/x_6194268.pdf . Singapore is an early adopter of technologies in the region and there are excellent opportunities for U.S. companies to sell applications and solutions to Singapore and through Singapore to neighboring countries. Singapore acts as a major distribution center for companies interested in selling to the region as reflected by re-export data. More than half of computer products imported into Singapore are re-exported to third countries.

Web Resources

Key websites

www.ida.gov.sg http://www.sitf.org.sg http://www.export.gov/market_research/index.asp

U.S. Commercial Service, Singapore Contact Ms. CHIA Swee Hoon, Senior Commercial Specialist Email: SweeHoon.Chia@trade.gov

TELECOMMUNICATION EQUIPMENT & SERVICES (TEL/TES)

Unit: USD millions

	2009	2010	2011 (estimated)	2012 (estimated)
Total Market Size	2863	4037	4400	4600
Total Local Production	1642	1938	2100	2200
Total Exports	7099	7918	8700	9100
Total Imports	8321	10016	11000	11500
Imports from the U.S.	994	1138	1200	1260
Exchange Rate: 1 USD	1.45	1.36	1.25	1.20

Total Market Size = (Total Local Production + Total Imports) – (Total Exports) Data Sources: Singapore Government Trade Statistics

Singapore is one of the most wired countries in the world, with a nation-wide network of fiber optic cables. It is building a super high-speed fiber optic broadband network called the Next Generation Nationwide Broadband Network (NGNBN) that will provide access speed of 1 gigabits per second (Gbps) or more. As of end-2010, 60% of homes and offices have access to the new, ultra high-speed, all-fiber Next Generation Nationwide Broadband Network (NGBN) . By mid-2012, 95% of the country will have access to the NGNBN. Besides a nationwide broadband network infrastructure, Singapore is well connected by multiple satellite and submarine cable systems with more than 67 terabits per second of potential capacity supporting international and regional telecoms connectivity. It has more than 830 Gbps of international internet bandwidth connectivity to economies such as the US, China, Japan, India, as well as some countries in Europe and ASEAN.

Sub-Sector Best Prospects

Best prospects include equipment, content, software and technologies for broadband, wireless broadband, and 3G. Singapore is a matured and sophisticated market for telecommunications products and services. The country is dependent on imports and

U.S. products are traditionally well received here. There are excellent opportunities to sell new applications and solutions to Singapore and through Singapore, as it is an early adopter and a major entrepot. The country serves as a major distribution center and springboard for companies interested in selling to the region as reflected by re-export data. Nearly 60% of telecommunications goods imported into Singapore are re-exported for third-country consumption.

Opportunities

The NGNBN provides excellent opportunities for U.S. vendors. The Singapore government Infocomm Development Authority (IDA) is seeking content and applications and retail service providers to participate in the rollout of the ultra high speed broadband network. U.S. companies interested in deploying services or partnering with service providers on the NGNBN should review http://www.ida.gov.sg/Infrastructure/20090731164857.aspx . In 2010, the IDA announced a Call for Proposal (CFP) to develop a program to support video services on the NGNBN. To support the development of services on the NGNBN, the government launched a second CFP for the Next Generation Services Innovation Program (NGSIP) . More information can be found at

http://www.ida.gov.sg/Infrastructure/20090807131841.aspx

There are also good opportunities for U.S. companies to sell solutions to existing telecom service operators in Singapore as they seek to offer new applications for the new broadband infrastructure. The three largest telecom service providers in Singapore: Singapore Telecommunications (SingTel) , StarHub, and M1, all announced retail service provider arms that will ride atop the NGNBN. M1, the smallest telco, announced in November 2010 it joined StarHub and SingTel in offering pay TV to consumers. They are all investing in infrastructure to support their planned new offerings.

Starhub, Singapore's second largest telecom services provider, plans to jointly build and operate a US$430 million submarine cable connecting East Asia's major business hubs. In January 2011, Starhub announced that its partners are NTT Communications, the Philippines Long Distance Telephone Co and Telekom Malaysia. The cable system, Asia Submarine-Cable Express (ASE) is a 7,200 km submarine cable linking Singapore directly to Japan, the Philippines and Hong Kong with a total carrying capacity exceeding 15 terabits per second and incorporating lates 40G optical technologies. The system will have connectivity to Malaysia and potential future connectivity to China and other Southeast Asian countries.

Web Resources

Key websites

www.ida.gov.sg http://www.sitf.org.sg/ http://www.atis.org.sg
http://www.export.gov/market_research/index.asp

U.S. Commercial Service, Singapore Contact Ms. CHIA Swee Hoon, Senior Commercial Specialist Email: SweeHoon.Chia@trade.gov

LABORATORY & SCIENTIFIC INSTRUMENTS (LAB)

Unit: USD millions

	2009	2010	2011 (estimated)	2012 (estimated)
Total Market Size	1164	1848	1885	1942
Total Local Production	1386	2026	2067	2129
Total Exports	2451	3361	3428	3531
Total Imports	2229	3183	3247	3344
Imports from the U.S.	797	1210	1234	1271
Exchange Rate: 1 USD	1.45	1.36	1.25	1.20

Total Market Size = (Total Local Production + Total Imports) – (Total Exports) Data Sources: Singapore Government Trade Statistics

The United States continues to dominate in the area of laboratory and scientific equipment and accounts for approximately 38% of total market share. Total imports of laboratory and scientific equipment rebounded in 2010, picking up momentum after the 2009 global market slowdown. Imports from the United States increased by a significant 50% from 2009, with 38% market share, up from 35% in 2009. There is a strong preference for American manufactured products and equipment, particularly in the field of laboratory equipment and instrumentation. Given the improvements in the economy in 2010, the total import of laboratory and scientific equipment also correspondingly grew.

This sector will see continual growth as the Singapore government has pledged S$12.88 billion to support R&D in Singapore from 2011 to 2015 under the Research, Innovation and Enterprise 2015 plan, with the primary aim of achieving total gross expenditure on R&D of 3.5% of GDP by 2015.

Sub-Sector Best Prospects

The areas that will see sustained demand for equipment are the biomedical sciences and laboratories, particularly in research and development, product testing, certification, consulting and education services, environmental and water technologies, specialty chemicals, petroleum refining, petrochemicals, plastics and interactive and digital media. Several of these sectors attracted new investment fueled by the Singapore government's development efforts over the last few years. With the global economy's unpredictable recovery, the challenge in the foreseeable future is to optimize production at these facilities.

Opportunities

The Singapore government established the National Research Council to provide a national framework for strategic research and development efforts. The areas of focus are the biomedical sciences, environmental and water technologies and interactive media. In the area of life sciences, Singapore has over the last decade proven itself to be a world-class research and development hub. It also hopes to capitalize on the rising trend of eco-sustainability. It plans to invest US$12.5 billion over the next five years, US$2.85 billion of this in biomedical sciences for the period 2011-2015. Singapore's premier biomedical research hub, Biopolis, will also be undergoing a US$61.5million to US$77 million expansion. Improvements will be made to laboratory designs and is expected to be completed by 2013.

The electronics sector, which accounts for 73% of Singapore's manufacturing, also presents good opportunities for laboratory and scientific instrumentation. Eastman Kodak has established its worldwide R&D HQ in Singapore and will be conducting various engineering development and design work. There are plans to double its R&D headcount over the next few years.

In the area of environmental and water technologies, efforts are spurred by the need to diversify Singapore's water resources. To date, the island state has successfully used innovative membrane technologies to produce clean water from both wastewater reclamation and seawater desalination. The US$1.3 billion development of the Jurong Island Petrochemical Complex, which is currently a work-in-progress, also presents an attractive market for laboratory instrumentation vendors.

Web Resources

Singapore Government Offices

Singapore Economic Development Board http://www.sedb.com

Singapore Biomedical Sciences Industry Cluster http://www.Biomed-Singapore.com

A*STAR (Agency for Science, Technology & Research) http://www.a-star.edu.sg

U.S. Commercial Service, Singapore Contact Luanne Theseira, Commercial Specialist Email: Luanne.Theseira@trade.gov

MEDICAL DEVICES (MED)

Unit: USD millions

	2009	2010	2011 (estimated)	2012 (estimated)
Total Market Size	586	756	778	793
Total Local Production	1358	1757	1809	1845
Total Exports	2015	2521	2597	2649
Total Imports	1243	1520	1566	1597
Imports from the U.S.	377	485	499	509
Exchange Rate: 1 USD	1.45	1.36	1.25	1.20

Total Market Size = (Total Local Production + Total Imports) – (Total Exports) Data Sources: Singapore Government Trade Statistics

Singapore serves as the healthcare and medical hub of the region, drawing over 350,000 patients a year with its high-quality healthcare. It is considered one of the world's leading medical travel destinations and its healthcare system is ranked sixth worldwide. Singapore's healthcare services are comparable to those of other industrialized economies. The government spends approximately 3.8% of GDP annually on healthcare and there are plans to raise this to US$1.37 billion a year in the next few years.

In 2010, import of medical equipment and supplies to Singapore registered an increase of 22% from 2009. This is likely due to the recovery of the economy and the pent-up demand from major healthcare institutions that may have held back purchases during the economic downturn. Correspondingly, total import from the United States grew by over 25% from 2009, representing 30% of the Singapore market.

Based on available trade figures for 2009 and 2010, market expectations for 2011 are that U.S exports of medical equipment to Singapore will continue to hold steady due to the nature of the healthcare industry. Overall, healthcare delivery in Singapore and the region is expected to see improvements as medical care is still considered a necessity. This should translate into a steady stream of transshipments through Singapore as the island-state is viewed as a major trade hub and launching pad for products into the region.

Medical devices are regulated under the Health Products Act. Singapore's Health Science Authority (HSA) , through its Centre for Medical Devices Regulation (CMDR) , oversees the system of statutory control aimed to safeguard the quality, safety and efficacy of medical devices available in Singapore. All medical devices, from high-risk stents for heart surgery to low-risk ones like mechanical wheelchairs, are licensed.

Sub-Sector Best Prospects

The Singapore government is focused on moving up the healthcare value chain through the provision of services that assist research and healthcare delivery in Singapore and the region. Over the next few years, it will pump nearly a billion dollars into the biomedical sciences sector with the aim of boosting health-care standards and clinical research capabilities. Singapore researchers are focused on 'bench to bedside' research with the hope of this making its way into mainstream medicine and benefit the larger population. To this end, U.S. firms that are able to provide cutting edge technology, laboratory and testing equipment and services that can help the research community will find Singapore a lucrative market.

Within the next two decades, Singapore will experience hyper-aging, in which more than 20% of the country's population is aged 65 years and above. Given this, more facilities for the elderly, such as nursing homes and rehabilitation centers, need to be built. The number of beds in community hospitals and nursing homes will be increased substantially over the next nine years. U.S. firms specializing in elder-care products and services will find a good market in Singapore.

There is growing emphasis on living a healthy lifestyle, with a focus on preventive care, and doing a better job of tackling chronic illnesses. U.S. firms with revolutionary or cutting-edge medical technology or focus on health screening and disease management would find Singapore an ideal place to sell their products.

Opportunities

Government hospitals account for 80% of the 11,830 hospital beds in Singapore. Singapore is renowned for its role as the healthcare hub for the region, treating patients from neighboring Malaysia, Brunei, Indonesia, Thailand, the Philippines and more recently, from the United States, Britain, Japan, Seychelles, China, Hong Kong and Bangladesh.

Demand for medical equipment comes from public and private hospitals and clinics. The Health Ministry is the largest consumer, accounting for nearly 70% of local demand. Parkway Healthcare, the largest private sector healthcare provider in Singapore, is also a significant consumer of medical equipment. More than 80% of local demand is met through imports and there is a premium placed on American-made products. U.S. manufacturers with revolutionary products will find Singapore a good market.

Most of the public sector hospitals have been extensively refurbished or totally rebuilt in recent years. The 550-bed public sector Khoo Teck Puat Hospital located in the northern part of the island was opened in late 2010. This facility will be supplemented by a new ambulatory or outpatient medical center offering specialist services, expected to be ready by 2013, and a 200-bed community hospital nearby. If there is a need, another outpatient medical center may be set up by 2015.

Two new public, acute general hospitals located in the western and eastern parts of the island are being planned. The one in the western part of the island is expected to be ready by 2014 and will have 700 beds with an adjoining 286-bed community hospital, scheduled to be built by 2015. The hospital in the east is expected to be ready by 2018. Other plans include upgrading and expanding the facilities at the National Heart Centre, National University Hospital and Singapore General Hospital.

Due to the global slowdown in 2009, the private sector's initial plans to have a 350-bed hospital costing between US$207 and US$345 million built by 2011 is now postponed to 2012. This facility will cater mainly to foreign patients who demand high-quality healthcare and services. A new 63-clinic medical center will be attached to the hospital. One of the older hospitals in Singapore, East Shore Hospital, completed their renovation program in 2010. In the longer term, the 153-bed hospital will have between 100 and 150 more beds and will add new specialist clinics for sports, medicine, dermatology, ophthalmology and neurology. Another private healthcare group will spend between $61.5 million and US$77 million to expand their flagship Raffles Hospital. This is expected to be completed by 2012.

Web Resources

Singapore Government Offices

Singapore Economic Development Board http://www.sedb.com

Ministry of Health (MOH) http://www.moh.gov.sg

Health Sciences Authority (HSA) http://www.hsa.gov.sg

Health Promotion Board (HPB) http://www.hpb.gov.sg

U.S. Commercial Service, Singapore Contact Luanne Theseira, Commercial Specialist Email: Luanne.Theseira@trade.gov

EDUCATION / TRAINING SERVICES (EDS)

	Sep 2002	Sep 2003	Sep 2004	Sep 2005	Sep 2006	Sep 2007	Sep 2008	Sep 2009	Sep 2010	Sep 2011
Number of visas issued to Singaporeans	1451	1617	1747	1944	2352	2363	2560	2676	2934	3168
% increase / decrease from previous year	-12.4	11.4	8.0	11.3	21.0	0	8.3	4.5	9.6	7.8
Total visas issued including foreign students	2088	2259	2590	2870	3418	3804	4349	4454	4870	5252
% increase / decrease from previous year	-10.0	8.2	14.7	10.8	19.1	11.3	14.3	2.4	9.3	7.8

Singapore emphasizes, supports and values higher education and human resource development. Many government agencies and private sector companies also offer full scholarships for top students to pursue their undergraduate and graduate studies in foreign universities, including in the United States.

Sub-Sector Best Prospects

There are presently close to 5,000 Singaporeans pursuing their tertiary education in the United States; two-thirds are undergraduates and a third are graduate students.

U.S. universities and colleges will find a receptive market in Singapore, provided they are willing to invest in long-term branding / marketing with accredited programs in disciplines that offer strong career growth and high income potential. The following degree courses are becoming increasingly important and are expected to see increased demand from Singaporean and third-country students studying in Singapore.

WEALTH MANAGEMENT / FINANCIAL PLANNING

Opportunities

The Singapore government is developing the country into the "global schoolhouse" for Asia. The education system is well known for its quality, which is why there is a strong demand from students in the region to study here. American universities, in addition to recruiting full-time students (both local and overseas) to study in the United States, may be able to tap viable opportunities offering their external degree and executive education programs to Singaporeans as well as international executives working in the region. However, a Private Education Bill was passed in November 2009 effectively establishing a non-tariff trade barrier for certain education institutions. The bill adversely affected the ability of some U.S. universities to offer external degree programs and has implications for other American education providers seeking to offer degree, diploma or certificate courses in Singapore.

Simply having proper recognition and/or accreditation in the foreign institution's own country is only a starting point for approval for a foreign institution seeking to offer programs or courses in Singapore. In addition to meeting Singapore's new standards, "national ranking" appears to be a key criterion for approval. The Council for Private Education was set up to regulate this new Bill and they are expected to complete by June-July 2011 the evaluation of all existing private education institutions and foreign degree programs that are conducted in Singapore.

In addition to Singaporeans, U.S. universities and colleges should also consider the large number of foreign students studying at the high school and university levels in Singapore. Today, there are 90,000 foreign students studying in Singapore and the government would like to increase that number to 150,000 within five years. Many foreign universities in recent years have established a presence in Singapore either by themselves or in collaboration with a local institution/organization to offer partial or full degree programs. Singaporean students find programs that allow them to complete at least part of their course work in Singapore a very attractive and financially viable alternative to completing their studies entirely in the United States.

Web Resources

Singapore Government Offices

Council for Private Education http://www.cpe.gov.sg

Ministry of Education http://www.moe.gov.sg

U.S. Commercial Service, Singapore Contact CHAN Y K, Commercial Specialist E-mail: yiukei.chan@trade.gov

FRANCHISING (FRA)

Singapore is home to more than 400 franchise concepts. Foreign franchises are well received and the United States is by far the largest supplier of foreign franchises in the country. There are American franchises in practically every industry. McDonald's, Burger King, KFC, Subway, Starbucks, Ben and Jerrys, Gymboree, New Horizons, Mister Minit, Avis, Toys R Us, On-line Trading Academy, Comfort Keepers, Contours Express, and many others have operations in Singapore. In 2009, several F&B concepts from the U.S. started operations here including Marble Slab and Froots. After many years of absence, several

U.S. franchises also made a comeback in 2009 including: Wendy's, Dunkin' Doughnut, Chili's, and TGIF. In 2010, Applebee's opened an outlet in Singapore and several other U.S. franchises including Cold Stone Creamery will open in 2011.

Sales turnover of franchises in Singapore amounted to US$5.7 billion in 2008 (latest available data) , according to the Franchising and Licensing Association of Singapore. Foreign franchises are estimated to account for 70% of franchise sales in the country. However, local franchise concepts have grown rapidly over the past few years and many of the larger ones are franchising abroad in Asia and several have opened outlets in the

Asset-rich Singapore firms and entrepreneurs continue to seek new business concepts to introduce into Singapore and the region. Many are looking to diversify their business and some are seeking investments for their children or to run their own business. However, potential franchisees are now more discerning. Best prospects include F&B concepts and child-related/training franchises. The success of selling a franchise in Singapore is based on a number of factors including brand name, up-front costs and royalties, the concept's uniqueness and the flexibility of the franchise agreement. U.S. franchisors should note that real estate in Singapore is very expensive and getting good locations is a challenge, especially for those in the retail and F&B business.

Singapore is the gateway to Southeast Asia. Its multi-ethnic society makes the country an ideal location for foreign franchisors to test their concepts and use the reaction to gauge the acceptance of their concepts in Asia. With its strategic location and well-developed infrastructure, Singapore serves as the regional showcase and distribution center for products and services from all over the world. Residents from the region travel often to Singapore for business and leisure, making Singapore a good springboard for U.S. franchisors wishing to enter the markets of Asia. There are also opportunities for U.S. franchisors to work with Singapore companies to enter third countries.

Web Resources

Key websites www.flasingapore.org www.iesingapore.gov.sg
http://www.export.gov/market_research/index.asp

U.S. Commercial Service, Singapore Contact Ms. CHIA Swee Hoon, Senior Commercial Specialist Email: SweeHoon.Chia@mail.doc.gov

AGRICULTURAL SECTORS

Processed Fruit & Vegetables

In USD Million

	2009	2010	2011 (estimated)	2012 (estimated)
Total Market Size	159	181	208	237
Total Local Production	0	0	0	0
Total Exports	65	78	88	103
Total Imports	224	259	296	340
Imports from U.S.	42	50	57	66
Exchange Rate 1 USD	1.45	1.36	1.25	1.2

With the overall improvement in the regional economies, the Singapore market for processed fruit and vegetables has similarly recovered from its low level of 2009. Buoyed by higher tourist arrivals and rising consumer incomes the Imports of processed fruit and vegetables have increased in 2010 by more than 15 percent over the preceding year . The rise in imports has also reflected the increase in demand in reexports to the neighboring ASEAN markets. The United States has maintained its market share of close to one fifth of the total imports due to local consumer preference for quality products.

Fruit & Vegetable Juices
PS&D 2009
Overview
In US$ Million

	2009	2010	2011 (estimated)	2012 (estimated)
Total Market Size	32	35	38	42
Total Local Production	0	0	0	0
Total Exports	16	18	20	22
Total Imports	48	53	58	64
Imports from U.S.	12	13	14	16
Exchange Rate 1 USD	1.45	1.36	1.25	1.20

Total Market Size = (Total Local Production + Total Imports) – (Total Exports) Data Sources: Global Trade Atlas

Fruit & Vegetables Juices

In line with the general improvement of the Singapore economy, total imports of fruit and vegetable juices rose by over 10 percent. The improvement in demand for fruit and vegetable juices may be attributed to the rise in consumer spending in the retail and restaurant industry. U.S. brands continue to have a significant market share of about 25 percent primarily due to consumer preference for quality products and established brands. The presence of lower priced fruit and vegetable juices from neighboring countries have not eroded U.S. market share as Singapore consumers are rather discerning in food purchasing preferences.

Pet Foods (Dog & Cat Food)

In US$ Million

	2009	2010	2011 (estimated)	2012 (estimated)
Total Market Size	20	21	22	24
Total Local Production	0	0	0	0
Total Exports	1	1	2	2
Total Imports	21	22	24	26
Imports from U.S.	8	9	10	12
Exchange Rate 1 USD	1.45	1.36	1.25	1.20

With rising consumer incomes in the last decade and with the improvement in the Singapore economic performance in 2010, Singaporeans are spending more and more of their disposable incomes on their pets. The opening of more and more pet food and accessories stores in suburban shopping malls have encouraged the consumer expenditure on pet food and supplies. The U.S. is a major supplier of pet foods to the Singapore market and occupy about 40 percent market share. Singapore pet owners tend to be very brand loyal in terms of purchasing pet foods and U.S. brands with their high quality image among Singapore consumers tend to enjoy this competitive advantage.

TRADE REGULATIONS, CUSTOMS AND STANDARDS

IMPORT TARIFFS

Singapore is generally a free port and an open economy. More than 99% of all imports into Singapore enter the country duty-free. For social and/or environmental reasons, Singapore levies high excise taxes on beer, wine and liquor, tobacco products, motor vehicles and petroleum products.

Singapore levies a 7% Goods and Services Tax (GST) . For dutiable goods, the taxable value for GST is calculated based on the CIF (Cost, Insurance and Freight) value plus all duties and other charges. In the case of non-dutiable foods, GST will be based on the CIF value plus any commission and other incidental charges whether or not shown on the invoice. If the goods are dutiable, the GST will be collected simultaneously with the duties. Special provisions pertain to goods stored in licensed warehouses and free trade zones. See http://www.iras.gov.sg and http://www.customs.gov.sg

Inland Revenue Authority of Singapore Comptroller of Goods & Service Tax 55 Newton Road Revenue House Singapore 307987 Tel: (65) 65/1800-356 8633 (General Helpline) Fax: (65) 6351-3553 Email: gst@iras.gov.sg Website: http://www.iras.gov.sg

Singapore Customs 55 Newton Road #10-01 Revenue House Singapore 307987 Tel: (65) 6355-2000 Fax: (65) 6250-8663 Email: customs_documentation@customs.gov.sg

Website: http://www.customs.gov.sg Contact: Mr. CHEAH Tuck Meng, Deputy Head, (Company Compliance Branch) Email: Cheah_Tuck_Meng@customs.gov.sg

(Note: Chinese family names often precede given names; they are indicated in upper case letters)

TRADE BARRIERS

Singapore maintains one of the most liberal trading regimes in the world, but U.S. companies face several trade barriers. The country maintains a tiered motorcycle operator licensing system based on engine displacement, which, along with a road tax based on engine size, places U.S. exports of large motorcycles at a competitive disadvantage.

Singapore's Agri-Food and Veterinary Authority (AVA) tests every imported shipment of meat and poultry and does not accept raw and uncooked poultry and meat products that contain salmonella bacteria that exceed AVA's unrealistic microbiological standards. This is not scientifically justifiable and has posed some difficulties for U.S. exporters. Details can be found at

http://www.ava.gov.sg/FoodSector/FoodTestingAndCertification/ExportHealthCertMeatFi shDairyProd/

After the discovery of BSE in the United States in December 2003, Singapore banned imports of all U.S. beef products, offals and variety meats. In January 2006, Singapore re-opened its markets to only U.S. boneless beef from animals under 30 months of age.

Current World Organization for Animal Health (OIE) guidelines for BSE provide for conditions under which all beef and beef products from countries of any risk classification for BSE can be safely traded when the appropriate specified risk materials are removed. The United States was officially categorized by the OIE as "controlled risk" for BSE in 2007. The United States continues to press Singapore to make science-based decisions based OIE guidelines, which allow for the full-range of beef and beef products from animals of any age.

The FTA that the U.S. signed with Singapore in 2004 allows the importation of chewing gum with therapeutic value for sale, subject to certain requirements. Previously, there was a blanket ban on all types of chewing gum.

In March 2010, the Media Development Authority (MDA) introduced new measures that will require pay TV companies to cross carry content subject to exclusive carriage provisions. A pay TV company with an exclusive contract for a channel would be required to share that content with other pay TV companies at their request. Content providers consider the measures an unnecessary interference in a competitive market that would deny content holders the ability to negotiate freely in the marketplace, and interferes with their ability to manage and protect their intellectual property. MDA plans to implement the measures in mid-2011.

A new Private Education Bill was passed in November 2009 effectively establishing a non-tariff trade barrier for certain education institutions. The bill adversely affected the ability of U.S. universities to offer external degree programs and has implications for other American education providers seeking to offer degree, diploma or certificate courses in Singapore. Simply having proper recognition and/or accreditation in the foreign institution's own country is only a starting point for approval for a foreign institution seeking to offer programs or courses in Singapore. In addition to meeting Singapore's new standards, "national ranking" appears to be a key criterion for approval. The Council for Private Education (www.cpe.gov.sg) was set up to regulate this new Bill and they are expected to complete by June 2011 the evaluation of all existing private education institutions and foreign degree programs that are conducted in Singapore.

Foreign companies also face barriers in certain other service sectors such as telecommunications, media, financial and professional services, and energy. Details can be found in the USTR Report on Foreign Trade Barriers that is available on-line at

http://www.ustr.gov/sites/default/files/uploads/reports/2010/NTE/2010_NTE_Singapore_f inal.pdf .

IMPORT REQUIREMENTS AND DOCUMENTATION

Companies must make an inward declaration for all goods imported into Singapore. All imports require an import permit although this is largely a statistical requirement for most goods. Details can be found at

http://www.customs.gov.sg/leftNav/trad/Permits+and+Documentation.htm

BONA FIDE TRADE SAMPLES

Import of trade samples for which the total value is below US$286 (S$400) are not subject to payment of duty and/or GST. In addition, no permit is required for their import. Bona fide trade samples (excluding liquors and tobacco) may be imported if they are imported solely for the purpose of soliciting orders for goods to be supplied from abroad, for demonstration in Singapore to enable manufacturers in Singapore to produce such articles to fulfill orders from abroad or by a manufacturer for the purpose of copying, testing or experimenting before they produce such articles in Singapore. More information can be found at

http://www.customs.gov.sg/leftNav/trad/imp/Importation+of+Trade+Samples.htm

Medical and Medicinal Products Import Regulations

All medical and medicinal products, prescription and over-the-counter pharmaceuticals imported or sold in Singapore are required to be licensed by the Health Sciences Authority. The onus of applying for a product license rests with the license holder, i.e., a locally registered company that is responsible for the safety, quality and efficacy of the product. If U.S. companies have concerns regarding product licensing, they should contact the Health Sciences Authority (http://www.hsa.gov.sg) or ask a potential distributor to submit samples to the Health Sciences Authority.

U.S. EXPORT CONTROLS

Companies wanting to export controlled items to Singapore must apply for licenses from the appropriate government agencies in the United States. U.S. goods being reexported from intermediary consignees in Singapore to ultimate consignees in third countries require specific licensing. Singapore is a major transshipment hub for the Asian market. While many items may not initially require an export license, exporters need to be aware that two-thirds of items exported to Singapore are re-exported to third countries that may have more stringent licensing requirements that require additional export licenses. The Bureau of Industry and Security (BIS) is responsible for implementing and enforcing the Export Administration Regulations (EAR) , which regulate the export and re-export of certain commercial items while other U.S government agencies regulate more specialized exports.

For example, the U.S. Department of State has authority over defense articles and defense services. A list of agencies involved in export controls can be found at www.bis.doc.gov or in Supplement No. 3 Part 730 of the EAR which is available on the Government Printing Office Website, www.gpo.gov

TEMPORARY ENTRY

Goods may be temporarily imported under the Temporary Import Scheme for the purpose of repairs, displays, exhibitions or other similar events without the payment of duty and/or GST. A banker's guarantee is required under the Temporary Import Scheme. The temporary imports are covered by a Customs Inward Permit or a Carnet. Goods temporarily imported must be re-exported within the prescribed period using a Customs Outward permit. GST has to be paid if the goods are not subsequently reexported. The procedures governing such importation can be found at

http://www.customs.gov.sg/leftNav/trad/imp/Temporary+Importation+for+Exhibitions+Auctions+and+Fairs.htm

ADMISSION TEMPORAIRE/TEMPORARY ADMISSION (ATA) CARNET

A foreign exhibitor may import exhibition goods into Singapore using an ATA carnet. When the exhibitor arrives in Singapore the carnet must be produced together with the goods to Customs at the entry point for verification and endorsement. When goods covered by a carnet are taken out of Singapore the foreign exhibitor must produce the carnet together with the goods to Customs at the exit point for verification and endorsement. GST will be recovered from the carnet holder on any item that is unaccounted for. For more information on Temporary Importation for Exhibition, Auction & Fairs or Temporary Import Scheme, please contact the following or visit

http://www.customs.gov.sg/leftNav/trad/imp/Temporary+Importation+for+Exhibitions+Auctions+and+Fairs.htm

Singapore Customs 55 Newton Road #10-01 Revenue House Singapore 307987 Tel: (65) 6355-2000 Fax: (65) 6250-8663 Email: customs_documentation@customs.gov.sg Website: http://www.customs.gov.sg

(Note: Chinese family names often precede given names; they are indicated in upper case letters)

LABELING AND MARKING REQUIREMENTS

Labels are required on imported food, drugs, liquors, paints and solvents and must specify the country of origin. Repackaged foods must be labeled to show (in English) the appropriate designation of food content printed in capital letters at least 1/16 inch high; whether foods are compounded, mixed or blended; the minimum quantity stated in metric net weight or measure; the name and address of the manufacturer or seller; and the country of origin.

A description (in English) of the contents of the package may be added to the face of the label provided the additional language is not contrary to or a modification of any statement on the label. Illustrations must accurately describe the true nature or origin of the food. Foods having defined standards must be labeled to conform to those standards and be free from added foreign substances. Packages of food described as "enriched", "fortified", "vitaminized" or in any other way that implies that the article contains added vitamins or minerals must show the quantity of vitamins or minerals added per metric unit. Special labels are required for certain foods, medicines and goods such as edible and non-edible animal fats as well as liquors, paints and solvents.

Labeling and advertising legislation applies to the sale of vitamins and dietary supplements. Generally, labeling laws required that: 1) the composition of the products be disclosed in English, 2) labels/packaging materials not contain any references to diseases/conditions as specified in the schedule to the Medicines (Advertisement & Sale) Act (http://agcvldb4.agc.gov.sg/) ; and 3) the advertising/sale promotion of the product in the public media be approved by the Health Sciences Authority.

PROHIBITED AND RESTRICTED IMPORTS

Special import licenses are required for certain goods, including strategic items, hazardous chemicals, films and videos, arms and ammunition, agricultural biotechnology products, food derived from agricultural biotechnology products, prescription drugs, overthe-counter drugs, vitamins with very high dosages of certain nutrients, and cosmetics and skin care products. The import of such items such as lighters in the shape of pistols or revolvers, firecrackers, handcuffs, shell casings, and silencers is prohibited.

Generally, the import of goods that the government determines as posing a threat to health, security, safety and social decency is controlled. A full list of prohibited products and controlled goods and their corresponding controlling agencies can be obtained from the Singapore Customs website,

http://www.customs.gov.sg/leftNav/trav/dut/Controlled+Goods.htm

Companies must make an outward declaration to export or re-export goods out of Singapore. Selected items are subjected to controls on exports of goods from Singapore. Items such as rubber, timber, granite, satellite dishes and receivers, and chlorofluorocarbons are subjected to export control and licensing. Items under export control must be endorsed or licensed by the appropriate government agencies before they can be exported. More information may be obtained at

http://www.customs.gov.sg/leftNav/trad/imp/Goods+Subject+to+Control.htm

CUSTOMS REGULATIONS AND CONTACT INFORMATION CUSTOMS REGULATIONS

In Singapore valuation for customs purposes is based on the Customs Valuation Code (CVC) . The primary basis for Customs value is the transaction value of the imported goods when sold for export to Singapore. Where goods are dutiable ad valorem or specific rates may be applied. An ad valorem rate, which is most commonly applied, is a percentage of the Customs value of the imported goods. A specific rate is a specified amount per unit of weight of other quantity.

Cost, insurance, freight, handling charges and all other charges incidental to the sale and delivery of the goods are taken into account when the duty is assessed. Exporters are required to ensure that the declared values of goods have not been undervalued or the Customs and Excise Department will increase the values declared. Severe penalties may be imposed on traders attempting to evade duty.

FREE TRADE ZONE/WAREHOUSES

Singapore has three Free Trade Zones (FTZ) authorities namely PSA Corporation Ltd, Jurong Port Pte Ltd and the Changi Airport Group (Singapore) Pte Ltd. The eight FTZs are Brani Terminal, Keppel Distripark, Pasir Panjang Terminal, Sembawang Wharves, Tanjong Pagar Terminal, Keppel Terminal, Jurong Port, Airport Logistics Park of Singapore and the Changi Airport Cargo Terminal Complex. They provide a wide range of facilities and services for storage and re-export of dutiable and controlled goods. Goods can be stored within the zones without any customs documentation until they are released in the market and they can also be processed and re-exported with minimum customs formalities. More information can be found at

http://www.customs.gov.sg/leftNav/trad/per/Documentation+in+a+Free+Trade+Zone.htm

GST is suspended for imported goods deposited in a FTZ and will only be payable upon removal from the FTZ for local consumption. GST is not payable on supply made in FTZ if the goods supplied are meant for transshipment or re-export.

The FTZs at the port facilitate entrepot trade and promote the handling of transshipment cargo. They offer free 72-hour storage for import/export of conventional and containerized cargo and 140-day free storage for transshipment/re-export cargo.

There are many warehouse space options available in Singapore. Some of the more popular ones are located close to the port and within easy reach of the airport and the Jurong industrial hub. These include the Tanjong Pagar, Alexandra and Pasir Panjang Distriparks which are home to many established multinationals. The distriparks, in varying designs and size, cater to Central Distribution Center operators, manufacturers, traders, freight forwarders and others.

http://www.customs.gov.sg/leftNav/trad/dir/Licensed+Premises+for+Zero+GST+Goods.h tm

STANDARDS

As the national standards and accreditation body, SPRING develops and promotes internationally-recognized quality and standards infrastructure to enhance competitiveness and facilitate trade. To do this, SPRING's strategies are to:

Enhance Quality and Standards Infrastructure

Drive Quality and Standards Implementation

Build Quality and Standards Resources

Facilitate Market Access

At the policy level, SPRING represents Singapore in the Asia Pacific Economic Cooperation (APEC) Sub-Committee on Standards & Conformance (SCSC) , the ASEAN Consultative Committee for Standards & Quality (ACCSQ) and the Pacific Area Standards Congress (PASC) .

SPRING is Singapore's representative to the International Organization for Standardization (ISO) . Singapore is also a member of the International Electrotechnical Commission (IEC) through the Singapore National Committee of the IEC.

Standards Organizations

Singapore's national standardization program is administered by SPRING Singapore. It establishes and publishes Singapore Standards by publication in the Government Gazette.

SPRING brings together representatives from industries, government agencies and academic institutions to enhance enterprise competitive and facilitate trade through standards. Where applicable, Singapore Standards are aligned to international standards to help ease entry into overseas markets for Singapore exports and lower technical barriers to trade.

SPRING helps to promote industry awareness and use of Singapore Standards and relevant international standards.

NIST Notify U.S. Service

Member countries of the World Trade Organization (WTO) are required under the Agreement on Technical Barriers to Trade (TBT Agreement) to report to the WTO all proposed technical regulations that could affect trade with other Member countries. Notify U.S. is a free, web-based e-mail subscription service that offers an opportunity to review and comment on proposed foreign technical regulations that can affect your access to international markets. Register online at Internet URL:

http://www.nist.gov/notifyus/

Conformity Assessment

A list of conformity assessment bodies accredited by the Singapore Accreditation Council (SAC) may be found here: http://www.sac-accreditation.gov.sg/directory.asp

Product Certification

A list of the designated product certification bodies for the Consumer Protection (Safety Requirements) Registration Scheme (CPS Scheme) administered by SPRING can be found here: http://www.spring.gov.sg/qualitystandards/cps/pages/conformity assessment-information.aspx

Accreditation

Besides being the national standards body in Singapore, SPRING also manages the Singapore Accreditation Council (SAC) , the national accreditation body. The SAC's primary function is to accredit conformity assessment bodies based on international standards.

Accreditation is an endorsement of an organization's competence, credibility, independence and integrity in carrying out its conformity assessment activities. This endorsement is manifested in the use of the SAC accreditation marks in the issuing of endorsed test/calibration/inspection reports or accredited certificates by its accredited organizations.

The Singapore Accreditation Council currently operates accreditation programs in the following areas:

Calibration and testing laboratories covering chemical, biological, environmental, medical, medical imaging, electrical, non-destructive testing, gaming and testing related to civil and mechanical engineering

Inspection bodies for areas such as industrial pressure vessels and lifting equipment, motor vehicle, structural steelwork and cargo

Quality management system (ISO 9001) certification bodies

Environmental management system (ISO 14001) certification bodies.

Product certification bodies

Occupational safety and health management system (OSHMS) certification bodies

Hazard Analysis and Critical Control Points (HACCP) food safety management system certification bodies

Food safety (ISO 22000) certification bodies

Business continuity management certification bodies

On October 2010, the SAC was formally recognised by the U.S. Environmental Protection Agency (EPA) for the ENERGY STAR Program.

More information is available on the website: http://www.sac-accreditation.gov.sg .

The Singapore Accreditation Council has signed a number of multilateral mutual recognition arrangements (MRAs/MLAs) . These include:

Asia Pacific Laboratory Accreditation Cooperation (APLAC) MRA for testing, calibration, medical (ISO 15189) and inspection

Pacific Accreditation Cooperation (PAC) MLA for quality management system certification and product certification

International Accreditation Forum (IAF) MLA for quality management system certification and product certification

Bilateral Agreement with MLA members of European Cooperation for Accreditation (EA) for testing and calibration

International Laboratory Accreditation Cooperation (ILAC) MRA for testing and calibration.

In addition, SPRING is also the Good Laboratory Practice (GLP) Compliance Monitoring Authority in Singapore. In Jan 2010, Singapore became a Mutual Acceptance of Data (MAD) adherent member of the Organisation for Economic Cooperation and Development (OECD) . This means that GLP studies conducted in Singapore for the health and safety assessment of chemicals will be accepted in more than 30 OECD and non-OECD member countries.

Singapore became the first country in Asia, and the third in the world (after the European Union and Canada) , to operate a Mutual Recognition Arrangement (MRA) on telecom equipment certification with the U.S. The MRA provides for direct entry of telecommunications into either market without the need for additional testing and certification. Under the Asian Pacific Economic Cooperation (APEC) Telecommunications MRA implemented between the U.S. and Singapore, products can be tested and certified in the United States for conformance with Singapore's technical requirements. A list of the recognized U.S. testing and certification agencies can be found at: http://www.ida.gov.sg/Policies%20and%20Regulation/20060609145118.aspx .

Publication of Technical Regulations

The Singapore Standards eShop offers Singapore Standards and Technical References for sale. Singapore Standards are nationally recognized documents, established by consensus. They are functional or technical requirements in the form of specifications for materials, product system or process, codes of practice, methods of test, terminologies, and guides etc.

Technical References (TR) are transition documents developed to help meet urgent industry demand for specifications or requirements on a particular product, process or service in an area where there is an absence of reference standards. Unlike Singapore Standards, TRs are not gazetted and are issued without going through the full consensus process. They are pre-standards 'tested' over two years before assessment on their suitability for approval as Singapore Standards. TRs can, therefore, become Singapore Standards after two years, continue as Technical References for further comments, or be withdrawn.

SPRING has appointed Toppan Leefung Pte Ltd to manage the sale of the Singapore Standards and Technical References, as well as international and overseas standards that SPRING is permitted to sell in Singapore. Toppan Leefung's contact details are:

Toppan Leefung Pte Ltd 1 Kim Seng Promenade #18-01 Great World City East Tower Singapore 237994 Operating Hours: Mon to Fri: 9.30am to 6.00pm Closed on Saturdays, Sundays and Public Holidays Customer Service Hotline: + (65) 6826 9691 Fax: + (65) 6820 3341 Email: singaporestandardseshop@toppanleefung.com

Singapore Standards eShop: http://www.singaporestandardseshop.sg

Labeling and Marking

The "SAFETY Mark" is given by SPRING for all registered controlled goods. The "SAFETY Mark" helps consumers and traders to identify registered controlled goods. All registered controlled goods must be individually marked with the "SAFETY Mark" either on the product or packaging. The "SAFETY Mark" comprises a "safety logo" enclosed in a square on

the left and the words "SAFETY MARK" within a rectangle on the right. Below these is a unique 8-digit registration number traceable to the registrant and the registered models.

U.S. suppliers (or their local representative) of controlled products planning to expand sales into Singapore should check with SPRING or other relevant regulatory authorities before exporting.

Telecommunication equipment imported for use in Singapore is subject to "Type Approval" by the Infocomm Development Authority of Singapore. More information can be obtained from the website: http://www.ida.gov.sg.

For the construction industry, the Building and Construction Authority uses the Construction Quality Assessment System (CONQUAS) to objectively rate building works. Details are available at the website: http://www.bca.gov.sg

Contacts

SPRING Singapore 1 Fusionopolis Walk #01-02 South Tower, Solaris Singapore 138628 Tel: (65) 6278 6666 Fax: (65) 6659 0640 Website: http://www.spring.gov.sg

Ms CHANG Kwei Fern, Director Accreditation Division Email: sac@spring.gov.sg

Mr Michael ONG, Director, Consumer Product Safety & Weights & Measure Division Email: enquiry@spring.gov.sg

Mr CHEONG Tak Leong, Deputy Director, Standards Division Email: stn@spring.gov.sg

Standards contact at Commercial Service, Singapore:

Ms CHIA Swee Hoon, Senior Commercial Specialist Email: Sweehoon.chia@trade.gov

TRADE AGREEMENTS

As a nation with a small domestic market that depends on imports for food, energy and industrial raw materials, Singapore places the highest priority on the multilateral trading system embodied by the World Trade Organization (WTO) . As a member of the WTO, Singapore believes that the WTO can provide a stable framework for developing sound multilateral rules that ensure that goods and services can flow freely with minimum impediment. The primary objective of Singapore's trade policy is to guard its trading interest by ensuring a free and open international trading environment.

In tandem with its support of the WTO, Singapore advocates that trade efforts are undertaken in the regional context such as APEC (Asia Pacific Economic Cooperation) , ASEM (Asia-Europe Meeting) and ASEAN (Association of Southeast Asia Nations) as well as bilateral Free Trade Agreements (FTAs) to accelerate the momentum of trade liberalization and strengthen the multilateral trading system. It has actively pursued a number of legally binding arrangements with trading partners. ASEAN is preparing a roadmap for an ASEAN Economic Community by 2020 that aims to create a single enlarged market of 550 million people.

Singapore has concluded FTAs with the United States, ASEAN, Australia, New Zealand, Hashemite Kingdom of Jordan, China, India, Japan, South Korea, Costa Rica, Switzerland, Liechtenstein, Norway & Iceland, Gulf Cooperation Council, Panama, Peru and with Brunei, Chile and New Zealand under the Trans-Pacific SEP (Strategic Economic Partnership) Agreement. FTA negotiations are ongoing with Canada, Mexico, Pakistan and the Ukraine. For more information, please visit http://www.iesingapore.gov.sg or http://www.fta.gov.sg

Web Resources Accounting and Corporate Regulatory Authority (ACRA) http://www.acra.gov.sg

Agri-Food & Veterinary Authority of Singapore (AVA) http://www.ava.gov.sg

Agency for Science, Technology & Research (ASTAR) http://www.a-star.edu.sg

Building & Construction Authority of Singapore http://www.bca.gov.sg

Civil Aviation Authority of Singapore (CAAS) http://www.caas.gov.sg

Consumer Association of Singapore (CASE) http://www.case.org.sg

Customs & Excise Department (CED) http://www.customs.gov.sg

Economic Development Board Singapore (EDB Singapore) http://www.edb.gov.sg

Energy Market Authority (EMA) http://www.ema.gov.sg

Enterprise One http://www.business.gov.sg

Hotel Licensing Board (HLB) http://www.hlb.gov.sg

Health Sciences Authority http://www.hsa.gov.sg

Infocomm Development Authority of Singapore (IDA Singapore) http://www.ida.gov.sg

International Enterprise Singapore (IE Singapore) http://www.iesingapore.gov.sg

Intellectual Property Office of Singapore (IPOS) http://www.ipos.gov.sg

International Revenue Authority of Singapore (IRAS) http://www.iras.gov.sg

Monetary Authority of Singapore (MAS) http://www.mas.gov.sg National Environment Agency (NEA) http://www.nea.gov.sg

Ministry of Defence http://www.mindef.gov.sg

Ministry of Education http://www.moe.gov.sg

Ministry of Environment & Water Resources http://www.mewr.gov.sg

Ministry of Finance http://www.mof.gov.sg

Ministry of Health http://www.moh.gov.sg

Ministry of Trade & Industry http://www.mti.gov.sg

Productivity and Standards Corporation Pte Ltd (PSB Corporation Pte Ltd) http://www.psbcorp.com

Singapore Productivity and Innovation for Growth (SPRING Singapore) http://www.spring.gov.sg http://www.safety.org.sg

Standards http://www.spring.gov.sg/qualitystandards/std/pages/about-standards.aspx

Singapore IT Standards http://www.itsc.org.sg

Singapore Standards eShop http://www.singaporestandardseshop.sg

Accreditation http://www.spring.gov.sg/qualitystandards/accreditation/pages/about-accreditation.aspx

Consumer Protection (Safety Requirements) Registration Scheme

http://www.spring.gov.sg/qualitystandards/cps/pages/consumer-protection-registration scheme.aspx

ASEAN Free Trade Area http://www.aseansec.org

TRADE AND PROJECT FINANCING

METHODS OF PAYMENT

Singapore has a well-developed financial system, which offers a full range of export finance instruments. Shipments are generally made under letters of credit and sight drafts (or bills of exchange) , depending on the exporter's preference and the extent of past dealings with the purchaser. Standard credit terms are generally 30 to 90 days and they are allocated on market terms. Quotations are generally made on a C.I.F. basis. Prices given in U.S. dollars should be clearly stated as such to avoid confusion with the Singapore dollar. Exporters making quotations in Singapore dollars should consult their banks for the prevailing exchange rate. Singapore uses the metric system, so it is often beneficial for price/quantity quotations to be prepared accordingly.

BANKING SYSTEM

Singapore is a reputable international financial center. It is a leading world foreign exchange trading center and trader in derivatives. There are about 900 local and foreign banking and financial institutions in Singapore that provide services relating to trade financing, foreign exchange, derivatives products, capital markets activities, loan syndication, underwriting, mergers and acquisitions, asset management, securities trading, financial advisory services and specialized insurance services.

The Monetary Authority of Singapore (MAS) performs all the functions of a central bank including the issuance of currency. The unit of legal tender is the Singapore dollar. The MAS is a wholly owned and controlled statutory board under the Ministry of Finance; it is responsible for all matters relating to banks and financial institutions. Besides regulating financial institutions, the MAS has a Financial Sector Promotion Department that promotes new financial activities, develops IT infrastructure and manpower resources for the financial sector, and designs appropriate incentives to attract international financial firms to conduct activities in Singapore.

Singapore has a deposit insurance program following the enactment of the Deposit Insurance Act in October 2005 which took effect from April 1 of the following year. The program compensates individuals and charities for the first S$20,000 (about US$16,000) of their Singapore dollar deposits in standard savings, current and fixed deposit accounts, net of liabilities, in the event that their bank or finance company fails. The program compensates depositors through a fund built up from contributions by full banks and finance companies.

In the worst case scenario where a bank or insurance company fails, especially in view of the current global financial crisis, a safety net is provided by deposit insurance and the policy owners' protection fund respectively. Deposit insurance, which is an explicit guarantee on deposits, provides a payout of up to S$20,000 to each individual depositor per bank. For deposits in excess of the payout, individual depositors can also claim from assets of the failed bank. Depositors and policyholders, in the case of an insurance company, would rank ahead of unsecured creditors and shareholders in their claims. The MAS, together with the Singapore Deposit Insurance Corporation (SDIC) that administers the deposit insurance scheme, will review the coverage limit regularly, taking into consideration the objectives of the scheme and international norms.

In October 2008, the Singapore government temporarily guaranteed all Singapore dollar and foreign currency deposits of individuals and non-bank customers in banks, finance companies and merchant banks licensed and supervised by the MAS. This was because of the widespread panic caused by the collapse of many well-known financial institutions then. This guarantee expired as of end 2010 but the expiry will not affect the operation of Singapore's deposit insurance scheme.

The MAS is known and respected as an effective regulator/supervisor of the financial services sector. The MAS currently requires branches of foreign banks operating in Singapore to meet the minimum BIS capital adequacy ratio (CAR) of 6.0%, but locally incorporated banks meet a more stringent ratio of 10.0%. Financial statements are in compliance with international standards and internationally recognized accounting firms perform audits. In October 2010, total assets/liabilities of Singapore's domestic banking sector amounted to US$423 billion, which is an increase from the previous year.

FOREIGN-EXCHANGE CONTROLS

Singapore has no significant restrictions on remittances, foreign exchange transactions and capital movements. It also does not restrict reinvestment or repatriation of earnings and capital. In addition, The U.S.-Singapore FTA underpins the shared commitment of the United States and Singapore to the free transfer of capital, unimpeded by regulatory restrictions.

U.S. BANKS AND LOCAL CORRESPONDENT BANKS

As of December 2010, there were 26 foreign full service licensees, 50 wholesale licensees, and 38 offshore licensees operating in Singapore. Of the 26 foreign full service licensees, the government has granted "qualifying full bank" (QFB) licenses to eight foreign banks, including one U.S. bank. Except in retail banking, Singapore laws do not distinguish operationally between foreign and domestic banks. The four U.S. banks with a license to provide full banking services are: Bank of America, Citibank N.A., Citibank Singapore Limited, and JPMorgan Chase Bank N.A.. The MAS maintains a full directory of local and foreign banks and financial institutions (including U.S.headquartered entities) that operate in Singapore. Access to this directory is free and is available at the following website: http://www.mas.gov.sg/fi_directory/index.html .

PROJECT FINANCING

Singapore is considered a developed country and does not receive development assistance from multilateral institutions.

U.S. government agencies such as the Export-Import Bank of the United States and the

U.S.Department of Agriculture, OPIC, as well as state and local bodies (e.g., Small Business Administration) offer a variety of programs to assist exporters with their financing and insurance needs. Firms seeking such assistance should contact their nearest Export Assistance Center (http://www.export.gov/comm_svc/eac.html) .

Web Resources Export-Import Bank of the United States: http://www.exim.gov Country Limitation Schedule: http://www.exim.gov/tools/country/country_limits.html OPIC: http://www.opic.gov Trade and Development Agency: http://www.tda.gov/ SBA's Office of International Trade: http://www.sba.gov/oit/ USDA Commodity Credit Corporation: http://www.fsa.usda.gov/ccc/default.htm

U.S.Agency for International Development: http://www.usaid.gov

(Insert a link to the applicable Multilateral Development Bank here and any other pertinent web resources.)

BUSINESS TRAVEL

BUSINESS CUSTOMS

Business discussions are usually conducted in a very straightforward manner. English is widely spoken and most businesspeople are skilled and technically knowledgeable. Most agents/distributors have visited the United States and often handle several American product lines. Corruption is virtually non-existent.

Many Singapore business people are of ethnic Chinese background, and many of them will have “Western” first names (e.g., Nancy Goh) . Those who do not will have only their Chinese name on their business card, in which case the family name is listed first. Mr. Chan Yiu Kei would be addressed as “Mr. Chan” and Ms. Wong Ai Lan as “Ms. Wong.”

The names of business people of Malay or Indian descent are written and spoken as given name followed by family name. For the sake of politeness and respect, it is wise to address a businessperson by the last name rather than the first name until invited to use a given name. When in doubt it is not impolite to ask. The common and polite Singaporean phrase is ‘How shall I address you?’

Business cards are a must as they are immediately exchanged during business and social meetings. The East Asian practice of presenting a business card with both hands is observed. There is no need to have special business cards printed in Chinese.

Located a few degrees from the Equator, Singapore has a constant tropical climate year-round. Daytime temperatures average between 85 and 90 degrees Fahrenheit. Humidity is very high and rain showers are frequent. Temperatures at night average between 76 and 80 degrees. All public buildings, indoor restaurants and taxis are air-conditioned.

Summer-weight suits/dresses, several dress-shirts, and an umbrella are recommended for the traveler. Singapore business dress is a long-sleeved shirt and tie for men, although one will not be out of place without a tie. Some formal meetings call for a coat and tie. Businesswomen wear light-weight attire. Evening dinner-dress is a shirt and tie for men but there isn’t a strict dress code for women.

Tipping is not customary in Singapore. Restaurants automatically add a 10% service charge and a 7% goods and services tax (GST) to the bill. Singapore's unit of currency is the Singapore dollar. Travelers' checks and currency may be exchanged in the baggage claim area at Changi Airport (at a reasonable rate) or at any hotel (at a less favorable rate) . Singapore features dozens of Government-authorized "money changers" located in major shopping centers, offering competitive rates and they will usually accept U.S. travelers' checks as well as major currencies. International credit cards are widely accepted in hotels, restaurants and retail shops. ATMs that accept

U.S. cards are widely available.

Travel Advisory

Americans traveling abroad should regularly monitor the Department of State's, Bureau of Consular Affairs' web site at http://travel.state.gov/, where the current Travel Warnings and Travel Alerts, as well as the Worldwide Caution, can be found. Up-to-date information on safety and security can also be obtained by calling 1-888-407-4747 toll-free in the U.S. and Canada or, for callers outside the U.S. and Canada, a regular toll line at 1-202-501-4444. These numbers are available from 8:00 a.m. to 8:00 p.m. Eastern Time, Monday through Friday (except U.S. federal holidays) .

The Department of State urges American citizens to take responsibility for their own personal security while traveling overseas. For general information about appropriate measures travelers can take to protect themselves in an overseas environment, see the Department of State's pamphlet A Safe Trip Abroad. (http://travel.state.gov/travel/tips/safety/safety_1747.html)

While in a foreign country, a U.S. citizen is subject to that country's laws and regulations, which sometimes differ significantly from those in the United States and may not afford the protections available to the individual under U.S. law. Penalties for breaking the law can be more severe than those in the United States for similar offenses. Persons violating Singapore laws, even unknowingly, may be expelled, arrested or imprisoned.

There are strict penalties for possession and use of drugs as well as for trafficking in illegal drugs. Visitors should be aware of Singapore's strict laws and penalties for a variety of actions that might not be illegal or might be considered minor offenses in the United States. Commercial disputes that may be handled as civil suits in the United States can escalate to criminal cases in Singapore and may result in heavy fines and prison sentences.

Singapore customs authorities enforce strict regulations concerning temporary import and export of items such as weapons, illegal drugs, certain religious materials and pornographic material. Singapore customs authorities' definition of "weapon" is very broad, and, in addition to firearms, includes many items which are not necessarily seen as weapons in the United States, such as dive knives, kitchen knives, handcuffs and expended shell casings. Carrying any of these items without permission may result in immediate arrest. All baggage is x-rayed at every port of entry, so checked baggage will also be inspected for regulated items.

Generally, there are four types of dutiable goods in Singapore: alcoholic beverages, tobacco, gasoline and motor vehicles. Travelers entering Singapore at any port of entry must approach an Immigration and Checkpoints Authority (ICA) officer at the "Red Channel" for payment of duty (e.g. alcohol and tobacco) and goods and services tax (GST) if you have dutiable goods which exceed the GST relief or duty-free concession. It is an offence to proceed to the "Green Channel" for clearance if you have items that are subject to payment of duty and/or GST.

The State Departments Consular Information Sheet on Singapore can be found at: http://travel.state.gov/travel/cis_pa_tw/cis/cis_1017.html

VISA REQUIREMENTS

U.S.citizens do not need a visa if their visit to Singapore is for business or social purposes and their stay is for 90 days or less. Travelers to the region should note that Singapore and some neighboring countries do not allow Americans to enter under any circumstances with fewer than six months of validity remaining on their passport. Travelers should note that there are also very strict penalties for overstaying their visas.

Specific information about entry requirements for Singapore may be obtained from the Embassy of the Republic of Singapore at 3501 International Place NW, Washington, DC 20008, tel. (202) 537-3100. Visit the Embassy of Singapore's web site at http://www.mfa.gov.sg/washington/ for the most current visa information.

U.S.companies should note that Singapore is part of the Visa Waiver Program and that eligible nationals of Singapore are able to travel to the United States without a visa for tourist and business travel of 90 days or less provided they possess an e-passport and an approved authorization through the Electronic System for Travel Authorization (ESTA) . Third country nationals living and working in Singapore may have to obtain a visa before visiting the United States. U.S. Companies that require travel of foreign businesspersons to the United States should be advised that security evaluations are handled via an interagency process. Visa applicants should go to the following links

State Department Visa Website: http://travel.state.gov/visa/

U.S.Embassy, Singapore: http://singapore.usembassy.gov/

ESTA: https://esta.cbp.dhs.gov

TELECOMMUNICATIONS

Telecommunications and Internet facilities in Singapore are state-of-the-art, providing high-quality communications with the rest of the world. For mobile phone users, third generation (3G) networks and services were rolled out in early 2005. Consumers can currently receive wireless data through their mobile phones at speeds of up to 21 megabits per second (Mbps) . Internet connections are available in most hotels. There are three main mobile telephony providers (and seven mobile virtual network operators or MVNOs) and 98 Internet Services Providers. The mobile penetration rate is above 140%. Household broadband penetration is at 80%.

Internet users can go online for free at close to 7,500 Wi-Fi hot spots island-wide at public places such as shopping malls, town centers and the business district. Called Wireless@SG, this wireless broadband service offers free Internet access at a speed of up to 1Mbps to anyone who signs up for an account. For those who require higher speeds on this nationwide network, they can take up higher speed paid-subscription plans offered by one of the three Wireless@SG operators. (http://www.infocomm123.sg/wireless) .

As of end-2010, 60% of homes and offices have access to the new, ultra high-speed, all-fiber Next Generation Nationwide Broadband Network (Next Gen NBN) . By mid-2012, 95% of the nation will have access to the Next Gen NBN. It is envisioned that this will eventually provide a nationwide ultra-high speed broadband access of 1 gigabit per second (Gbps) and more, to all physical addresses including homes, schools, government buildings, businesses and hospitals. Besides a nationwide broadband network infrastructure, Singapore is well connected by multiple satellite and submarine cable systems with more than 67 terabits per second (Tbps) of potential capacity supporting international and regional telecoms connectivity. It has more than 830 Gbps of international internet bandwidth connectivity to economies such as the US, China, Japan, India, as well as some countries in Europe and ASEAN.

TRANSPORTATION

Situated at the crossroads of international shipping and air routes, Singapore is a center for transportation and communication in Southeast Asia. With more than 80 airlines serving 196 cities in 60 countries, Singapore's Changi Airport has established itself as a major aviation hub in the Asia Pacific region. Singapore was the world's second busiest container port in 2010. The country is linked by road and rail to Malaysia.

Taxis are abundant, metered, safe, inexpensive and air-conditioned, and most drivers speak English. Drivers should be given place names for the destination as these are often more familiar than street names. Traffic flow is good. The Government limits the total number of cars on the road through heavy fees/taxes and imposes a surcharge on vehicles entering the Central Business District during peak hours. In addition, an exceptionally clean, efficient subway system links the major business/shopping areas.

LANGUAGE

English is widely spoken in Singapore. It is the language of business, government, education and the media. Many business people are highly educated and have traveled extensively

HEALTH

Good medical care is widely available in Singapore and high-end medical tourism is a growing business. Doctors and hospitals expect immediate payment for health services by credit card or cash and generally do not accept U.S. health insurance. Recipients of health care should be aware that the Ministry of Health auditors in certain circumstances may be granted access to patient medical records without the consent of the patient, and in certain circumstances, physicians may be required to provide information relating to the diagnosis or treatment without the patient's consent.

MEDICAL INSURANCE: The Department of State strongly urges Americans to consult with their medical insurance company prior to traveling abroad to confirm whether their policy applies overseas and whether it will cover emergency expenses such as a medical evacuation. Please see information on medical insurance overseas .

OTHER HEALTH INFORMATION: Information on vaccinations and other health precautions may be obtained from the Centers for Disease Control and Prevention's automated information line for international travelers at 877-FYI-TRIP (877-394-8747) or via http://wwwn.cdc.gov/travel/default.aspx. For information about outbreaks of infectious diseases abroad consult the World Health Organization's website at http://www.who.int/en . The World Health Organization also provides additional health information at http://www.who.int/ith . The Singapore Ministry of Health's web site, http://www.moh.gov.sg/ , contains helpful health information.

LOCAL TIME, BUSINESS HOURS, AND HOLIDAYS

Singapore is twelve hours ahead of Eastern Daylight Savings or thirteen hours ahead of Eastern Standard Time. Normal business hours are 8:30 a.m. - 5:00 p.m., Monday-Friday. Government of Singapore agencies and many private sector companies are closed for business on Saturday. Shops are normally open every day from 10:00 am – 9:00 p.m.

The American Embassy closes on American and local holidays. The dates on which holidays are observed are listed below: * The following Monday will be a public holiday.

OFFICIAL DATE	U.S. HOLIDAY	LOCAL HOLIDAY	DATE OBSERVED
January 1	New Year's Day	New Year's Day	Friday, December 31
3rd Mon in January	Birthday of Martin Luther King, Jr.		Monday, January 17
February 3 – 4		Chinese New Year	Thursday, February 3 Friday, February 4
3rd Mon in Feb	Washington's Birthday		Monday, February 21
April 22		Good Friday	Friday, April 22
*May 1 (Sunday)		Labor Day	Monday, May 2
May 17		Vesak Day	Tuesday, May 17
Last Mon in May	Memorial Day		Monday, May 30
July 4	Independence Day		Monday, July 4
August 9		National Day	Tuesday, August 9

August 30		Hari Raya Puasa	Tuesday, August 30
1st Mon in September	Labor Day		Monday, September 5
2nd Mon in October	Columbus Day		Monday, October 10
** October 26		Deepavali	Wednesday, October 26
*November 6 (Sunday)		Hari Raya Haji	Monday, November 7
November 11	Veteran's Day		Friday, November 11
4th Thu in November	Thanksgiving		Thursday, November 24
*December 25 (Sunday)	Christmas	Christmas	Monday, December 26
*January 1, 2012 (Sunday)	New Year	New Year	Monday, January 2

** The date for Deepavali, October 26, 2011, will be checked against the Indian Almanac when it is available. Should there be a change in this date, the Ministry of Manpower will issue a press release to announce the change.

TEMPORARY ENTRY OF MATERIALS AND PERSONAL BELONGINGS

There is no restriction on the temporary entry of laptop computers, software and exhibition materials into the country. Please see Chapter 5 on temporary goods entry requirement.

Web Resources http://www.customs.gov.sg/topNav/hom/ http://www.mfa.gov.sg/washington/ http://travel.state.gov/travel/cis_pa_tw/cis/cis_1017.html http://www.cdc.gov/travel/seasia.htm http://travel.state.gov/visa/ http://wwwn.cdc.gov/travel/default.aspx. http://www.who.int/en http://www.who.int/ith

https://esta.cbp.dhs.gov http://www.moh.gov.sg/ http://singapore.usembassy.gov/ http://travel.state.gov/travel/cis_pa_tw/cis/cis_1470.html

IMPORTANT CONTACTS

Singapore Government Agencies

Accounting & Corporate Regulatory Authority – http://www.acra.gov.sg

Agency for Science, Technology and Research (ASTAR) – http://www.a-star.edu.sg

Building & Construction Authority – http://www.bca.gov.sg

Central Provident Fund Board – http://www.cpf.gov.sg

Centre for Drug Administration (CDA) – http://www.hsa.gov.sg

Centre for Forensic Medicine (CFM) – http://www.hsa.gov.sg

Centre for Medical Device Regulation (CMDR) – http://www.hsa.gov.sg

Civil Aviation Authority of Singapore – http://www.caas.gov.sg

Economic Development Board – http://www.sedb.com

Health Promotion Board – http://www.hpb.gov.sg

Immigration & Checkpoints Authority – http://www.ica.gov.sg

Infocomm Development Authority of Singapore – http://www.ida.gov.sg

Inland Revenue Authority of Singapore – http://www.iras.gov.sg

Institute for Infocomm Research – http://www.i2r.a-star.edu.sg

Institute of Microelectronics – http://www.ime.a-star.edu.sg

Intellectual Property Office of Singapore – http://www.ipos.gov.sg

International Enterprise Singapore – http://www.iesingapore.gov.sg

JTC Corporation – http://www.jtc.gov.sg

Land Transport Authority (LTA) – http://www.lta.gov.sg

Media Development Authority – http://www.mda.gov.sg

MediaCorp – http://www.mediacorp.com.sg

Ministry of Community Development,

Youth and Sports – http://www.mcys.gov.sg Ministry of Defence – http://www.mindef.gov.sg

Ministry of Education – http://www.moe.edu.sg

Ministry of Finance – http://www.mof.gov.sg

Ministry of Health – http://www.moh.gov.sg

Ministry of Information, Communications and the Arts – http://www.mica.gov.sg Ministry of Law – http://www.minlaw.gov.sg

Ministry of Manpower – http://www.mom.gov.sg

Ministry of National Development – http://www.mnd.gov.sg

Ministry of the Environment and Water Resources – http://www.mewr.gov.sg

Ministry of Trade and Industry – http://www.mti.gov.sg Ministry of Transport – http://www.mot.gov.sg

Monetary Authority of Singapore – http://www.mas.gov.sg

PSA Corporation Limited – http://www.psa.com.sg

Public Utilities Board – http://www.pub.gov.sg

Singapore Customs – http://www.customs.gov.sg

Singapore Power Ltd. – http://www.singaporepower.com.sg

Singapore Science Centre – http://www.science.edu.sg

Singapore Sports Council – http://www.ssc.gov.sg

Singapore Tourism Board – http://www.stb.com.sg

Spring Singapore – http://www.spring.gov.sg

Urban Redevelopment Authority – http://www.ura.gov.sg

Singapore government website – http://www.gov.sg

Singapore website - http://www.sg

Trade Associations/Chambers of Commerce in Singapore

American Chamber of Commerce in Singapore – http://www.amcham.org.sg

Association of Process Industry – http://www.aspri.com.sg

Association of Small and Medium Enterprises – http://www.asme.org.sg

Association of the Telecommunications Industry of Singapore – http://www.atis.org.sg

General Insurance Association of Singapore – http://www.gia.org.sg

The Institution of Engineers, Singapore – http://www.ies.org.sg

Instrumentation & Control Society Singapore – http://www.singics.org.sg

Life Insurance Association Singapore – http://www.lia.org.sg

Motor Traders Association of Singapore – http://www.mta.org.sg

Packaging Council of Singapore – http://www.packaging.org.sg

Real Estate Developers' Association of Singapore – http://www.redas.com

Recording Industry Association (Singapore) – http://www.rias.org.sg

Singapore Association of Pharmaceutical Industries (SAPI) – http://www.sapi.org.sg

Singapore Business Federation – http://www.sbf.org.sg

Singapore Chinese Chamber of Commerce and Industry – http://www.sccci.org.sg

Singapore Computer Society – http://www.scs.org.sg

Singapore Cycle & Motor Traders' Association – http://www.autoparts.com.sg

Singapore Dental Association – http://www.sda.org.sg

Singapore Exchange Ltd. – http://www.sgx.com

Singapore Furniture Industries Council – http://www.singaporefurniture.com

Singapore Indian Chamber of Commerce and Industry – http://www.sicci.com

Singapore Industrial Automation Association – http://www.siaa.org

Singapore Infocomm Technology Federation – http://www.sitf.org.sg

Singapore Institute of Architects – http://www.sia.org.sg

Singapore Institute of Planners- http://www.sip.org.sg

Singapore Institute of Surveyors & Valuers – http://www.sisv.org.sg

Singapore International Chamber of Commerce – http://www.sicc.com.sg

Singapore Jewellers Association – http://www.sja.org.sg

Singapore Malay Chamber of Commerce – http://www.smcci.org.sg

Singapore Manufacturers' Federation – http://www.smafederation.org.sg

Singapore Medical Association – http://www.sma.sg

Singapore Plastic Industry Association – http://www.spia.org.sg

Singapore Precision Engineering & Tooling Association – http://www.speta.org

Singapore Retailers Association – http://www.retail.org.sg/

Singapore Shipping Association – http://www.ssa.org.sg

Singapore Society of Radiographers – http://www.ssr.org.sg

Singapore Timber Association – http://www.singaporetimber.com

Textile and Fashion Federation (Singapore) – http://www.taff.org.sg

The Association of Banks in Singapore – http://www.abs.org.sg

The Singapore Contractors Association Ltd. (SCAL) – http://www.scal.com.sg

US - Asean Business Council, Inc. – http://us-asean.org

LIST OF BANKS

American Express Bank Ltd.
16 Collyer Quay
Hitachi Tower
Singapore 049318
Tel: (65) 538-4833 Fax: (65) 534-3022
Website: www.americanexpress.com
General Manager: Mr. Edward Sadler

Bank of America
9 Raffles Place
Republic Plaza Tower 1
#18-00
Singapore 048619
Tel: (65) 239-3101 Fax: (65) 239-3137
Website: bankofamerica.com
President Asia: Mr. Calm McCarthy

The Chase Manhattan Bank
168 Robinson Road
#14-00 Capital Tower
Singapore 068912
Tel: (65) 291-1298 Fax: (65) 392-7375
Website:
Chief Executive Officer:

Citibank
3 Temasek Avenue
#14-00 Centennial Tower
Singapore 039190
Tel: (65) 224-2611 Fax: (65) 224-8172
Website: www.citibank.com.sg
Country Chief Officer: Mr. Sunil Sreenivasan

Development Bank of Singapore Ltd.
6, Shenton Way,
DBS Building, Tower 1, 46th Floor,
Singapore 068809
Tel : (65) 878-1111 Fax : (65) 222-7543
Website: www.dbs.com.sg
Chief Executive Officer: Mr. Philippe Paillart

Bank One
9 Raffles Place
#29-02 Republic Plaza
Singapore 048619
Tel: (65) 438-2488 Fax: (65) 438-2070
Website: www.international.bankone.net
First VP & Region Head, Southeast Asia: Mr. DennisPortelli

First Union National Bank
80 Raffles Place, UOB Plaza 2
#11-20
Singapore 048624

Tel: (65) 395-2525 Fax: (65) 395-2526
Website: www.firstunion.com/international
Senior Vice President: Ms. Gwynno Master

Bank of Hawaii
77 Robinson Road
#10-03 SIA Building
Singapore 068896
Tel: (65) 538-5248 Fax: (65) 536-9430
Website: www.boh.com
General Manager: Mr. Donald J. Huse

Merrill Lynch International Bank Ltd
2 Raffles Link
Marina Bayfront
Singapore 039392
Tel: (65) 331-3888 Fax: (65) 331-3500
Website: www.ml.com
Chairman: Mr. Raymond YU

Morgan Guaranty Trust Co. Of New York
6 Shenton Way
#32-08 DBS Building Tower 2
Singapore 068809
Tel: (65) 220-8144 Fax: (65) 326-9981
Website: www.jpmorgan.com
Managing Director: Ms. Jeanette Wong

The Bank of New York
1 Temasek Avenue
#02-01 Millenia Tower
Singapore 039192
Tel: (65) 432-0222 Fax: (65) 337-4302
Website: bankofny.com
Managing Director: Mr. Jai Arya

The Northern Trust Company
80 Raffles Place
46th Floor, UOB Plaza 1
Singapore 048624
Tel: (65) 437-6666 Fax: (65) 437-6609
Website: ntrs.com
General Manager: Mr. Jeffrey Conover

Overseas-Chinese Banking Corporation Ltd.
65, Chulia Street OCBC Centre
Singapore 049513
Tel: (65) 535-7222 Fax: (65) 533-7955
Website: ocbc.com.sg
CEO: Mr. Alex Au

Overseas Union Bank Ltd.
1, Raffles Place,
OUB Centre,
Singapore 048616
Tel: (65) 533-8686 Fax: (65) 530-2213
Website: www.oub2000.com.sg
Vice-Chairman & CEO: Mr. Peter SEAH

HSBC Republic Bank (Suisse) SA

21 Collyer Quay
21 Floor, HSBC Building
Singapore 049320
Tel: (65) 224-0077 Fax: (65) 225-5769
Managing Director: Mr. John C. Hanson

United Overseas Bank Group Ltd.
80, Raffles Place, OUB Plaza,
Singapore 048624
Tel: (65) 539-2000 Fax: (65) 534-2334
Website: www.uobgroup.com
Chairman: Mr. WEE Cho Yaw

SELECTED BUSINESS OPPORTUNITIES WITH THE GOVERNMENT

REGISTRATION AS A GOVERNMENT CONTRACTOR/SUPPLIER OF EXPENDITURE & PROCUREMENT

Policies Unit(EPPU) , Ministry of Finance

FREQUENTLY ASKED QUESTIONS ON REGISTRATION AS A GOVERNMENT SUPPLIER

1.	**Question:**	Where is EPPU located?
	Answer:	EPPU is located at the Treasury at 100 High Street, #03-02, Singapore 179434.
2.	**Question:**	What are the official working hours of EPPU?
	Answer:	8.30a.m.to 5.00p.m. from Mondays to Fridays (Office is however closed from 12.30p.m. to 1.30p.m.) 8.30a.m. to 1.00p.m on Saturdays.
3.	**Question:**	How to apply as a Government Supplier?
	Answer:	Applicants for registration must complete the prescribed Form A , (Application As A Government Supplier) and submit together with the latest audited financial accounts , evidence of the relevant track record , Performance Report from client and the Non-refundable processing fee.
4.	**Question:**	How to obtain the EPPU application form?
	Answer:	The Application Form as well as the Guidelines can be downloaded through Internet (The Web Site address is http://www.gebiz.gov.sg/) , or by mail (to provide a self addressed return envelope with a cheque of $5/-) , or from EPPU, MOF at the Treasury, 100 High Street, #03-02, Singapore 179434.
5.	**Question:**	What are the processing fees for registration as a new Government supplier?
	Answer:	$60/- per Registration Head of Supply subject to a maximum of $600/- (for 10 Heads of Supply, or more) for new applications and up-grading.
6.	**Question:**	What are the criteria adopted by EPPU?
	Answer:	Based on the following 2 fundamental criteria, viz: a. Financial Resources - Supplier must have a positive net worth of at least 5% of the financial grade which they are applying (Net Worth is defined as paid-up capital and accumulated reserves) b. Experience - Supplier must adduce evidence of relevant performance track records of contract values from a single client company (either from the government or private sector) over one year. The amounts should not less than four times below the financial grade which they are applying.
7.	**Question:**	Can a newly set-up company be registered as a Government Supplier?
	Answer:	Where supplier has no audited financial statement and relevant track records, it will be considered based entirely on its net worth multiplied by 20 times less 4 levels of the financial grade.
8.	**Question:**	How to apply for Supplementary/Replacement Registration Card ?

	Answer:	Fax request to EPPU and post a cheque of $10/- for each Supplementary/ Replacement Registration Card.
9.	**Question:**	What is the highest Financial Grade/Limit be granted for a Sole proprietorship or Partnership companies?
	Answer:	Sole proprietorship or partnership companies will only be considered for registration up to grade S4 ($500,000) for all heads. These companies will only be considered for upgrading of registration if they are incorporated as private limited or public companies.
10.	**Question:**	What is the time taken for an application to be approved?
	Answer:	Generally, the lead time is 7 days for new applications.
11.	**Question:**	Can one application form be used to apply for many heads?
	Answer:	You can apply at least 8 Supply Heads under the prescribed Form, if the space is not enough, you can use a separate sheet of form (photocopy them) .
12.	**Question:**	We have registered with BCA for the construction head, must we registered with EPPU as well?
	Answer:	BCA is the authority for evaluating and approval for all the Construction and Engineering Heads and EPPU is the authority for evaluating and approval for the general supply of goods and services; supplier would therefore need to register only with EPPU for the general supply/service heads.

REGISTRATION AS A GOVERNMENT SUPPLIER WITH MINISTRY OF FINANCE - EPPU (GUIDELINES FOR APPLICANTS)

1 Current practice requires business entities desiring to supply goods and/or services, classified under the Heads of Supply given in Appendix A, to the Public Sector (i.e. Government Ministries/Departments, Hospitals, Schools, institutions, Statutory Boards, and other public sector organisations) to be registered with the Expenditure & Procurement Policies Unit (**EPPU**) , Ministry of Finance at The Treasury, 100 High Street, #03-02, Singapore 179434.

2 If the goods and/or services provided by the business entity do not fall within the broad categories given in Appendix **A**, the applicant should contact the **EPPU** for advice before submitting its application.

3 Registration under each Head Of Supply may be for one of the Financial Categories shown in Appendix **B**.

4 The Criteria For Registration is given in Appendix **C**. The **EPPU** is not bound to accept any application notwithstanding that the applicant may have complied with the minimum requirements as set out therein nor is it bound to assign any reasons for approving or rejecting any application or for upgrading/downgrading/cancelling a firm's registration status.

5 Applicants are advised to read the contents of this "**Guide**" carefully and ensure that they fully satisfy the minimum requirements stipulated herein for registration under a particular Head of Supply or Financial Category, before submitting an application.

APPLICATION PROCEDURES

6 Applications for registration shall be made on **Form A** – "Application For Registration As A Government Supplier" which can be purchased from the **EPPU**, Ministry of Finance at The Treasury, 100 High Street, #03-02, Singapore 179434 or downloaded from the **Internet** (our Web Site address is

http://www.gebiz.gov.sg/) . Enquiries on registration procedures and guidelines may be referred to the Suppliers' Registration Officer at Telephone No **3333428** during normal office hours.

7 Applications must be clearly written in **BLOCK LETTERS or TYPEWRITTEN** in English and submitted to the **EPPU** together with a **crossed cheque** for the appropriate non-refundable processing fee (see paragraph 22) . One (1) set of the following documents must accompany the original application:-

(i) A set of the latest **Certified/Audited Financial Reports** or Profit & Loss Account and Balance Sheet in English to certify the company's capital, current assets, current liabilities, sales turnover, profit/loss after tax and accumulated profit/loss carried forward to the next financial year.

(ii) Evidence of **RELEVANT** Track Records (to be translated into English if the documents are in other languages) to prove that the company has undertaken the jobs/contracts/sales when requested by EPPU.

8 All firms have to be registered with the Registry of Companies and Businesses (**RCB**) at the time of application. You may contact **RCB** at **No. 10 Anson Road, #05-01/15 International Plaza, Singapore 079903,** or **Telephone No: 3253731, Telex : RS 28395 RCBSIN, Fax No: 2251676** for general information of registration. The **RCB** print-out for local firms will be generated at the **EPPU** (if necessary) .

9 Applications from newly registered companies which have no audited statement of accounts would be considered on condition that they meet the financial requirements in Appendix B.

10 Sole proprietorship or partnership companies will only be considered for registration up to financial grade **S4** ($500,000) for all heads of supply. Further upgrading of registration status will only be considered if they are incorporated as private limited or public companies.

11 Companies incorporated under foreign jurisdiction must furnish a certified true copy of the following document issued by the Registrar of Companies (**RCB**) in Singapore, before their application would be considered:

Form 79- Return by Foreign Company Giving Particulars of Directors and Changes of Particulars; and

12 Companies seeking to register under financial categories above $500,000/- must be companies duly incorporated under the laws of Singapore or under the laws of a foreign jurisdiction that would have the same effect as if the companies have been incorporated in Singapore.

13 To encourage business, the **EPPU** is prepared to register companies that do not have the required experience/track record but have substantial financial resources. They may be registered up to three grades below the grades which they would normally be granted.

14 The applicant shall let **EPPU** officers examine the originals of all accompanying documents which form part of the application when requested.

PROCESSING OF APPLICATIONS

15 Applications are considered by a Registration Committee. It is implied that applicants have authorised the Committee to make all enquiries relating to the application it deems necessary.

16 In processing the applications, references may be obtained from the applicant's clients, customers, and from any other person or authority the Committee considers necessary. The speed of their response to the Committee's enquiries will determine the time taken to process the applications. To speed up the processing, applicants should submit the particulars of their current clients, preferably Local Government/Statutory Boards.

OUTCOME OF APPLICATIONS

17 Applicants will be informed on the outcome of their applications as soon as possible by post.

APPROVAL

8 If the application is approved, the applicant will be issued with a "Supplier's Registration Card" which will state the Heads of Supply and Financial Categories approved and the validity period of the registration (see paragraph 24

APPLICATION FOR UPGRADING

19 Registered firms that have acquired sufficient experience in their current financial categories may apply for upgrading to higher financial categories. In processing such applications, the Committee will consider whether applicants have demonstrated a sufficient standard of service and financial capabilities in projects undertaken since obtaining registration under the current financial categories to justify upgrading. (Please see Appendix B.)

CHANGE OF PARTICULARS

20 A firm registered with the **EPPU** is required to advise the Unit immediately in writing of any changes in its management status or any other pertinent particulars eg. Change of address, which may occur from time to time. Copies of the necessary supporting documents, eg Form 13 issued by the Registrar of Companies and Businesses (**RCB**) , must be submitted with the written advice. It should be noted that registration

status is accorded to a firm on the basis of its particulars at the time of application and the Unit reserves the right to revoke or modify the registration status in the event of any development or change in the firm's particulars which in the opinion of the Unit renders the firm unsuitable to be accorded the current registration status.

PROCESSING FEE

21 **An appropriate non-refundable processing fee as indicated below,** (only cheques marked **"NOT NEGOTIABLE"** OR **ACCOUNT PAYEE ONLY"** and made payable to The Expenditure and Procurement Policies Unit will be accepted) , shall accompany each application:-

Fee For New, Upgrading & Additional Registration

$60/- per Registration Head of Supply, subject to a maximum of **$600**/-(for **10** Heads of Supply, or more)

Example: Processing Fee for Registration Under 4 Heads
ie 4 x $60/- = $240/-

Processing Fee for Registration for 10 Heads Or More - a fixed sum of $600/-

Fee For Renewal Of Registration

$60/- for renewal of registration **for 1** Head of Supply

$100/- for renewal of registration **for 2 or more** Heads of Supply.

22 All fees are **NON-REFUNDABLE** irrespective of whether an application is approved or not.

CONDITIONS OF REGISTRATION

23 Registration status shall be accorded only to firms which the **EPPU** considers as having sufficient resources, experience and technical expertise to undertake contracts of a nature and size as

defined by the Registration Head of Supply and the Financial Category allocated. See Appendix **C** for Criteria for Registration. The stipulations in this "Guide" shall be taken as defining only the minimum requirements expected of an applicant.

VALIDITY OF REGISTRATION & RENEWAL

24 The validity period of any approved registration is three (3) years or shorter, depending on the circumstances, and will automatically lapse unless an application to renew is received before the expiry date. Applications for renewal shall be made on prescribed forms sent by **EPPU.** It should be submitted one and a half (1½) months **BEFORE** the expiry of the validity period of the registration. Each renewal is normally valid for three (3) years, unless otherwise stated.

AUTHORITY OF THE EXPENDITURE & PROCUREMENT POLICIES UNIT

25 The Registration Committee, whilst being the sole arbiter for emplacement of applicants under the Registration Heads of Supply and Financial Categories mentioned in this "Guide", also reserves the right to renew the registration status of the registered firms from time to time.

The following courses of action may inter alia, be taken at its sole discretion:-

(i) Upgrading or Downgrading of registration status, and financial categories;

(ii) Reducing or Amending the validity period;

(iii) Cancelling the firm's registration and deleting it from the Unit's Register.

26 The **EPPU** is not bound to accept any application or assign reasons for rejection or approval (see paragraph 4) .

27 The Supplier's Registration Card (original) must be produced as and when requested for, by any Tender Issuing Authority. New applicants who need to submit tenders, pending approval of their application, may submit the official receipts issued by the EPPU as proof of submission of their applications when requested for by the Tender Issuing Authority.

28 The Supplier's Registration Card is the property of the **EPPU** and must be surrendered to the Unit whenever a registered firm is debarred or has its registration terminated for any reason.

EXPENDITURE & PROCUREMENT
POLICIES UNIT (**EPPU**)
MINISTRY OF FINANCE

APPENDIX A

REGISTRATION HEADS OF SUPPLY

Applicants should ensure that the products/services they are currently handling fall within the Head of Supply for which they wish to be registered.

1. Applicants may apply for registration under one or more of the Heads of Supply set out below. The appropriate **non-refundable processing fees** (see Clause 21 of Guidelines) must be paid at time of application.

2. Applicants would be required upon request to adduce evidence that they have undertaken contracts to manufacture, supply, construct, service or install the items falling under each of the particular Registration Heads of Supply applied for. The evidence may be contract documents, purchase or works orders or the names of clients for whom work was done or to whom supplies were delivered.

3. Applicants should note that where debarment is imposed upon a registered firm and it is subsequently found that one or more of its partners or directors are at the same time partners or directors of one or more firms registered with the **EPPU**, each of these other firms may be similarly debarred by virtue of this relationship.

(A) HEADS OF REGISTRATION

S/No	Head Reference	Head Description	Examples of Goods/Services Covered
1.	EPU/AVP/10	Audio Visual, Photographic & Optical Products	Audio and audio visual equipment, accessories and supplies, white boards (excludes CATV systems) . Photographic equipment and supplies, including processing services. Optical equipment and supplies, eg films etc.
2.	EPU/CAA/10	Textiles, Clothing and Accoutrements	Textiles, Uniforms (including those for Armed Forces) , pyjamas, boots and shoes, belts, socks, gloves, headwear and tailoring services..
3.	EPU/CMP/10	Computer Hardware and software Products	Readily available hardware and software products, modems, accessories and computer cabling excluding computer suppliers eg diskettes, computer ribbons.
4.	EPU/CMP/20	Software Development	Software development on tailor-made basis , projects on turnkey basis and Internet Service Provider for all Internet related services and any other types of IT services.
5.	EPU/CNE/10	Communication and Navigation Systems	All communication equipment such as VHF sets, and radar system. This Head also covers equipment eg PABX systems and encoder.
6.	EPU/ECS/10	Electrical &Electronic Components	Connectors, passive components printed circuit boards, relays, solenoids, semiconductors, switches and other related items
7.	EPU/FBV/10	Food & Beverages	Food & beverages, wet & dry rations, canned food stuff, cooked food, catering services and pet food.
*8.	EPU/FFG/10	Fire Fighting, Safety & Rescue Equipment	Fire extinguishers, fire hoses, fire fighting foam and chemicals, special fire fighting tools (which do not fall under hardware & tools) , fire blankets, beaters for dousing fires, fire fighting apparel (excludes fire fighting systems) . Rescue and life support systems, ear plugs.
9.	EPU/FUR/10	Furniture, Racking, Upholstery, Painting	Manufacturing, repair and supply of wooden and metal furniture, racks and storage systems and non-mechanical office equipment, ie filing cabinets, card index cabinets, compactus, storage boxes, key cabinets including services for upholstery and spray painting.
10.	EPU/HEQ/10	Domestic Equipment &	Refrigerators, washing machines, cookers,

S/No	Head Reference	Head Description	Examples of Goods/Services Covered
		Supplies	kettles, irons, fans, television, vacuum cleaners, sewing machines, weighing scales, air-conditioners, dehumidifiers, detergents, disinfectants, soaps, toiletries, mattresses, pillows, blankets, toilet paper, towers, crockery, tarpaulin, canvas and PVC sheeting, flags, banners, curtains, polythene bags, fertilizers.
11.	EPU/HWT/10	Hardware & Tools	Workshop machinery (woodworking & metalworking) , general hardware and tools, including fastening and anchoring systems, wire-grip hoist, material handling equipment, eg trolleys..
12.	EPU/LTE/10	Laboratory Testing And Survey Equipment	Laboratory, testing, measuring, caliberating, scientific and Survey equipment. Excludes medical laboratory equipment.
13.	EPU/MAR/10	Shipbuilding, Repair and Marine Supplies	Shipbuilding, repairs, refurbishing marine and related supplies, echo sounders, diving equipment.
*14.	EPU/MSS/10	Military Spares	All military spares for vehicles, vessels and aircraft.
15.	EPU/OFE/10	Office Equipment and Supplies, Computer Supplies	Typewriters (both manual and electronic) , shredding machines, safes, photocopiers, duplicators, scanners, offset machines, word processors, calculators, dictating machines and microfilming equipment, facsimile machine (but excluding stationery items and printing) . ATM tellers, queue posts. Computer diskettes, ribbons and other related items.
16.	EPU/SCD/10	Scrap Dealers	Sales of Scrap materials, etc.
17.	EPU/SPE/10	Sports, Recreational Equipment and Supplies	Sports, recreational equipment, trophies, flowers, gifts, souvenirs, plaques and musical instruments, tents, toys, playthings, children's instructional manuals, camping equipment.
18	EPU/STA/10	Stationery and Printing	Stationery products such as paper, writing instruments etc and printing of forms and other materials, sign-crafts, books, teaching aids
*19	EPU/WAA/10	Weapons, Weapon Systems and Ammunition	All arms, ammunition (including blanks) , pyrotechnics such as thunder flashes, etc., military aircraft, military vessels and vehicles such as tanks and Armoured Personnel Carriers, hand-cuffs.

***It is the company's responsibility to obtain the relevant valid license to carry out jobs/supplies for Supply Reference EPU/FFG/10, EPU/MSS/10 and EPU/WAA/10.**

(B) HEADS OF REGISTRATION UNDER SERVICES

S/No	Head Reference	Head Description	Examples of Goods/Services Covered

S/No	Head Reference	Head Description	Examples of Goods/Services Covered
20.	EPU/SER/11	Service (Transportation, Towing)	Land, sea and air transport (inclusive of package tours) , rental of vehicles, cranes and vehicle appraisal services
21.	EPU/SER/12	Service (Laundry)	
22.	EPU/SER/13	Service (Audio Visual Production)	Photography, video CD production.
23.	EPU/SER/14	Service (Photocopying)	
24.	EPU/SER/15	Service (Microfilming)	
25.	EPU/SER/16	Service (Bookbinding)	
26.	EPU/SER/17	Service(Exhibition/Event Management)	EVENT MANAGEMENT, BOOTHS, STAGE, BACKDROP & LIGHTING ETC
27.	EPU/SER/18	Service (Advertising, Graphics)	Graphics Design
28.	EPU/SER/19	Service (Data Entry, Supply of Manpower)	Supply of skilled and unskilled manpower
29.	EPU/SER/20	Service(Publishing)	Mass Production and Distribution Capability, Editorial Service/Graphic artists support, Filming/Plating and Electronic Publishing
30.	EPU/SER/21	Service (Maintenance of System, Equipment & Computers)	Including domestic equipment
31.	EPU/SER/28	Service (Courier, Distribution of Publications)	Addressing, mailing, postal services.
32.	EPU/SER/29	Service (Maintenance of Musical Instruments)	Maintenance, Tuning & Repair of Musical Instruments
33.	EPU/SER/30	Service (Management)	Management of Car-parks, Food-courts, Kiosks & real estate management.
34.	EPU/SER/31	Service (Laboratory Testing)	Testing, monitoring
35.	EPU/SER/32	Service (Public Relations Counselling	Promotional Work
36.	EPU/SER/33	Service (Survey)	
37.	EPU/SER/34	Service (Consultant)	Professional services eg accounting, auditing , architectural, legal, insurance, engineering, veterinary services etc.

S/No	Head Reference	Head Description	Examples of Goods/Services Covered
38.	EPU/SER/35	Service (Training of Personnel)	Including recruitment & providing of manpower as trainers.
39.	EPU/SER/36	Service (Disposal & Treatment of Waste Chemicals, etc)	
40.	EPU/SER/37	Service (Undertaker)	
41.	EPU/SER/38	Service (Hiring of Miscellaneous items)	Hiring of Office Equipment, Vending Machine, Furniture, Temporary shelter including tables and chairs, etc
42.	EPU/SER/39	Service(Rental of Premises)	Includes warehousing, training, recreation, hotels, lodging services etc
43.	EPU/SER/40	Service (Marine)	For seaport, underwater services including hydrographic survey but excludes construction
44.	EPU/SER/41	Service (Childcare/Social)	Includes creche, old folks home services. Staff must be trained and possess the Childcare Certificate
45.	EPU/SER/42	Service (Storage)	For storage of computer media, documents
*46.	EPU/SER/43	Service (Security)	Supply of manpower, equipment and guard dogs, includes security escort service
47.	EPU/SER/44	Service (Grooming)	Hairdressing, manicure etc
48.	EPU/SER/46	Service (Cleaning)	All forms of cleaning eg toilet cleaning and maintenance of Aquariums and fish pond etc. This however excludes laundry service, cleaning and maintenance of building which comes under BCA.

***It is the company's responsibility to obtain the relevant valid license to carry out jobs for Supply Reference EPU/SER/43.**

(C) HEADS OF REGISTRATION UNDER MEDICAL/EQUIPMENTS

S/No	Head Reference	Head Description	Examples of Goods/Services Covered
49	EPU/XRF/21	X-Ray films	Medical X-ray films, Dental X-ray films
50	EPU/XRC/22	X-Ray related Chemicals and accessories	X-ray developer, starter, replenisher, X-ray shields etc
51	EPU/MEG/23	Medial Gases	Compressed Medical Oxygen, Liquid Nitrogen
52	EPU/BTS/24	Blood Bags and Administration Sets	Blood collection bags, blood cell processing sets, collection system etc
53	EPU/DLC/25	Dispensing and Laboratory Containers and Consumables	Bottles lotion, bags polythene, bag lab specimen, tubes blood test etc

S/No	Head Reference	Head Description	Examples of Goods/Services Covered
54	EPU/SUR/26	Surgical Implants	Heart valves and pacemakers, orthopaedic implants and appliances, intraocular lens etc
55	EPU/SGI/27	Surgical consumables and Instruments	Sutures, surgical dressing, catheters and cannulas, hospital consumables, condoms etc
56	EPU/MLS/28	Medical Laboratory Services	Outpatient Laboratory Testing, Microbiological Testing Services etc
*57	EPU/DEN/29	Dental Equipment and Materials	Crowns, bridges, dental castings etc
*58	EPU/LAB/30	Laboratory Equipment and accessories	Liquid Chromatograph, Gas Chromatograph etc
*59	EPU/MED/31	Medical Equipment and accessories	Patient monitoring equipment, Dialysis equipment and Anaesthetic equipment, hospital furniture, health-related equipment, Rehabilitation & Physiotherapy equipment etc
**60	EPU/DAP/32	Drugs and Pharmaceuticals	Paracetamol, Aspirin and Atenolol etc
61	EPU/RAP/33	Radio Pharmaceuticals	Radioactive cobalt, radioactive iodine etc
**62	EPU/LCR/34	Laboratory Chemicals and Reagents	Screening test kits, blood grouping reagents etc
63	EPU/VAC/35	Vaccines and Biological	Serums, antigens, antitoxins etc
64	EPU/MTM /36	Medical Training Materials	Instructional aids/computer programmes, charts, CD-Rom on health matters etc
65	EPU/HNS /37	Health Supplements/Non-scheduled Poisons	Health food, drug & pharmaceuticals not containing Poisons
66	EPU/DEL/38	Dental Laboratory	Lab services related to the making of dental crowns, bridges and others
67	EPU/AAD/39	Antiseptics and Disinfectants	Disinfectant solutions, such as Glutaraldehyde, Hibiscrub, Printol etc
68	EPU/STE/40	Sterilization Services	Provision of sterilization services to medical establishments

***It is the company's responsibility to obtain the relevant professional certificate of technicians to service the equipment supplied for Supply Reference EPU/DEN/29, EPU/LAB/30 and EPU/MED/31.**

**** It is the company's responsibility to obtain the relevant valid license to carry out jobs/supplies for Supply Reference EPU/DAP/32 {Poison Licence (Form A or Form C) }, EPU/LCR/34 {Hazardous Substance Licence (issued by ENV) }.**

APPENDIX B

REGISTRATION REQUISITES TRACK RECORD, PAID-UP CAPITAL

Reg Grade	Tendering Capacity ($)	Capital Net Worth ($)	Track Record (largest Contract Value or Aggregate Sales/Service from 1 client within 1 Year ($)	Turnover/Sales ($)
S1	50,000	2,500	12,000	50,000
S2	100,000	5,000	25,000	100,000
S3	250,000	12,500	62,500	250,000
S4	500,000	25,000	125,000	500,000
S5	1,000,000	50,000	250,000	1,000,000
S6	3,000,000	150,000	750,000	3,000,000
S7	5,000,000	250,000	1,250,000	5,000,000
S8	10,000,000	500,000	2,500,000	10,000,000
S9*	>10,000,000	1,500,000	>2,500,000	>10,000,000 *Paid Up Capital must be at least $1.5m
S10**	>30,000,000	4,500,000	7,500,000	>15,000,000 **Paid Up Capital must be at least $2m

1 **FOR LIMITED PRIVATE COMPANIES**

"CAPITAL NET WORTH" shall be taken to mean the sum of paid-up capital, revenue reserves, preference shares plus accumulated profit or less accumulated losses.

2 **FOR OTHER FIRMS AND BUSINESSES**

2.1 "CAPITAL NET WORTH" shall be taken to mean the sum of cash, current account, fixed deposits and bonds that are currently allocated for the applicant's business under reference plus profit or less total liabilities (ie accumulated losses or withdrawal) .

3 **FOR BOTH THE PRIVATE COMPANIES AND OTHER FIRMS**

3.1 The capital net worth must be in the **positive** at the time of application.

3.2 Subject to the value of contracts normally undertaken, a company is generally eligible for registration in a financial category not exceeding twenty times the value of its positive capital (or capital net worth) . A company seeking registration in the registration Grade **S9 & S10** must have a capital paid-up of at least $1.5 and 2 million respectively.

3.3 Applicants are required to submit their applications, as directed on the application forms.

3.4Applicants should not apply for registration in financial categories way beyond the normal value of contracts undertaken. An applicant is normally eligible for registration in a financial category approximately four times the highest contract value undertaken. For example if the normal value of contracts undertaken by the applicant is in the region of $100,000, registration in financial categories up to $500,000 may be approved. An application in the financial category of $1 million may not be approved.

APPENDIX C

CRITERIA FOR REGISTRATION

1 The stipulations set out below shall be taken as defining the minimum requirements expected of an applicant.

2 Registration shall be approved only in respect of those applicants whom the **EPPU** considers as having sufficient resources, experience and expertise to undertake contracts awarded under the registration sought.

3 In the case of an application by a sole proprietor or partnership, the applicant shall satisfy the **EPPU** that:-

(a) he/she is at least 21 years of age
(b) he/she possesses the minimum requisites stated below for the Head and Category of Registration sought and any additional requirements as may from time to time be stipulated by the **EPPU**.

4 In the case of an application from a registered company or other corporate body, the **EPPU** must be satisfied that the managing directors and/or other principal officers of the registered company or other corporate body, as the case may be, fulfil the aforesaid attributes.

CAPITAL/CAPITAL NET WORTH

5 Applications must be solvent and be backed by a sound financial and technical organisation. See Appendix B for meaning of capital or capital net worth. For first-time or re-application cases, applicants must ensure that their "capital net worth "is not in the negative, otherwise, the application will be rejected.

EXPERIENCE

6 Applicants are expected to have maintained a business or other commercial undertaking for the trading, supply, manufacture, construction and/or installation of the respective type of materials, equipment, or supplies falling under the particular Head of Registration applied for.

7 The applicant's business should also have an annual turnover, for the last one year, corresponding to the description of the financial category applied for. This figure will be looked at in relation to the values of the individual contracts awarded to the company.(Please see Appendix B.)

EXAMPLE

8 An applicant applying for registration as a supply contractor for stationery (Head EPU/STA/10) in the financial category of $100,000 will have to adduce evidence that his current business concern in Stationery has an annual turnover in the region of $100,000 and that at least one contract exceeds $25,000. If individual contracts do not exceed $25,000, registration may be approved for a lower financial category, ie $50,000.00.

9 Applicants for registration are to furnish summaries of their trading transactions, which will indicate that they have undertaken supply/trade of the required magnitude, and the name and address of the client (with the highest contract value) who shall be person of good repute and who can testify to the extent and quality of the applicant's supplies and services under the relevant Heads.

OFFICE EQUIPMENT & COMPUTER PRODUCTS

10 Applicants for registration under Office Equipment or Computer Products are generally expected to have agencies for the products handled. They are also expected to have the resources necessary to provide back-up service for the equipment.

INFORMATION ON EPPU HEAD REFERENCES & HEAD DESCRIPTION

S/NO	HEAD REFERENCES	HEAD DESCRIPTION	GOODS/SERVICES COVERED
1.	EPU/AVP/10	Audio Visual,Photographic & Optical Products	Audio and audio visual equipment, accessories and supplies, white boards (excludes CATV systems) . Photographic equipment and supplies, including processing services. Optical equipment and supplies, eg films etc.
2.	EPU/CAA/10	Textiles, Clothing and Accoutrements	Textiles, Uniforms (including those for Armed Forces) , pyjamas, boots and shoes, belts, socks, headwear and tailoring services, gloves.
3.	EPU/CMP/10	Computer Hardware and software Products	Readily available hardware and software products, modems, accessories (including computer cabling) .
4.	EPU/CMP/20	Software Development	Software development on tailor-made basis or projects on turnkey basis and Internet Service Provider for all Internet related services and any other types of IT services.
5.	EPU/CNE/10	Communication and Navigation Systems	All communication equipment as VHF sets and radar system. This Head also covers equipment and systems, encoder.
6.	EPU/ECS/10	Electronic Components	Connectors, passive components printed circuit boards, relays, solenoids, semiconductors, switches and other related items.
7.	EPU/FBV/10	Food & Beverages	Food and beverages, wet and dry rations, canned food stuff, cooked food, catering services and pet food.
*8.	EPU/FFG/10	Fire Fighting, Safety & Rescue Equipment	Fire extinguishers, fire hoses, fire fighting foam and chemicals, special fire fighting tools (which do not fall under hardware & tools) , fire blankets, beaters for dousing fires, fire fighting apparel (excludes fire fighting systems) . Rescue and life support systems, ear plugs.
9.	EPU/FUR/10	Furniture, Racking, Upholstery, Painting	Manufacturing, repair and supply of wooden and metal furniture, racks and storage systems and non-mechanical office equipment, ie filing cabinets, card index cabinets, compactus, storage boxes, key cabinets including services for upholstery and spray painting.

10.	EPU/HEQ/10	Domestic Equipment & Supplies	Refrigerators, washing machines, cookers, kettles, irons, fans, television, vacuum cleaners, sewing machines, weighing scales, air-conditioners, dehumidifiers,detergents, disinfectants, soaps, toiletries, mattresses, pillows, blankets, toilet paper, towers, crockery, tarpaulin, canvas and PVC sheeting, flags, banners, curtains, polythene bags, fertilizers.
11.	EPU/HWT/10	Hardware & Tools	General hardware and tools, including fastening and anchoring systems, wire-grip hoist.
12.	EPU/LTE/10	Laboratory Testing And Survey Equipment	Laboratory, testing, measuring, caliberating, scientific and Survey equipment. Excludes medical laboratory equipment.
13.	EPU/MAR/10	Shipbuilding, Repair and Marine Supplies	Shipbuilding, repairs, refurbishing marine and related supplies, echo sounders, diving equipment.
*14.	EPU/MSS/10	Military Spares	All spares for military vehicles, vessels and aircraft.
15.	EPU/OFE/10	Office Equipment and Supplies, Computer Supplies	Typewriters (both manual and electronic) , shredding machines, safes, photocopiers, duplicators, scanners, offset machines, word processors, calculators, dictating machines and microfilming equipment, facsimile machine (but excluding stationery items and printing) . ATM tellers, queue posts. Computer diskettes, ribbons and other related items.
16.	EPU/SCD/10	Scrap Dealers	Sales of Scrap materials, etc.
17.	EPU/SPE/10	Sports, Recreational Equipment and Supplies	Sports, recreational equipment, trophies, gifts, souvenirs, plaques and musical instruments, tents, toys, playthings, children's instructional manuals, camping equipment.
18.	EPU/STA/10	Stationery and Printing	Stationery products such as paper, writing instruments etc and printing of forms and other materials, sign-crafts, books, teaching aids.
*19.	EPU/WAA/10	Weapons, Weapon Systems and Ammunition	All arms, ammunition (including blanks) , pyrotechnics such as thunder flashes, etc., military aircraft, military vessels and vehicles such as tanks and Armoured Personnel Carriers, hand-cuffs.
20.	EPU/SER/11	Service (Transportation, Towing)	Land, sea and air transport (inclusive of package tours) , rental of vehicles, cranes.

21.	EPU/SER/12	Service (Laundry)	
22.	EPU/SER/13	Service (Audio Visual Production)	Photography
23.	EPU/SER/14	Service (Photocopying)	
24.	EPU/SER/15	Service (Microfilming)	
25.	EPU/SER/16	Service (Bookbinding)	
26.	EPU/SER/17	Service (Exhibition)	Booths, stage, backdrop & Lighting
27.	EPU/SER/18	Service (Advertising, Graphics)	Graphics Design
28.	EPU/SER/19	Service (Data Entry, Supply of Manpower)	Supply of skilled and unskilled manpower
29.	EPU/SER/20	Service (Publishing)	Mass Production and Distribution Capability, Editorial Service/Graphic artists support, Filming/Plating and Electronic Publishing
30.	EPU/SER/21	Service (Maintenance of Equipment & Computers)	Including domestic equipment
31.	EPU/SER/28	Service (Courier, Distribution of Publications)	Addressing, mailing
32.	EPU/SER/29	Service (Maintenance of Musical Instruments)	Maintenance, Tuning & Repair of Musical Instruments
33.	EPU/SER/30	Service (Management)	Management of Car-parks, Food Courts, Kiosks etc
34.	EPU/SER/31	Service (Laboratory Testing)	Testing, monitoring
35.	EPU/SER/32	Service (Public Relations Counselling	Promotional Work
36.	EPU/SER/33	Service (Survey)	
37.	EPU/SER/34	Service (Consultant)	
38.	EPU/SER/35	Service (Training of Personnel)	
39.	EPU/SER/36	Service (Treatment of Waste Chemicals, etc)	
40.	EPU/SER/37	Service (Undertaker)	
41.	EPU/SER/38	Service (Hiring of Miscellaneous items)	Hiring of Office Equipment, Vending Machine, Furniture, Temporary shelter including tables and chairs, etc

42.	EPU/SER/39	Service(Rental of Premises)	For warehousing, training, recreation etc.
43.	EPU/SER/40	Service (Marine)	For seaport, underwater services including hydrographic survey but excludes construction
44.	EPU/SER/41	Service (Childcare)	Staff must be trained and possessed the Childcare Certificate
45.	EPU/SER/42	Service (Storage)	For storage of computer media, documents
*46.	EPU/SER/43	Service (Security)	Supply of manpower, equipmentand guard dogs, includes securityescort service
47.	EPU/SER/44	Service (Grooming)	Hairdressing, manicure etc
48.	EPU/SER/46	Service (Cleaning)	All forms of cleaning excludes laundry service. Also excludes cleaning and maintenance of building which comes under CIDB.
49.	EPU/XRF/21	X-Ray films	Medical X-ray films, Dental X-ray films
50.	EPU/XRC/22	X-Ray Processing Chemicals and Contrast Media	X-ray developer, starter, replenisher, X-ray shields etc
51.	EPU/MEG/23	Medical Gases	Compressed Medical Oxygen, Liquid Nitrogen
52.	EPU/BTS/24	Blood Bags and Administration Sets	Blood collection bags, blood cell processing sets, collection system etc
53.	EPU/DLC/25	Dispensing and Laboratory Containers and Consumables	Bottles lotion, bags polythene, bag lab specimen, tubes blood test etc
54.	EPU/SUR/26	Surgical Implants	Heart valves and pacemakers, orthopaedic implants and appliances, intraocular lens
55.	EPU/SGI/27	Surgical Consumables Instruments	Sutures, surgical dressing , catheters and cannulas, hospital consumables, condoms etc
56.	EPU/MLS/28	Medical Laboratory Services	Outpatient Laboratory Testing, Microbiological Testing Services etc
57.	EPU/DEN/29	Dental Equipment and Materials	Crowns, bridges, dental castings
58.	EPU/LAB/30	Laboratory Equipment	Liquid Chromatograph, Gas Chromatograph etc
59.	EPU/MED/31	Medical Equipment	Patient monitoring equipment, Dialysis equipment and Anaesthetic equipment, hospital furniture, health-related equipment, Rehabilitation & Physiotherapy equipment

			etc
60.	EPU/DAP/32	Drugs and Pharmaceuticals	Paracetamol, Aspirin and Atenolol etc
61.	EPU/RAP/33	Radiopharmaceuticals	Radioactive cobalt, radioactive iodine etc
62.	EPU/LCR/34	Laboratory Chemicals and Reagents	Screening test kits, blood grouping reagents etc
63.	EPU/VAC/35	Vaccines and Biologicals	Serums, antigens, antitoxins
64.	EPU/MTM/36	Medical Training Materials	Instructional aids/computer programmes, charts, CD-Rom on health matters etc
65.	EPU/HNS/37	Health Supplements/Non-scheduled Poisons	Health food, drug & pharmaceuticals not containing Poisons
66.	EPU/DEL/38	Dental Laboratory	Lab Services related to the making of dental crowns, bridges and others
67.	EPU/AAD/39	Antiseptics and Disinfectants	Disinfectant solutions, such as Glutaraldehyde, Hibiscrub, Printol etc
68.	EPU/STE/40	Sterilization Services	Provision of sterilization services to medical establishments

SELECTED BUSINESS OPPORTUNITIES IN HEALTH SECTOR

PRE-QUALIFICATION OF CONTRACTORS FOR ADDITION, ALTERATION AND INTERIOR RENOVATION WORKS FOR THE SINGHEALTH GROUP

Singapore Health Services Pte Ltd (SingHealth) invites interested Contractors complying with the following requirements to apply for pre-qualification to tender for Addition, Alteration and Interior Renovation Works for the SingHealth Group which comprises of the following:

HOSPITALS

Singapore General Hospital
Changi General Hospital
KK Women's and Children's Hospital
Ang Mo Kio Community Hospital

SPECIALITY CENTRES

Singapore National Eye Centre
National Heart Centre
National Cancer Centre
National Dental Centre

POLYCLINICS

Bedok
Bukit Merah
Geylang

Institute of Health
Marine Parade
Queenstown
Tampines

Requirements:

A **Eligibility**

Either one of the listed category:

- BCA Registered Contractor, CR06 - L1 ($100,000) and above,
- BCA Registered Contractor, CW01 - G1 ($500,000) and above,
- Contractor registered with other recognised Authorities or Organisations.

B **Experience**

Preferably has experience in Hospital and Health Institution projects. However, those with experience in interior decoration works for hotel, office or other commercial buildings will also be considered.

Collection of Pre-qualification Document:

The Pre-qualification Document will be available for collection at:

Facilities Development Department
Singapore General Hospital
Block 8 Level 2
Outram Road
Singapore 169608

between **16 and 17 Apr 2010** from 1400 hours to 1700 hours.

Submission of Pre-qualification Document:

Completed documents should be submitted to the above address **not later than 1500 hours on Friday 27 Apr 01**.

Enquires:
Contact Person: Yvonne Goh
Tel: 326 6334

EXPORTS REGULATIONS

For non-controlled and non-dutiable items, you may export your goods first and obtain the Export Permits within 3 days after export. If you are not a TradeNet user, you may:

1. appoint a TradeNet Service Centre to apply for your export permit;
2. provide the export invoice and bill of lading/air waybill to your appointed TradeNet Service Centre for them to apply for your export permit;
3. collect the Export Cargo Clearance Permit (CCP) from the TradeNet Service Centre after it has been approved.

SEPARATE APPLICATIONS

Separate applications are required for:

Non-controlled goods
Controlled goods (subject to **one** competent authority in **one** application)
One Ocean B/L or one Master AWB (for direct consignments)
One House B/L or One House AWB (for consolidated shipments)
Different types of trade within the same consignment
Different final destinations within the same consignment
Used personal effects and commercial goods within the same consignment

GENERAL CONDITIONS OF APPROVAL

1. The permit is valid for one month from the date of approval.
2. All unused permits for non-controlled items must be cancelled electronically through TradeNet by the expiry date. Unused permits for controlled items must be returned to the I&E Office for cancellation by the expiry date. You are also required to inform the competent authority of the cancellation.

Please note that there may be other specific conditions of approval relating to specific transactions or types of goods exported. Failure to comply with these conditions is an offence.

USAGE OF THE CCP

Hand the photocopy of the first print of the CCP to the shipping agent (for sea consignments) ;
Show the original first print of the CCP to the airline agent (for direct air consignments) ;
Submit the permit details to the airline agent/cargo agent electronically via Air Cargo EDI System (for direct/consolidated air consignments;
Show the original first print of the CCP to Customs at the checkpoint/gate when the goods are sent in to the controlled area/Free Trade Zone (FTZ) ;

You may also appoint a freight forwarder or a cargo agent to handle the documentation and arrange for the shipment of the goods for you.

EXPORT CONTROL

Items under export control may either be under quota, subject to endorsement or licence or be prohibited from export.

We will only allow such exports when the conditions of the relevant authorities are met.

EXPORT OF GOODS UNDER ATA CARNET

In Singapore, ATA Carnets are issued only by the Singapore International Chamber of Commerce (SICC) . You should apply to the SICC for an ATA Carnet for goods temporarily exported from Singapore.

You must present the ATA Carnet (endorsed by Customs) to the carrier's agent to effect shipment of the goods. The B/L No. or AWB No. should be indicated on the top right hand corner of the ATA Carnet. The carrier's agent will:

1. retain a copy of the ATA Carnet.
2. indicate in the manifest, the ATA Carnet No. against the item which was exported under the ATA Carnet.

Where some or all of the goods are not re-imported, you must obtain the necessary export permits.

LIST OF CONTROLLED GOODS: EXPORTS

	ITEMS	COMPETENT AUTHORITY
	All goods to	
1)	Iraq	Prohibited, TDB
	SPECIFIC Goods	
1)	Animals	AVA
2)	Arms & explosives	AEB
3)	Articles of clothing intended as protection against attack, including bullet-proof vests.	AEB
4)	Chemicals, toxic and precursors	NA, CWC
5)	Chlorofluorocarbons (CFCs)	TDB
6)	Fish and fishery products (including fin fish, crustaceans and molluscs)	AVA
7)	Ginseng roots	AVA
8)	Handcuffs	AEB
9)	Halons	TDB
10)	Helmets, steel	AEB
11)	Irradiating apparatus	RPI
12)	Meat and meat products	AVA
13)	Precursor Chemicals	CNB
14)	Radio-active materials	RPI
15)	Rhinoceros horn, worked, unworked or prepared and waste and powder of this product	Prohibited, AVA
16)	Rice (excluding rice bran)	TDB
17)	Rubber	TDB
18)	Singapore-made textiles, garments & textile articles for export to Canada, the European Union countries or the United States of America	TDB
19)	Timber:	
	a) Logs, plywood, sawn timber, railway sleepers	TDB
	b) Timber and wood (CITES listed)	AVA
20)	Toys guns/pistols/revolvers	AEB
21)	Waste lead-acid batteries and waste batteries made with lead, cadmium or mercury	PCD
22)	Exports to Libya: (* sanctions on Libya suspended with effect from 5 Apr 99 until further notice)	
	a) Arms and related material of all types including but not restricted to:	

	i) weapons;	
	ii) ammunition;	
	iii) military equipment	
	iv) military vehicles; and	
	v) paramilitary police equipment;	
	b) aircraft of all types;	
	c) components or spare parts of any item falling within paragraph (a) or (b) ;	
	d) equipment for the manufacture or maintenance of any item falling within paragraph (a) , (b) or (c)	Prohibited, TDB
	e) with the exception of emergency equipment and equipment directly related to civilian air traffic control -	
	i) materials destined for the construction, improvement or maintenance of Libyan civilian or military airfields or associated facilities or equipment;	
	ii) components destined for the maintenance of any Libyan civil or military airfields or associate facilities or equipment;	
	f) the items specified below or any types of equipment or supplies for the manufacture or maintenance of such items.	
	1. Pumps of medium or large capacity (being equal to or larger than 350 cubic metres per hour) or drivers (being gas turbines or electric motors) designed for use in the transportation of crude oil and natural gas.	
	2. Equipment designed for use in crude oil export terminals being -	
	a. loading buoys or single point moorings (SPM) ;	
	b. flexible hoses for connection between underwater manifolds (PLEM) and single point mooring and floating hoses of large sizes (from 12 inches to 16 inches) ; and	Prohibited, TDB
	c. anchor chains.	
	3. Equipment not specifically designed for use in crude oil export terminals but which, because of their large capacity, can be used for this purpose, being -	
	a. loading pumps of large capacity (4,000 cubic metres per hour) and small head (10 bars) ;	
	b. boosting pumps within the same range of flow rates;	
	c. inline pipe line inspection tools or cleaning devices (being pigging tools of 16 inches and above) ; and	
	d. large capacity metering equipment (1,000 cubic metres per hour and above) .	
	4. Refining equipment being -	

	a. boilers meeting the American Society of Mechanical Engineers 1 standards;	
	b. furnaces, fractionation columns or catalytic reactors meeting the American Society of Mechanical Engineers 8 standards;	Prohibited, TDB
	c. pumps meeting the American Petroleum Institute 610 standards; and	
	d. prepared catalysts including catalysts containing platinum or molybdenum.	
	5. Spare parts destined for the items in paragraphs 1 to 4.	
23)	Exports to Angola:	
	a) Petroleum;	
	b) petroleum products;	
	c) any arms and related material (including weapons and ammunition, military vehicles, military equipment and paramilitary equipment) ;	Prohibited, TDB
	d) any component for any goods specified in paragraph (c) ;	
	e) any goods specially designed or prepared for use, or normally used in the manufacture or maintenance of any goods specified in paragraph (c) or (d) ;	
	f) aircraft or aircraft components;	
	g) equipment used in mining or mining services;	
	h) motorized vehicles or watercraft; and	
	i) spare parts for motorized vehicles or watercraft.	
24)	Exports to Rwanda:	
	a) Arms and related materials of all types including -	Prohibited, TDB
	i) weapons;	
	ii) ammunition;	
	iii) military vehicles;	
	iv) military equipment; and	
	v) paramilitary police equipment	
	b) spare parts of any item falling within paragraph (a) .	
25)	Exports to Liberia:	
	a) Weapons and military equipment	Prohibited, TDB
26)	Exports to Somalia:	
	a) Weapons and military equipment	Prohibited, AEB
27)	Exports to Sierra Leone:	
	a) arms and related material of all types including weapons and ammunition, military vehicles and equipment, paramilitary equipment; and	Prohibited, TDB
	b) spare parts for the items listed in (a)	

28)	Exports to Federal Republic of Yugoslavia, including Kosovo:	
	a) arms and related material of all types including	
	i) weapons	Prohibited, TDB
	ii) ammunition	
	iii) military vehicles	
	iv) military equipment; and	
	b) spare parts for the items listed in (a)	

LIST OF CONTROLLED GOODS: IMPORTS

	ITEMS	COMPETENT AUTHORITY
	All goods from	
1)	Iraq	Prohibited, TDB
	SPECIFIC Goods	
1)	Amusement machines, coin or disc-operated, including pin-tables, shooting galleries & cinematograph machines	PELU, Police
2)	Animals, birds and products thereof	AVA
3)	Arms & explosives	AEB
4)	Articles of asbestos	PCD
5)	Articles of clothing intended as protection against attach, including bullet-proof vests.	AEB
6)	Batteries (primary) , alkaline, zinc-carbon and mercury oxide	PCD
7)	Cartridges/cassettes/audio compact diskettes - pre-recorded	FPD
8)	Chemicals:	
	a) poisons and hazardous	PCD
	b) toxic and precursors	NA, CWC
9)	Chewing Gum	Prohibited, TDB
10)	Chlorofluorocarbons (CFCs)	TDB
11)	Cigarette lighters - pistol/revolver shaped	Prohibited, TDB
12)	Cosmetics and cosmestic products (except medicated skin and face lotions and creams which are controlled by DAD)	CCU
13)	Diesel oil/fuel	PCD
14)	Diamonds & diamond related products from Angola	TDB
15)	Films, cinema/video/laser discs	FPD
16)	Fire crackers	Prohibited, TDB
17)	Fishes and fishery products (including fin fish, crustaceans and molluscs)	AVA
18)	Food items (excluding fresh/chilled vegetables and fruits)	FCD

19)	Fruits (fresh/chilled)	AVA
20)	Fruit/jackpot machines	CED
21)	Ginseng roots	AVA
22)	Gramophone records	FPD
23)	Handcuffs	AEB
24)	Halons	TDB
25)	Hair dye & hair care preparations	
	a) with poison	DAD
	b) without poison	CCU
26)	Helmets:	
	a) Industrial safety	DIS
	b) Steel	AEB
27)	Industrial safety items:	
	a) Belts	
	b) Harnesses	
	c) Life line	DIS
	d) Safety lines	
	e) Nets	
28)	Irradiating apparatus	RPI
29)	Mastering equipment and replication equipment for any of the following:	
	a) CD (compact disc)	
	b) CD-ROM (compact disc-read only memory)	
	c) VCD (video compact disc)	TDB
	d) DVD (digital video disc)	
	e) DVD-ROM (digital video disc-read only memory) .	
30)	Meat and meat products of animals and birds	AVA
31)	Medicines/medicaments/pharmaceutical	DAD
32)	Medicaments, veterinary	AVA
33)	Milk powder - skimmed (coloured for animal feed) Fresh milk/skimmed/pasteurised from Peninsular Malaysia/Sabah/Sarawak, refer to AVA for endorsement	AVA
34)	Nitro-cellulose	AEB
35)	Organic fertilizer	AVA
36)	Plants with/without soil, flowers and seeds	AVA
37)	Poppy seeds (kaskas)	CNB
38)	Precursor Chemicals	CNB
39)	Publications	FPD
40)	Rhinoceros horn, worked, unworked or prepared and worked and powder of this product	Prohibited, AVA
41)	Rice (excluding rice bran)	TDB

42)	Radio-active materials	RPI
43)	Surface-active agents, anionic	PCD
44)	Tableware and kitchenware of :	FCD
	a) porcelain or china	
	b) lead crystal	
45)	Tapes, pre-recorded	FPD
46)	Telecommunication equipment:	
	Radiocommunication	
	a) Ham radios	
	b) Paging equipment	
	c) Radar equipment	
	d) Radio alarms	
	e) Radio telephones	
	f) Receivers	IDA
	g) Ship's radios	
	h) Transceivers	
	i) Transmitters	
	j) Walkie-talkie	
	k) Wireless microphones	
47)	Timber and wood (CITES listed)	AVA
48)	Toy currency note, toy coin or goods bearing the imprint of the Singapore currency note or coin	BCCS
49)	Toy guns/pistols/revolvers	AEB
50)	Toy walkie-talkie	IDA
51)	Vegetables (fresh/chilled)	AVA
52)	Volcanic rock aggregates of a size which does not exceed 40 millimetres	Prohibited, TDB
53)	Waste lead-acid batteries and waste batteries made with lead, cadmium or mercury	PCD

IMPORT REGULATIONS: QUESTIONS AND ANSWERS

IMPORTS PROCEDURES

You are encouraged to take speedy delivery of the goods that you import. If you are not a TradeNet User, you may:

1. appoint a TradeNet Service Centre to apply for your import permits.
2. provide the supplier's invoice and bill of lading/air waybill to your appointed TradeNet Service Centre for them to apply for your import permits.
3. collect the Import Cargo Clearance Permit (CCP) from the TradeNet Service Centre after it has been approved.

SEPARATE APPLICATIONS

Separate applications are required for:

Non-dutiable, non-controlled goods
Non-dutiable, controlled goods (subject to **one** competent authority in **one** application)
Dutiable and non-dutiable goods
One Ocean B/L or one Master AWB (for direct consignments)
One House B/L or One House AWB (for consolidated shipments)
Different types of trade within the same consignment
Different countries of origin within the same consignment
Used personal effects and commercial goods within the same consignment

GENERAL CONDITIONS OF APPROVAL

1. The permit is valid for:
    - One month from the date of approval for manual permits
    - One month from the date of approval for "IG" non-GST payment permits
    - 14 days for "IG" GST payment permit

   unless otherwise specified in the conditions.

2. All unused permits for non-controlled and non-dutiable items must be cancelled electronically through TradeNet by the expiry date. Unused permits for controlled items must be returned to the I&E Office for cancellation by the expiry date. You are also required to inform the competent authority of the cancellation.

Please note that there may be other specific conditions of approval relating to specific transactions or types of goods imported. Failure to comply with these conditions is an offence.

DELIVERY

To take delivery of the goods, you need to:

hand the photocopy of the first print of the CCP to the shipping agent in exchange for a delivery order (for sea consignments) ;
show the original first print of the CCP to the airline/cargo agent (for direct air consignments) ;
submit the permit details to the airline agent/cargo agent electronically via Air Cargo EDI System (for direct/consolidated air consignments) ;
show the original first print of the CCP to Customs at the checkpoint/gate when the goods are taken out of the controlled area/Free Trade Zone (FTZ) .

You may also appoint a freight forwarder or a cargo agent to handle the documentation and take delivery of goods for you.

IMPORT CONTROL

Items under import control may either require endorsement or a licence before import is allowed or they may be prohibited from import.

For controlled items, you are reminded not to enter into any financial commitment or contractual obligations before the necessary licences or approvals are obtained.

IMPORT OF HIGH-TECHNOLOGY PRODUCTS

Certain high-technology products are subject to export control by the exporting country. In this case, the exporter in the exporting country will ask the Singapore importer for an **Import Certificate and Delivery Verification (ICDV)** from Singapore.

The I&E Office will issue the ICDV to you upon your application. The purpose of the ICDV is to ensure that the items are in fact imported into Singapore and are not diverted or re-export to a proscribed destination.

IMPORT OF GOODS UNDER ATA CARNET

Import permits are not required for goods imported under ATA Carnet. However, if the goods to be imported are under import control (refer to list of controlled goods) , you must obtain the endorsement/approval from the relevant competent authority before the arrival of the controlled goods in Singapore.

You must present the ATA Carnet (endorsed by Customs) to the carrier's agent to take delivery of the goods. The B/L No. or AWB No. should be indicated on the top right hand corner of the ATA Carnet. The carrier's agent will:

1. retain a copy of the ATA Carnet.
2. indicate in the manifest, the ATA Carnet No. against the item which was imported under the ATA Carnet.

Where some or all of the goods are not re-exported, you must also obtain the necessary import permit(s) .

APPLICATION FOR CENTRAL REGISTRATION (CR) NUMBER

Question
I have recently incorporated my company in Singapore. Do I need to apply for a Central Registration (CR) Number from the TDB?

Answer
You are required to register with the TDB to obtain a CR Number if your company wishes to import goods into or export goods from Singapore. The CR number is for use in all import, export and transhipment permits, certificates and any other documents issued by the TDB.

Question
How can my company apply for a CR Number from the TDB?

Answer
You can do so by accessing the TDB Traders Registration System (TTRS) from any computer terminal with Internet access. The website address is:

http://www.asianconnect.com/TDB/TRS/crnum.html

Question
How soon can I use the CR Number? Is there a validity period for the CR Number issued?

Answer
You can use the CR Number to submit TDB Permit applications and other documents through the TradeNet on the next working day. The CR Number is valid for two years from the date of issue.

Question
My freight forwarder applies an Import Permit on my behalf. However, my company's Central Registration (CR) Number was rejected by the TradeNet System. What was the reason for the rejection?

Answer
You probably did not renew your company's registration with the TDB before the expiry date. You can register your company with the TDB from the Internet via TTRS.

Question
I have not registered a business with the Registry of Companies and Businesses (RCB) . Can I apply for the CR Number as an individual?

Answer
The CR Number is issued to a company or a business but not to individuals.

Question
I cannot remember if I have applied earlier for a CR Number for my company. How can I find out if my company is already registered with TDB?

Answer
You can check whether your company is registered with the TDB by accessing the "Query of Own Accesscode/Registration Number" from the TTRS homepage. Upon receipt of your request, the system will fax a copy of the **Notification Slip** to you on the same day.

Question
I have recently changed my company's name. Is it necessary for me to register for a CR Number with TDB under the new company's name?

Answer
If there is no change in the registration number issued by the Registry of Companies and Businesses (RCB) , you can update your record with us through the Internet - TDB Trade Register System (TTRS) . The website is:

http://www.asianconnect.com/TDB/TRS/crnum.html

If there is a change in the registration number issued by the RCB, you can register the new company from our TTRS website, and cancel the registration of the old company if it has ceased operations.

Question
I have converted from a sole-proprietorship to a private limited company. Can I retain the CR Number of the sole-proprietorship for the private limited company?

Answer
You cannot retain the CR Number because your private limited company with the Registry of Companies and Businesses (RCB) is a separate entity from the sole-proprietorship. You have to register with the TDB to obtain a CR Number for the private limited company through TTRS and cancel the registration of the sole-proprietorship.

APPLYING FOR A CENTRAL REGISTRATION NUMBER

If you have goods to be imported into Singapore or exported from Singapore, whether commercial or non-commercial, you are required to register your company/firm with the Imports & Exports Office as an importer, exporter, common carrier and others. The I&E Office will issue to you a Central Registration Number (CR No.) . The registration applies to local companies/organisations. You can apply for your registration through **Internet.**

Applying through Internet - TDB Traders Registration System (TTRS)

Access into Internet at the following address -

http://www.asianconnect.com/TDB/TRS/crnum.html

Follow closely the instructions as given in the TTRS.
Your application will be automatically approved within 15 minutes of submission. **Immediately** print the notification letter which provides the CR No. of your company/firm.
If your application is not approved automatically, it will be routed to TDB for on-line processing. If your application is in order, TDB will process and approve your application. You will receive by fax the notification letter of your CR No usually on the following day.
You can call the SNS Helpdesk at Tel No. 7755977 if you encounter difficulty accessing into the TTRS.
If you require help in the data entry under the TTRS, please call the TDB Helpdesk at Tel No. 3376690.

Change of Particulars

You need to notify us when you change any particulars of your company/firm registered with us, eg. address, telephone number, fax number. You should update the changes of your company/firm's particulars through TTRS.

If your company's name has been changed but your Registration No. with the Registrar of Companies and Businesses (RCB) **remains the same**, you need to update the change of the company's name through TTRS.

If your company's name and RCB Registration/Incorporation No. have been changed, you need to re-apply for a new CR No. This applies especially to sole-proprietorships/ partnerships converting to private limited companies. **It is an offence to import and export under a Company's name which is no longer valid or in the name of a company/firm which is no longer in existence.**

Cancellation of Registration

When your company/firm ceases operations or terminates its registration/ incorporation as a business, you must cancel your registration with us through TTRS.

Renewal of Registration

We will fax to you a "Notification of Renewal of Registration" before the expiry of your registration with us. Upon receipt of the Notification, you should immediately renew your registration with us through TTRS. It is therefore very important that you update your fax number registered with us regularly.

If you do not have a fax number, we will send the Notification to you by post. However, for convenience you should renew your registration through the TTRS.

APPLYING FOR A CENTRAL REGISTRATION NUMBER

If you have goods to be imported into Singapore or exported from Singapore, whether commercial or non-commercial, you are required to register your company/firm with the Imports & Exports Office as an importer, exporter, common carrier and others. The I&E Office will issue to you a Central Registration Number (CR No.) . The registration applies to local companies/organisations. You can apply for your registration through **Internet.**

Applying through Internet - TDB Traders Registration System (TTRS)

Access into Internet at the following address -

http://www.asianconnect.com/TDB/TRS/crnum.html

Follow closely the instructions as given in the TTRS.
Your application will be automatically approved within 15 minutes of submission. **Immediately** print the notification letter which provides the CR No. of your company/firm.
If your application is not approved automatically, it will be routed to TDB for on-line processing. If your application is in order, TDB will process and approve your application. You will receive by fax the notification letter of your CR No usually on the following day.
You can call the SNS Helpdesk at Tel No. 7755977 if you encounter difficulty accessing into the TTRS.
If you require help in the data entry under the TTRS, please call the TDB Helpdesk at Tel No. 3376690.

Change of Particulars

You need to notify us when you change any particulars of your company/firm registered with us, eg. address, telephone number, fax number. You should update the changes of your company/firm's particulars through TTRS.

If your company's name has been changed but your Registration No. with the Registrar of Companies and Businesses (RCB) **remains the same**, you need to update the change of the company's name through TTRS.

If your company's name and RCB Registration/Incorporation No. have been changed, you need to re-apply for a new CR No. This applies especially to sole-proprietorships/ partnerships converting to private limited companies. **It is an offence to import and export under a Company's name which is no longer valid or in the name of a company/firm which is no longer in existence.**

Cancellation of Registration

When your company/firm ceases operations or terminates its registration/ incorporation as a business, you must cancel your registration with us through TTRS.

Renewal of Registration

We will fax to you a "Notification of Renewal of Registration" before the expiry of your registration with us. Upon receipt of the Notification, you should immediately renew your registration with us through TTRS. It is therefore very important that you update your fax number registered with us regularly.

TDB PERMIT APPLICATIONS

Question
I have applied for a Joint "TT" Permit. Must I apply for a TDB Export Permit ("OU") ?

Answer
A Joint "TT" Permit serves as a TDB Transhipment Permit and Customs Transhipment Permit. It covers both inward and outward movement of transhipment cargo. The "TT" Permit is to be applied only for goods which are covered under a "Through Bill of Lading" or a "Through Air Waybill" transhipment. Hence, you need not apply for a TDB Export Permit ("OU") .

Question
I am handling shipments for a number of exporters. Can I submit an Export Permit application for all the exporters?

Answer
This is not allowed because only one exporter's name and his CR number can be declared in one Permit application. When requested by TDB, an exporter should support his application with the invoice issued under his company's name for the sale of the goods.

Question
My consignment was imported under ATA Carnet for exhibition purposes. Must I apply for an Export Permit if I want to export the consignment to another destination?

Answer
You need not apply for an Export Permit to export the consignment that was originally imported under ATA Carnet. You must obtain the endorsement from Customs on the ATA Carnet before export and produce the endorsed ATA Carnet to the Carrier's Agent to effect the shipment of goods.

Question
I am a local importer and I intend to store some imported goods in the Free Trade Zone for re-export at a later date. What should I key in for type of trade when I apply for an Import Permit?

Answer
For non-controlled goods, the trade type is "1" for the trade type field. For controlled goods, the trade type is "3" for the trade type field.

Question
I have one unit of machine packed in 10 cartons. What should I key in the quantity field and the total outer pack field?

Answer
For the quantity field, you should key in "1" NMB. For the total outer pack field, you should key in "10" CAR.

Question
A consignment is imported by a local company and stored in Changi FTZ. The same cargo is later sold to another local company that wants to export it overseas. How do I declare the Import/Export Permit applications when the importer and exporter are two different companies and the cargo is kept within the FTZ?

Answer
Firstly, you must declare an IG Permit, declaration purpose type "1", supported by an Inward Air Waybill and an invoice from the overseas supplier for the cargo imported and remained in the FTZ. You will then request the local exporter, who has taken ownership of the cargo from the importer, to provide you with the export invoice to declare the Export Permit (OU) application for the same consignment to be re-exported overseas.

Question
Can I apply for one Import or Export Permit for several Bills of Lading?

Answer
This is not allowed. You have to apply for one Permit for one Bill of Lading or one Air Waybill.

JOINT PERMIT APPLICATIONS

Question
The importer is a local trading company. Cargo is discharged at vessel location, "CW" for re-export to another country. The connecting vessel is at location "PPW". Must I apply for any Permit?

Answer
Import and Export Permits are required for all imports and exports by companies in Singapore. Since your

goods are imported for re-export, you should apply for a Joint "IT" Permit for import. For export, you should apply for TDB "OU" Permit.

Question
The importer is a MES company. What type of Permit should I apply for import and re-export on his behalf? The cargo is cleared from the Customs checkpoint for temporary storage and repacking in Singapore.

Answer
For import, you should apply for a Joint "ME" Permit, declaration purpose type "ME". For export, you should apply for a TDB "OU" Permit.

IMPORT CERTIFICATE AND DELIVERY VERIFICATION

HOW TO APPLY FOR AN IMPORT CERTIFICATE

(For goods under export control in the exporting country)

Application

You can apply for an Import Certificate (IC) if the goods to be imported into Singapore are subject to export control in the exporting country or the IC is requested by the exporting country. The "Application for an Import Certificate" can be purchased from the **SNP Corporation Ltd** (Tel: 333 9703) at $4.50 per set of 10.

First, you will need a letter or declaration from the exporter that an IC is required. We may ask you to provide a letter of confirmation from the foreign exporter's Government authority that the goods are subject to export control.

You must submit **three copies** (original, 1st and 2nd copies) of the IC application to the Trade Development Board. Affix a S$10/- **TDB revenue stamp** which can also be purchased from some branches of the Singapore Post Pte Ltd on the 1st copy of the Application (not the original copy) .

All the particulars stated must be true and correct.

How to complete the IC Application form

Item	Instructions
1.	Type the applicant's full name, address and telephone number
2.	If you do not have a CR No., you must apply for one. See [CR No.]
3.	Type the exporter's full name and address.
4.	Type the end-user's full name and address. You must also attach a declaration from the end-user that the goods to be imported are for his use.
5.	You will need to indicate whether the goods are for use in Singapore or for re-export. If the goods are for re-export, you will need to state the country/countries where the goods will be re-exported.
6.	Indicate whether you need or do not need a Delivery Verification Certificate for the goods after delivery in Singapore.
7.	Declaration must be signed by an authorised person, giving his full name and designation.
8.	A maximum of 5 items can be typed into one IC. Prepare a carry-forward set of IC when the space for the 5 items is fully used. No TDB revenue stamp is required for the carried-forward set of IC. A

	maximum of 10 items is permitted in one set of IC.
9.	Description of goods refers to codes and descriptions in the Singapore Trade Classification and Customs Duties, 1996 (STCCD,1996) . The description must match the particulars in the end-user's and foreign exporter's declarations, including brand, model number and technical specifications.
10.	Commodity/item codes are HS codes obtainable from the STCCD, 1996. The full 9-digit HS Code should be given.
11.	For each item, state the quantity in numbers and the unit, eg. 12 pcs.
12.	For each item, state the CIF value in S$.
13.	When the IC is approved, it will be signed by an authorised TDB officer on behalf of the Trade Development Board. An IC No. will be given. The validity period of the IC will be stated.
14.	TDB revenue stamp affixed on the 1st copy (not the original copy) .
15.	Refer to How to Apply for a Delivery Verification

Approval of IC

If the application is approved, the Trade Development Board will return the signed original and 2nd copy of the IC to you. Please forward the original copy of the IC to your exporter in the exporting country immediately.

Conditions of Import

If the Trade Development Board has issued an IC to you, you should not:

1. import those goods or cause or permit them to be imported into any country other than Singapore;
2. dispose of those goods before they have been imported into Singapore; or
3. export those goods or cause or permit them to be exported from Singapore after they have been imported into Singapore.

except with the written approval of the Trade Development Board.

Validity of IC

The approved IC is valid for one year from the date of issue. This means that you must import the goods as stated in the IC into Singapore within one year.

You may, **before expiry** of the IC, apply to the Trade Development Board for an extension of the validity period. Any extension granted will be for a period not exceeding another year. In this case, you must import the goods within the period of the extension granted by the Trade Development Board.

Arrival of Goods

When the goods arrive in Singapore, you must submit an import permit application to the Trade Development Board through TradeNet to take delivery of the goods and the quantity specified in Singapore. In the item description field, besides the item description, you have to state the **ICDV number** against the item description.

In addition, you have to state "IC" in the Exception Type Indicator field of the import permit application to indicate that you are submitting an ICDV permit for processing. If the IC item to be imported falls under a **partially-controlled HS code** and you would like the import permit application to be routed to the relevant competent authority for endorsement, you have to indicate **both** "CA" and "IC" in this field. You have to key in the indicators one after another.

You also have to indicate the **ICDV number** for **each item** declared in the "Other Reference Number" field of the import permit application. You should also provide the relevant quantity unit of the item at the HS level i.e. item quantity and/or the "Description of Goods" field, based on the quantity unit declared in the ICDV Certificate.

Example (a) :

If the ICDV Certificate quantity unit is "NMB" and HS quantity unit is by Value (" - ") , you would have to key in "NMB" in the item quantity unit field.

Example (b) :

If the ICDV Certificate quantity is Kilometres (KM) and HS quantity unit is by "TNE", you would have to key in "TNE" in the item quantity unit field and "KM" in the "Description of Goods" field.

If the items imported in one consignment are covered by different ICDVs, you can declare them in one import permit application but you must state **all** the different ICDVs involved in the "Description of Goods" field. However, you are **not allowed** to combine ICDV items with non-ICDV items in the same import permit application.

If you are not the end-user, you must deliver the goods to the end-user named in the IC together with all the relevant accompanying documents.

Re-export of Goods

You must first get approval from the Trade Development Board **before** re-exporting goods that have been imported into Singapore under an IC.

If in the IC issued to you, you have indicated that the goods are for re-export, you have to produce an **End-User Certificate** from the **consignee** to whom you are re-exporting to and a copy of the IC when you apply for the **export permit**.

If you have not indicated in the IC issued to you that the goods are for re-export and you subsequently wish to re-export the goods, you must produce:

1. the export licence from the exporter's Government authority granting approval for the re-export of the goods from Singapore to the country you wish to re-export;
2. the End-User Certificate from the consignee to whom you are re-exporting to.

When the Trade Development Board is satisfied with the documents submitted, you may then submit the export permit application for approval through TradeNet before you re-export the goods.

The application of the export permit through TradeNet is the same as the application of the import permit for the ICDV items.

Free Trade Zone

If the goods imported under the IC were to remain in the Free Trade Zone (FTZ) pending re-export, you are still required to obtain the **import permit** and the **export permit** from the Trade Development Board.

You have to follow the **same** procedures to take delivery of the goods first before re-exporting them.

Notification of Changes

You are **not allowed** to make any **amendments** to the application against which an approved IC has been issued. If at any time after the issue of an IC, a change occurs in any representation, statement, declaration or undertaking in or accompanying the application for the IC, you should immediately **notify** the Trade Development Board giving particulars of the change in writing.

If at any time a **change** occurs in the name or address of the end-user of any goods imported under an IC, the end-user should, **within 14 days** of such a change, inform the Trade Development Board giving particulars of the change in writing.

Cancellation

If the goods subject to an IC are **not imported**, you should **return** the IC to the Trade Development Board for **cancellation**.

If you have **not imported** the goods before the expiry period of the IC, and **no extension** has been required or granted, you should **return** the IC to the Trade Development Board for **cancellation**.

Surprise Checks

The Trade Development Board reserves the right to conduct surprise checks on the goods imported under an IC after you have imported the goods into Singapore. You should extend your fullest co-operation to the officers who are conducting these checks.

Penalties

If you contravene any of the provisions of the IC issued to you, or make a false declaration in any material particular, you will be guilty of an offence and will be liable on conviction to a fine not exceeding **$100,000** or **three times** the value of the goods (whichever is greater) ; or to **imprisonment** of up to **12 months**; or to **both** such fine and imprisonment. Heavier penalties will be imposed for second and subsequent offences.

For enquiries, please call tel no. 7373 575

HOW TO APPLY FOR A DELIVERY VERIFICATION CERTIFICATE

Application

Before you apply for an IC, please find out from your exporter whether a **Delivery Verification** Certificate (DVC) is needed. You should then indicate whether or not you need a DVC under **item 6** of the IC application.

If your exporter needs a DVC, you have to obtain the DVC (**item 15** of the IC application) from the Trade Devleopment Board.

Verification

Verification for Complete Delivery

This refers to the verification of the delivery of the goods in the IC when imported in one shipment. For complete verification, you must submit:

1. the **2nd copy** of the IC. You must complete **item 15** of the IC application by typing the name of the vessel or flight number by which the goods arrived in Singapore, the date of arrival and the quantity of the goods;
2. indicate import permit no. and approval date on the top right-hand corner of **item 15 of the IC**;
3. Bill of Lading or Air Waybill; and
4. **original copy** of the **Declaration** of Goods Imported into Singapore under an Import Certificate by the Importer.

to the Trade Development Board for verification of delivery of the goods and the quantity stated in Singapore.

The Trade Development Board will certify that the goods and the quantity stated have arrived in Singapore based on the evidence of these documents.

Verification for Partial Delivery

This refers to the verification of the delivery of the goods in the IC when such goods were imported partially or in different shipments, i.e. more than 2 shipments.

For goods partially delivered in Singapore, you should submit 2 copies of the "Statement of Delivery Verification for Partial Delivery" to the Trade Development Board for verification. Please attach the following documents to your Statement:

1. import permit no. and approval date on the top right-hand corner of **item 15 of the IC**;
2. Bill of Lading or Air Waybill;
3. **original copy** of the **Declaration** of Goods Imported into Singapore under an Import Certificate by the Importer and
4. the 2nd copy of the IC (when the last consignment listed in the IC has been delivered) .

The Trade Development Board will endorse the Delivery Verification Certificate (**item 15** of the IC application) when the delivery of the whole consignment as stated in your IC is completed.

Verification For Goods Remaining in the Free Trade Zone (FTZ)

This applies to the import (by sea only) of the goods in the IC which remain in the FTZ pending re-export from the same FTZ.

You will be required to appoint an authorised security agency to confirm the product, brand, model number and quantity of the goods stored in the FTZ.

The Trade Development Board will verify the DVC based on the **confirmation** by the security agency.

The Trade Development Board will not endorse the DVC if there are discrepancies in the particulars in the documents submitted for verification. These discrepancies may appear in the brand, model no., quantity, goods description, value, etc.

Verification of delivery of the goods in Singapore if required, must be done within **14 days** of the **arrival** of all the goods or any quantity in Singapore. If you do not submit your documents for verification within 14 days, the **Trade Development Board reserves the right not to verify the DVC**. Similarly, the Trade Development Board will not be able to verify the delivery of your goods into Singapore if you fail to indicate **"IC"** in the appropriate column when you are applying for an import permit through TradeNet.

After verification, you should, without delay, send the DVC to the exporter.

HS CLASSIFICATION

Question
Why do you say it is incorrect to classify "flours of animal meat and meat offal for animal feed" under HS code 0210 90 000?

Answer
HS code 0210 90 000 covers "edible flours of animal meat and meat offal". You should classify "flours of animal meat and meat offal for animal feed" under HS code 2301 10 000 as they are unfit for human consumption.

Chapter 03

Question
What is the HS code for "frozen swordfish fillet"? Can they be classified under HS code 0304 90 000?

Answer
"Frozen swordfish fillet" is classified under HS code 0304 20 000. "Fish fillet" refers to strips of meat cut parallel to the backbone of the fish and constituting the right or left side of a fish insofar as the head, guts, fins and bones have been removed and the two sides are not joined together, for example by the back or belly.

HS code 0304 90 000 refers to "frozen fish meat" whether or not minced from which the bones have been removed.

Question
What is the HS classification for "frozen sea crawfish", "frozen freshwater crawfish" and "frozen cooked crawfish meat"? Are they classified under the same HS code?

Answer
No, they are classified separately as follows:

Product Description	HS Code
Frozen sea crawfish (whether in shell or not)	0306 11 900
Frozen freshwater crawfish (whether in shell or not)	0306 19 000
Frozen cooked crawfish meat (prepared)	1605 40 000

Question
Is "sea-cucumber" classified under HS code 0707 00 000?

Answer
"Sea-cucumber" or "beche-de-mer" or "trepang" should be classified under HS code 0307 99 100 if frozen and HS code 0307 99 210 when dried, salted or in brine.

"Sea-cucumbers" are not classified under HS code 0707 00 000 (for fresh or chilled cucumber) because they are not vegetables.

Chapter 05

Question
Where do you classify "frozen pigs' maws"? Are they classified under HS heading 0206 ?

Answer
"Frozen pigs' maws" are classified under HS code 0504 00 000 as "frozen guts, bladders, stomachs of animals (other than fish) ". They are not classified under HS heading 0206 as "edible offal of swine". Examples of frozen edible offal of swine under HS code 0206 49 000 are pigs' kidneys, feet and tails.

Question
Can I classify "frozen fish stomach" under HS code 0504 00 000?

Answer
No, "frozen fish stomach" should be classified under the HS code 0511 91 000 as "products of fish" because HS code 0504 00 000 covers "bladders and stomachs of animals, excluding fish".

Chapter 07

Question
What is the HS classification for "fennel"?

Answer
Fennel, in its various forms, is classified separately as follows:

Product Description	HS Code
Fresh Fennel	0709 90 000
Frozen Fennel (Uncooked or cooked by steaming or boiling in water)	0710 80 000
Fennel seeds	0909 50 000
Essential oil of Fennel	3301 29 000

Question
Can I classify "fresh sweet potato" under HS code 0701 90 000?

Answer
"Fresh sweet potato" is classified specifically under HS code 0714 20 000. HS code 0701 90 000 covers "fresh or chilled potatoes".

Chapter 12

Question
Where do you classify "herbs eg. tangkui and other herbs which you can buy from the Chinese sinseh shop"?

Answer "Chinese herbs which you buy from the Chinese sinseh shop" are classified under HS code 1211 90 100.

Chapter 15

Question
Can we classify "refined peanut oil" under HS code 1515 90 000 as "other fixed vegetable fats and oils"?

Answer
"Refined peanut oil" is classified together with "ground-nut oil" in HS code 1508 90 000. It is not classified under HS code 1515 90 000 as "other fixed vegetable fats and oils". Examples of items that can be classified under HS code 1515 90 000 are almond oil, wheat-germ and walnut oil.

Question
Are "red palm stearin" and "stearic acid" classified under the same HS code 2915 70 000?

Answer
"Red palm stearin" is classified under HS code 1511 90 000 as "refined palm oil and its fractions" whereas "stearic acid" is classified under HS code 2915 70 000 if it is chemically pure. "Stearic acid" which is industrial monocarboxylic fatty acids is classified under HS code 3823 11 000.

Question
Where do you classify "palm olein"? Is it classified under HS code 3823 12 000 ?

Answer
No, "palm olein" is classified under HS code 1511 90 000 as "refined palm oil and its fractions". HS code 3823 12 000 covers commercial oleic acid or olein, which is an industrial monocarboxylic fatty acid.

Question
What is "beeswax" and where is it classified?

Answer
"Beeswax" is classified under HS code 1521 90 000. It is the substance which bees build the hexagonal cells of the combs in the hives. In the natural state, it has a granular structure and is light yellow, orange or sometimes brown, with a particularly agreeable smell. It is used for the manufacture of candles, waxed cloth or paper, mastics, polishes, etc.

Chapter 16

Question
Can I have the HS classification for canned foods?

Answer
Canned foods are classified according to the type of canned foods. If it is canned meat, classify under HS heading 1602.

For canned fish, you can classify under HS heading 1604 and for canned vegetables, classify under HS headings 2010 to 2005 by the different types of vegetables.

Question
Where do you classify "baby food "?

Answer
"Baby food" is generally classified as "homogenised food preparations" according to the ingredients. They are classified as follows:

HS code	Product Description
1602 10 000	Homogenised food preparations containing mainly meat
2104 20 100	Homogenised composite food preparations containing meat

2104 20 900	Homogenised composite food preparations not containing meat
2005 10 000	Homogenised food preparations containing vegetables
2007 10 000	Homogenised food preparations containing fruits

However, if you have preparations of flour, meal, starch or malt for infant feeding, you should classify them under HS heading 19.01 according to the type of packing and whether or not they are based on goods of headings 04.01 to 04.04.

Question
What is the HS classification for "frozen sea crawfish", "frozen freshwater crawfish" and "frozen cooked crawfish meat"? Are they classified under the same HS code?

Answer
No, they are classified separately as follows:

Product Description	HS Code
Frozen sea crawfish (whether in shell or not)	0306 11 900
Frozen freshwater crawfish (whether in shell or not)	0306 19 000
Frozen cooked crawfish meat (prepared)	1605 40 000

Chapter 19

Question
Are "3-in-1 cereals" in packet form classified under HS code 1104 19 900?

Answer
No, you cannot classify "3-in-1 cereals" in packet form under the HS code 1104 19 900 because the HS code covers "other rolled or flaked cereal grains". "3-in-1 cereals" which do not contain cocoa are classified under the HS code 1901 90 940 as "preparations of flour, meal, starch or malt extract, not containing cocoa, not for infant feeding". For "3-in-1 cereals" which contain cocoa", they are classified under HS code 1901 90 960 as "preparations of flour, meal, starch or malt extract, containing cocoa, not for infant feeding".

Question
Can I classify "sweetened condensed filled milk" in HS code 0402 99 000?

Answer
"Sweetened condensed filled milk" refers to canned milk that has the butterfat substituted or blended with vegetable oil. It is classified under HS code 1901 90 930 as "preparations of goods of headings nos. 04.01 to 04.04, not containing cocoa or containing less than 5% by weight of cocoa calculated on a totally defatted basis, not elsewhere specified or included". HS code 0402 99 000 covers sweetened condensed milk which do not contain any vegetable oil or vegetable fats.

Question
What is "crispbread"? Can I classify under HS code 1905 40 000? **Answer**
"Crispbread" which is also known as "knackebrot" is a dry crisp bread usually in thin rectangular or round pricked pieces. It is made from a dough of flour, meal, groats or wholemeal of rye, oats, barley or wheat and leavened by means of yeast, sour dough or other leavening agents or by compressed air. It is classified under HS code 1905 10 000.

HS code 1905 40 000 covers "rusks, toasted bread and similar toasted products", whether or not sliced or ground, with or without the addition of butter or other fats, sugar, eggs or other nutritive substances.

Chapter 20

Question
Can I have the HS classification for canned foods?

Answer
Canned foods are classified according to the type of canned foods. If it is canned meat, classify under HS heading 1602.

For canned fish, you can classify under HS heading 1604 and for canned vegetables, classify under HS headings 2010 to 2005 by the different types of vegetables.

Chapter 21

Question
Can I classify "Tom Yam soup base without meat content" under HS code 2922 42 100?

Answer
"Tom Yam soup base without meat content" is classified under HS code 2104 10 900. HS code 2922 42 100 refers to chemically pure monosodium glutamate powder or granules put up in packings for retail sale as a flavour enhancer for soups, sauces and other dishes.

Question
What is the HS code for "canned vegetarian food"? Can I classify it under HS code 2005 90 000?

Answer
"Canned vegetarian food" is classified under HS code 2106 10 000. You cannot classify it under HS code 2005 90 000 under "other prepared or preserved mixtures of vegetables" because "canned vegetarian food" is made mostly from protein concentrates and textured protein substances.

Question
Can I classify "natural honey enriched with bee's royal jelly" under HS code 0409 00 000 as "natural honey"?

Answer
"Natural honey enriched with bee's royal jelly" should be classified under HS code 2106 90 900 as "food supplements" which are normally placed in packages with indications that they maintain general health or well-being.

Question
Is "canned vegetarian mock duck" classified under HS code 1602 39 000?

Answer
"Canned vegetarian mock duck" is usually made from gluten, soya bean flour or textured protein substances. It is classified under HS code 2106 10 000 as "protein concentrates and textured protein substances". Since it is not a meat product, it should not be classified under HS code 1602 39 000 as the code covers "other prepared or preserved meat, meat offal or blood of the species Gallus Domesticus".

Question
Where do you classify "aspartame"?

Answer
"Aspartame", as a pure chemical, is classified under HS code 2924 29 000. However, food preparations using "aspartame" for sweetening purposes are classified under HS code 2106 90 400.

Chapter 22

Question
Can I classify "natural water" under HS code 2851 00 900?

Answer
"Natural water", filtered, sterilised, purified or softened is classified under HS code 2201 10 000. HS code 2851 00 900 covers only distilled water, re-distilled or electro-osmotic water, conductivity water and water of similar purity, including water treated with ion exchange media.

Chapter 26

Question
Are "residues of nickel" classified as "nickel waste and scrap" under HS code 7503 00 000.

Answer
"Residues of nickel" should be classified under HS code 2620 90 900 as "other ash and residues" because they are extracted from nickel ores and concentrates found under HS code 2604 00 000.

It cannot be classified under HS code 7503 00 000 because waste and scrap under Chapter 75 are defined under Note 8(a) of Section XV as "metal waste and scrap from the manufacture or mechanical working of metals, and metal goods definitely not usable as such because of wear or other reasons".

Chapter 27

Question
Is "peat" used as a fertiliser classified under HS code 3101 00 100 ?

Answer
"Peat" used as a fertiliser is classified under HS heading 27.03, depending on whether or not they are agglomerated, by applying Rule 3(a) of the Interpretative Rules of the HS, that is, HS heading 27.03 provides the specific description of "peat" instead of HS heading 31.01. "Peat" is formed from partly carbonised vegetable material and is generally used as potting soil.

Question
Where do you classify "methane"?

Answer "Methane" as a liquefied gas, is classified under HS code 2711 19 000 whereas "methane" in the gaseous state is classified under HS code 2711 29 000.

Chapter 28

Question
I have a consignment of "silver cyanides". Can I classify them under HS code 2837 19 000 as "other cyanides and cyanide oxides"?

Answer
"Silver cyanides" are classified under HS code 2843 29 000 as "other silver compounds". Some examples of "other cyanides and cyanide oxides" classified under HS code 2837 19 000 are potassium cyanides and calcium cyanides.

Question
Are "silver nitrates" classified under HS code 7106 10 000?

Answer
"Silver nitrates" are classified specifically under HS code 2843 21 000. HS code 7106 10 000 covers silver usually in the form of finely divided powder, obtained by various mechanical or chemical processes. They are used in metallurgy and in the manufacture of metallising preparations for electronic applications and of conducting cements.

Chapter 29

Question
Are "red palm stearin" and "stearic acid" classified under the same HS code 2915 70 000?

Answer
"Red palm stearin" is classified under HS code 1511 90 000 as "refined palm oil and its fractions" whereas "stearic acid" is classified under HS code 2915 70 000 if it is chemically pure. "Stearic acid" which is industrial monocarboxylic fatty acids is classified under HS code 3823 11 000.

Question
Where do you classify "aspartame"?

Answer
"Aspartame", as a pure chemical, is classified under HS code 2924 29 000. However, food preparations using "aspartame" for sweetening purposes are classified under HS code 2106 90 400.

Question
What is the HS code for "formic acid"? Is it classified under HS code 2936 29 000?

Answer
"Formic acid" is classified under HS code 2915 11 000. It is a mobile, colourless liquid, gives off slight fumes when exposed to air, has an irritating odour and is caustic. It is found in nature and obtained synthetically. It is used in dyeing, in tanning, in the coagulation of latex, in medicine as an antiseptic, or in organic synthesis.

HS code 2936 29 000 is used to classify "folic acid" under "other vitamins, not put up as medicament".

Question
What is the HS code for "Non-irradiated ergosterol"?

Answer
"Non-irradiated ergosterol" or provitamin D2 is found in the ergot of rye, in brewer's yeast, in mushrooms and in other fungi. It is classified under HS code 2936 10 000 if it is not formulated as vitamins.

If formulated as vitamins but not put up in measured doses or in forms or packing for retail sale, "non-irradiated ergosterol" as provitamin D2 is classified under HS code 3003 90 100. When put up in measured doses or in forms for retail sale, it is classified under HS code 3004 50 000 as "other medicaments containing vitamins or other products of heading 29.36".

Chapter 30

Question
Where do you classify "sulphur" used as medicaments for the treatment of white spots on the skin ?

Answer
"Sulphur", when formulated as a medicament, is classified under HS code 3003 90 900 when not put up in packings for retail sale and HS code 3004 90 900 if put up in packings for retail sale.

However, as a mineral product, "sulphur" is classified under the HS code 2503 00 000. Sublimed or precipitated "sulphur" is classified under HS code 2802 00 000.

Question
Are painter's fillings classified under HS code 3208 90 390?

Answer
"Painters' fillings" are classified specifically under HS code 3214 10 000. They are used to prepare surfaces (eg. indoor walls) for painting by levelling out irregularities and, if necessary, filling in cracks, holes or porous surfaces. HS code 3208 90 390 covers "other paints not containing insecticide derivatives".

Question
What is the HS classification for "ink cartridge", "inked ribbon cartridge", "toners for laser printers" and "toner cartridges for photocopiers? Are they classified under the same HS code?

Answer
No, they are classified separately as follows:

Product Description	HS Code
Ink cartridge (filled with ink)	3215 90 900 (Other inks)
Ink cartridge (empty) , of plastic	3926 90 900 (Other articles of plastic)
Inked ribbon cartridge (for typewriter use)	9612 10 000 (Typewriter or similar ribbons, inked or otherwise prepared for giving, impressions, whether or not on spools or in cartridges)
Toners for laser printers	3707 90 000 (Other chemical preparations for photographic uses)
Cartridges for photocopiers (with or without toner)	9009 90 000 (Parts and accessories for photocopying apparatus)

Question
What is the HS code for "Non-irradiated ergosterol"?

Answer
"Non-irradiated ergosterol" or provitamin D2 is found in the ergot of rye, in brewer's yeast, in mushrooms and in other fungi. It is classified under HS code 2936 10 000 if it is not formulated as vitamins.

If formulated as vitamins but not put up in measured doses or in forms or packing for retail sale, "non-irradiated ergosterol" as provitamin D2 is classified under HS code 3003 90 100. When put up in measured doses or in forms for retail sale, it is classified under HS code 3004 50 000 as "other medicaments containing vitamins or other products of heading 29.36".

Chapter 33

Question
Can I classify "face toner" under HS code 3707 90 000?

Answer
"Face toner" should be classified under HS code 3304 99 100 as "face lotions". HS code 3707 90 000 covers "photographic toners" which are used to modify the colour of the photo image.

Question
Why is "eye brow pencil" classified under HS code 3304 20 000 and not under HS code 9609 20 000?

Answer
"Eye brow pencil" is classified under HS code 3304 20 000 as an eye make-up preparation. HS code 9609 20 000 covers pencils which are used as stationery.

Question
I have a new product which is a "freshener" for under-garments suitably used in hot and humid Asian countries. It comes in the form of a small flat pouch to be attached to the undergarment. Where can I classify this new product ?

Answer
"Freshener" for under-garments in the form of a small flat pouch to be attached to the undergarment is classified under HS code 3307 90 900 as "other perfumery, cosmetic or toilet preparations, not elsewhere specified or included".

Chapter 35

Question
Where do you classify "glue"?

Answer
"Prepared glues", when packed for retail sale in packages not exceeding a net weight of 1 kg, are classified under HS code 3506 10 000. However, if the packaging exceeds a net weight of 1 kg, "prepared glue" should be classified according to its material composition. "Rubber glue", in packings which exceed a net weight of 1 kg, is classified under HS code 4005 20 000. If the glue is made of plastic, you should classify it according to the specific types of plastic under Chapter 39.

Chapter 37

Question
Where do you classify "plastic film" ?

Answer
For sensitised "plastic film", you should classify according to the usage under Chapter 37 as "photographic or cinematographic goods". If the "plastic film" is non-sensitised, you should classify it according to the specific types of plastic compositions under HS headings 39.19, 39.20 or 39.21.

Chapter 38

Question

Can I classify "cade oil" under HS code 3301 29 000?

Answer
"Cade oil" also known as "juniper tar oil" used in medicine and soap making is classified under HS code 3807 00 900. HS code 3301 29 000 refers to juniper oil which is an essential oil other than those of citrus fruits.

Question
"Is insect repellent cream" classified under HS code 3004 90 900 ?

Answer
"Insect repellent cream" is applied on the skin to repel pests and insects. Since it is not for therapeutic use, it should not be classified under the HS code 3004 90 900 as "other medicaments put up for retail sale". "Insect repellent cream" is classified under HS code 3808 10 900 as "other insecticides".

Question
What is the HS code for "fabric softener"? Can it be classified under HS code 3402 13 000?

Answer
"Fabric softener" is classified under HS code 3809 91 000 as "finishing agents, dye carriers to accelerate the dyeing or fixing of dyestuffs and other products and preparations, of a kind used in the textile or like industries".

Question
Are "red palm stearin" and "stearic acid" classified under the same HS code 2915 70 000?

Answer
"Red palm stearin" is classified under HS code 1511 90 000 as "refined palm oil and its fractions" whereas "stearic acid" is classified under HS code 2915 70 000 if it is chemically pure. "Stearic acid" which is industrial monocarboxylic fatty acids is classified under HS code 3823 11 000.

Question
Can I classify "silica gel" under HS code 2811 22 000 ?

Answer
"Silica gel" should be classified under HS code 3824 90 900 as "other chemical products and preparations not elsewhere specified or included". HS code 2811 22 000 covers silicon dioxide.

Chapter 39

Question
Under which textile chapter can we classify "vulcanised fibre"?

Answer
"Vulcanised fibre" is the expression for "plastics". It is not classified under any of the textile chapters.

"Vulcanised fibre" plates, sheets, film, foil and strip which are non-cellular and not reinforced, laminated, supported or similarly combined with other materials are classified under HS code 3920 72 000.

Question
My invoice showed the description of goods as "laminating films". Can you advise which HS code I should use to classify these products ?

Answer
"Laminating films" are classified based on their material composition. As "laminating films" are mostly made of plastic, they are classified under HS heading 3920 based on the specific type of plastic.

Question
Where is "vulcanised fibre" classified? Is it the same as plastics?

Answer
Based on Note 1 of Chapter 39, any reference to "plastics" throughout the Nomenclature also includes vulcanised fibre. The expression, however, does not apply to materials regarded as textile materials. "Vulcanised fibre" plates, sheets, film, foil and strip, non-cellular and not reinforced, laminated, supported or similarly combined with other materials are classified under HS code 3920 72 000.

Question
What is the HS classification for "ink cartridge", "inked ribbon cartridge", "toners for laser printers" and "toner cartridges for photocopiers? Are they classified under the same HS code?

Answer
No, they are classified separately as follows:

Product Description	HS Code
Ink cartridge (filled with ink)	3215 90 900 (Other inks)
Ink cartridge (empty) , of plastic	3926 90 900 (Other articles of plastic)
Inked ribbon cartridge (for typewriter use)	9612 10 000 (Typewriter or similar ribbons, inked or otherwise prepared for giving, impressions, whether or not on spools or in cartridges)
Toners for laser printers	3707 90 000 (Other chemical preparations for photographic uses)
Cartridges for photocopiers (with or without toner)	9009 90 000 (Parts and accessories for photocopying apparatus)

Question
Where do you classify "plastic film" ?

Answer
For sensitised "plastic film", you should classify according to the usage under Chapter 37 as "photographic or cinematographic goods". If the "plastic film" is non-sensitised, you should classify it according to the specific types of plastic compositions under HS headings 39.19, 39.20 or 39.21.

Chapter 37

Question
Where do you classify "glue"?

Answer
"Prepared glues", when packed for retail sale in packages not exceeding a net weight of 1 kg, are classified under HS code 3506 10 000. However, if the packaging exceeds a net weight of 1 kg, "prepared glue" should be classified according to its material composition. "Rubber glue", in packings which exceed a net weight of 1 kg, is classified under HS code 4005 20 000. If the glue is made of plastic, you should classify it according to the specific types of plastic under Chapter 39.

Question
What is the HS classification for "tyres of a size 1000-20 16 PR" and "tyres of a size 165 x 65 R13"?

Answer
"Tyres of a size 1000-20 16PR" are classified under HS code 4011 20 000 as "tyres of a kind used on buses or lorries" while "tyres of a size 165 x 65 R13" are classified under HS code 4011 10 000 as "tyres of a kind used on motor cars"(including station wagons and racing cars) .

Chapter 42

Question
Are "dog's clothings" classified under HS code 6211 32 000?

Answer
"Dog's or other animal's clothings" are classified separately from "other woven cotton garments for men or boys" under HS code 6211 32 000. "Dog's clothings" are classified under HS code 4201 00 000 as "saddlery and harness for any animal (including traces, leads, knee pads, muzzles, saddle cloths, saddle bags, dog coats and the like) , of any material.

Question
Can we classify "blankets for horses" under HS code 6301 90 000?

Answer
No, "blankets for horses" should not be classified under HS code 6301 90 000 as "other blankets and travelling rugs". They are classified under HS code 4201 00 000 which includes "saddlery and harness for any animal (including traces, leads, knee pads, muzzles, saddle cloths, saddle bags, dog coats and the like) , of any material".

Question
Can I classify "soft carrying bag of polyester" under HS code 3923 29 000?

Answer
"Soft carrying bag of polyester" should be classified under HS code 4202 92 000 as "travelling bags, toilet bags, sports bags, shopping bags, etc., with outer surface of plastic sheeting or of textile materials". HS code 3923 29 000 covers plastic bags which are not for prolonged usage.

Question
Is "cotton cosmetic bag" classified under HS code 6305 20 000?

Answer
"Cotton cosmetic bag" is classified under HS code 4202 32 000 as "articles of a kind normally carried in the pocket or handbag". It should not be classified under HS code 6305 20 000 as the code covers "cotton sacks and bags of a kind used for the packing of goods".

Question
Can we classify "trunks (suitcases) made of steel" under HS code 7326 90 900?

Answer
"Trunks (suitcases) made of steel" are classified specifically under HS code 4202 19 000 as travelling-bags. They should not be classified based on their material composition under HS code 7326 90 900 as "other articles of iron or steel."

Question
What is the HS classification for "belts"?

Answer
"Belts" are classified according to their material composition and usage. If the belts are made of leather and are used as clothing accessories, the HS code is 4203 30 000. However, if the leather belt is used at the worksite for the purpose of industrial safety, it is classified under HS code 4205 00 100. Belts for orthopaedic use are classified under HS code 9021 19 000.

Question
Can I classify "catgut" under HS code 3006 10 000?

Answer
"Catgut" which is manufactured by twisting-strips of cleaned and dried gut, especially sheep's gut is used mainly in the manufacturing of rackets, of fishing tackle and of machinery is classified under HS code 4206 10 000. HS code 3006 10 000 covers sterile surgical catgut.

Chapter 44

Question
What is "wood wool" ? Is there a HS code for such an item ?

Answer
"Wood wool" consists of fine slivers of wood, curled or twisted to form a tangled mass. It is used mainly for packing or stuffing purposes and is specifically classified under HS code 4405 00 000.

Question
Can I classify "particleboard" under HS code 4412 99 000?

Answer
"Particleboard" is classified under HS code 4410 19 000. It is a flat product manufactured in various lengths, widths and thicknesses by pressing or extrusion. It is usually made from wood chips or particles obtained by the mechanical reduction of roundwood or wood residues. It may also be produced from other ligneous materials such as fragments obtained from bagasse, bamboo, cereal straw or from flax or hemp shives.

Particleboard is normally agglomerated by means of an added organic binder, usually a thermosetting resin, which generally does not exceed 15 % of the weight of the board.

HS code 4412 99 000 covers laminated wood, other than those at least one outer ply of non-coniferous wood, not containing any plies of tropical wood or any layers of particle board.

Question
What is the HS code for "wooden houses for pets"? Can I classify them under HS code 9403 60 900?

Answer
"Wooden houses for pets" such as rabbit-hutches, cages and kennels of wood are classified under HS code 4421 90 000 as "other articles of wood". HS code 9403 60 900 refers to other wooden furniture.

Chapter 48

Question
What is the HS code for "carbon paper"?

Answer
"Carbon paper" in strips or rolls of a width exceeding 36 cm or in rectangular (including square) sheets with one side exceeding 36 cm and the other side exceeding 15 cm in the unfolded state, is classified under the HS code 4809 10 000. However, "carbon paper," of a width not exceeding 36 cm, whether or not put up in boxes, is classified under HS code 4816 10 000.

Question
What is the HS code for "surgical face-masks" ?

Answer
"Surgical face-masks" are classified according to the material composition. For paper "surgical face-masks", you should classify under the specific HS code 4818 50 100. If the "surgical face-masks" are made of textile, the specific HS code is 6307 90 300.

Question
What is the HS code for "baby wipes"?

Answer
"Baby wipes" are wet cleansing tissues and are classified under HS code 4818 20 000.

Chapter 49

Question
Where do you classify "pictures that are framed"?

Answer
"Pictures, whether or not framed" are classified under HS code 4911 91 000.

Chapter 53

Question
What are "raw coconut fibres (coir) "? Are they classified under HS code 5702 20 000?

Answer
"Raw coconut fibres (coir) " are vegetable textile fibres obtained from the external covering of the nut. They are coarse, brittle and brown in colour, whether in mass or in bundles and are classified under HS code 5305 11 000. HS code 5702 20 000 on the other hand covers "woven floor coverings of coconut fibres (coir) , not tufted or flocked".

Chapter 58

Question
What is the HS code for "polyester embroidery"?

Answer
"Polyester embroidery" in the piece, in strips, in roll form or in motifs is classified under HS heading 58.10.

They are classified under HS code 5810 10 000 if they do not have visible ground, that is, their ground fabric has been eliminated, for example, by a chemical process or by cutting out.

However, if they have a visible ground, they are classified under HS code 5810 92 000 as "other embroidery of man-made fibres".

Chapter 59

Question
Can we classify "textile backdrop" as "made-up textile articles" under HS code 6307 90 900?

Answer
"Textile backdrop" refers to a piece of painted cloth hung across the back of a stage. It is classified specifically under HS code 5907 00 000 as "textile fabrics impregnated, coated or covered, including painted canvas being theatrical scenery, studio back-cloths and the like".

Chapter 61

Question
Where do you classify "men's cotton polo shirts"?

Answer
"Men's cotton polo shirts" which are knitted or crocheted are classified under HS code 6105 10 000 as "men's shirts, knitted or crocheted, of cotton". However, if these are woven shirts, they are classified under the HS code 6205 20 000 as "men's shirts, of cotton".

Chapter 62

Question
What is the HS code for "boys' cotton judo suits" ?

Answer
"Boys' cotton judo suits" are classified as "other cotton garments for men or boys" under HS code 6211 32 000.

Chapter 63

Question
What is the HS code for "surgical face-masks"?

Answer
"Surgical face-masks" are classified according to the material composition. For paper "surgical face-masks", you should classify under the specific HS code 4818 50 100. If the "surgical face-masks" are made of textile, the specific HS code is 6307 90 300.

Question
Can I classify "umbrella cases or covers" as "umbrella parts" under HS code 6603 90 000?

Answer
"Umbrella cases or covers" are usually made of textile. They should be classified under HS code 6307 90 900 as "articles of textile". HS code 6603 90 000 covers umbrella parts, trimmings and accessories such as shafts, spikes, runner, rib etc.

Chapter 65

Question
Do you classify "leather hat" under HS code 4205 00 900?

Answer
"Leather hat" is classified under HS code 6506 99 000 as "other headgear of other materials". It should not be classified under HS code 4205 00 900 as "other articles of leather or of composition leather".

Chapter 68

Question
"Paper" is classified under Chapter 48. Is it correct to classify "abrasive paper" under HS code 4811 29 000 ?

Answer
"Abrasive paper" should be classified under HS code 6805 20 000 as "natural or artificial abrasive powder or grain, on a base of paper or paperboard". HS code 4811 29 000 covers "other gummed or adhesive paper or paperboard" which are not cut to size.

Question
Can I classify "cement bricks" under HS code 6904 10 000?

Answer
"Cement bricks" are classified under HS code 6810 11 000 as "building blocks and bricks of cement, of concrete or of artificial stone, whether or not reinforced". HS code 6904 10 000 covers "ceramic building bricks".

Question
Where do you classify "fire fighter's suits"?

Answer
"Fire fighter's suits" are normally made of asbestos. They are classified under HS code 6812 50 000 as "clothing of asbestos".

Chapter 69

Question
Can I classify "ceramic cornices" under HS code 6913 10 000?

Answer
"Ceramic cornices" are architectural ornaments for use on walls and are classified under HS code 6905 90 000. HS code 6913 10 000 covers statuettes and other ornamental ceramic articles of porcelain or china.
Chapter 70

Question
Where do you classify "Corning tableware"?

Answer
"Corning tableware" is opaque and is more heat resistant than ordinary glass tableware. It should be classified under HS code 7013 10 000 as "glassware of a kind used for table, of glass-ceramics".

Chapter 71

Question
What is the HS code for "spent catalyst" used in the recovery of gold ? Is it classified under HS code 7115 10 000 ?

Answer
"Spent catalyst" used in the recovery of gold is classified under HS code 7112 10 000. Please see Chapter Note 1(d) of Chapter 38. HS code 7115 10 000 refers to the classification of "catalysts in the form of wire cloth or grill, of platinum".

Question
Is "waste and scrap photographic film containing silver" classified under HS code 4707 30 000?

Answer
"Waste and scrap photographic film containing silver" normally used principally for the recovery of precious metal is classified under HS code 7112 90 000. HS code 4707 30 000 on the other hand covers paper or paperboard made mainly of mechanical pulp such as newspapers, journals and similar printed matters normally presented in compressed bales and used for pulping.

Question
Where do you classify "designer's jewellery" ?

Answer
"Designer's jewellery" made from gold or silver is classified under HS heading 71.13. For "designer's jewellery" of other materials, it is classified under HS heading 71.17.

Question
What is the HS code for "forks made of sterling silver" ?

Answer
"Forks made of sterling silver" is classified under the HS code 7114 11 000 as "articles of silversmiths' wares, whether or not plated or clad with other precious metal".

Chapter 73

Question
What is the HS code for "tin cans used for canning food"? Are they classified under HS code 8001 20 000?

Answer
"Tin cans used for canning food" are normally made of iron or steel. They are classified under HS code 7310 21 000 as "cans which are to be closed by soldering or crimping, of a capacity of less than 50 litres". However, if they are made of tin, they are classified under HS code 8007 00 000 as "other articles of tin".

It is incorrect to classify under HS code 8001 20 000 because it covers unwrought tin alloys.

Question
What is the HS code for "staples" ?

Answer
"Staples" of iron or steel which are not in strips, pointed at both ends and are used for electric wiring, fencing and picture frames, are classified under the HS code 7317 00 900.

Other "staples" of base metal, in the form of strips and are used for office stapling machines, are classified under HS code 8305 20 000.

Chapter 74

Question
Are "cables" classified under HS code 7413 00 000?

Answer
"Cables" which are not electrically insulated are classified according to their material composition. For example, copper "cables" which are not electrically insulated are classified under HS code 7413 00 000 whereas iron or steel "cables" which are not electrically insulated are classified under the HS code 7312 10 000. However, electrically insulated "cables" are classified under HS heading 8544.

Question
Are "cables" classified under HS code 7413 00 000?

Answer
"Cables" are classified by material composition if they are not electrically insulated as follows:

Material Composition	HS Code
Copper	7413 00 000
Iron or steel	7312 10 000

However, they are classified under HS heading 8544 if they are electrically insulated.

Question
What is the HS code for "token coins" used in game machines?

Answer
"Token coins" used in game machines are classified according to their material composition. They are classified under HS code 7419 99 000 if made of copper and HS code 7616 99 000 if made of aluminium

Chapter 75

Question
Can I classify "tubes, pipes and fittings of nickel" under 3917 40 000?

Answer
"Tubes, pipes and fittings of nickel" which are usually used in apparatus for the chemical, food, papermaking industries, etc., in the manufacture of steam condensers, hypodermic needles, etc. because of their resistance to corrosion are classified under HS code 7507 20 000. HS code 3917 40 000 covers fittings of plastics for tubes, pipes and hoses.

Chapter 76

Question
What is the HS code for "token coins" used in game machines?

Answer
"Token coins" used in game machines are classified according to their material composition. They are classified under HS code 7419 99 000 if made of copper and HS code 7616 99 000 if made of aluminium

Chapter 78

Question
What is "lead foil"? Is it classified under HS code 7801 99 000?

Answer
"Lead foil" is mainly used for packing (especially for lining tea chests or cases for silk) . In some cases, the foil is clad or coated with tin or other metals. It is classified under HS code 7804 11 000 if the thickness of the foil (excluding any backing) does not exceed 0.2mm. HS code 7801 99 000 covers lead (other than refined lead) , unwrought, in cast anodes, other than those containing by weight of antimony as the principal other element.

Chapter 80

Question
Where do you classify "pewterware"?

Answer
"Pewterware" usually refers to ornamental articles and tableware made of tin. It is classified under HS code 8007 00 000 as "articles of tin".

Question
What is the HS code for "tin cans used for canning food"? Are they classified under HS code 8001 20 000?

Answer
"Tin cans used for canning food" are normally made of iron or steel. They are classified under HS code 7310

21 000 as "cans which are to be closed by soldering or crimping, of a capacity of less than 50 litres". However, if they are made of tin, they are classified under HS code 8007 00 000 as "other articles of tin".

It is incorrect to classify under HS code 8001 20 000 because it covers unwrought tin alloys.

Chapter 82

Question
What is the HS code for "hand saws"?

Answer
Manual "Hand saws" for wood, metal, stone or other materials are classified under HS code 8202 10 000. "Hydraulic saws" for working in the hand or those with a self-contained non-electric motor is classified under HS code 8467 81 000. For electric "hand saws" which have a self-contained motor and are used as an electro-mechanical tool for working in the hand, you should classify under HS code 8508 20 000.

Question
Where do you classify "drills"?

Answer
Drills are classified as follows :

	Type of drill	HS code
a)	manually operated	8205 10 000
b)	pneumatic	8467 11 100
c)	with self-contained electric motor	8508 10 000

Question
Should I declare separate HS codes for "handtools in sets" such as spanners, screwdrivers, pliers and socket sets that come together with the tool box?

Answer
"Handtools in sets" should be declared under HS code 8206 00 000. You need not declare separate HS codes for the tools such as spanners and screwdrivers.

Chapter 83

Question
Are "door guards fitted with chain" classified as "iron or steel chain and parts" under HS code 7315 12 000 ?

Answer
"Door guards fitted with chains" should be classified under HS code 8302 41 000 as "other mountings, fittings and similar articles suitable for buildings".

Question
What is the HS code for "staples" ?

Answer
"Staples" of iron or steel which are not in strips, pointed at both ends and are used for electric wiring, fencing and picture frames, are classified under the HS code 7317 00 900.

Other "staples" of base metal, in the form of strips and are used for office stapling machines, are classified under HS code 8305 20 000.

Chapter 84

Question
What is the HS code for "compressors for refrigerators"? Is it classified under HS code 8414 40 000?

Answer
"Compressors for refrigerators" are classified under HS code 8414 30 000 as "compressors of a kind used in refrigerating equipment" whereas HS code 8414 40 000 covers "air compressors mounted on a wheeled chassis for towing".

Question
Can I classify "grape crushing machine" for wine under HS code 8509 40 000?

Answer
"Grape crushing machine" which is used in the manufacture of wine usually consists of two grooved cylinders or of a single cylinder fitted with beaters that extracts the juice from the grapes without crushing the seeds or stems is classified under HS code 8435 10 000.

HS code 8509 40 000 refers to "fruits or vegetable juice extractors" for household use.

Question
Can I classify "compressed air grease gun" under HS code 8205 59 000?

Answer
The "grease gun" which is operated by compressed air should be classified under HS code 8467 19 900 as "other pneumatic tools for working in the hand". HS code 8205 59 000 covers "other manual hand tools".

Question
What is the HS code for "hand saws" ?

Answer
Manual "Hand saws" for wood, metal, stone or other materials are classified under HS code 8202 10 000. "Hydraulic saws" for working in the hand or those with a self-contained non-electric motor is classified under HS code 8467 81 000. For electric "hand saws" which have a self-contained motor and are used as an electro-mechanical tool for working in the hand, you should classify under HS code 8508 20 000.

Question
Please advise the HS classification for computers.

Answer
For a portable computer, the HS code is 8471 30 000.
If it comprises in the same housing, at least a CPU, an input or output unit, the HS code is 8471 41 XXX.

For computers presented in the form of a system, the HS code is 8471 49 XXX.

Question
What is the HS code for "banknote counter"? Can I classify it under HS code 8470 30 000 as "other calculating machines" since it is used for counting dollar notes in the bank?

Answer
"Banknote counter" is classified together with "coin-counting machines" under HS code 8472 90 000 as "other office machines".

Question
Are "automatic teller machines" classified under HS code 8476 89 000?

Answer
"Automatic teller machines" which customers deposit, draw and transfer money and see the balances of their accounts without direct contact with bank personnel are classified under 8472 90 000. HS code 8476 89 000 is for classifying money-changing machine.

Question
What is the HS code for printed circuit board?

Answer
If assembled and is for computer use, printed circuit board is classified under HS code 8473 30 100.

If unassembled, printed circuit board is classified under HS heading 8534.

Question
Where do you classify "vending machines" for dispensing cold drinks such as coke and 7-up?

Answer
"Vending machines" for dispensing coke and 7-up are classified under HS code 8476 21 000 as "automatic beverage-vending machine incorporating a refrigerating device".

Chapter 85

Question
What is the HS code for "hand saws" ?

Answer
Manual "Hand saws" for wood, metal, stone or other materials are classified under HS code 8202 10 000. "Hydraulic saws" for working in the hand or those with a self-contained non-electric motor is classified under HS code 8467 81 000. For electric "hand saws" which have a self-contained motor and are used as an electro-mechanical tool for working in the hand, you should classify under HS code 8508 20 000.

Question
Can I classify "electric tooth brush" under HS code 9603 21 000?

Answer
"Electric tooth brush" should be classified under HS code 8509 80 000. You can classify ordinary tooth brush in HS code 9603 21 000.

Question
Where should I classify "home sauna" apparatus ?

Answer
"Home sauna" apparatus consists of an infra-red radiator of enamelled sheet steel for use as stool and a cylindrical cabin consisting of four separate parts (namely a shutter made of slats of wood or plastics or of imitation leather, a carpet cover, a cabin top of imitation leather and a thermometer in a wooden casing) . The various components are put together, before use, to take heat baths at home. The "home sauna" apparatus is classified under the HS code 8516 79 900 as "other electro-thermic appliances".

Question
Can I classify "electric irons for domestic use" under HS code 8451 30 000?

Answer
"Electric irons for domestic use" should be classified under the HS code 8516 40 000. HS code 8451 30 000 covers "industrial ironing machines for pressing garments".

Question
Where do you classify "walkman"?

Answer
"Walkman" is a pocket-size cassette-player. It is classified under HS code 8519 92 000 as pocket-size cassette-players.

Question
What is the HS code for "telephone answering machine with recording device"? Is it classified under HS code 9030 40 000?

Answer
"Telephone answering machine with recording device" is classified under HS code 8520 20 000 while those not incorporating a sound recording device is classified under HS code 8519 99 900. HS code 9030 40 000 refers to telephone hand test set with rotary and tone dialling capabilities, used to test the installation and maintenance of telecommunication lines and systems.

Question
What is the HS classification for CD-Rom for computer use?

Answer
Blank CD-Rom for computer use is classified under HS code 8523 90 200 but recorded CD-Rom is under HS code 8524 31 000.

Question
What is the HS classification for video compact disc?

Answer
Blank video compact disc is classified under HS code 8523 90 100. If it is recorded, it is classified under HS code 8524 39 000.

Question
What is the HS code for "magnetic stripe access card (magnetic card key) " which is normally used to open the door of a hotel room?

Answer
Blank "magnetic stripe access card (magnetic card key) " is classified under HS code 8523 30 000 as "unrecorded card incorporating a magnetic stripe".

If the "magnetic stripe access card (magnetic card key) " has been programmed and is used as a key to open the door of the hotel room, it is classified under HS code 8524 60 000 as "recorded card incorporating a magnetic stripe".

Question
What is the HS code for "audio pancake" of a width not exceeding 4 mm?

Answer
"Audio pancake" which is an unrecorded magnetic audio tape, in the form of jumbo rolls or pancakes (maximum width of 4 mm) is classified under HS code 8523 11 900.

Question
Where do you classify "telephone cards"?

Answer
"Telephone cards" with stored value are classified under HS code 8524 60 000. For "telephone cards" without stored value, they are classified under HS code 8523 30 000. However, "telephone cards" which are kept as "collectors' pieces" are under HS code 9705 00 900.

Question
Where do you classify "cartridges for video game" ?

Answer
"Magnetic tape cartridges for video games" are classified under HS codes 8524 51 100, 8524 52 100 or 8524 53 100, depending on the width of the magnetic tapes.

However, if you have video games cartridges containing integrated circuits as the recording media, they are classified under HS code 8524 99 100 as "other video recorded media".

Question
Where do I classify "decoder for video camera"? Is it classified under HS code 8522 90 900 as "parts and accessories suitable for use solely or principally with the apparatus of headings Nos. 85.19 to 85.21"?

Answer
"Decoder for video camera" is classified as "other transmission apparatus for radio-telephony, radio-telegraphy, radio-broadcasting or television" under HS code 8525 10 900.

Question
What is the HS classification for radio cassette recorder?

Answer
Battery operated radio cassette recorder is classified under HS code 8527 13 000. For mains operated, it is classified under HS code 8527 31 000.

Question
Can I classify "video monitors " under HS code 8471 60 210?

Answer
"Video monitors " are receivers connected directly to the video camera or recorder by means of co-axial cables, so that all the radio-frequency circuits are eliminated. They are generally used for closed-circuit television. They are classified under HS code 8528 21 000 whereas HS code 8471 60 210 covers specifically "colour computer monitors".

Question
Can I classify "electronic brass bells" under HS code 7419 99 000?
Answer
"Electronic brass bells" generally consist of an electro-magnetically operated appliance which causes a small hammer to vibrate and strike a bell dome. They are classified under HS code 8531 80 000 as "other electric sound or visual signalling apparatus". HS code 7419 99 000 covers "other articles of copper".

Question
What is the HS code for "control panel" ?

Answer
A "control panel" consists of an assembly of switches, fuses etc. on a board, panel or console or mounted in a cabinet or desk. It usually incorporates meters and sometimes subsidiary apparatus such as transformers, valves, voltage regulators. It is classified according to the voltage under HS heading 85.37. For "control panels" which do not exceed 1,000 V, they are classified under the HS code 8537 10 100. HS code 8537 20 100 covers "control panels" of voltage exceeding 1,000 V.

The following are some examples of products classified under HS heading 85.37 :

1. numerical control panels with built-in data processing machine, generally used to control machine tools ;

2. programmed switchboards to control apparatus which allows the choice of operations to be followed. E.g. those used in washing machines ; and

3. programmable controllers which are digital apparatus using a programmable memory for storing instructions for implementing specific functions.

Question
Is 'infra-red lamps' classified under HS code 9018 20 000?

Answer
"Infra-red lamps" are filament lamps specially designed to produce infra-red rays. The interior of the lamp is usually coppered or silvered to form a reflector. They are classified under HS code 8539 49 000. HS code 9018 20 000 covers infra-red ray apparatus used in medical, surgical, dental or veterinary sciences.

Question
Is "wafers for integrated circuit" classified under HS code 1905 30 300?

Answer
"Wafers for integrated circuit" are electronic goods. They are classified under HS code 8542 90 000.

HS code 1905 30 300 covers wafers (thin light biscuits usually eaten with ice-cream) baked between patterned metal plates.

Question
My consignment was described in the invoice as "Intel pentium 75 MHZ". Where should I classify this product ?

Answer
"Intel pentium 75 MHZ" is classified under HS code 8542 19 000 as "other digital integrated circuits".

Question
Can I classify "lead frames for integrated circuits" under HS code 7806 00 000 as "other articles of lead"?

Answer
"Lead frames for integrated circuits" are "parts for integrated circuits". They should be classified under HS code 8542 90 000 as "parts for electronic integrated circuits and microassemblies".

Question
Are "sound mixers" classified under HS code 8509 40 000?

Answer
"Sound mixers" are classified under HS code 8543 89 000 as "other electrical machines and apparatus

having individual functions, not specified or included elsewhere in Chapter 85". The products covered under HS code 8509 40 000 are "electrical domestic food mixers" such as food grinders and mixers.

Question
Are "cables" classified under HS code 7413 00 000?

Answer
"Cables" are classified by material composition if they are not electrically insulated as follows:

Material Composition	HS Code
Copper	7413 00 000
Iron or steel	7312 10 000

However, they are classified under HS heading 8544 if they are electrically insulated.

Chapter 87

Question
Where do you classify "car safety airbags"?

Answer
"Car safety airbags" are classified under HS code 8708 99 000 as "motor vehicle parts".

Chapter 90

Question
What is the HS classification for "belts"?

Answer
"Belts" are classified according to their material composition and usage. If the belts are made of leather and are used as clothing accessories, the HS code is 4203 30 000. However, if the leather belt is used at the worksite for the purpose of industrial safety, it is classified under HS code 4205 00 100.

Belts for orthopaedic use are classified under HS code 9021 19 000.

Question
Is "mock-up TV (model) " classified under HS heading 85.28?

Answer
"Mock-up TV (model) " is classified under HS code 9023 00 000 as "models designed for demonstrational purposes (e.g. in education or exhibitions) , unsuitable for other uses".

Question
I have a consignment for one testing machine. How should I classify the machine?

Answer
Please state the use of the testing machine. For eg. testing machine to test the hardness of metal is classified under the HS code 9024 10 000.

For test benches (which consist of a frame and a measuring or calibrating instrument) used for testing engines and motors, electrical generators, pumps, speed indicators or tachometers, they are classified under HS code 9031 20 000.

Question
Can I classify "saccharimeters" under HS code 2925 11 000?

Answer
"Saccharimeters" are special polarimeters designed for determining the strength of sugar solutions and are classified under HS code 9027 80 900. HS code 2925 11 000 refers to "saccharin and its salts" which is an odourless, white crystalline powder having a very sweet taste and its sodium and ammonium salts have a lower sweetening power but more soluble.

Question
What is the HS code for "oscillometers"?

Answer
"Oscillometers", being instruments for testing watch movements are classified under HS code 9031 80 000 whereas oscillometers, being diagnostic medical instruments for measuring blood pressure are classified under HS code 9018 90 900.

Chapter 92

Question
Can I classify "body for zither" under HS code 9202 90 000?

Answer
"Body for zither" is classified under HS code 9209 92 000 as "parts for musical instruments of Heading No. 9202". HS code 9202 90 000 refers to zithers which are plucked string instruments having a flat sound-box of approximately trapezoidal shape, and a large number of strings usually metal.

Question
Where do you classify "mirrors" which form parts of furniture?

Answer
"Mirrors" which form parts of furniture, for example, wardrobe doors, are classified under HS code 9403 90 000 as "furniture parts".

Question
Where do you classify "illuminated barber lights or signs" normally placed in front of barber shop?

Answer
"Illuminated barber lights or signs" are classified under HS code 9405 60 000 as "illuminated lighting fittings".

Question
Where do you classify "doll's parts and accessories"?

Answer
"Doll's parts and accessories" are classified under the HS code 9502 91 000. However "glass eyes for dolls without moving mechanism" are classified under HS code 7018 90 000.

Chapter 95

Question
Do you classify "balloons for children" under "articles of rubber"?

Answer
No, they are classified under HS code 9503 90 900 as other toys. They are not classified under "articles of rubber" even though they are made of rubber because the balloons are essentially toys meant for children to play.

Question
What is the HS code for "bubble blow soap in liquid form for children to play" ? Can it be classified as "soap" under HS code 3401 11 900 ?

Answer
"Bubble blow soap in liquid form for children to play" is classified under HS code 9503 90 900 as "other toys". We do not classify the product as "soap" because its end-use is not for washing.

Question
Where do you classify "children's plastic rocking horse"? Is it classified under HS code 9508 00 000 ?

Answer
"Children's plastic rocking horse" is classified as "other toys" under 9503 90 900.

Question
What is the HS code for "plastic ultra-man toy which has the size of a three year old boy (with motor) "? Can we classify it as "other plastic articles" under HS code 3926 90 900?

Answer
"Plastic ultra-man toy which has the size of a three year old boy" is a "toy model" and is classified under HS code 9503 80 900 as "other toys and models, incorporating a motor".

Question
Can I classify "toy tea sets" under HS code 6911 10 000?

Answer
"Toy tea sets" are classified under HS code 9503 70 000 as "other toys, put up in sets" whereas HS code 6911 10 000 refers to tea sets of porcelain or china.

Question
Are "dumb bells" used for general physical exercise classified under 8306 10 000?

Answer
"Dumb bells" used for general physical exercise are classified under HS code 9506 91 000 as "articles and equipment for general physical exercise". HS code 8306 10 000 refers to non-electric bells of base metal for religious worship, public buildings, fire-engines, animal bells and bicycles etc.

Chapter 96

Question
Can I classify "feather duster" under HS code 6701 00 000?

Answer
"Feather duster" is normally used for dusting furniture, shelves, shop windows, etc. It should be classified under HS code 9603 90 000.

You cannot classify it under HS code 6701 00 000 based on the "material composition" even though it consists of a bundle of feathers mounted on a handle.

Question
What is the HS code for "overnight travelling kit which consists of a toothbrush, a tube of toothpaste, a comb, a mirror, an eyebrow tweezer and a small towel"? Should I itemise and classify the items according to their specific HS codes?

Answer
"Overnight travelling kit which consists of a toothbrush, a tube of toothpaste, a comb, a mirror, an eyebrow tweezer and a small towel" is classified under the specific HS code 9605 00 000 as "travel sets for personal toilet". There is no need to classify the items separately according to their specific HS codes.

Question
Can I classify "highlighters" under HS code 3213 10 000?

Answer
"Highlighters" are classified under HS code 9608 20 000. You should not classify them under HS code 3213 10 000 as "colours in sets" because "colours in sets" refer to water colours, oil paints, etc. in sets.

Question
Can I classify "pumps for fountain pen" under HS code 8413 91 000?

Answer
"Pumps for fountain pen" are parts of fountain pen classified under HS code 9608 99 000 whereas HS code 8413 91 000 refers to parts of pumps for liquids, whether or not fitted with a measuring device.

Question
What is the HS classification for "ink cartridge", "inked ribbon cartridge", "toners for laser printers" and "toner cartridges for photocopiers? Are they classified under the same HS code?

Answer
No, they are classified separately as follows:

Product Description	HS Code
Ink cartridge (filled with ink)	3215 90 900 (Other inks)
Ink cartridge (empty) , of plastic	3926 90 900 (Other articles of plastic)
Inked ribbon cartridge (for typewriter use)	9612 10 000 (Typewriter or similar ribbons, inked or otherwise prepared for giving, impressions, whether or not on spools or in cartridges)
Toners for laser printers	3707 90 000 (Other chemical preparations for photographic uses)
Cartridges for photocopiers (with or without toner)	9009 90 000 (Parts and accessories for photocopying apparatus)

Chapter 97

Question
Are "butterflies encased in a frame "classified under HS code 0106 00 900?

Answer
"Butterflies encased in a frame" are classified under HS code 9705 00 900 as "collectors' pieces". It should not be classified under HS code 0106 00 900 because the code covers "other live animals".

Question
Where do you classify "telephone cards"?

Answer
"Telephone cards" with stored value are classified under HS code 8524 60 000. For "telephone cards" without stored value, they are classified under HS code 8523 30 000. However, "telephone cards" which are kept as "collectors' pieces" are under HS code 9705 00 900.

STARTING A BUSINESS IN SINGAPORE

LICENSING AND REGISTRATION OF BUSINESS ORGANISATIONS

6. There are no restrictions on the types of businesses that may be set-up in Singapore, but some have to apply for special licences from the Government e.g. banks, finance companies, insurance and stock-broker firms. Some items require a licence before manufacturing for eg. cigarettes, beer or stout or fire crackers.
7. Every business in Singapore must be registered with the Registry of Companies and Businesses.

FORMATION OF REPRESENTATIVE OFFICE

A foreign company may establish a representative office in Singapore to undertake promotional and liaison activities on behalf of its parent company. The office, however, directly or on behalf of its parent company, must not be engaged in business; undertake transhipment of goods; or open or negotiate any letters of credits. Approval for the establishment of a representative office must be obtained from the Singapore Trade Development Board.

TYPES OF BUSINESS ORGANISATIONS

8. Persons who wish to carry on business in Singapore must seek registration either under the Business Registration Act (Cap. 32) or the Companies Act (Cap. 50) .

These two Acts regulate businesses and companies in Singapore respectively. They are administered by the Registry of Companies and Businesses.

9. The types of business organisation which may be registered in Singapore are:

Under the **Business Registration Act:**
a. Sole Proprietorships
b. Partnerships

Under the **Companies Act:**
a. Companies incorporated in Singapore
b. Foreign companies

REGISTRATION

10. Briefly, the formalities which must be completed before a company can be registered under the Companies Act are as follows:

a. Application must be made to the Registry of Companies and Businesses for approval of the name of the company.

b. A memorandum and articles of association should be drawn up for the purposes of registration. The requirements for the memorandum are specified in Section 22 of the Companies Act.

c. These must be filed with the Registry of Companies and Businesses.

FOREIGN COMPANIES

A foreign company should, before it establishes a place of business or commences to carry on business in Singapore, lodge with the Registry of Companies and Businesses for registration relevant information including:

a certified copy of the certificate of its incorporation or registration in its place of incorporation. For more details please refer to the Registry of Companies and Businesses Website.

The agent of a foreign company is answerable for the doing of all acts, matters and things as are required to be done by the foreign company under the Act and is personally liable for any penalties imposed on the foreign company for any contravention of such requirements.

A foreign company is not regarded as carrying on business in Singapore by reason of the fact that it maintains a bank account in Singapore, effects any sale through an independent contractor, invests its funds or holds any property.

To ascertain whether the foreign company is "carrying on business in Singapore", it is often advisable to obtain professional advice from lawyers and public accountants.

Company law in Singapore is very similar to company law in the UK and Australia, with procedures for registration, submission of returns etc, varying only slightly according to local requirements. It is advisable to employ the services of a firm of solicitors or accountants to attend to the formalities of registering a company.

GOODS MANUFACTURED

Manufacturing the following items need to be approved by the Singapore government

First Schedule	Second Schedule
1. Air-conditioners	1. Cigarettes
2. Beer and stout	2. Matches
3. Cigars	
4. Chewing gum, bubble gum, dental chewing gum	
5. Drawn steel products	
6. Firecrackers	
7. Pig iron and sponge iron	
8. Rolled steel products	

9. Refrigerators	
10. Steel ingots, billets, blooms and slabs	

REGISTERING A COMPANY INSINGAPORE

WHAT IS A BUSINESS FIRM?

Under The Business Registration Act, "business" includes every form of trade, commerce, craftmanship, calling, profession and any activity carried on for the purposes of gain but does not include any office, employment or occupation, or any of the businesses specified in the First Schedule.

List of exempted entities/individuals:

(a)	Individuals carrying on any of the businesses specified in the First Schedule.*
(b)	Statutory authority or other body established under any written law.
(c)	Institution, society or person specified in the First Schedule to the Income Tax Act.
(d)	Registered Society.
(e)	Registered co-operative society.
(f)	Registered mutual benefit organisation.
(g)	Person carrying on any business consisting solely of the exercise of any profession which under the law can be exercised only by those who posses certain prescribed qualifications and whose names are registered in the manner prescribed by the law (e.g. doctors, lawyers) .
(h)	Charitable institutions which is exempt from tax under the Income Tax Act.
(i)	The Public Trustee or the Offical Assignee of the property of a bankrupt.
(j)	A foreign company carrying on business in Singapore which is registered under the Companies Act and carries on the business under its corporate name.
(k)	Any other person or class of persons for the time being exempted by the Minister, by notification of the Gazette, from all provisions of this Act.
(l)	Any company registered under the Companies Act or any previous legislation carrying on business under a business name that consists of its corporate name.

***Businesses specified in the First Schedule :**

1.	Any business of a licensed hawker who sells or exposes for sale any drink, goods, wares or merchandise of any kind whatsoever, or who offers for hire his skill in handicraft or craftmanship.
2.	Any business of a craftsman who -
(a)	exercises his craft on his own domestic premises;
(b)	does not display the products of his craftsmanship for sale in public; and
(c)	does not employ any person other than members of his immediate family for the purpose of his business.

3. Any business of -

(a) a **taxi driver**;

(b) a **trishaw rider**;

(c) a **sampan man** plying his sampan for hire; or

(d) a **farmer, a fish pond keeper or a prawn pond keeper** who

  (i) does not employ any person other than members of his immediate family;

  (ii) does not own the land on which his farm or pond stands; and

  (iii) does not charge members of the public any fee for admission.

A business firm is either a sole-proprietorship or a partnership. Individuals and companies, being "legal persons", may set up and own a business firm. However, a business firm, not being a legal entity, cannot register another business firm.

Individuals and companies registering business firms need not be Singaporeans or incorporated in Singapore. But in all cases, the manager of a business firm must be a Singaporean, Singapore Permanent Resident, Singapore Employment Pass Holder or Dependant's Pass Holder.

1. SOLE-PROPRIETORSHIP

A sole-proprietorship is a business firm owned by one person or one company. There are no partners. The sole-proprietor has absolute say in the running of the business firm.

2. PARTNERSHIP

A partnership is made up of more than one person or company. To avoid possible disputes, it is preferable that a partnership agreement is drawn up.

Partnerships may have between two and twenty partners. Once there are more than twenty partners, the business entity must be registered as a company under the Companies Act, Cap.50.

SETTING UP A BUSINESS FIRM IN SINGAPORE

To register a business firm:

You will have to submit an **Application for Approval of Name (Form A)** for the purpose of obtaining a business name. A non-refundable fee of S$15.00 per name is payable. This form is submitted at the same time as the **Application to Register a Business (Form B)** . We will process your application and inform you of the outcome within 24 hours. The same forms are used for the application to register sole-proprietorships and partnerships.

Once the application is submitted, you will be given an appointment to return the next working day. However, if your application is submitted on a Friday, your appointment will be scheduled on the following Monday. In the meantime, RCB will do a computer search to check if the names proposed in Form A are similar or identical to names already on our register of businesses/companies.

At the same time, RCB will decide if the application needs to be referred to another authority for approval or comments. For example, if you intend to carry out activities involving video and laser disc rental business, your application will be referred to the Board of Film Censors, the licensing agency. When an application has been referred to another authority, it may take another 14 days to 2 months before the outcome is known.

A proposed business name will not be approved if it is identical to, or so nearly resembles the name of another company, foreign company or business, as to be calculated to mislead. Undesirable names, including restricted names or vulgar names will also not be approved.

If a referral is needed or if the name is not available, meaning it has been used or found unsuitable, you will be told when you return to RCB for the appointment with RCB's front office service personnel.

If the name applied for is available and acceptable, and no referral is required, all it takes is just one working day and a payment of S$105.00 for registration. You will then be issued a Certificate of Registration which is valid for three years.

From 1 January 1994, self-employed persons applying to register a business are required to contribute to their Medisave Account. If you are already a business owner, your contribution must be paid up-to-date before you apply for a new or another licence. You may wish to call the **Central Provident Fund Board (CPFB)** at their toll-free number **1800-226 3877** for more information.

Forms A and B are available free-of-charge from our reception desk. You may also request for these forms to be sent to you by mail. Just call our toll-free number : **1-800-222-6266**. Press **11411** to record your request.

QUESTION-AND-ANSWER SESSION FOR BUSINESS REGISTRATION DEPARTMENT

1.	**Can you comment on limited liability practices in Singapore?**
	Corporations (including societies registered under the Co-operative Societies Act) are the only limited liability entities in Singapore.
2.	**Can a company register a sole proprietorship? If so, what is the liability? What about directors?**
	Yes, a company can register a sole-proprietorship (RCB may require a local manager to be appointed) . As with all other unincorporated entities, liability of the sole-proprietorship is unlimited. Directors of the owner-company may, in certain circumstances, be rendered liable for the business, as the Business Registration Act includes directors in the definition of persons who are responsible for the management of the business.
3.	**Must the names describe the businesses?**
	There is no legal requirement as such. However, descriptive names are to be used if it would make the business name distinct from those of other entities for the purposes of making an application for the registration of a business name.
4.	**If the applicant is unable to apply in person at the Registry, the applicant can sign Forms A + B in the presence of an Advocate & Solicitor / Public Accountant, but not in the presence of a Practicing Chartered Secretary. Will RCB consider this?**
	With effect from 1 April 2000, the signing of forms may also be verified by a practising member of the Singapore Association of the Institute of Chartered Secretaries and Administrators (SAICSA) .
5.	**Who can witness the Forms B and Forms D etc? Approved company auditor, Advocate & Solicitor, others? Please advise.**
	With effect from 1 April 2000, the signing of business forms may be witnessed and verified by an Advocate or Solicitor, a Certified Public Accountant, or a practising member of the Singapore Association of the Institute of Chartered Secretaries and Administrators (SAICSA) , for forms executed in Singapore. For forms signed overseas, they should be witnessed by a Notary Public.
6.	**We understand that for incorporation of companies, the date of incorporation will be one day after the documents are lodged. Please explain whether the same policy is applied for business registrations? Can we request for a special date?**

	The Certificate of Registration will be dated the day it is issued and collected by the applicant. In most cases, the Certificate of Registration will be dated the next working day from the date of the application, as applicants will be advised to attend at the Registry then for an appointment to check if their application has been approved. As the date is dependent on the date of payment, there is no need to accommodate requests for special dates.
7.	**Does the Registry cap the number of business names a private limited company wishes to register?**
	No.
8.	**There exists ABC Pte Ltd. Can a person, who is also a director of ABC Pte Ltd, register a business name known as ABC?**
	No, the names are considered identical. From the example, if ABC Pte Ltd wishes to register ABC Trading, we would allow this provided the name does not fall foul of section 11 of the Business Registration Act and ABC Pte Ltd provides a letter of consent for the use of the name "ABC".
9.	**If a sole proprietor dies, must notification be filed? If so, who is responsible? Who will be fined for not filing or late filing?**
	Yes - the next-of-kin or the estate of the deceased will be responsible for notifying us. As for failure to file or in cases of late filing, similarly, the estate will be penalised.
10.	**Can we handle incorporation of companies, registration of business & corporate secretarial services in HDB flats?**
	Business activities may be conducted in HDB flats, if the business qualifies under the Technopreneur Home Office Scheme. Please contact the National Science & Technology Board (NSTB) (hotline: 779 7066) for more details on eligibility, or visit their website www.nstb.gov.sg for more information.
11.	**Societies & Clubs (non- profit organizations) - who do they register with?**
	The Registry of Societies.
12.	**Re: Form A & B** **Commencement date and the date of appointment of a manager - can this be earlier than the date of submission of registration documents?**
	If the dates of commencement of the business and appointment of the manager precede the date of the Certificate of Registration of the sole-proprietorship/partnership, this would mean that business had been carried on prior to registration, which is an offence under the Business Registration Act.
13.	**If the sole-proprietor intends to use the business name for a Private Limited company, when should the date of cessation be? Should the Form D be dated on the date when we submit the incorporation documents?**
	We have no objection to the business firm being terminated within 3 months of the date of incorporation. If the business owner wishes to extend the date of termination beyond the 3 month period, he/she must submit the request in writing to RCB citing the reason(s) for the extension.
14.	**If EP holders appoint a local manager & later the former disappears, what can the local manager do in order for him to cease the business?**
	I am assuming that the EP holders are the owners/partners of the business. To terminate a business, all the partners are required to execute Form D. However, if the Certificate of Registration is not renewed, the business will be cancelled after one year from the date of expiry of the Certificate pursuant to section 13 of the Business Registration Act.

Form No.	Type of Form & Section No. of Companies Act
5	Return of Proprietor/Partners of Firm of Auditor(s)
6	Statutory Declaration of Compliance
7	Certificate of Identity
11	Notice of Resolution
14	Application for Approval and Reservation of Name for a Company to be incorporated under the Companies Act
14A	Application for Approval and Reservation of Name for Change of Name by an existing Company
14B	Application for Approval and Reservation of Name for Registration of a Foreign Company
16A	Assent by Members to Application to convert Company to Unlimited Company
16B	Statutory Declaration by Director or Secretary Verifying Execution
18	Statutory Declaration of Compliance by Company that has not issued Prospectus
21	Notice of Increase in Number of Members
22	Statutory Declaration of Compliance by Company that has issued Prospectus
24	Return of Allotment of Shares
25	Statement containing Particulars of Shares allotted otherwise than for Cash
26	Statement of Amount or Rate of Commission and Brokerage
27	Notice of Redemption of Redeemable Preference Shares
28	Notice of Increase in Share Capital
28A	Notice of Increase in Share Capital (Foreign Companies and Local Companies with Share Capital denominated in Foreign Currency)
29A	Notice of Intention to Propose Special Resolution to give Financial Assistance for the Acquisition of Shares or Units in Company
29B	Notice to Non-resident who has Interest in Voting Shares of Company
29C	Notice of Purchase or Acquisition of Shares
30	Notice of Place where Register of Holders of Debentures is kept, or of Change in that Place
30A	Application for Declaration as an Exempt Purchaser under Section 106C (g)
30B	Report by Issuer to Registrar of Intention to sell Shares or Debentures under Section 106I (1) pursuant to an Exemption under Division 5A
30C	Register to be maintained under Section 106I (2) by the Issuer
30D	Notice of Sale of Shares or Debentures Acquired under Section 106C or 106D
31	Notice of Place where Register of Interest Holders is kept, or of Change in that Place
32	Return by Management Company
33	Affidavit Verifying Execution of Charge created by Company and Correctness of Statement

34	Statement of Particulars in respect of Charge
35	Statement containing Particulars of a Series of Debentures
36	Particulars when more than one issue is made of Debentures in a series
37	Affidavit in respect of Property acquired by Company or Foreign Company while Property is subject to a Charge
38	Affidavit in respect of Charge created by Foreign Company before Registration of Foreign Company in Singapore
38A	Affidavit in respect of Property Acquired by Foreign Company while Property is subject to a Charge before Registration of Foreign Company in Singapore
41	Memorandum of Satisfaction of Registered Charge
42	Memorandum where Property or Undertaking is Released from Registered Charge or has ceased to form part of Company's Property or Undertaking
44	Notice of Situation of Registered Office and of Office Hours at time of Incorporation
44A	Notice of Change of Situation of Registered Office and of Office Hours
45	Consent to Act as Director and Statement of Non-Disqualification to act as Director
45A	Consent to act as Director and Statement of Non-Disqualification to act as Director with Leave of Court
45B	Consent to act as Secretary
46	Undertaking by Director to take and pay for Qualification Shares
47	Statutory Declaration by Director of Registration of Qualification Shares
48	Statutory Declaration by Director of Entitlement to Qualification Shares
48C	Report on Conduct of Director of Insolvent Company
49	Return giving Particulars in Register of Directors, Managers, Secretaries and Auditors and Changes of Particulars
51	Statutory Report of a Public Company
52	Copy of Minute by Representative of Holding Company relating to Proceedings of Subsidiary Company
53	Notice of Place where Register of Members and Index kept, or of Change in that Place
54	Notice of Situation of Office where Branch Register of Members kept, or of Change in Situation or Discontinuance
55	Annual Return of Company not having a Share Capital
56	Certificate for Inclusion in Public Company's Annual Return that does not include List of Members
57	Notice of Dissenting Shareholder
58	Notice of Non-Assenting Shareholder
59	Notice of Appointment of Receiver or Receiver and Manager
60	Notice by Receiver or Receiver and Manager of Cessation of Office

61	Statement of Affairs
61A	Statement of Affairs
62	Affidavit Verifying Statement of Affairs
62A	Affidavit Verifying Statement of Affairs
63	Account of Receipts and Payments by Receiver or Receiver and Manager
63A	Petition for Judicial Management Order
63B	Notice of Petition for Judicial Management
63C	Affidavit of Service of Petition for Judicial Management Order
63D	Affidavit Verifying Petition for Judicial Management Order
63E	Notice of Intention to appear on Petition for Judicial Management Order
63F	List of Parties Wishing to attend the Hearing of a Petition for Judicial Management Order
63G	Notice to Judicial Manager of Judicial Management Order
63H	Order of Court for Judicial Management
63I	Notice of Judicial Management Order
63J	Notice of Judicial Management Order for Publication
63K	Notice by Judicial Manager of Cessation of Office
63L	Notice of Judicial Manager to Creditors of First Meeting
63M	Notice of Judicial Manager to Directors and Officers of Company to attend First Meeting of Creditors
63N	Notice of Judicial Manager's Meeting of Creditors
63O	Affidavit of Posting of Notices of Meeting
63P	Memorandum of Adjournment of Meeting of Creditors in relation to Judicial Management
63Q	Memorandum of Proceedings at Adjourned First Meeting of Creditors in relation to Judicial Management
63R	List of Creditors Present at a Meeting of Creditors
63S	Notice to Prove Debt or Claim for Publication
63T	Notice to Creditors of a Company under Judicial Management to Prove Debt or Claim
63U	Notice to Persons claiming to be Creditors of a Company under Judicial Management to Prove Debt or Claim
63V	Notice of Rejection of Proof of Debt
63W	Notice of Report of Result of Meeting of Creditors on Proposals or Revised Proposals of Judicial Manager
64	Notice by Inspector Investigating the Affairs of a Company
65	Notice of Winding-Up Order and Particulars of Liquidator(s)
65A	Statutory Declaration by Directors of Company's Inability to Continue Business by reason of

	its Liabilities
66	Statutory Declaration of Solvency
67	Notice of Meeting of Creditors
68	Notice of Holding of Meeting of Creditors
69	Return by Liquidator relating to Final Meeting
70	Notice of Appointment and Situation of Office of Provisional Liquidator/Liquidator (Winding Up by the Court)
71	Notice of Appointment and Situation of Office of Liquidator (Members' Voluntary Winding Up)
72	Notice of Appointment and Situation of Office of Provisional Liquidator(s) / Liquidator(s) (Creditors' Voluntary Winding Up)
73	Notice of Change in Situation of Office of Provisional Liquidator(s) /Liquidator(s)
74	Notice by Provisional Liquidator(s) /Liquidator(s) of Cessation
75	Liquidator's Account of Receipts and Payments and Statement of the Position in the Winding Up
76	Particulars of Unclaimed Assets Payable to Companies Liquidation Account
77	Statutory Declaration as to Proof of Debt General Form
78	Statutory Declaration as to Proof of Debt Employees' Group Form
79	Return by Foreign Company Giving Particulars of Directors and Changes of Particulars of Directors
80	Statutory Declaration by Agent of Foreign Company
81	Notice by Agent of Foreign Company of Cessation of Agency
82	Notice by Foreign Company of Cessation of Agency
84	Notice of Change relating to Foreign Company
85	Notice of Cessation of Agency or Appointment of Agent of Foreign Company
85A	Notice of Change of Address of Agent of Foreign Company
86	Notice of Change of Address of Registered Office of Foreign Company in Place of Incorporation or Origin
87	Statutory Delcaration Verifying Balance-Sheet of Foreign Company
87A	Statutory Declaration that Foreign Company is not required to hold Annual General Meeting and prepare Balance-Sheet
88	Notice by Foreign Company with Share Transfer or Share Registration Office and not otherwise Carrying on Business in Singapore
89	Notice by Foreign Company of Commencement of Business other than Share Transfer or Share Registration Office
90	Notice by Foreign Company of Cessation of Business
91	Notice by Agent of Foreign Company of Liquidation or Dissolution of Company

92	Notice of Intention to Apply for Exemption from section 400 (1)
93	Lodgement of Order of Court
94	General Lodgment Form
AR	Annual Return of Company having a Share Capital

REGISTERING A COMPANY

TYPES OF COMPANIES

IN SINGAPORE, THE THREE MAIN TYPES OF COMPANIES ARE :

1.**Private Limited Companies :** Number of shareholders is limited to 50 or less.

2.**Public Companies :** Number of shareholders can be more than 50 members and the company may raise capital by offering shares and debentures to the public. A public company must register a prospectus with the Registrar before making any public offer of shares and debentures.

3.**Branches of Foreign Companies :** These are companies whose country of origin are outside Singapore and who wish to set up a branch in Singapore. The companies are registered and not incorporated under the Companies Act, Chapter 50.

HOW TO REGISTER A LOCAL COMPANY IN SINGAPORE

As the registration of a local company is rather technical, it would be wise if you seek professional assistance from a firm of local solicitors or accountants.

OBTAINING A COMPANY NAME

A company cannot be incorporated unless the proposed name has been approved by us first. Names for all companies in Singapore must conform to certain guidelines laid down in the Companies Act, Chapter 50.

You are required to submit Form 14 (Application for Approval and Reservation of Name for a company) under the Companies Act, Chapter 50. For each proposed company name, a fee of S$15.00 has to be paid. You must declare if the proposed company name includes a trade mark or patent name, or the name of another company/business existing elsewhere and produce the unconditional written consent of the owner of the trade mark or patent, or the other company for the use of the name. You are also required to declare that you will change the name if it is found otherwise.

If approved, the company name will be reserved for two months. Should you need more time, RCB may grant an extension of two months upon submission of an application for an extension of time and payment of S$5.00.

A proposed company name will not be approved if it is identical to, or so nearly resembles the name of another company, foreign company or business firm as to be mistaken for it. Undesirable names, including offensive or vulgar names will also not be approved.

Certain types of activities need the necessary approval and licence from other Government authorities before the proposed business activity can begin. For example, the authority which issues Travel Agency Licence in Singapore is the Singapore Tourism Board (STB) . As such an application to register a company carrying on the activity of a Travel Agency will be referred to STB to ensure compliance with STB's guidelines. When an application has been referred to another authority, it may take another 14 days to 2 months.

It usually takes us 5 working days to process the application for approval of name.

REGISTERING THE COMPANY

After the company name has been approved, you can proceed to register the company. You would have to prepare and file the following incorporation documents :

1.Memorandum & Articles of Association setting out the objects and by-laws of the proposed company.

2.Statutory Declaration of Compliance (Form 6) .

3.Certificate of Identity (Form 7) .

4.Notice of Situation of Registered Office and of Office Hours at time of Incorporation (Form 44) .

5.Consent to Act as Director & Statement of Non Disqualification to Act as Director (Form 45) .

A further 5 working days will be required for us to incorporate your company and issue the Certificate of Incorporation upon lodgement of the relevant incorporation documents.

Every company must have at least 2 directors one of whom must be locally resident ie Singapore citizen, Singapore Permanent Resident, Singapore Employment Pass or Dependent Pass Holder. Please refer to the procedure for application of an employment pass by a foreigner who wishes to act as a local director of a new company.

A filing fee of S$10.00 per document filed and a registration fee based on the authorised share capital of the proposed company is payable. The minimum registration fee payable is S$1,200.00 based on an authorised share capital of S$100,000.00. fee.

TDB TRADERS REGISTRATION SYSTEM (TTRS)

When your Business has been registered with RCB and if your Business activity is importing and/or exporting of goods, you can register with the Trade Development Board (TDB) for such purpose via TDB Trade Register System (TTRS)

HOW TO REGISTER A FOREIGN COMPANY IN SINGAPORE

What is a Foreign Company?

A foreign company is one that is incorporated outside Singapore. A foreign company has to register its branch in Singapore under the Companies Act before it can commence business in Singapore. Any foreign company wishing to register a branch is advised to engage a professional eg. lawyer or an accountant to assist in the preparation and filing of the necessary documents for registration.

REGISTRATION OF A FOREIGN COMPANY

As the registration of a foreign company is rather technical, it would be wise if you seek professional assistance from a firm of local solicitors or accountants.

Usually, it takes 5 working days to register the foreign company and issue the Certificate of Registration.

You are required to submit Form 14B (Application for Approval and Reservation of Name for Registration of a foreign company) under the Companies Act, Chapter 50. For each proposed foreign company name, a fee of S$15 has to be paid. When the name has been approved and is being reserved, you would have to file following documents and effect registration before commencing business :

A copy of the foreign company's Certificate of Incorporation or Registration certified, not more than 3 months before, by the authority which issued the certificate.

A copy of the foreign company's charter, statute or memorandum and articles or other instrument constituting or defining its constitution certified, not more than 3 months before, by the authority which incorporated the foreign company; or a notary public; or a director, manager or secretary of the foreign company in the form of an affidavit.

A memorandum of appointment or power of attorney appointing two or more locally resident persons (i.e. Singapore Citizen, Singapore Permanent Resident,Singapore Employment Pass Holder or Dependent Pass Holder) authorized to accept service of process and any notices required to be served on the foreign company. The memorandum of appointment or power of attorney must be verified by a person stating that he was present and did see :-

(a) the seal of the foreign company duly affixed to the memorandum of appointment or power of attorney; or

(b) executed on behalf of the foreign company in such a manner as to be the memorandum of appointment or power of attorney duly binding on the company.

Please refer to the procedure for application of an employment pass by a foreigner who wishes to act as a local agent of a new company.

4. A return giving particulars of directors of the foreign company at time of registration (Form 79) . Where the return includes directors resident in Singapore who are members of the local board of directors, a memorandum duly executed stating the powers of the local directors must also be filed.
5. Notice of Situation of Registered Office and of Office Hours at time of Incorporation (Form 44) .
6. Statutory Declaration by Agent of Foreign Company (Form 80) .

A filing fee of S$10.00 per document and a registration fee based on the authorized share capital of the foreign company is payable. The minimum registration fee payable is S$1,200.00 based on an authorized share capital equivalent to S$100,000.00.

TDB TRADERS REGISTRATION SYSTEM (TTRS)

When your Business has been registered with RCB and if your your Business activity is importing and/or exporting of goods, you can register with the Trade Development Board (TDB) for such purpose via TDB Trade Register System **(TTRS)** .

GENERAL INFORMATION ON COMPANIES

Appointment of Officers/Auditors

All companies must have a minimum of two directors at least, one of whom must be either a Singaporean, a Singapore Permanent Resident, Singapore Employment Pass Holder or Dependent Pass Holder. Any person above the age of 21 may be appointed as a director. However, some individuals eg. bankrupts, are disqualified from being directors. A director cannot resign unless there are two other directors remaining in the company, one of whom must be a local resident.

Every company must have at least one secretary appointed within 6 months of the date of incorporation. The secretary must have the requisition knowledge and experience to discharge the functions of a secretary of the company and who is either of the following:

7. a secretary of a company for at least 3 of the 5 years immediately preceding the abovementioned date of my appointment as secretary of the abovenamed company.
8. a qualified person under the Legal Profession Act (Cap. 161) .
9. an accountant registered with the Institute of Certified Public Accountants of Singapore.
10. a member of the Singapore Association of the Institute of Chartered Secretaries and Administrators.
11. a member of the Association of International Accountants (Singapore Branch) .
12. a member of the Institute of Company Accountants. Singapore Branch.

An auditor for a company must be appointed within 3 months from the date of incorporation.

Every foreign company registered with RCB must have two agents acting on its behalf in Singapore. These agents must be Singaporeans, Singapore Permanent Residents, Singapore Employment Pass Holders or Dependent Pass Holders.

NOTIFICATION OF CHANGES TO PARTICULARS

You are to notify the Registrar of changes to registered particulars through the lodgment of various prescribed forms. Indicated below are some examples of such changes.

Type of change	**What form to lodge**	**When to lodge**	**Filing Fees S$**
Change of registered office address	Form 44A	Within 14 days	10.00
Appointment of Company's Secretary	From 45B & 49	Within 1 month of appointment	10.00 each
Annual Return	AR Form	Within 1 month of Annual General Meeting	20.00
Allotment of Shares	Form 24	Within 1 month	10.00
Changes of Particulars in Register of Directors, Managers, Secretaries and Auditors	Form 49	Within 1 month	10.00
Appointment of Company's Director	Forms 45 & 49	Within 1 month	10.00 each

This table is not a comprehensive list of the changes to company particulars. Please seek professional assistance from your company secretary or from a firm of local solicitors or accountants if in doubt.

CLARIFICATION OF CLERICAL OR TYPOGRAPHICAL ERRORS BY STATUTORY DECLARATIONS

Section 12B of the Companies Act, Chapter 50, provides that if any particular recorded in a register is erroneous or defective, the court may by order, direct the Registrar to rectify the register.

In practice where the error is obviously minor in nature and which resulted from clerical or typographical mistakes, the Registrar may allow for clarification by way of a Statutory Declaration ("SD") . In cases where the errors are of substantial nature, eg. errors in share capital which are not due to clerical mistakes, the Registrar will not allow clarification by way of an SD and a Court Order will be required. For rectification of errors in charge documents, Court Orders are required to be obtained under Section 137 of the Companies Act, Chapter 50 and lodged with RCB.

Any person who proposes to lodge such an SD must submit their request in writing together with a draft SD for the Registrar's approval. The request should set out the relevant facts and attach documentary proofs, if any. The draft SD must contain pertinent facts and be clear as it will be on public record. Lodgement can only be effected after approval has been given.

No application fee is payable for submitting the draft SD and the applicant will be notified in writing on the outcome of his application. If the SD is approved, the applicant will have to submit the duly executed SD with a prescribed Form 94 (General Lodgement Form) and $10 filing fee (by cheque) for lodgement. Such documents will not be processed at the counter and the receipt for the lodgement of documents will be posted to the applicant subsequently.

For further inquiries, please call 325

Penalty Information

A penalty will be imposed if the forms are lodged later than the period prescribed in the Companies Act.

Annual Return/Annual General Meeting

Every company is required to hold its Annual General Meeting (AGM) within 18 months of its incorporation to present its audited accounts to its shareholders. These audited accounts must not be made up to a date older than 6 months from the date of the AGM. After that, an AGM must be held once every calendar year but not later than 15 months from the date of the last meeting. Please note that failure to comply with this statutory requirement will render the company and all its officers liable to prosecution. The company's Annual Return together with the audited accounts must then be filed with the Registrar not later than one month from the date of the Annual General Meeting.

Any application for the extension of time to hold the AGM must be made prior to the due dates stipulated under section 175 and 201 of the Companies Act, Cap. 50 for holding the Annual General Meeting and for filing the Annual Return. The prescribed application fee of S$25.00 is payable per section. An application made after the said due dates shall not be considered.

Prosecution Information

The Registrar shall commence prosecution action against officers of companies that have failed to hold the Annual General Meeting and file the Annual Return by the due dates prescribed under Sections 175, 197 and 201 of the Companies Act. Such offences may be compounded if the defaults are rectified prior to the date of mention. Defendants may enquire on the exact amount of composition fine payable by calling the Compliance Control Department at Tel : **(65) 325 3723**. Please be informed that you are not required to attend Court if the matter is compounded before the first mention.

TDB TRADERS REGISTRATION SYSTEM (TTRS)

You are now able to obtain approval for registration with TDB almost instantaneously from the convenience of any computer terminal with Internet access.

After registration, you will be able to use the **Central Registration (CR) Number** to submit trade Permit applications and other documents through TradeNet after one working day from the date of issue of the CR Number.

The Internet address for the TTRS is:

"http://www.asianconnect.com/TDB/TRS/crnum.html"

The TTRS provides round-the-clock service for companies engaged in import and export to **apply** for as well as to **renew, amend and cancel** your registration with TDB. It will also send a Notice of Renewal to you. The Notice of Renewal will provide the "accesscode" for you to access the TTRS for submission of renewals, notification of changes and cancellation of registration through the system.

You may also obtain your own accesscode by accessing the **"Query of Own Accesscode/Registration Number"** on the TTRS Home Page. Upon receipt of your request, the system will fax a copy of the Notification Slip to you on the same day

If you have any further enquiries on the TTRS, you can call the following officers:

Ms Ruby Goh	433 4581
Miss Patricia Poh	433 4629
Helpdesk	337 6690

BUSINESS TRAVEL

BUSINESS CUSTOMS

Business discussions are usually conducted in a very straightforward manner. English is widely spoken, and most businesspeople are skilled and technically knowledgeable. Most agents/distributors have visited the United States and often handle several U.S. product lines. Corruption is virtually non-existent.

Many Singapore business people are of ethnic Chinese background, and many of them will have "Christian" first names (e.g., Nancy Goh, Jeannie Sim) . Those who do not will have only their Chinese name on their business card, in which case the family name is listed first. Mr. Ho Weng Hee would be addressed as "Mr. Ho" and Ms. Wong Ai Lan as "Ms. Wong". For the sake of politeness and respect, it is wise to address a business person by the last name rather than the first name - unless an immediate rapport is developed.

Business cards are a must as they are immediately exchanged during business and social meetings. The East Asian practice of presenting a business card with both hands is observed. There is no need to have special business cards printed in Chinese, however.

TRAVEL ADVISORY AND VISAS

While in a foreign country, a U.S. citizen is subject to that country's laws and regulations which sometimes differ significantly from those in the United States and do not afford the same protections available to the individual under U.S. law. Penalties for breaking the law can be more severe than in the United States for similar offences. Persons violating the law, even unknowingly, may be expelled, arrested or imprisoned.

Visitors should be aware of Singapore's strict laws and penalties for a variety of offences that might be considered minor in the United States, including jaywalking, littering and spitting, as well as the importation and sale of chewing gum. Singapore imposes a mandatory caning sentence on males for vandalism offences. Caning may also be imposed for immigration violations and other offences. Penalties for possession, use, or trafficking in illegal drugs are strict, and convicted offenders can expect jail sentences and fines. Singapore has a mandatory death penalty for many narcotics offences. Commercial disputes that may be handled as civil suits in the U.S. can escalate to criminal cases in Singapore and result in heavy fines and prison sentences. There are no jury trials in Singapore. Judges hear cases and decide sentencing. The Singapore Government does not provide legal assistance except in capital crimes cases.

A valid U.S. passport is required for tourist and business travel to Singapore. No visa is necessary for U.S. citizens visiting Singapore. To facilitate regional travel, it is advisable to replace any passport that has less than six months validity.

HOLIDAYS

The American Embassy closes on American and local holidays. The dates on which holidays are observed in 2002 are listed below:

January 1, Tuesday - New Year's Day
January 21, Monday - Birthday of Martin Luther King, Jr.
February 12 & 13,
Tuesday & Wednesday - Lunar New Year
February 18, Monday - Washington's Birthday
February 23, Saturday - Hari Raya Haji
March 29, Friday - Good Friday
May 1, Wednesday - Labor Day (Singaporean)
May 27, Monday - Vesak Day
May 27, Monday - Memorial Day
July 4, Thursday - Independence Day
August 9, Friday - National Day (Singaporean)
September 2, Monday - Labor Day (American)
October14, Monday - Columbus Day
November 4, Monday - Deepavali**
November 11, Monday - Veteran's Day
November 28, Thursday - Thanksgiving
December 6, Friday - Hari Raya Puasa
December 25, Wednesday - Christmas Day
** This date may change according to the Indian Almanacs.

Business travelers to Singapore seeking appointments with U.S. Embassy Singapore officials are encouraged to schedule an appointment with Commercial Officers prior to departure from the U.S. The Commercial section may be reached by telephone at 65/476-9037, fax at 65/476-9080, or email at, commerce@pacific.net.sg.

WORKWEEK

Singapore is twelve hours ahead of Eastern Daylight Savings (or thirteen hours ahead of E.S.T) . Business hours normally are 8:30 a.m. - 5:00 p.m., Monday-Friday, 8:30 am – 1:00 p.m., Saturday. Shops are normally open from 10:00 am – 9:00 p.m.

BUSINESS INFRASTRUCTURE

Taxis are abundant, metered, inexpensive and air-conditioned, and most drivers speak English. Drivers should be given place names for the destination as these are often more familiar than street names. Traffic flow is quite good. The Government limits the total number of cars on the road through heavy fees/taxes and imposes a surcharge on vehicles entering the Central Business District during much of the day. In addition, an exceptionally clean, efficient, subway system links the major business/shopping areas.

Singapore's unit of currency is the Singapore dollar. Travelers' checks and currency may be exchanged in the baggage claim area at Changi Airport (at a reasonable rate) or at any hotel (at a less favorable rate) . Singapore features dozens of Government-authorized "money changers" located in major shopping centers, who offer competitive rates and will usually accept U.S. travelers' checks as well as major currencies. International credit cards are widely accepted in hotels, restaurants and retail shops.

In addition to having one of the world's best airports and container ports, Singapore features an exceptionally modern telecommunications system. Public telephones accepting cash cards or cash are located throughout. 'Cyber cafes' are also gaining in popularity, and internet connections are available in most hotels. Electrical current is 220V, 50HZ.

Located a few degrees from the Equator, Singapore has a constant tropical climate year-round. Daytime temperatures average between 85 and 90 degrees Fahrenheit. Humidity is very high and rain showers are frequent. Temperatures at night average between 76 and 80 degrees. All public buildings, indoor restaurants and taxis are air-conditioned.

Summer-weight suits/dresses, several dress-shirts, an umbrella and swimsuit are recommended for the traveller. Singapore business dress is shirt and tie for men, although one will not be out of place occasionally wearing a jacket. Businesswomen wear conservative, light-weight attire. Evening dinner-dress is a shirt and tie for men, a dress for women.

Tipping is not customary in Singapore. Restaurants automatically add a 10% service charge and a 3.0% goods and services tax to the bill.

TEMPORARY ENTRY OF GOODS

There is no restriction on the temporary entry of laptop computers, software and exhibition materials into the country. Please see Chapter 6 on temporary goods entry requirement.

SUPPLEMENTS

BANKRUPTCY LAWYERS IN SINGAPORE

Ali Budiardjo, Nugroho, Reksodiputro
Ali Budiardjo, Nugroho, Reksodiputro
Singapore, Singapore
Counsellors at Law
Phone+65 6236-0282
Ali Budiardjo, Nugroho, Reksodiputro (ABNR) was founded in 1967 by professionals with a deep respect for the law and a keen interest in assisting clients, both foreign and domestic, to achieve their commercial goals within the Indonesian legal environment.
ABNR has the insight...

Law Firm's Overview
Ashurst
Ashurst
Singapore, Singapore
International Law Firm
Phone+65 6221 2214
Ashurst's Singapore office opened in 1996 and now comprises some 40 lawyers, including eight partners. Carl Dunton is the managing partner in Singapore.
Ashurst Singapore acts for many top Asian and international corporations, financial institutions and multilateral agencies...

Law Firm's Overview
Baker & McKenzie
Baker & McKenzie
Singapore, Singapore
Global Full Service Law Firm
Phone+65 6338 1888
Baker & McKenzie's member firm in Singapore, Baker & McKenzie.Wong & Leow is part of one of the world's leading and most internationally diverse law firms. With broad global coverage and comprehensive local knowledge gained from over 30 years of operating in Singapore,...

Law Firm's Overview
Clifford Chance LLP
Clifford Chance LLP
Singapore, Singapore
M&A, Corporate, Private Equity, Banking, Finance and Industry Specialists
Phone+65 64 102200
Clifford Chance is one of the world's leading law firms, with 29 offices in 20 countries and some 3,200 legal advisers.
A single partnership, the firm has unrivalled scale and depth of legal resources across the four key markets of the Americas, Asia, Europe and the Middle East...

Law Firm's Overview
Clyde & Co LLP
Clyde & Co LLP
Singapore, Singapore
International Law Firm
Phone+65 65446500
Clyde & Co is a leading international law firm which works worldwide across 120 countries. Our work is cross-border, high profile and complex. With over 1300 staff based in 24 offices worldwide, we have genuine in-depth knowledge of our chosen industries.
Our history in the...

Law Firm's Overview

Conyers Dill & Pearman
Conyers Dill & Pearman
Singapore, Singapore
Corporate, Intellectual Property and Litigation Law Firm
Phone+65 62236006
Conyers Dill & Pearman is one of the largest offshore law firms in the world.
The firm has operations in Anguilla, Bermuda, British Virgin Islands, Cayman Islands, Hong Kong, London and Singapore. The firm advises on the laws of Anguilla, Bermuda, the British Virgin Islands...

Law Firm's Overview
Dechert LLP
Dechert LLP
Singapore, Singapore
International Asset Management, Corporate & Securities and Litigation Law Firm
Phone+65 6808 6340
Deeply committed to the Asia region, Dechert opened our newest office in 2014 in Singapore, one of the world's major financial hubs, with a particular emphasis on servicing client needs across Southeast and South Asia. Dechert's Singapore office advises investment funds, their managers...

Law Firm's Overview
Dentons
Dentons
Singapore, Singapore
International Law Firm
Phone+65 65321024
SNR Denton is a new name in the legal marketplace. At the same time, SNR Denton is a firm with a 225-year pedigree of excellence and professionalism in service to law firm clients. A spirit of multidisciplinary collaboration and teamwork infuses the culture of the firm—across sectors...

Law Firm's Overview
DLA Piper
DLA Piper
Singapore, Singapore
Global Law Firm
Phone+65 6512 9595
DLA Piper became one of the largest legal service providers in the world in 2005 through a merger of unprecedented scope in the legal sector. While large in scale, the merger strategy was simple – to create an international legal practice capable of taking care of the most important...

Law Firm's Overview
Duane Morris LLP
Duane Morris LLP
Singapore, Singapore
IP, Telecommunications, Information Technologies, Energy, Endangered Species
Phone+65 68293300
Duane Morris LLP, a full-service law firm with more than 700 attorneys in 24 offices in the United States and internationally, offers innovative solutions to the legal and business challenges presented by today's evolving global markets.
Evolving from a partnership of prominent...

Law Firm's Overview
Eversheds
Eversheds
Singapore, Singapore
Global Legal Services
Phone+65 65725555
Eversheds, which operates as one team, from 45 offices in 28 countries, is one of the world's largest corporate law firms. Committed locally, but connected globally, with over 40 offices based in the world's major economic centres, with a proven track record of delivering consistently...

Law Firm's Overview
Fragomen, Del Rey, Bernsen and Loewy, LLP
Fragomen, Del Rey, Bernsen and Loewy, LLP
Singapore, Singapore
Global Corporate and Immigration Law Firm
Phone+65 6334 0766
Fragomen's Singapore Immigration Team is exclusively focused on specializing in all aspects of Singapore immigration services. Through dedication to technical excellence combined with a highly efficient and commercial approach, we are able to effectively use the Ministry of Manpower's...

Law Firm's Overview
Freshfields Bruckhaus Deringer LLP
Freshfields Bruckhaus Deringer LLP
Singapore, Singapore
International Full-Service Law Firm
Phone+65 6908 0408
Freshfields Bruckhaus Deringer LLP is a leader among international law firms, providing business law advice of the highest quality throughout Europe, the Middle East, Asia and the US.
With over 2,500 lawyers in 27 key business centers around the world, we provide a comprehensive...

Law Firm's Overview
Gibson, Dunn & Crutcher
Gibson, Dunn & Crutcher
Singapore, Singapore
International Full-Service Law Firm
Phone+65 6507 3600
Gibson Dunn's lawyers in the Singapore office have lived and worked extensively in the region and possess both an established presence and an in-depth understanding of the legal and cultural environment. They are deeply experienced in transactional work for high-profile financial...

Law Firm's Overview
Jones Day
Jones Day
Singapore, Singapore
Worldwide Full Service Law Firm
Phone+65 6538 3939
Jones Day lawyers have been advising clients in Southeast Asia for more than 20 years. The Jones Day Singapore Office comprises approximately 30 lawyers who have lived and worked in the region for many years and who understand the unique cultures and ways of doing business in the...

Law Firm's Overview
K&L Gates LLP
K&L Gates LLP
Singapore, Singapore
Full-Service International Law Firm
Phone+65 6507-8100
K&L Gates LLP represents leading global corporations, growth and middle-market companies, capital markets participants and entrepreneurs in every major industry group as well as public sector entities, educational institutions, philanthropic organizations and individuals. Our...

Law Firm's Overview
King & Spalding LLP
King & Spalding LLP
Singapore, Singapore
International Full-Service Law Firm
Phone+65 6303 6000
King & Spalding's Singapore office serves as the firm's Asia-Pacific hub for our energy projects and international arbitration practices. Our team of five partners and 11 other fee-earners help clients meet the opportunities and challenges of the Asian market by offering local...

Law Firm's Overview
Latham & Watkins LLP
Latham & Watkins LLP
Singapore, Singapore
Full-Service International and Business Law Firm
Phone+65 6536 1161
Latham has been advising clients in Singapore and across Asia-Pacific for more than 20 years. Lawyers in the Singapore office represent corporations, financial institutions and governmental agencies on complex corporate and financing transactions, offering innovative advice on many...

Law Firm's Overview
Nabarro LLP
Nabarro LLP
Singapore, Singapore
International Commercial Law Firm
Phone+65 66453280
Nabarro is a major UK commercial law firm renowned for the positive and practical way we work. Our no-nonsense approach and wide-ranging expertise help clients achieve their objectives across many sectors, both public and private.
Our commitment to clarity is revealed in our understanding...

Law Firm's Overview
O'Melveny & Myers LLP
O'Melveny & Myers LLP
Singapore, Singapore
International Law Firm
Phone+65 65931800
At O'Melveny & Myers LLP, our clients come from many industries, nations, and developmental stages. Their diversity spurs our own diversity and reach. We were one of the first US law firms to open offices in Beijing and Tokyo. We now have the largest China practice of any US-based...

Law Firm's Overview
Shearman & Sterling LLP
Shearman & Sterling LLP
Singapore, Singapore
A Global Law Firm
Phone+65 62303800
Shearman & Sterling LLP, a global law firm, has been advising many of the world's leading corporations and financial institutions, governments and governmental organizations for more than 135 years. Our lawyers are committed to providing legal advice that is insightful and valuable...

Law Firm's Overview
Sidley Austin LLP
Sidley Austin LLP
Singapore, Singapore
International Full Service Law Firm
Phone+65 62303900
Sidley Austin LLP is a global law firm, with approximately 1600 lawyers in 17 offices. We provide a broad range of legal services to meet the needs of our diverse client base. The strategic establishment of our offices in the key corporate and financial centers of the world has enabled...

Law Firm's Overview
Squire Sanders
Squire Sanders
Singapore, Singapore
International Full-Service Law Firm
Phone+65 6922-8668
Our lawyers in Singapore work closely with our global and Asia Pacific network of lawyers so the most comprehensive knowledge and resources are available to our clients on each matter. We ensure that the right team is available to provide the right advice to our clients.

Law Firm's Overview
Walkers
Walkers
Singapore, Singapore
Corporate and International Finance Law Firm
Phone+65 65954670
Walkers based in the Cayman Islands with offices in the British Virgin Islands, Dubai, Hong Kong, Jersey and London, offers high-level skills across the legal spectrum. The firm was named 2006 "Offshore Law firm of the Year" by The Lawyer, who credited Walkers with "'the strategic...

Law Firm's Overview
White & Case LLP
White & Case LLP
Singapore, Singapore
A Global Law Firm
Phone+65 62256000
White & Case, founded in New York in 1901, has lawyers in the United States, Latin America, Europe, the Middle East, Africa and Asia. Our clients are public and privately held commercial businesses and financial institutions, as well as governments and state-owned entities, involved...

Law Firm's Overview

STRATEGIC GOVERNMENT AND BUSINESS CONTACTS

U.S. GOVERNMENT CONTACTS

Ambassador Steven J. Green
American Embassy
PSC 470
FPO AP 96534
Tel: (65) 476-9167 Fax: (65) 476-9337

Jonathan M. Bensky
Commercial Counselor
American Embassy
PSC 470-FCS
FPO AP 96534
Tel: (65) 476-9037 Fax: (65) 476-9080

William T. Monroe
Economic/Political Counselor
American Embassy
PSC 470-E/P
FPO AP 96534
Tel: (65) 476-9424 Fax: (65) 476-9389

Dale Good
Agricultural Trade Officer
American Embassy
PSC 470-ATO
FPO AP 96534
Tel: (65) 737-1233 Fax: (65) 732-8307

Major David Hyres
Office Of Defense Cooperation
American Embassy
PSC 470-SAO
FPO AP 96534
Tel: (65) 476-9379 Fax: (65) 476-9483/9101

Chan Yiu Kei
U.S.-Asia Environmental Partnership Director
American Embassy
PSC 470-FCS
FPO AP 96534
Tel: (65) 476-9026 Fax: (65) 476-9311

SINGAPORE GOVERNMENT AGENCIES

Role and Functions Of EPC Agencies	
Economic Development Board 250 North Bridge Road #24-00 Raffles City Tower Singapore 179101 Tel: (65) 336-2288 Fax: (65) 339-6077	□ Lead agency for industrial planning, development and promotion of investments in manufacturing, services and local business. □ Within a strategic and economic

www.sedb.com	framework, the Board will assist investors in setting up operations speedily.
Housing Development Board HDB Centre 3451 Jalan Bukit Merah Singapore 159459 Tel: (65) 273-9090 Fax: (65) 279-6097 www.hdb.gov.sg	□ Public Housing Authority that plans, designs and develops quality housing and related facilities for sale and rental and upgrade and redevelop older estates. □ Provides efficient services in estate management, housing adminstration and mortage financing.
Jurong Town Corporation Jurong Town Hall 301 Jurong Town Hall Road Singapore 609431 Tel: (65) 560-0056 Fax: (65) 565-5301 www.jtc.gov.sg	□ Principal developer and manager of industrial estates and related facilities. □ Offers manufacturers a wide range of facilities from industrial land, high and low risk factories to R&D and Business Park facilities.
Ministry of Education Kay Siang Road Singapore 248922 Tel: (65) 473-9111 Fax: (65) 475-6128 www.moe.edu.sg	□ Formulates and implements education policies which seek to maximise the potential of our students. □ Responsible for the development and administration of all schools and junior colleges and for overseeing the institutions of higher learning.
Ministry of Manpower 18 Havelock Road Singapore 059764 Tel: (65) 534-1511 Fax: (65) 534-4840 http://www.gov.sg/mom	□ Responsible for promoting stable and peaceful industrial relations, safeguarding workers' safety, health and welfare. □ Formulating and implementing the foreign worker policy.
Ministry of Trade and Industry 8 Shenton Way #48-01 Treasury Building Singapore 068811 Tel: (65) 225-9911 Fax: (65) 220-1215 www.gov.sg/mti	□ Overall economic planning, analysis and coordination of economic policy. □ Development and promotion of trade and industry.
National Computer Board NCB Building 71 Science Park Drive Singapore 118253 Tel: (65) 778-2211 Fax: (65) 778-9641 www.ncb.gov.sg	□ National information technology (IT) authority dedicated to the development of IT in Singapore. □ Spearhead implementation of Singapore's IT2000 Masterplan.
National Science and Technology Board 16 Science Park Drive #01-03 The Pasteur Singapore Science Park	□ National agency for the promotion of R&D activities in the industrial and services sectors.

Singapore 118227 Tel: (65) 779-7066 Fax: (65) 777-1711 www.nstb.gov.sg	□ Spurs R&D efforts and capability build-up in niche areas of technology through its five research institutes and four centres for R&D activites.
Port of Singapore Authority PSA Building 460 Alexandra Road Singapore 118221 Tel: (65) 274-7111 Fax: (65) 274-4677 www.psa.com.sg	□ Responsible for the provision and maintenance of efficient port facilities and services. □ Operates six port terminals for all types of vessels including container ships, cargo freighters, coasters, lighters and passenger lines.
Singapore Productivity and Standards Board PSB Building 2 Bukit Merah Central Singapore 159835 Tel: (65) 278-6666 Fax: (65) 278-6665 www.psb.gov.sg	□ Spearheads the drive to raise Singapore's productivity and competitiveness through manpower development, economic restructuring and technical progress. □ As of 8 April 1996, it takes over the roles of the National Productivity Board (NPB) , the Singapore Institute of Standards and Industrial Research (Sisir) and the smalland medium-sized enterprise development function of the Economic Development Board (EDB) .
Singapore Tourism Board Tourism Court 1 Orchard Spring Lane Singapore 247729 Tel: (65) 736-6622 Fax: (65) 736-9423 www.stb.com.sg	□ Develops and promotes tourism and related facilties and services in Singapore. □ Promotes Singapore as a venue for conventions, exhibitions, sporting events, incentive travel and other tourism businesses.
Singapore Trade Development Board 230 Victoria Street 07-00 Bugis Junction Office Tower Singapore 188024 Tel: (65) 337-6628 Fax: (65) 337-6698 www.tdb.gov.sg	□ National trade promotion agency to develop Singapore's international trade. □ Provides assistance and information on setting up trading or distribution operation in Singapore.
Urban Redevelopment Authority 45 Maxwell Road Singapore 069118 Tel: (65) 221-6666 Fax: (65) 224-8752	□ Authority responsible for national planning and conservation. □ It plans, facilitates and regulates the physical development of Singapore into a tropical city of excellence.

Central Provident Fund Board
CPF Building, 79 Robinson Road
Singapore 068897
Tel: (65) 220-2422 Fax: (65) 224-5869
Chairman: Dr. Andrew Chew

Civil Aviation Authority of Singapore
Singapore Changi Airport, P.O. Box 1
Singapore 918141
Tel: (65) 542-1122 Fax: (65) 542-1231
Director-General: Mr. Wong Woon Liong

Communications (Ministry of)
460 Alexandra Road, #39-00 PSA Building
Singapore 119963
Tel: 65-270 7988 Fax: 65-375 7734
Minister: Mr. Mah Bow Tan

Customs and Excise Department
55 Newton Road, Revenue House #07-00
Singapore 307987
Tel: (65) 272-8222 Fax: (65) 250-9606/9
Director-General: Mr. Koh Chong Hwa

Defence (Ministry of)
Upper Bukit Timah Road, Gombak Drive, MINDEF Building
Singapore 669638
Tel: (65) 760-8828 Fax: (65) 762-0112
Minister: Dr. Tony Tan

Economic Development Board
250 North Bridge Road, #24-00 Raffles City Tower
Singapore 179101
Tel: (65) 336-2288 Fax: (65) 339-6077
Chairman: Mr. Philip Yeo

Education (Ministry of)
Kay Siang Road, Singapore 248922
Tel: (65) 473-9111 Fax: (65) 473-1891
Minister: Mr. Teo Chee Hian

Environment (Ministry of the)
Environment Building, 40 Scotts Road
Singapore 228231
Tel: (65) 732-7733 Fax: (65) 731-9456
Minister: Mr. Yeo Cheow Tong

Finance (Ministry of)
100 High Street, #06-03/#10-01 The Treasury
Singapore 179434
Tel: (65) 225-9911 Fax: (65) 332-7435
Minister: Dr. Richard Hu Tsu Tau

Health (Ministry of)
16 College Road, College of Medicine Building
Singapore 169854
Tel: (65) 223-7777 Fax: (65) 224-1677
Minister: Mr. Yeo Cheow Tong

Immigration Department
10 Kallang Road
Singapore 208718
Tel: (65) 391-6100 Fax: (65) 298-0843
Controller: Mr. Lu Cheng Yang

Information and the Arts (Ministry of)
460 Alexandra Road, #37-00 PSA Building
Singapore 119963
Tel: (65) 270-7988 Fax: (65) 375-7886
Minister: BG (NS) George Yeo

Institute of Technical Education
10 Dover Drive, Singapore 138683
Tel: (65) 775-7800 Fax: (65) 776-2172
Director: Dr. Law Song Seng

Inland Revenue Authority of Singapore
55 Newton Road, Revenue House
Singapore 307987
Tel: (65) 356-8300 Fax: (65) 351-3636
Commissioner: Mr. Koh Cher Siang

Jurong Town Corporation
301 Jurong Town Hall Road
Singapore 609431
Tel: (65) 560-0056 Fax: (65) 565-5301
Chairman: Mr. Lim Neo Chian

Manpower (Ministry of)
18 Havelock Road, #07-01
Singapore 059764
Tel: (65) 534-1511 Fax: (65) 534-4840
Minister: Dr. Lee Boon Yang

Law (Ministry of)
The Treasury, 100 High Street, #08-02
Singapore 179434
Tel: (65) 332-8840 Fax: (65) 332-8842
Minister: Prof. S. Jayakumar

Land Transport Authority (LTA)
460 Alexandra Road, PSA Building, #28-00
Singapore 119963
Tel: (65) 375-7100 Fax: (65) 375-7203
Executive Director: Mr. Low Tien Sio

Nanyang Technological University
Nanyang Avenue, Singapore 639798
Tel: (65) 791-1744 Fax: (65) 791-9516
President: Dr. Cham Tao Soon

National Computer Board
71 Science Park Drive, NCB Building
Singapore 118253
Tel: (65) 778-2211 Fax: (65) 778-9564
Chief Executive: Mr. Stephen Yeo

National Development (Ministry of)
5 Maxwell Road, #22-00, Tower Block MND Complex
Singapore 069110
Tel: (65) 222-1211 Fax: (65) 325-7254
Minister: Mr. Lim Hng Kiang

National Institute of Education
469 Bukit Timah Road
Singapore 259756
Tel: (65) 469-5151 Fax: (65) 463-2960
Director: Professor Leo Tan

National Science and Technology Board
10 Science Park Road, #01-01/03, The Alpha
Singapore Science Park 2, Singapore 117684
Tel: (65) 779-7066 Fax: (65) 773-2795
Executive Director: Mr. Chong Lit Cheong

National University of Singapore
10 Kent Ridge Crescent
Singapore 119260
Tel: (65) 775-6666 Fax: (65) 779-5481
Vice-Chancellor: Professor Lim Pin

Ngee Ann Polytechnic
535 Clementi Road
Singapore 599489
Tel: (65) 466-6555 Fax: (65) 467-6502
Principal: Mr. Khoo Chin Hean

Port Cooperation Limited
460 Alexandra Road, PSA Building
Singapore 119963
Tel: (65) 274-7111 Fax: (65) 274-4677
Chief Executive Officer: Mr. Koo Teng Chye

Productivity and Standards Board
2 Bukit Merah Central, PSB Building
Singapore 159835
Tel: (65) 278-6666 Fax: (65) 278-6665
Chief Executive: Mr. Lee Suan Hiang

Public Utilities Board
111 Somerset Road, #15-01 PUB Building
Singapore 238164
Tel: (65) 235-8888 Fax: (65) 731-3020
Chief Executive Officer: Mr. Ong Ho Sim

Public Works Department
5 Maxwell Road, #20-00 Tower Block
MND Complex, Singapore 069110
Tel: (65) 325-8833 Fax: (65) 325-8848
Director-General: Mr. Chua Koon Hoe

Registry of Companies and Businesses
10 Anson Road, #05-01/15 International Plaza
Singapore 079903
Tel: (65) 227-8551 Fax: (65) 225-1676
Registrar: Ms. Jocelyn Ong

Registry of Trade Marks and Patents
51 Bras Basah Road, #04-01 Plaza by the Park
Singapore 189554
Tel: (65) 330-2700 Fax: (65) 339-0252
Registrar: Ms. Liew Woon Yin

Singapore CableVision Pte. Ltd.
2D Ayer Rajah Crescent, A.O.S. Building
Singapore 139938
Tel: (65) 773-5088 Fax: (65) 870-1742
President: Mr. Yong Lum Sung

Singapore Environmental Management &
Engineering Services Pte.
Ltd. (SEMES)
40 Scotts Road, #11-00 Environment Building
Singapore 228231
Tel: (65) 738-9720 Fax: (65) 738-9719
General Manager: Mr. Donald Goh

Singapore Polytechnic
500 Dover Road
Singapore 139651
Tel: (65) 775-1133 Fax: (65) 772-1985
Principal: Mr. Low Wong Fook

Singapore Power Ltd
111 Somerset Road, #16-01 PUB Building
Singapore 238164
Tel: (65) 733-1668 Fax: (65) 831-8190
Chairman: Mr. Ho Kwon Ping

Singapore Science Centre
15 Science Centre Road
Singapore 609081
Tel: (65) 560-3316 Fax: (65) 565-9533
Ag Director: Dr. Chew Tuan Chiong

Singapore Sports Council
15 Stadium Road, National Stadium, Kallang
Singapore 397718
Tel: (65) 340-9570 Fax: (65) 346-4953
Executive Director: Col (RET) Kwan Yue Yeong

Singapore Tourist Board
1 Orchard Spring Lane, Tourism Court
Singapore 247729
Tel: (65) 736-6622 Fax: (65) 736-9423
Chief Executive Officer: Mr. Yeo Khee Leng

Singapore Trade Development Board
230 Victoria Street #07-00
Bugis Junction Office Tower, Singapore 188024
Tel: (65) 337-6628 Fax: 65) 337-6898
Chief Executive Officer: Mr. Barry Desker

Television Corporation of Singapore
Caldecott Hill, Andrew Road
Singapore 299939
Tel: (65) 256-0401 Fax: (65) 253-2312
Chief Executive (Channels 5 & 8) : Mr. Lee
Cheok Yew

Television 12
12 Prince Edward Road, #05-00 Bestway
Building
Singapore 079212
Tel: (65) 225-8133 Fax: (65) 225-3238
Chief Executive (Channel 12) : Mr. Lim Hup Seng

Trade and Industry (Ministry of)
100 High Street, #09-01 The Treasury

Singapore 179434
Tel: (65) 225-9911 Fax: (65) 332-7260
Minister: Mr. Lee Yock Suan

Urban Redevelopment Authority
45 Maxwell Road, URA Building
P.O. Box 1393, Robinson Road, Singapore 069118
Tel: (65) 221-6666 Fax: (65) 224-8752
Chief Executive Officer & Chief Planner: Dr. Tan Kim Siew

TRADE ASSOCIATIONS/CHAMBERS OF COMMERCE IN SINGAPORE

Association of Small and Medium Enterprises
8 Queen Street, #02-06
Singapore 188535
Tel: (65) 338-5868 Fax: (65) 338-6859
President: Mr. Derek Goh

Singapore Chinese Chamber of Commerce and Industry
47 Hill Street, #09-00 Chinese Chamber of Commerce Building
Singapore 179365
Tel: (65) 337-8381 Fax: (65) 339-0605
President: Mr. Tay Beng Chuan

Singapore Federation of Chambers of Commerce and Industry
47 Hill Street, #03-01 Chinese Chamber of Commerce Building
Singapore 179365
Tel: (65) 338-9761/2 Fax: (65) 339-5630
President: Mr. Kwek Leng Joo

Singapore Indian Chamber of Commerce and Industry
101 Cecil Street, #23-01 Tong Eng Building
Singapore 069533
Tel: (65) 222-2855, (65) 222-2505 Fax: (65) 223-1707
Chairman: Mr. D.D. Gupta

Singapore International Chamber of Commerce
6 Raffles Quay, #10-01 John Hancock Tower
Singapore 048580
Tel: (65) 224-1255 Fax: (65) 224-2785
Chairman: Mr. P.I. Overmyer

Singapore Malay Chamber of Commerce
72A Bussorah Street
Singapore 199485
Tel: (65) 297-9296 Fax: (65) 392-4527
President: Mr. Haj Jalil Haron

Singapore Confederation of Industries
20 Orchard Road, SMA House
Singapore 238830
Tel: (65) 338-8787 Fax: (65) 338-3787
President: Mr. Robert Chua

Singapore Retailers Association
31-A, Ann Siang Road
Singapore 069711
Tel: (65) 223-6221 Fax: (65) 223-6621
President: Mr. Teh Ban Lian

Singapore/US Business Council
250 North Bridge Road
Raffles City Tower
#24-00
Singapore 179101
Tel: (65) 336-2288 /330-6750
Fax: (65) 339-6077 / 337-7528
Chairman: Mr. Tony Tan

SINGAPORE CONTACTS BY INDUSTRY

AEROSPACE

Singapore Technologies Aerospace Ltd.
540 Airport Road, Paya Lebar
Singapore 539938
Tel: (65) 287-1111 Fax: (65) 280-9713
President: Mr. Gary Yeo

AUTOMATION

Singapore Industrial Automation Association
151 Chin Swee Road, #03-13 Manhattan House
Singapore 169876
Tel: (65) 734-6911 Fax: (65) 235-5721
Executive Director: Mr. Stephen Teng

AUTOMOTIVE

Singapore Cycle & Motor Traders' Association
Blk. 261 Waterloo Centre, #03-09 Waterloo Street
Singapore 180261
Tel: (65) 339-7648 Fax: (65) 336-6181
Executive Secretary: Mr. Boo Yeow Thong

Singapore Motor Cycle Trade Association
40 Sam Leong Road
Singapore 207930
Tel: (65) 297-1991 Fax: (65) 297-1313
Administrative Officer: Mr. Yin Nam Kwang

BANKING, FINANCE AND INSURANCE

Banks in Singapore (The Association of)
10 Shenton Way, #12-08 MAS Building
Singapore 079117

Tel: (65) 224-4300 Fax: (65) 224-1785
Director: Mrs. Ong-Ang Ai Boon

General Insurance Association of Singapore
48 Amoy Street
Singapore 069874
Tel: (65) 221-8788 Fax: (65) 227-2051
President: Mr. Albert Koh

Life Insurance Association
1 Selegie Road
Paradiz Center, #06-17A
Singapore 188306
Tel: (65) 338-3340 Fax: (65) 336-0654
President: Mr. N.A. Ganesan

Monetary Authority of Singapore
10 Shenton Way, MAS Building
Singapore 079117
Tel: (65) 225-5577 Fax: (65) 229-9491
Managing Director: Mr. Koh Yong Guan

Stock Exchange of Singapore Ltd.
20 Cecil Street, #26-01/08 The Exchange
Singapore 049705
Tel: (65) 535-3788 Fax: (65) 535-6994
President: Mr. Lim Choo Peng

COMPUTERS

GINTIC Institute of CIM
71 Nanyang Drive
Singapore 638075)
Tel: (65) 793-8383 Fax: (65) 791-6377
Director: Dr. Li Yee Hsun

Kent Ridge Digital Labs
21 Heng Mui Keng
Singapore 119613
Tel: (65) 874-2096 Fax: (65) 775-0938
Chief Exec. Officer: Dr. Juzat Motiwalla

Microcomputer Trade Association of Singapore
219 Henderson Road, #06-03 Henderson Industrial Park
Singapore 159556
Tel: (65) 278-2855 Fax: (65) 275-3032
Chairman: Mr. Tan Chin Ngiap

National Computer Board
71 Science Park Drive, NCB Building
Singapore 118253
Tel: (65) 778-2211 Fax: (65) 778-9564
Chief Executive: Mr. Stephen Yeo

Singapore Computer Society
1 Maritime Square
#11-07A World Trade Center
Singapore
Tel: (65) 377-3011 Fax: (65) 377-3022
President: Dr. Alex Siow

Singapore Federation of Computer Industry
71 Science Park Drive, NCB Building
Singapore 118253
Tel: (65) 775-1927 Fax: (65) 778-4968
Chairman: Mr. William Liu

CONSTRUCTION/PROPERTY

Association of Consulting Engineers, Singapore
51 Anson Road, #02-65 Anson Center
Singapore 079904
Tel: (65) 324-2682 Fax: (65) 324-2581
President: Dr. Kog Yue Choong

Construction Industry Development Board
9 Maxwell Road, #03-00 National Development Building,
MND Complex, Annex A
Singapore 069112
Tel: (65) 225-6711 Fax: (65) 225-7301
Chief Executive Officer: Mr. Lam Siew Wah

Institution of Engineers, Singapore
70 Bukit Tinggi Road
Singapore 289758)
Tel: (65) 469-5000 Fax: (65) 467-1108
President: Associate Prof. Ong Ser Huan

Real Estate Developers' Association of Singapore
190 Clemenceau Avenue, #07-01 Singapore Shopping Centre
Singapore 239924
Tel: (65) 336-6655 Fax: (65) 337-2217
President: Mr. Daniel Teo

Singapore Contractors Association Ltd. (SCAL)
Construction House,
1 Bukit Merah Lane 2
Singapore 159760
Tel: (65) 278-9577 Fax: (65) 273-3977
President: Mr. Tan Kian Hoon

Singapore Institute of Architects
72-B, Tras Street
Singapore 079011
Tel: (65) 226-2668 Fax: (65) 226-2663
President: Mr. Tham Tuck Cheong

Singapore Institute of Planners
c/o 23 Duxton Hill
Singapore 089606
Tel: (65) 225-0322 Fax: (65) 324-6580
President: Dr. Foo Ah Fong

Singapore Institute of Surveyors & Valuers

20 Maxwell Road, #10-09B Maxwell House
Singapore 069113
Tel: (65) 222-3030 Fax: (65) 225-2453
President: Associate Prof. Lim Lan Yuan

ELECTRONICS

GINTIC Institute of Manufacturing Technology
Nanyang Technological University
71 Nanyang Drive, Nanyang Avenue
Singapore 638075
Tel: (65) 793-8383 Fax: (65) 791-2927
Director: Dr. Frans M. A. Carpay

Institute of Microelectronics
11 Science Park Road, Science Park II
Singapore 117685
Tel: (65) 779-7522 Fax: (65) 778-8516
Director: Dr. Bill Chen

National Science and Technology Board
10 Science Park Road, #01-01/02/03 The Alpha
Science Park 2
Singapore 117684
Tel: (65) 779-7066 Fax: (65) 777-1711
Director, Development Division: Mrs. Adams-Yau Lee Ying

Singapore Economic Development Board
#24-00 Raffles City Tower, 250 North Bridge Road
Singapore 179101
Tel: (65) 336-2288 Fax: (65) 339-6077
Deputy Director: Mr. Lai Yeow Hin

Singapore Industrial Automation Association
151 Chin Swee Road, #03-13 Manhattan House
Singapore 169876
Tel: (65) 734-6911 Fax: (65) 235-5721
Executive Director: Mr. Stephen Teng

Singapore Trade Development Board
230 Victoria Street #07-00
Bugis Junction Office Tower
Singapore 188024
Tel: (65) 337-6628 Fax: (65) 337-5253
Manager : Mr. Francis Tay

ENVIRONMENT

Singapore Environmental Management & Engineering Services Pte.
Ltd.
40 Scotts Road, #11-00 Environment Building
Singapore 228231
Tel: (65) 738-9720 Fax: (65) 738-9719
General Manager: Mr. Donald Goh

Singapore Association for Environmental Companies (SAFECO)
20 Orchard Road, SMA House
Singapore 238830
Tel: (65) 338-8578 Fax: (65) 334-5740
Manager: Ms. Josephine Ong

Clean Technology & Environmental Management (CTEM)
20 Orchard Road, SMA House
Singapore 238830
Tel: (65) 338-8787 Fax: (65) 338-5906
Administrator: Ms. Kavita Gandhi

FILM, VIDEO & MUSIC

International Federation of the Phonographic Industry
163 Tras Street
#04-00 Lian Huat Building
Singapore 079026
Tel: (65) 220-6744 Fax: (65) 220-4177
Regional Director: Ms. Leong May Seey

Rediffusion (Singapore) Pte. Ltd.
6 Harper Road, #04-01/08 Leong Huat Building
Singapore 369674
Tel: (65) 383-2633 Fax: (65) 383-2622
Managing Director: Mr. Wong Ban Kuan

Singapore CableVision Pte. Ltd.
2D Ayer Rajah Crescent, Level 3, A.O.S. Building
Singapore 139938
Tel: (65) 872-0188 Fax: (65) 870-1742
President: Mr. Yong Lum Sung

Singapore Phonogram & Videogram Association
67A Tras Street
Singapore 079006
Tel: (65) 220-4166 Fax: (65) 220-9452
Administrative Executive: Mr. Nicole Tan

FOOD EQUIPMENT

Singapore Association of Food Equipment Manufacturers & Suppliers
c/o Focus Management Pte Ltd
20 Maxwell Road, #06-03 Maxwell House
Singapore 069113
Tel: (65) 324-3114 Fax: (65) 222-3703
Honorary Secretary: Mr. Tan Choon Boon

FOOD

Singapore Fruits and Vegetables Importers & Exporters Association
Blk 1 Wholesale Centre, #02-07
Singapore 110021

Tel: (65) 775-3676 Fax: (65) 773-1336
Contact: Mr. Tay Khiam Back, Chairman

Singapore Fruits Importers
& Exporters Exchange Pte Ltd
Blk 1 Wholesale Centre
#02-17/19
Singapore 110021
Tel: (65) 779-4488 Fax: (65) 779-3003
Contact: Mr. Tan Lik Huat

U.S. Meat Export Federation
541 Orchard Road
#15-03, Liat Towers
Singapore 238881
Tel: (65) 733-4255 Fax: (65) 732-1977
Contact: Mr. Eric Choon, Asean Director

U.S. Poultry and Egg Export Council
541 Orchard Road
#15-04, Liat Towers
Singapore 238881
Tel: (65) 737-1726 Fax: (65) 737-1727
Contact: Ms. Margaret Say, Regional Director

U.S. Wheat Associates
541 Orchard Road
#15-02, Liat Towers
Singapore 238881
Tel: (65) 737-4311
Fax: (65) 733-9359
Contact: Mr. Mark Samson, Vice President for South Asia

American Soya Bean Association
541 Orchard Road
#11-03, Liat Towers
Singapore 238881
Tel: (65) 737-6233
Fax: (65) 737-5849
Contact: Mr. John Linblom, Regional Director

JEWELRY

Diamond Exchange of Singapore
545 Orchard Road, #11-02
Far East Shopping Centre
Singapore 238882
Tel: (65) 738-6162 Fax: (65) 737-0993
President: Mr. S.J. Khafi

Singapore Jewelers Association
38C North Canal Road
Singapore 059294
Tel: (65) 535-2989 Fax: (65) 533-0867
President: Mr. Wan Shung Ming

MARINE

Association of Singapore Marine Industries
1 Maritime Square, #09-10 World Trade Centre
Singapore 099253
Tel: (65) 270-7883 Fax: (65) 273-1867
President: Mr. Hung Chiang Gnee

Singapore Shipping Association
456 Alexandra Road, #09-02 NOL Building
Singapore 119962
Tel: (65) 278-3464 Fax: (65) 274-5079
President: Mr. Lua Cheng Eng

MEDICAL

Singapore Medical Association
2 College Road, Level 2, Alumni Medical Centre
Singapore 169850
Tel: (65) 223-1264 Fax: (65) 224-7827
Executive Secretary: Ms. Chua Gek Eng

Singapore Dental Association
2 College Road
Singapore 169850
Tel: (65) 220-2588 Fax: (65) 224-7967
President: Mr. Patrick Tseng
Honorary Secretary: Dr. Shahul Hameed

Pharmaceutical Industry (Singapore Association of)
151 Chin Swee Road, #02-13A, 14 Manhattan House
Singapore 169876
Tel: (65) 738-0966 Fax: (65) 738-0977
President: Mr. Tan Chwee Choon

Plastic Surgeons (Singapore Association of)
(address same as Academy of Medicine)

Singapore Society of Ophthalmology
Singapore National Eye Centre Pte Ltd
11 Third Hospital Avenue
Singapore 168751
Tel: (65) 227-7255 Fax: (65) 227-7290
Medical Director: Professor Arthur Lim

Singapore Society of Radiographers
c/o Department of Diagnostic Imaging
National University Hospital, No. 5 Lower Kent Ridge Road
Singapore 119074
Tel: (65) 772-5272 Fax: (65) 772-5219
President: Mr. Albert Low

PACKAGING

Packaging Industry Council of Singapore
c/o Singapore Confederation of Industry

20 Orchard Road, SMA House
Singapore 238830
Tel: (65) 338-8787 Fax: (65) 338-3358
Chairman: Mr. C. S. Wong

PRESS

Straits Times Press (1975) Ltd.
Times House, 390 Kim Seng Road
Singapore 239495
Tel: (65) 737-0011 Fax: (65) 732-0131
Editor: Mr. Leslie Fong

SECURITY AND SAFETY EQUIPMENT

Chartered Industries of Singapore Pte. Ltd.
249 Jalan Boon Lay
Singapore 619523
Tel: (65) 265-1066; Fax: (65) 261-6932
President: Mr. Loh Chuck Yam

Command Control Communications and Computer Systems Organization
No.1 Depot Road, #22-01 Defence Technology Tower A
Singapore 109679
Tel: (65) 373-2577 Fax: (65) 373-3418
Director: Col. Larry Ang

Commercial and Industrial Security Corporation
20 Jalan Afifi, CISCO Center
Singapore 409179
Tel: (65) 747-2888 Fax: (65) 747-2275
General Manager/Chief Executive Officer: Mr. Chan Boon Kiong

Defense Materials Organization
Ministry of Defense
Depot Road, Defense Technology Tower A, Level 18
Singapore 109679
Tel: (65) 373-4678 Fax: (65) 273-1078
Director: Col. Soh Kong Pheng

Defence Science Organization
20 Science Park Drive, Singapore Science Park
Singapore 118230
Tel: (65) 772-7005 Fax: (65) 775-9011
Director: Professor Quek Tong Soon

Ministry of Defence, Defence Procurement Division
Depot Road, 3rd Storey, Defense Technology Tower A
Singapore 109679
Tel: (65) 373-4072 Fax: (65) 276-8443
Assistant Director: Mr. Ng Kit Seng

Systems and Computer Organization
No. 1 Depot Road
#08-01
Singapore 109679
Tel: (65) 373-2600 Fax: (65) 273-9052
Director: Mr. Lai Kim Fatt

TELECOMMUNICATIONS

Intraco Ltd
230 Victoria Street, #12-00 Bugis Junction Towers
Singapore 188024
Tel: (65) 337-0011 Fax: (65) 337-7200
Chief Executive Officer: Mr. Bernard Chen

Singapore Telecommunications Ltd
31 Exeter Road, Comcentre
Singapore 239732
Tel: (65) 838-3388 Fax: (65) 732-8300
Chief Executive Officer/President: BG (NS) Lee Hsien Yang

ST Telecommunications Pte. Ltd.
3 Lim Teck Kim Road, #10-02 Singapore Technologies Building
Singapore 088934
Tel: (65) 220-5335 Fax: (65) 222-1020
President: Mr. Lee Theng Kiat

Telecommunication Authority of Singapore
35 Robinson Road, TAS Building
Singapore 068876
Tel: (65) 323-3888 Fax: (65) 323-0964
Director-General: Mr. Leong Keng Thai

TEXTILES/APPARELS

Sewing Machine Traders Association
135 Middle Road, #03-02 Bylands Building
Singapore 188975
Tel: (65) 338-2256 Fax: (65) 339-4976
Secretary: Ms. Molly Teo

Singapore Master Tailors' Association
3E Lorong 12 Geylang
Singapore 398984
Tel: (65) 748-3878 Fax: (65) 747-4200
Chairman: Ms. Tham Siew Leng

Singapore Textiles & General Merchants Association
148 Neil Road
Singapore 088877
Tel: (65) 223-8061 Fax: (65) 222-3501
President: Mr. Kwong Chi Khiong

Textile and Fashion Federation
60 Martin Road, #07-16 TradeMart Singapore

Singapore 239065
Tel: (65) 735-8390 Fax: (65) 735-8409
President: Mr. Patrick Lee

TIMBER/FURNITURE

Singapore Timber Exporters' Association
2 Finlayson Green, #09-08 Asia Insurance Building
Singapore 049247
Tel: (65) 224-2437 Fax: (65) 225-7987
President: Mr. Anthony K. Y. Lo

Singapore Timber Manufacturers' Association
341B Beach Road
Singapore 199567
Tel: (65) 298-0709 Fax: (65) 291-9844
President: Mr. Neo Koon Boo

Singapore Precision Engineering and Tooling Association
14 Balestier Road
Singapore 329679
Tel: (65) 291-6430 Fax: (65) 292-4517
President: Dr. Ricky Souw

Singapore Furniture Industries Council
2 Jurong East Street 21, #02-110/111 IMM Building
Singapore 609601
Tel: (65) 568-2626 Fax: (65) 568-2922
President: Mr. Choo Yong See

SINGAPORE MARKET RESEARCH FIRMS

D. Richmond & Associates Pte Ltd
Ms. Dee Richmond, Ph.D.
Managing Director
70A Prinsep Street
Singapore 188662
Tel: (65) 338-3812
Fax: (65) 338-3813

Market Behaviour (Singapore) Pte Ltd
Dr. Thomas Tan
Managing Director
19 Keppel Road #03-10
Jit Poh Building
Singapore 089058
Tel: (65) 222-2432
Fax: (65) 222-2436

Research Singapore (Pte) Ltd
Mrs. Ho Chin See
Managing Director
51 Newton Road
#09-01 Goldhill Plaza
Singapore 308900
Tel: (65) 252-8595
Fax: (65) 253-4287

Acorn Marketing & Research
Mr. Kenneth Tan
Director
241 River Valley
River Valley Road
Singapore 238298
Tel: (65) 733-6565
Fax: (65) 732-6128

Applied Research Corporation
Mr. Ong Chor Eong
Managing Director
Engineering Block E4-04-11
National University of Singapore
Kent Ridge
Singapore 119260
Tel: (65) 775-5822
Fax: (65) 773-0924

Frank Small & Associates (SEA) Pte Ltd
Mr. Mirko Mlatac
Managing Director
Marketing & Research Consultants
Asia-Pacific Region Specialists
510 Thomson Road
#15-03 SLF Building
Singapore 298135
Tel: (65) 258-9911
Fax: (65) 258-2672

MAJOR COMMERCIAL BANKS IN SINGAPORE

Overseas Union Bank Ltd.
Mr. Peter Seah Lim Huat
President & Chief Executive Officer
1, Raffles Place,
OUB Centre,
Singapore 048616
Tel : 533-8686
Fax : 530-2213

United Overseas Bank Group Ltd.
Mr. Wee Cho Yaw
Chairman & Chief Executive Officer
80, Raffles Place, OUB Plaza,
Singapore 048624
Tel : 539-2000
Fax : 534-2334

Oversea-Chinese Banking Corporation Ltd.
Mr. Lee Seng Wee
Chairman & Chief Executive Officer
65, Chulia Street,
Singapore 049513
Tel : 535-7222
Fax : 535-5219

Development Bank of Singapore Ltd.
Mr. Ng Kee Choe
Deputy President
6, Shenton Way,
DBS Building, Tower 1,
46th Floor,
Singapore 068809
Tel : 220-1111
Fax : 323-9112

The Chase Manhattan bank
Mr. Morgan McGrath
Regional Manager
150 Beach Road
35th Floor Gateway West
Singapore 189720
Tel: 291-1298
Fax: 392-7375

Bank of America
Mr. Colm McCarthy
Vice President/Regional Manager
9 Raffles Place
Republic Plaza Tower 1
#18-00
Singapore 048619
Tel: 239-3101
Fax: 239-3137

Citibank
Mr. Shehzad Naqvi
Country Corporate office GF Head
UIC Building, 8th Floor
Singapore 068808
Tel: 224-8172
Fax: 224-2611

U.S.-BASED MULTIPLIERS RELEVANT FOR SINGAPORE

Embassy of the Republic of Singapore-Washington
1 International N.W. Washington, D.C. 20008
Tel: (202) 537-3100; Fax: (202) 537-0876
Ambassador: Prof. Ms. Chan Heng Chee

Singapore Economic Development Board-Boston
8th Floor, One International Place, Boston, MA 02110-2600
Tel: (617) 261-9981; Fax: (617) 261-9983
Centre Director: Mr. Jonathan Kwa

Singapore Economic Development Board-Chicago
Two Prudential Plaza, 180 N. Stetson Ave., Suite 970
Chicago, IL 60601-6712
Tel: (312) 565-1100; Fax: (312) 565-1994
Centre Directors: Ms. Aw Kah Peng

Singapore Economic Development Board-Los Angeles
2029 Century Park East, Suite 1540, Los Angeles, CA 90067
Tel: (310) 553-0199; Fax: (310) 557-1044
Centre Director: Mr. Lim Beng Yong Simon

Singapore Economic Development Board-New York
55 East 59th St., New York, NY 10022-11122
Tel: (212) 421-2200; Fax: (212) 421-2206
Regional Director: Mr. Ng Nam Sin

Singapore Economic Development Board-San Francisco
210 Twin Dolphin Dr., Redwood City, CA 94065-1402
Tel: (415) 591-9102; Fax: (415) 591-1328
Regional Director (Western U.S.) : Mr. Barry Sim Mong Huat
Centre Directors: Mr. Quek Swee Kuan, Mr. Png Cheong Boon, Mr.
Seow
Wee Seong (Int'l Manpower) and Mr. Joseph Chow (SBI) .

Singapore Economic Development Board-Washington
1100 New York Avenue
NW, Suite #440 Washington DC 20005
Tel: (202) 223-2570/2571; Fax: (202) 223-2572
Centre Director: Mr. Beh Swan Gin

Singapore Trade Development Board-New York
55 East 59th Street, Suite 21B
New York 10022
Tel: (212) 421-2207; Fax: (212) 888-2897
Centre Director: Mr. Satvinder Singh

Singapore Trade Development Board-Washington
Embassy of the Republic of Singapore-USA
3501 International Place, NW
Washington DC 20008
Tel: (202) 537-3100; Fax: (202) 537-0876
First Secretary (Economics) : Ms. Kathy Lai

U.S.-ASEAN Council for Business & Technology, Inc.
1400 L St. N.W., Suite 375, Washington, D.C. 20005
Tel: (202) 289-1911; Fax: (202) 289-0519
Executive Director: Mr. Ernest Bower

U.S. Chamber of Commerce
International Division
1615 H St. N.W., Washington, D.C. 20062
Tel: (202) 473-5486
President: Mr. Richard L. Lesher

IMPORTANT U.S. GOVERNMENT CONTACTS IN THE UNITED STATES

TPCC Trade Information Center number in Washington:
1-800-USA-TRADE

U.S. Department of State Office of Business Affairs: Tel:
202-746-1625, Fax: 202-647-3953

U.S. Department of Commerce MAC Country Desk Officer: Mr. Kevin Boyd, Tel: 202-482-3646, Fax: 202-482-3316

U.S. Department of Agriculture, Foreign Agricultural Service,
Trade Assistance and Promotion Office: Tel: 202-720-7420

Overseas Private Investment Corporation: Tel: 202-336-8799, Fax:
202-408-5155

Other American Organizations in Singapore

American Chamber of Commerce in Singapore
1 Scotts Road #16-07 Shaw Centre
Singapore 228208
Tel: (65) 235-0077 Fax: (65) 732-5917
Executive Director: Ms. Claire Adams

Port of Charleston
c/o Jardine Transport Services
1 Maritime Square, Lobby D
#10-40 World Trade Centre
Singapore 099253
Tel: (65) 374-8209, Fax: (65) 275-3313
E-mail: lakhbir.singh@jtsjsa.com.sg
Manager (Business Development) :Mr. Lakbir Singh

State of Indiana, Wisconsin and Missouri
c/o US-ASEAN Business Council
70-A Prinsep Street
Singapore 188662
Tel: (65) 339-8885, Fax: (65) 339-1982
E-mail: jrasean@pacific.net.sg
Director: Ms. Joyce Rasmussen

Port of Los Angeles
c/o PIERS Resource & Services Pte Ltd
Blk 334, Kreta Ayer Road
#03-10, Singapore 080334
Tel: (65) 324-6823, Fax: (65) 324-6825
Managing Director: Mr. K. C. Tan

State of Mississippi, ASEAN Office
7, Temasek Boulevard
#12-02C Suntec City Tower 1
Singapore 038987
Tel: (65) 338-6377 Fax: (65) 337-6377
Director (ASEAN) : Mr. Simon Beh

State of Massachussetts
161A Telok Ayer Street
Singapore 068615
Tel: (65) 323-1882, Fax: (65) 323-1682
Trade Representative (ASEAN) : Mr. Sitoh Yih Pin

Port Authority of New York and New Jersey
24 Port Road
#03-00 Office Block CWT
Distripark (HQ)
Singapore 619097
Tel: (65) 261-1061 Fax: (65) 261-1659
E-mail: desmondtamaki@compuserde.com
Regional Director: Mr. Desmond Tamaki

Port of Olympia
#09-00, South Point
200 Cantonment Road
Singapore 089763
Tel: (65) 326-4350, Fax: (65) 226-2804
Director: Mr. Francis Aurol

State of Oklahoma
Department of Commerce
International Trade & Investment
7500A Beach Road #12-302, The Plaza
Singapore 199591
Tel: (65) 2979095 Fax: (65) 2979766
E-mail:
stanley_ang.odoc@notes.compuserve.com
Director (ASEAN) : Mr. Stanley Ang

Port of Seattle
Singapore Representative Office
Tel: (65) 235-5762, 96826904 (Handphone)
Fax: (65) 7355889, (65) 7360820 (Home)
Director: Mr. Kirpa Ram Vij

Port of Tacoma
c/0 Henry Noon Co.
Citylink #05-05
102F Pasir Panjang Road
Singapore 118530
Tel/Handphone: (65) 9-652-9364, Fax:(65) 254 7251
Director: Mr. Keith Hiller

US-ASEAN Council for Business and Technology
70-A Prinsep Street
Singapore 188662
Tel: (65) 339-8885, Fax: (65) 339-1982
E-mail: jrasean@pacific.net.sg
Regional Director: Ms. Joyce Rasmussen

United States Education Information Center
12 Prince Edward Road
#01-03 Bestway Building
Shenton Way, Singapore 079212
Tel: (65) 226-6996 Fax: (65) 223-0550
Director: Ms. Hong Nih Ly

U.S. BANKS IN SINGAPORE

American Express Bank Ltd.
16 Collyer Quay
Hitachi Tower
Singapore 049318
Tel: (65) 538-4833
Fax: (65) 534-3022

Bank of America NT & SA
9 Raffles Place
Republic Plaza Tower 1, #18-00
Singapore 048619
Tel: (65) 223-6688
Fax: (65) 239-3068

Bank of Hawaii
4 Shenton Way
#19-01 Shing Kwan House
Singapore 068807
Tel: (65) 221-0500
Fax: (65) 224-1144

Bankers Trust Company
5 Temasek Boulevard
#08-00 Suntec City Tower
Singapore 038985
Tel: (65) 336-2838
Fax: (65) 331-4868

Citibank N.A.
5 Shenton Way
#06-00
UIC Building
Singapore 068808
Tel: (65) 224-2611
Fax: (65) 224-9844

CoBank, ACB
50 Raffles Place
Level 37, Shell Tower
Singapore 048623
Tel: (65) 320-8427
Fax: (65) 320-8426

CoreStates Bank NA
6 Battery Road
#13-03
Singapore 049909
Tel: (65) 224-6177
Fax: (65) 224-6176

First Chicago NBD
9 Raffles Place
#29-02 Republic Plaza
Singapore 048619
Tel: (65) 438-2488
Fax: (65) 438-2070

Marine Midland Bank N.A.
21 Collyer Quay
#12-00 Hong Kong Bank Building
Singapore 049320
Tel: (65) 225-7282
Tel: (65) 225-1519

Merrill Lynch International Bank Ltd
2 Raffles Link
4th & 5th Storey
Marina Bayfront
Singapore 039392
Tel: (65) 334-3368
Fax: (65) 331-3500

Morgan Guaranty Trust Co. Of New York
6 Shenton Way
#32-08
DBS Building Tower 2
Singapore 068809
Tel: (65) 220-8144
Fax: (65) 326-9981

Nations Bank, N.A.
80 Raffles Place
#30-20 UOB Plaza 2
Singapore 048624
Tel: (65) 230-2300
Fax: (65) 230-2302

Republic National Bank of New York
143 Cecil Street
#01-00 GB Building
Singapore 069542
Tel: (65) 224-0077
Fax: (65) 225-5769

The Philadelphia National Bank
6 Battery Road
#13-03
Standard Chartered Building
Singapore 049909
Tel: (65) 224-6177
Fax: (65) 224-6170

The Northern Trust Company
80 Raffles Place
#46-02 UOB Plaza 1
Singapore 048624
Tel: (65) 437-6666
Fax: (65) 437-6659

The First National Bank of Boston
150 Beach Road
#07-00 Gateway West
Singapore 189720
Tel: (65) 296-2366
Fax: (65) 296-0998

The Chase Manhattan Bank N.A.
150 Beach Road
Gateway West
#35-00
Singapore 189720
Tel: (65) 291-1298
Fax: (65) 392-7259

The Bank of New York
1 Temasek Avenue
#02-01 Millenia Tower
Singapore 039192
Tel: (65) 432-0222
Fax: (65) 337-4302

STOCK BROKERS; MEMBER COMPANIES

ABN AMRO Asia Securities (Singapore) Pte Limited
63 Chulia Street #11-02 Singapore 049514

Tel: 536 7688 Fax: 536 4788/538 6972

BNP Paribas Peregrine Securities Pte Ltd
30 Cecil Street #19-01 Prudential Tower Singapore 049712
Tel: 438 9888 Fax: 535 8859

BT Brokerage & Associates Pte Ltd
20 Collyer Quay, #19-00, Tung Centre, Singapore 049319
Tel: 224 9233 Fax: 224 9180

CLSA Singapore Pte Ltd
9 Raffles Place #19-20/21 Republic Plaza II Singapore 048619
Tel: 534 3268 Fax: 533 8922

Credit Suisse First Boston (Singapore) Securities Pte Ltd
1 Raffles Link #03-01 North Lobby Singapore 039393
Tel: 212 2000 Fax: 212 3100

Daiwa Securities SB Capital Markets Investment Services Pte Ltd
6 Shenton Way #26-08 DBS Building Tower Two Singapore 068809
Tel: 220 3666 Fax: 221 8853

DBS Securities Singapore Pte Ltd
22 Malacca Street, DBS Securities Building, Singapore 048980
Tel: 533 9688 Fax: 535 7785
http://www.dbss.com.sg (WAP service)

DMG & Partners Securities Pte Ltd^*
20 Raffles Place, #22-01, Ocean Towers, Singapore 048620
Tel: 533 1818 Fax: 532 6211
www.dmg.com.sg

Fraser Securities Pte Ltd^+
10 Collyer Quay, #27-01, Ocean Building, Singapore 049315
Tel: 535 9455 Fax: 535 1745 / 534 4826
www.fraserdirect.com.sg

G K Goh Stockbrokers Pte Ltd^+
50 Raffles Place #33-00 Singapore Land Tower Singpaore 048623
Tel: 225 1228 Fax: 225 1522
www.gkgoh.com / www.gohdirect.com

Grand Orient Securities Pte Ltd*
10 Collyer Quay, #10-00, Ocean Building, Singapore 049315
Tel: 236 1111 Fax: 536 6539

ING Baring Securites (Singapore) Pte Ltd
9 Raffles Place #19-01 Republic Plaza Singpaore 048619
Tel: 535 3688 Fax: 535 3233

Jardine Fleming Singapore Securities Pte Ltd
9 Raffles Place #42-01 Republic Plaza Singapore 048619
Tel: 532 1933

J.M. Sassoon & Co (Pte) Ltd^*
1 Raffles Place, #44-00, OUB Centre, Singapore 048616
Tel: 535 2888 Fax: 533 7956
www.sass-i.com.sg

Kay Hian Private Limited^*
80 Raffles Place, #30-01, UOB Plaza 1, Singapore 048624
Tel: 533 2936 Fax: 532 6919
www.kayhian.com

Keppel Securities Pte Ltd^*
10 Hoe Chiang Road, #08-01, Keppel Towers, Singapore 089315
Tel: 221 5688 Fax: 226 1543
www.vianet.com.sg

Kim Eng Securities Pte Ltd*
9 Temasek Boulevard, #39-00, Suntec City Tower Two, Singapore 038989
Tel: 336 9090 Fax: 339 6003

Lim & Tan Securities Pte Ltd^*
10 Collyer Quay #12-00 Ocean Building Singapore 049315
Tel: 533 0595 Fax: 533 2368
www.limtan.com.sg or www.eq.com.sg

Lum Chang Securities Pte Ltd^*
16 Raffles Quay, #28-01, Hong Leong Building, Singapore 048581
Tel: 223 8282 Fax: 225 6801
http://www.investline.com.sg

Merrill Lynch (Singapore) Pte Ltd
1 Temasek Avenue #28-01 & #29-01 Millenia Tower Singapore 039192
Tel: 330 7888 Fax: 330 7800

Millennium Securities Pte Ltd
80 Robinson Road #02-00 Singapore 068898
Tel: 224 5877 Fax: 224 6632

Nomura Securities Singapore Pte Ltd
6 Battery Road #34-01 Singapore 049909
Tel: 420 1811 Fax: 420 1888

OCBC Securities Private Limited*
18 Church Street #06-00 OCBC Centre South Singapore 049479
Tel: 535 2882 Fax: 532 2768

Ong & Company Private Limited^
24 Raffles Place, #12-01/06 & #07-03/07, Clifford Centre Singapore 048621
Tel: 533 3368 Fax: 538 6212
www.ongline.com (WAP service)

OUB Securities Pte Ltd^*
50 Collyer Quay, #01-01, Overseas Union House, Singapore 049321
Tel: 225 1166 Fax: 225 6884
www.oub.com.sg

Phillip Securities Pte Ltd^*
95 South Bridge Road, #11-17, Pidemco Centre, Singapore 058717
Tel: 533 6001 Fax: 535 3834
www.phillip.com.sg

RHB-Cathay Securities Pte Ltd
9 Raffles Place, #25-01/#26-01, Republic Plaza, Singapore 048619
Tel: 538 0268 Fax: 538 8227

Summit Securities (S) Pte Ltd
20 Raffles Place, #15-01/05, Ocean Towers, Singapore 048620
Tel: 533 3388 Fax: 532 6333/532 6356
Internet: www.ses.com.sg/tsang

UBS Warburg & Associates (Singapore) Pte Ltd^*
9 Raffles Place, #32-01, Republic Plaza, Singapore 048619
Tel: 538 1818 Fax: 536 9649
http://www.wits.com.sg

UOB Securities Pte Ltd^*
80 Raffles Place, #18-00, UOB Plaza 1, Singapore 048624
Tel: 535 6868 Fax: 533 1747
http://www.uob.com.sg/investment

INTERNATIONAL MEMBERS; MEMBER COMPANIES

ABN Amro Asia Securities (S'pore) Pte Ltd
63 Chulia Street #11-02 Singapore 049514
Tel: 536 7688 Fax: 538 6972

Credit Lyonnais Securities (Singapore) Pte Ltd
9 Raffles Place #19-20/21 Republic Plaza II Singapore 048619
Tel: 534 3268 Fax: 533 8922

Daiwa Securities SB Capital Markets Investment Services Pte Ltd
6 Shenton Way, #26-08, DBS Building Tower Two, Singapore 068809
Tel: 220 3666 Fax: 221 8853

ING Baring Securities (Singapore) Pte Ltd
9 Raffles Place, #19-01, Republic Plaza, Singapore 048619
Tel: 535 3688 Fax: 535 3233

Jardine Fleming Singapore Securities Pte Ltd
9 Raffles Place #42-01 Republic Plaza Singapore 048619
Tel: 532 1933 Fax: 532 1922

Merrill Lynch (Singapore) Pte Ltd
1 Temasek Avenue, #28-01 & #29-01, Millenia Tower, Singapore 039192
Tel: 330 7888 Fax: 330 7800

Nomura Securities Singapore Pte Ltd
6 Battery Road, #34-01, Singapore 049909
Tel: 420 1811 Fax: 420 1888

BASIC TITLES ON SINGAPORE

Title	ISBN
Singapore A "Spy" Guide - Strategic Information and Developments	143304448X
Singapore A Spy" Guide"	1438743262
Singapore Air Force Handbook	1438743270
Singapore Air Force Handbook	1433044498
Singapore Army Weapon Systems Handbook	1433061902
Singapore Army Weapon Systems Handbook	1433061902
Singapore Army Weapon Systems Handbook	1433061902
Singapore Army, National Security and Defense Policy Handbook	1438743289
Singapore Army, National Security and Defense Policy Handbook	1433044501
Singapore Banking & Financial Market Handbook	1438743297
Singapore Banking & Financial Market Handbook	143304451X
Singapore Banks and Financial Companies Registration Handbook	1433068125
Singapore Business and Investment Opportunities Yearbook	1438743300
Singapore Business and Investment Opportunities Yearbook	1433044528
Singapore Business and Investment Opportunities Yearbook Volume 1 Strategic Information and Opportunities	1438777876
Singapore Business and Investment Opportunities Yearbook Volume 2 Leading Export-Import, Business, Investment Opportunities and Projects	1577519817
Singapore Business Intelligence Report - Practical Information, Opportunities, Contacts	1438743319
Singapore Business Intelligence Report - Practical Information, Opportunities, Contacts	1433044536
Singapore Business Law Handbook - Strategic Information and Basic Laws	1438771002
Singapore Business Law Handbook - Strategic Information and Basic Laws	1438743327
Singapore Business Law Handbook - Strategic Information and Basic Laws	1433044544
Singapore Business Law Handbook - Strategic Information and Basic Laws	1438771002
Singapore Clothing & Textile Industry Handbook	1438743335
Singapore Clothing & Textile Industry Handbook	1433044552

Title	ISBN
Singapore Company Laws and Regulations Handbook	1433070588
Singapore Constitution and Citizenship Laws Handbook - Strategic Information and Basic Laws	1438779801
Singapore Country Guide	1438743343
Singapore Country Guide	1433044560
Singapore Country Study Guide - Strategic Information and Developments Volume 1 Strategic Information and Developments	1438775547
Singapore Customs, Trade Regulations and Procedures Handbook	1438743351
Singapore Customs, Trade Regulations and Procedures Handbook	1433044579
Singapore Diplomatic Handbook - Strategic Information and Developments	143874336X
Singapore Diplomatic Handbook - Strategic Information and Developments	1433044587
Singapore Ecology & Nature Protection Handbook	1438743378
Singapore Ecology & Nature Protection Handbook	1433044595
Singapore Ecology & Nature Protection Laws and Regulation Handbook	1433074907
Singapore Economic & Development Strategy Handbook	1438743386
Singapore Economic & Development Strategy Handbook	1433044609
Singapore Education System and Policy Handbook	1433068133
Singapore Education System and Policy Handbook	1438768133
Singapore Education System and Policy Handbook	1433068133
Singapore Energy Policy, Laws and Regulation Handbook	1433072661
Singapore Export-Import Trade and Business Directory	1438743394
Singapore Export-Import Trade and Business Directory	1433044617
Singapore Foreign Policy and Government Guide	1438743408
Singapore Foreign Policy and Government Guide	1433044625
Singapore Government and Business Contacts Handbook	1438743416
Singapore Government and Business Contacts Handbook	1433044633
Singapore Government Encyclopedic Directory	1438743424
Singapore Government Encyclopedic Directory	1433044641
Singapore Healthcare Sector Organization, Management and Payment Systems Handbook - Strategic Information, Programs and Regulations	9781433085987
Singapore Immigration Laws and Regulations Handbook - Strategic Information and Basic Laws	143878340X
Singapore Industrial and Business Directory	1438743432
Singapore Industrial and Business Directory	143304465X
Singapore Insolvency (Bankruptcy) Laws and Regulations Handbook - Strategic Information and Basic Laws	9781433085635
Singapore Internet and E-Commerce Investment and Business Guide - Strategic and Practical Information: Regulations and Opportunities	1438743440
Singapore Internet and E-Commerce Investment and Business Guide - Strategic and Practical Information: Regulations and Opportunities	1433044668
Singapore Investment and Business Guide - Strategic and Practical Information	1438768729
Singapore Investment and Business Guide - Strategic and Practical Information	1438743459
Singapore Investment and Business Guide - Strategic and Practical Information	1438768729
Singapore Investment and Business Guide - Strategic and Practical Information	1433044676
Singapore Investment and Business Guide Volume 2 Business, Investment Opportunities and Incentives	1577518764
Singapore Investment and Trade Laws and Regulations Handbook	1433076594
Singapore Justice System and National Police Handbook	1438743467
Singapore Justice System and National Police Handbook	1433044684

Title	ISBN
Singapore Labor Laws and Regulations Handbook - Strategic Information and Basic Laws	1438781601
Singapore Land Ownership and Agriculture Laws Handbook	1438759916
Singapore Media Companies and Information Market Handbook	9781577515227
Singapore Medical & Pharmaceutical Industry Handbook	1438743475
Singapore Medical & Pharmaceutical Industry Handbook	1433044692
Singapore Recent Economic and Political Developments Yearbook	1433062526
Singapore Recent Economic and Political Developments Yearbook	1433062526
Singapore Recent Economic and Political Developments Yearbook	1433062526
Singapore Research & Development Policy Handbook	143306281X
Singapore Research & Development Policy Handbook	143306281X
Singapore Research & Development Policy Handbook	143306281X
Singapore Starting Business (Incorporating) in Singapore Guide	1433047128
Singapore Starting Business (Incorporating) in....Guide	1433068141
Singapore Tax Guide	1438743483
Singapore Tax Guide VOL 1 Business Taxation	1433044706
Singapore Taxation Laws and Regulations Handbook	143308094X
Singapore Telecom Laws and Regulations Handbook	143308242X
Singapore Telecommunication Industry Business Opportunities Handbook	1438743491
Singapore Telecommunication Industry Business Opportunities Handbook	1433044714
Singapore Transportation Policy and Regulations Handbook	143306815X
Singapore: How to Invest, Start and Run Profitable Business in Singapore Guide - Practical Information, Opportunities, Contacts	9781433084522

Equatorial Guinea Company Laws and Regulations Handbook
Eritrea Company Laws and Regulations Handbook
Estonia Company Laws and Regulations Handbook
Ethiopia Company Laws and Regulations Handbook
Falkland Islands Company Laws and Regulations Handbook
Faroes Company Laws and Regulations Handbook
Fiji Company Laws and Regulations Handbook
Finland Company Laws and Regulations Handbook
France Company Laws and Regulations Handbook
Gabon Company Laws and Regulations Handbook
Gambia Company Laws and Regulations Handbook
Georgia Company Laws and Regulations Handbook
Germany Company Laws and Regulations Handbook
Ghana Company Laws and Regulations Handbook
Gibraltar Company Laws and Regulations Handbook
Greece Company Laws and Regulations Handbook
Greenland Company Laws and Regulations Handbook
Grenada Company Laws and Regulations Handbook
Guam Company Laws and Regulations Handbook
Guatemala Company Laws and Regulations Handbook
Guernsey Company Laws and Regulations Handbook
Guinea Company Laws and Regulations Handbook
Guinea-Bissau Company Laws and Regulations Handbook
Guyana Company Laws and Regulations Handbook
Haiti Company Laws and Regulations Handbook
Honduras Company Laws and Regulations Handbook
Hungary Company Laws and Regulations Handbook
Iceland Company Laws and Regulations Handbook
India Company Laws and Regulations Handbook
Indonesia Company Laws and Regulations Handbook
InternationalCompany Laws and Regulations Handbook
Iran Company Laws and Regulations Handbook
Iraq Company Laws and Regulations Handbook
Ireland Company Laws and Regulations Handbook
Israel Company Laws and Regulations Handbook
Italy Company Laws and Regulations Handbook
Jamaica Company Laws and Regulations Handbook
Japan Company Laws and Regulations Handbook
Jersey Company Laws and Regulations Handbook
Jordan Company Laws and Regulations Handbook
Kazakhstan Company Laws and Regulations Handbook
Kenya Company Laws and Regulations Handbook
Kiribati Company Laws and Regulations Handbook
Korea, North Company Laws and Regulations Handbook
Korea, South Company Laws and Regulations Handbook
Kosovo Company Laws and Regulations Handbook
Kuwait Company Laws and Regulations Handbook
Kyrgyzstan Company Laws and Regulations Handbook
Laos Company Laws and Regulations Handbook
Latvia Company Laws and Regulations Handbook
Lebanon Company Laws and Regulations Handbook
Lesotho Company Laws and Regulations Handbook
Liberia Company Laws and Regulations Handbook
Libya Company Laws and Regulations Handbook
Liechtenstein Company Laws and Regulations Handbook
Lithuania Company Laws and Regulations Handbook
Luxembourg Company Laws and Regulations Handbook
Macao Company Laws and Regulations Handbook
Macedonia Company Laws and Regulations Handbook
Madagascar Company Laws and Regulations Handbook
Madeira Company Laws and Regulations Handbook
Malawi Company Laws and Regulations Handbook
Malaysia Company Laws and Regulations Handbook
Maldives Company Laws and Regulations Handbook
Mali Company Laws and Regulations Handbook
Malta Company Laws and Regulations Handbook
Man Company Laws and Regulations Handbook
Marshall Islands Company Laws and Regulations Handbook
Mauritania Company Laws and Regulations Handbook
Mauritius Company Laws and Regulations Handbook
Mayotte Company Laws and Regulations Handbook
Mexico Company Laws and Regulations Handbook
Micronesia Company Laws and Regulations Handbook
Moldova Company Laws and Regulations Handbook
Monaco Company Laws and Regulations Handbook
Mongolia Company Laws and Regulations Handbook
Monserrat Company Laws and Regulations Handbook
Morocco Company Laws and Regulations Handbook
Mozambique Company Laws and Regulations Handbook
Myanmar Company Laws and Regulations Handbook
Namibia Company Laws and Regulations Handbook
Nauru Company Laws and Regulations Handbook
Nepal Company Laws and Regulations Handbook
Netherlands Company Laws and Regulations Handbook
New Caledonia Company Laws and Regulations Handbook
New Zealand Company Laws and Regulations Handbook
Nicaragua Company Laws and Regulations Handbook
Niger Company Laws and Regulations Handbook
Nigeria Company Laws and Regulations Handbook
Niue Company Laws and Regulations Handbook
Northern Mariana Islands Company Laws and Regulations Handbook
Norway Company Laws and Regulations Handbook
Oman Company Laws and Regulations Handbook
Pakistan Company Laws and Regulations Handbook
Palau Company Laws and Regulations Handbook

Palestine Company Laws and Regulations Handbook
Panama Company Laws and Regulations Handbook
Papua New Guinea Company Laws and Regulations Handbook
Paraguay Company Laws and Regulations Handbook
Peru Company Laws and Regulations Handbook
Philippines Company Laws and Regulations Handbook
Pitcairn Islands Company Laws and Regulations Handbook
Poland Company Laws and Regulations Handbook
Polynesia French Company Laws and Regulations Handbook
Portugal Company Laws and Regulations Handbook
Qatar Company Laws and Regulations Handbook
Romania Company Laws and Regulations Handbook
Russia Company Laws and Regulations Handbook
Rwanda Company Laws and Regulations Handbook
Saint Kitts and Nevis Company Laws and Regulations Handbook
Saint Lucia Company Laws and Regulations Handbook
Saint Vincent and The Grenadines Company Laws and Regulations Handbook
Samoa (American) Company Laws and Regulations Handbook
Samoa (Western) Company Laws and Regulations Handbook
San Marino Company Laws and Regulations Handbook
Sao Tome and Principe Company Laws and Regulations Handbook
Saudi Arabia Company Laws and Regulations Handbook
Scotland Company Laws and Regulations Handbook
Senegal Company Laws and Regulations Handbook
Seychelles Company Laws and Regulations Handbook
Sierra Leone Company Laws and Regulations Handbook
Singapore Company Laws and Regulations Handbook
Slovakia Company Laws and Regulations Handbook
Slovenia Company Laws and Regulations Handbook
Solomon Islands Company Laws and Regulations Handbook
Somalia Company Laws and Regulations Handbook
South Africa Company Laws and Regulations Handbook
Spain Company Laws and Regulations Handbook
Sri Lanka Company Laws and Regulations Handbook
St. Helena Company Laws and Regulations Handbook
St. Pierre & Miquelon Company Laws and Regulations Handbook
Sudan Company Laws and Regulations Handbook
Suriname Company Laws and Regulations Handbook
Swaziland Company Laws and Regulations Handbook
Sweden Company Laws and Regulations Handbook
Switzerland Company Laws and Regulations Handbook
Syria Company Laws and Regulations Handbook
Taiwan Company Laws and Regulations Handbook
Tajikistan Company Laws and Regulations Handbook
Tanzania Company Laws and Regulations Handbook
Thailand Company Laws and Regulations Handbook
Togo Company Laws and Regulations Handbook
Tonga Company Laws and Regulations Handbook
Trinidad and Tobago Company Laws and Regulations Handbook
Tunisia Company Laws and Regulations Handbook
Turkey Company Laws and Regulations Handbook
Turkmenistan Company Laws and Regulations Handbook
Turks & Caicos Company Laws and Regulations Handbook
Tuvalu Company Laws and Regulations Handbook
Uganda Company Laws and Regulations Handbook
Ukraine Company Laws and Regulations Handbook
United Arab Emirates Company Laws and Regulations Handbook
United Kingdom Company Laws and Regulations Handbook
United States Company Laws and Regulations Handbook
Uruguay Company Laws and Regulations Handbook
Uzbekistan Company Laws and Regulations Handbook
Vanuatu Company Laws and Regulations Handbook
Vatican City Company Laws and Regulations Handbook
Venezuela Company Laws and Regulations Handbook
Vietnam Company Laws and Regulations Handbook
Virgin Islands, British Company Laws and Regulations Handbook
Wake Atoll Company Laws and Regulations Handbook
Wallis & Futuna Company Laws and Regulations Handbook
Yemen Company Laws and Regulations Handbook
Serbia Company Laws and Regulations Handbook
Zambia Company Laws and Regulations Handbook
Zimbabwe Company Laws and Regulations Handbook

WORLD INSOLVENCY (BANKRUPTCY) LAWS AND REGULATIONS HANDBOOK LIBRARY

STRATEGIC INFORMATION AND BASIC LAWS

UPDATED ANNUALLY: PLEASE CONTACT IBP, INC FOR ISBN NUMBERS

978 ISBN	COMPLETE FULL TITLE
9781433084997	Afghanistan Insolvency (Bankruptcy) Laws and Regulations Handbook - Strategic Information and Basic Laws
9781433085000	Albania Insolvency (Bankruptcy) Laws and Regulations Handbook - Strategic Information and Basic Laws
9781433086793	Algeria Insolvency (Bankruptcy) Laws and Regulations Handbook - Strategic Information and Basic Laws
9781433085017	Angola Insolvency (Bankruptcy) Laws and Regulations Handbook - Strategic Information and Basic Laws
9781433086250	Antigua and Barduba Insolvency (Bankruptcy) Laws and Regulations Handbook - Strategic Information and Basic Laws
9781433085024	Argentina Insolvency (Bankruptcy) Laws and Regulations Handbook - Strategic Information and Basic Laws
9781433086786	Armenia Insolvency (Bankruptcy) Laws and Regulations Handbook - Strategic Information and Basic Laws
9781433085031	Australia Insolvency (Bankruptcy) Laws and Regulations Handbook - Strategic Information and Basic Laws
9781433086779	Austria Insolvency (Bankruptcy) Laws and Regulations Handbook - Strategic Information and Basic Laws
9781433085048	Azerbaijan Insolvency (Bankruptcy) Laws and Regulations Handbook - Strategic Information and Basic Laws
9781433086762	Bahamas Insolvency (Bankruptcy) Laws and Regulations Handbook - Strategic Information and Basic Laws
9781433085055	Bahrain Insolvency (Bankruptcy) Laws and Regulations Handbook - Strategic Information and Basic Laws
9781433086243	Bangladesh Insolvency (Bankruptcy) Laws and Regulations Handbook - Strategic Information and Basic Laws
9781433085062	Barbados Insolvency (Bankruptcy) Laws and Regulations Handbook - Strategic Information and Basic Laws
9781433086755	Belarus Insolvency (Bankruptcy) Laws and Regulations Handbook - Strategic Information and Basic Laws
9781433085079	Belgium Insolvency (Bankruptcy) Laws and Regulations Handbook - Strategic Information and Basic Laws
9781433086748	Belize Insolvency (Bankruptcy) Laws and Regulations Handbook - Strategic Information and Basic Laws
9781433085086	Benin Insolvency (Bankruptcy) Laws and Regulations Handbook - Strategic Information and Basic Laws
9781433086731	Bermuda Insolvency (Bankruptcy) Laws and Regulations Handbook - Strategic

978 ISBN	COMPLETE FULL TITLE
	Information and Basic Laws
9781433085093	Bhutan Insolvency (Bankruptcy) Laws and Regulations Handbook - Strategic Information and Basic Laws
9781433086595	Bolivia Insolvency (Bankruptcy) Laws and Regulations Handbook - Strategic Information and Basic Laws
9781433085109	Bosnia and Herzegovina Insolvency (Bankruptcy) Laws and Regulations Handbook - Strategic Information and Basic Laws
9781433086236	Brazil Insolvency (Bankruptcy) Laws and Regulations Handbook - Strategic Information and Basic Laws
9781433086236	Bulgaria Insolvency (Bankruptcy) Laws and Regulations Handbook - Strategic Information and Basic Laws
9781433085123	Burkina Faso Insolvency (Bankruptcy) Laws and Regulations Handbook - Strategic Information and Basic Laws
9781433086717	Cabo Verde Insolvency (Bankruptcy) Laws and Regulations Handbook - Strategic Information and Basic Laws
9781433085130	Cambodia Insolvency (Bankruptcy) Laws and Regulations Handbook - Strategic Information and Basic Laws
9781433086847	Cameroon Insolvency (Bankruptcy) Laws and Regulations Handbook - Strategic Information and Basic Laws
9781433085147	Canada Insolvency (Bankruptcy) Laws and Regulations Handbook - Strategic Information and Basic Laws
9781433086694	Cayman Insolvency (Bankruptcy) Laws and Regulations Handbook - Strategic Information and Basic Laws
9781433085154	Central African Republic Insolvency (Bankruptcy) Laws and Regulations Handbook - Strategic Information and Basic Laws
9781433086687	Chad Insolvency (Bankruptcy) Laws and Regulations Handbook - Strategic Information and Basic Laws
9781433085161	Chile Insolvency (Bankruptcy) Laws and Regulations Handbook - Strategic Information and Basic Laws
9781433086670	China Insolvency (Bankruptcy) Laws and Regulations Handbook - Strategic Information and Basic Laws
9781433085178	Colombia Insolvency (Bankruptcy) Laws and Regulations Handbook - Strategic Information and Basic Laws
9781433086663	Comoros Insolvency (Bankruptcy) Laws and Regulations Handbook - Strategic Information and Basic Laws
9781433085208	Congo Democratic Republic Insolvency (Bankruptcy) Laws and Regulations Handbook - Strategic Information and Basic Laws
9781433085185	Costa Rica Insolvency (Bankruptcy) Laws and Regulations Handbook - Strategic Information and Basic Laws
9781433086229	Croatia Insolvency (Bankruptcy) Laws and Regulations Handbook - Strategic Information and Basic Laws
9781433085192	Cyprus Insolvency (Bankruptcy) Laws and Regulations Handbook - Strategic Information and Basic Laws
9781433086212	Czech Insolvency (Bankruptcy) Laws and Regulations Handbook - Strategic Information and Basic Laws
9781433086656	Denmark Insolvency (Bankruptcy) Laws and Regulations Handbook - Strategic Information and Basic Laws
9781433085215	Dominican Republic Insolvency (Bankruptcy) Laws and Regulations Handbook - Strategic Information and Basic Laws
9781433086649	Ecuador Insolvency (Bankruptcy) Laws and Regulations Handbook - Strategic Information and Basic Laws
9781433085222	Egypt Insolvency (Bankruptcy) Laws and Regulations Handbook - Strategic Information and Basic Laws

978 ISBN	COMPLETE FULL TITLE
9781433086632	El Salvador Insolvency (Bankruptcy) Laws and Regulations Handbook - Strategic Information and Basic Laws
9781433085239	Estonia Insolvency (Bankruptcy) Laws and Regulations Handbook - Strategic Information and Basic Laws
9781433086625	Ethiopia Insolvency (Bankruptcy) Laws and Regulations Handbook - Strategic Information and Basic Laws
9781433085246	European Union Insolvency (Bankruptcy) Laws and Regulations Handbook - Strategic Information and Basic Laws
9781433086076	Fiji Insolvency (Bankruptcy) Laws and Regulations Handbook - Strategic Information and Basic Laws
9781433085253	Finland Insolvency (Bankruptcy) Laws and Regulations Handbook - Strategic Information and Basic Laws
9781433086199	France Insolvency (Bankruptcy) Laws and Regulations Handbook - Strategic Information and Basic Laws
9781433085260	Gabon Insolvency (Bankruptcy) Laws and Regulations Handbook - Strategic Information and Basic Laws
9781433086311	Gambia Insolvency (Bankruptcy) Laws and Regulations Handbook - Strategic Information and Basic Laws
9781433085277	Georgia Republic Insolvency (Bankruptcy) Laws and Regulations Handbook - Strategic Information and Basic Laws
9781433086175	Germany Insolvency (Bankruptcy) Laws and Regulations Handbook - Strategic Information and Basic Laws
9781433085284	Ghana Insolvency (Bankruptcy) Laws and Regulations Handbook - Strategic Information and Basic Laws
9781433086618	Gibraltar Insolvency (Bankruptcy) Laws and Regulations Handbook - Strategic Information and Basic Laws
9781433085291	Greece Insolvency (Bankruptcy) Laws and Regulations Handbook - Strategic Information and Basic Laws
9781433086168	Grenada Insolvency (Bankruptcy) Laws and Regulations Handbook - Strategic Information and Basic Laws
9781433085307	Guatemala Insolvency (Bankruptcy) Laws and Regulations Handbook - Strategic Information and Basic Laws
9781433086601	Guyana Insolvency (Bankruptcy) Laws and Regulations Handbook - Strategic Information and Basic Laws
9781433085314	Haiti Insolvency (Bankruptcy) Laws and Regulations Handbook - Strategic Information and Basic Laws
9781433086977	Honduras Insolvency (Bankruptcy) Laws and Regulations Handbook - Strategic Information and Basic Laws
9781433085321	Hong Kong Insolvency (Bankruptcy) Laws and Regulations Handbook - Strategic Information and Basic Laws
9781433086151	Hungary Insolvency (Bankruptcy) Laws and Regulations Handbook - Strategic Information and Basic Laws
9781433085338	Iceland Insolvency (Bankruptcy) Laws and Regulations Handbook - Strategic Information and Basic Laws
9781433086144	India Insolvency (Bankruptcy) Laws and Regulations Handbook - Strategic Information and Basic Laws
9781433085345	Indonesia Insolvency (Bankruptcy) Laws and Regulations Handbook - Strategic Information and Basic Laws
9781433086991	Iran Insolvency (Bankruptcy) Laws and Regulations Handbook - Strategic Information and Basic Laws
9781433085352	Iraq Insolvency (Bankruptcy) Laws and Regulations Handbook - Strategic Information and Basic Laws
9781433086137	Ireland Insolvency (Bankruptcy) Laws and Regulations Handbook - Strategic Information

To order and for additional analytical and marketing information, please contacts
International Business Publications, USA at:
P.O. Box 15343, Washington, DC 20003, USA. Phone: (202) 546-210 Fax: (202) 546-32
E-mail: ibpusa@comcast.net

978 ISBN	COMPLETE FULL TITLE
	and Basic Laws
9781433085369	Island of Jersey Insolvency (Bankruptcy) Laws and Regulations Handbook - Strategic Information and Basic Laws
9781433086724	Israel Insolvency (Bankruptcy) Laws and Regulations Handbook - Strategic Information and Basic Laws
9781433085376	Italy Insolvency (Bankruptcy) Laws and Regulations Handbook - Strategic Information and Basic Laws
9781433087080	Ivory Coast Insolvency (Bankruptcy) Laws and Regulations Handbook - Strategic Information and Basic Laws
9781433085383	Jamaica Insolvency (Bankruptcy) Laws and Regulations Handbook - Strategic Information and Basic Laws
9781433087073	Japan Insolvency (Bankruptcy) Laws and Regulations Handbook - Strategic Information and Basic Laws
9781433085390	Jersey Insolvency (Bankruptcy) Laws and Regulations Handbook - Strategic Information and Basic Laws
9781433087066	Jordan Insolvency (Bankruptcy) Laws and Regulations Handbook - Strategic Information and Basic Laws
9781433085406	Kazakhstan Insolvency (Bankruptcy) Laws and Regulations Handbook - Strategic Information and Basic Laws
9781433086120	Kenya Insolvency (Bankruptcy) Laws and Regulations Handbook - Strategic Information and Basic Laws
9781433085413	Kiribati Insolvency (Bankruptcy) Laws and Regulations Handbook - Strategic Information and Basic Laws
9781433086113	Korea Insolvency (Bankruptcy) Laws and Regulations Handbook - Strategic Information and Basic Laws
9781433085420	Kuwait Insolvency (Bankruptcy) Laws and Regulations Handbook - Strategic Information and Basic Laws
9781433086106	Kyrgyz Republic Insolvency (Bankruptcy) Laws and Regulations Handbook - Strategic Information and Basic Laws
9781433085437	Latvia Insolvency (Bankruptcy) Laws and Regulations Handbook - Strategic Information and Basic Laws
9781433087059	Lebanon Insolvency (Bankruptcy) Laws and Regulations Handbook - Strategic Information and Basic Laws
9781433085444	Lesotho Insolvency (Bankruptcy) Laws and Regulations Handbook - Strategic Information and Basic Laws
9781433087042	Liechtenstein Insolvency (Bankruptcy) Laws and Regulations Handbook - Strategic Information and Basic Laws
9781433085451	Lithuania Insolvency (Bankruptcy) Laws and Regulations Handbook - Strategic Information and Basic Laws
9781433086090	Luxembourg Insolvency (Bankruptcy) Laws and Regulations Handbook - Strategic Information and Basic Laws
9781433085468	Macedonia Insolvency (Bankruptcy) Laws and Regulations Handbook - Strategic Information and Basic Laws
9781433086083	Madagascar Insolvency (Bankruptcy) Laws and Regulations Handbook - Strategic Information and Basic Laws
9781433085475	Malaysia Insolvency (Bankruptcy) Laws and Regulations Handbook - Strategic Information and Basic Laws
9781433087110	Malta Insolvency (Bankruptcy) Laws and Regulations Handbook - Strategic Information and Basic Laws
9781433085482	Marshall Islands Insolvency (Bankruptcy) Laws and Regulations Handbook - Strategic Information and Basic Laws
9781433087035	Mexico Insolvency (Bankruptcy) Laws and Regulations Handbook - Strategic Information and Basic Laws

To order and for additional analytical and marketing information, please contacts
International Business Publications, USA at:
P.O. Box 15343, Washington, DC 20003, USA. Phone: (202) 546-210 Fax: (202) 546-32
E-mail: ibpusa@comcast.net

978 ISBN	COMPLETE FULL TITLE
9781433085499	Micronesia Insolvency (Bankruptcy) Laws and Regulations Handbook - Strategic Information and Basic Laws
9781433087097	Moldova Insolvency (Bankruptcy) Laws and Regulations Handbook - Strategic Information and Basic Laws
9781433085505	Monaco Insolvency (Bankruptcy) Laws and Regulations Handbook - Strategic Information and Basic Laws
9781433087028	Mongolia Insolvency (Bankruptcy) Laws and Regulations Handbook - Strategic Information and Basic Laws
9781433085512	Montenegro Insolvency (Bankruptcy) Laws and Regulations Handbook - Strategic Information and Basic Laws
9781433087011	Mozambique Insolvency (Bankruptcy) Laws and Regulations Handbook - Strategic Information and Basic Laws
9781433085529	Nepal Insolvency (Bankruptcy) Laws and Regulations Handbook - Strategic Information and Basic Laws
9781433086441	Netherlands Insolvency (Bankruptcy) Laws and Regulations Handbook - Strategic Information and Basic Laws
9781433085536	New Zealand Insolvency (Bankruptcy) Laws and Regulations Handbook - Strategic Information and Basic Laws
9781433086465	Nicaragua Insolvency (Bankruptcy) Laws and Regulations Handbook - Strategic Information and Basic Laws
9781433085543	Niger Insolvency (Bankruptcy) Laws and Regulations Handbook - Strategic Information and Basic Laws
9781433087004	Nigeria Insolvency (Bankruptcy) Laws and Regulations Handbook - Strategic Information and Basic Laws
9781433085550	Norway Insolvency (Bankruptcy) Laws and Regulations Handbook - Strategic Information and Basic Laws
9781433086205	Pakistan Insolvency (Bankruptcy) Laws and Regulations Handbook - Strategic Information and Basic Laws
9781433085567	Palau Insolvency (Bankruptcy) Laws and Regulations Handbook - Strategic Information and Basic Laws
9781433086564	Panama Insolvency (Bankruptcy) Laws and Regulations Handbook - Strategic Information and Basic Laws
9781433085574	Papau New Guinea Insolvency (Bankruptcy) Laws and Regulations Handbook - Strategic Information and Basic Laws
9781433086557	Paraguay Insolvency (Bankruptcy) Laws and Regulations Handbook - Strategic Information and Basic Laws
9781433085581	Peru Insolvency (Bankruptcy) Laws and Regulations Handbook - Strategic Information and Basic Laws
9781433087127	Philippines Insolvency (Bankruptcy) Laws and Regulations Handbook - Strategic Information and Basic Laws
9781433085598	Poland Insolvency (Bankruptcy) Laws and Regulations Handbook - Strategic Information and Basic Laws
9781433086540	Portugal Insolvency (Bankruptcy) Laws and Regulations Handbook - Strategic Information and Basic Laws
9781433085604	Romania Insolvency (Bankruptcy) Laws and Regulations Handbook - Strategic Information and Basic Laws
9781433086854	Russia Insolvency (Bankruptcy) Laws and Regulations Handbook - Strategic Information and Basic Laws
9781433085611	Saudi Arabia Insolvency (Bankruptcy) Laws and Regulations Handbook - Strategic Information and Basic Laws
9781433086533	Senegal Insolvency (Bankruptcy) Laws and Regulations Handbook - Strategic Information and Basic Laws
9781433085628	Serbia Insolvency (Bankruptcy) Laws and Regulations Handbook - Strategic Information

978 ISBN	COMPLETE FULL TITLE
	and Basic Laws
9781433086526	Sierra Leone Insolvency (Bankruptcy) Laws and Regulations Handbook - Strategic Information and Basic Laws
9781433085635	Singapore Insolvency (Bankruptcy) Laws and Regulations Handbook - Strategic Information and Basic Laws
9781433087103	Slovak Republic Insolvency (Bankruptcy) Laws and Regulations Handbook - Strategic Information and Basic Laws
9781433086519	Slovenia Insolvency (Bankruptcy) Laws and Regulations Handbook - Strategic Information and Basic Laws
9781433085642	Solomon Islands Insolvency (Bankruptcy) Laws and Regulations Handbook - Strategic Information and Basic Laws
9781433086502	South Africa Insolvency (Bankruptcy) Laws and Regulations Handbook - Strategic Information and Basic Laws
9781433085659	Spain Insolvency (Bankruptcy) Laws and Regulations Handbook - Strategic Information and Basic Laws
9781433086984	Sri Lanka Insolvency (Bankruptcy) Laws and Regulations Handbook - Strategic Information and Basic Laws
9781433085666	St. Kitts & Nevis Insolvency (Bankruptcy) Laws and Regulations Handbook - Strategic Information and Basic Laws
9781433086496	Sweden Insolvency (Bankruptcy) Laws and Regulations Handbook - Strategic Information and Basic Laws
9781433085673	Switzerland Insolvency (Bankruptcy) Laws and Regulations Handbook - Strategic Information and Basic Laws
9781433086489	Taiwan Insolvency (Bankruptcy) Laws and Regulations Handbook - Strategic Information and Basic Laws
9781433085680	Tajikistan Insolvency (Bankruptcy) Laws and Regulations Handbook - Strategic Information and Basic Laws
9781433086472	Tanzania Insolvency (Bankruptcy) Laws and Regulations Handbook - Strategic Information and Basic Laws
9781433085697	Thailand Insolvency (Bankruptcy) Laws and Regulations Handbook - Strategic Information and Basic Laws
9781433085703	Togo Insolvency (Bankruptcy) Laws and Regulations Handbook - Strategic Information and Basic Laws
9781433086960	Trinidad and Tobago Insolvency (Bankruptcy) Laws and Regulations Handbook - Strategic Information and Basic Laws
9781433085710	Tunisia Insolvency (Bankruptcy) Laws and Regulations Handbook - Strategic Information and Basic Laws
9781433086953	Turkey Insolvency (Bankruptcy) Laws and Regulations Handbook - Strategic Information and Basic Laws
9781433085727	Tuvalu Insolvency (Bankruptcy) Laws and Regulations Handbook - Strategic Information and Basic Laws
9781433086946	Uganda Insolvency (Bankruptcy) Laws and Regulations Handbook - Strategic Information and Basic Laws
9781433085734	Ukraine Insolvency (Bankruptcy) Laws and Regulations Handbook - Strategic Information and Basic Laws
9781433086939	United Arab Emirates Insolvency (Bankruptcy) Laws and Regulations Handbook - Strategic Information and Basic Laws
9781433085741	United Kingdom Insolvency (Bankruptcy) Laws and Regulations Handbook - Strategic Information and Basic Laws
9781433086328	Uruguay Insolvency (Bankruptcy) Laws and Regulations Handbook - Strategic Information and Basic Laws
9781433085758	USA Insolvency (Bankruptcy) Laws and Regulations Handbook - Strategic Information and Basic Laws

To order and for additional analytical and marketing information, please contacts
International Business Publications, USA at:
P.O. Box 15343, Washington, DC 20003, USA. Phone: (202) 546-210 Fax: (202) 546-32
E-mail: ibpusa@comcast.net

978 ISBN	COMPLETE FULL TITLE
9781433086922	Uzbekistan Insolvency (Bankruptcy) Laws and Regulations Handbook - Strategic Information and Basic Laws
9781433085765	Venezuela Insolvency (Bankruptcy) Laws and Regulations Handbook - Strategic Information and Basic Laws
9781433086915	Vietnam Insolvency (Bankruptcy) Laws and Regulations Handbook - Strategic Information and Basic Laws
9781433085116	Virgin Islands, British Insolvency (Bankruptcy) Laws and Regulations Handbook - Strategic Information and Basic Laws
9781433085772	Zambia Insolvency (Bankruptcy) Laws and Regulations Handbook - Strategic Information and Basic Laws
9781433086458	Zimbabwe Insolvency (Bankruptcy) Laws and Regulations Handbook - Strategic Information and Basic Laws

WORLD BUSINESS LAW HANDBOOK LIBRARY

VOLUME 1 STRATEGIC INFORMATION AND BASIC LAWS

UPDATED ANNUALLY: PLEASE CONTACT IBP, INC FOR ISBN NUMBERS
Ultimate directories for conducting export-import operations in the country. Largest exporters and importers, strategic government and business contacts, selected export-import regulations and more...

Price: $149 each

Afghanistan Business Law Handbook Volume 1 Strategic Information and Basic Laws
Aland Business Law Handbook Volume 1 Strategic Information and Basic Laws
Albania Business Law Handbook Volume 1 Strategic Information and Basic Laws
Algeria Business Law Handbook Volume 1 Strategic Information and Basic Laws
Andorra Business Law Handbook Volume 1 Strategic Information and Basic Laws
Angola Business Law Handbook Volume 1 Strategic Information and Basic Laws
Anguilla Business Law Handbook Volume 1 Strategic Information and Basic Laws
Antigua and Barbuda Business Law Handbook Volume 1 Strategic Information and Basic Laws
Antilles (Netherlands) Business Law Handbook Volume 1 Strategic Information and Basic Laws
Argentina Business Law Handbook Volume 1 Strategic Information and Basic Laws
Armenia Business Law Handbook Volume 1 Strategic Information and Basic Laws
Aruba Business Law Handbook Volume 1 Strategic Information and Basic Laws
Australia Business Law Handbook Volume 1 Strategic Information and Basic Laws
Austria Business Law Handbook Volume 1 Strategic Information and Basic Laws
Azerbaijan Business Law Handbook Volume 1 Strategic Information and Basic Laws
Bahamas Business Law Handbook Volume 1 Strategic Information and Basic Laws
Bahrain Business Law Handbook Volume 1 Strategic Information and Basic Laws
Bangladesh Business Law Handbook Volume 1 Strategic Information and Basic Laws
Barbados Business Law Handbook Volume 1 Strategic Information and Basic Laws
Belarus Business Law Handbook Volume 1 Strategic Information and Basic Laws
Belgium Business Law Handbook Volume 1 Strategic Information and Basic Laws
Belize Business Law Handbook Volume 1 Strategic Information and Basic Laws
Benin Business Law Handbook Volume 1 Strategic Information and Basic Laws
Bermuda Business Law Handbook Volume 1 Strategic Information and Basic Laws
Bhutan Business Law Handbook Volume 1 Strategic Information and Basic Laws
Bolivia Business Law Handbook Volume 1 Strategic Information and Basic Laws
Bosnia and Herzegovina Business Law Handbook Volume 1 Strategic Information and Basic Laws
Botswana Business Law Handbook Volume 1 Strategic Information and Basic Laws
Brazil Business Law Handbook Volume 1 Strategic Information and Basic Laws
Brunei Business Law Handbook Volume 1 Strategic Information and Basic Laws
Bulgaria Business Law Handbook Volume 1 Strategic Information and Basic Laws
Burkina Faso Business Law Handbook Volume 1 Strategic Information and Basic Laws

Burundi Business Law Handbook Volume 1 Strategic Information and Basic Laws
Cambodia Business Law Handbook Volume 1 Strategic Information and Basic Laws
Cameroon Business Law Handbook Volume 1 Strategic Information and Basic Laws
Canada Business Law Handbook Volume 1 Strategic Information and Basic Laws
Cape Verde Business Law Handbook Volume 1 Strategic Information and Basic Laws
Cayman Islands Business Law Handbook Volume 1 Strategic Information and Basic Laws
Central African Republic Business Law Handbook Volume 1 Strategic Information and Basic Laws
Chad Business Law Handbook Volume 1 Strategic Information and Basic Laws
Chile Business Law Handbook Volume 1 Strategic Information and Basic Laws
China Business Law Handbook Volume 1 Strategic Information and Basic Laws
Colombia Business Law Handbook Volume 1 Strategic Information and Basic Laws
Comoros Business Law Handbook Volume 1 Strategic Information and Basic Laws
Congo Business Law Handbook Volume 1 Strategic Information and Basic Laws
Congo, Democratic Republic Business Law Handbook Volume 1 Strategic Information and Basic Laws
Cook Islands Business Law Handbook Volume 1 Strategic Information and Basic Laws
Costa Rica Business Law Handbook Volume 1 Strategic Information and Basic Laws
Cote d'Ivoire Business Law Handbook Volume 1 Strategic Information and Basic Laws
Croatia Business Law Handbook Volume 1 Strategic Information and Basic Laws
Cuba Business Law Handbook Volume 1 Strategic Information and Basic Laws
Cyprus Business Law Handbook Volume 1 Strategic Information and Basic Laws
Czech Republic Business Law Handbook Volume 1 Strategic Information and Basic Laws
Denmark Business Law Handbook Volume 1 Strategic Information and Basic Laws
Djibouti Business Law Handbook Volume 1 Strategic Information and Basic Laws
Dominica Business Law Handbook Volume 1 Strategic Information and Basic Laws
Dominican Republic Business Law Handbook Volume 1 Strategic Information and Basic Laws
Ecuador Business Law Handbook Volume 1 Strategic Information and Basic Laws
Egypt Business Law Handbook Volume 1 Strategic Information and Basic Laws
El Salvador Business Law Handbook Volume 1 Strategic Information and Basic Laws
Equatorial Guinea Business Law Handbook Volume 1 Strategic Information and Basic Laws
Eritrea Business Law Handbook Volume 1 Strategic Information and Basic Laws
Estonia Business Law Handbook Volume 1 Strategic Information and Basic Laws
Ethiopia Business Law Handbook Volume 1 Strategic Information and Basic Laws
Falkland Islands Business Law Handbook Volume 1 Strategic Information and Basic Laws
Faroes Islands Business Law Handbook Volume 1 Strategic Information and Basic Laws
Fiji Business Law Handbook Volume 1 Strategic Information and Basic Laws
Finland Business Law Handbook Volume 1 Strategic Information and Basic Laws
France Business Law Handbook Volume 1 Strategic Information and Basic Laws
Gabon Business Law Handbook Volume 1 Strategic Information and Basic Laws
Gambia Business Law Handbook Volume 1 Strategic Information and Basic Laws
Georgia Business Law Handbook Volume 1 Strategic Information and Basic Laws
Germany Business Law Handbook Volume 1 Strategic Information and Basic Laws
Ghana Business Law Handbook Volume 1 Strategic Information and Basic Laws
Gibraltar Business Law Handbook Volume 1 Strategic Information and Basic Laws
Greece Business Law Handbook Volume 1 Strategic Information and Basic Laws
Greenland Business Law Handbook Volume 1 Strategic Information and Basic Laws
Grenada Business Law Handbook Volume 1 Strategic Information and Basic Laws
Guam Business Law Handbook Volume 1 Strategic Information and Basic Laws
Guatemala Business Law Handbook Volume 1 Strategic Information and Basic Laws
Guernsey Business Law Handbook Volume 1 Strategic Information and Basic Laws
Guinea Business Law Handbook Volume 1 Strategic Information and Basic Laws
Guinea-Bissau Business Law Handbook Volume 1 Strategic Information and Basic Laws

Guyana Business Law Handbook Volume 1 Strategic Information and Basic Laws
Haiti Business Law Handbook Volume 1 Strategic Information and Basic Laws
Honduras Business Law Handbook Volume 1 Strategic Information and Basic Laws
Hungary Business Law Handbook Volume 1 Strategic Information and Basic Laws
Iceland Business Law Handbook Volume 1 Strategic Information and Basic Laws
India Business Law Handbook Volume 1 Strategic Information and Basic Laws
Indonesia Business Law Handbook Volume 1 Strategic Information and Basic Laws
Iran Business Law Handbook Volume 1 Strategic Information and Basic Laws
Iraq Business Law Handbook Volume 1 Strategic Information and Basic Laws
Ireland Business Law Handbook Volume 1 Strategic Information and Basic Laws
Israel Business Law Handbook Volume 1 Strategic Information and Basic Laws
Italy Business Law Handbook Volume 1 Strategic Information and Basic Laws
Jamaica Business Law Handbook Volume 1 Strategic Information and Basic Laws
Japan Business Law Handbook Volume 1 Strategic Information and Basic Laws
Jersey Business Law Handbook Volume 1 Strategic Information and Basic Laws
Jordan Business Law Handbook Volume 1 Strategic Information and Basic Laws
Kazakhstan Business Law Handbook Volume 1 Strategic Information and Basic Laws
Kenya Business Law Handbook Volume 1 Strategic Information and Basic Laws
Kiribati Business Law Handbook Volume 1 Strategic Information and Basic Laws
Korea, North Business Law Handbook Volume 1 Strategic Information and Basic Laws
Korea, South Business Law Handbook Volume 1 Strategic Information and Basic Laws
Kosovo Business Law Handbook Volume 1 Strategic Information and Basic Laws
Kurdistan Business Law Handbook Volume 1 Strategic Information and Basic Laws
Kuwait Business Law Handbook Volume 1 Strategic Information and Basic Laws
Kyrgyzstan Business Law Handbook Volume 1 Strategic Information and Basic Laws
Laos Business Law Handbook Volume 1 Strategic Information and Basic Laws
Latvia Business Law Handbook Volume 1 Strategic Information and Basic Laws
Lebanon Business Law Handbook Volume 1 Strategic Information and Basic Laws
Lesotho Business Law Handbook Volume 1 Strategic Information and Basic Laws
Liberia Business Law Handbook Volume 1 Strategic Information and Basic Laws
Libya Business Law Handbook Volume 1 Strategic Information and Basic Laws
Liechtenstein Business Law Handbook Volume 1 Strategic Information and Basic Laws
Lithuania Business Law Handbook Volume 1 Strategic Information and Basic Laws
Luxembourg Business Law Handbook Volume 1 Strategic Information and Basic Laws
Macao Business Law Handbook Volume 1 Strategic Information and Basic Laws
Macedonia Business Law Handbook Volume 1 Strategic Information and Basic Laws
Madagascar Business Law Handbook Volume 1 Strategic Information and Basic Laws
Madeira Business Law Handbook Volume 1 Strategic Information and Basic Laws
Malawi Business Law Handbook Volume 1 Strategic Information and Basic Laws
Malaysia Business Law Handbook Volume 1 Strategic Information and Basic Laws
Maldives Business Law Handbook Volume 1 Strategic Information and Basic Laws
Mali Business Law Handbook Volume 1 Strategic Information and Basic Laws
Malta Business Law Handbook Volume 1 Strategic Information and Basic Laws
Man Business Law Handbook Volume 1 Strategic Information and Basic Laws
Marshall Islands Business Law Handbook Volume 1 Strategic Information and Basic Laws
Mauritania Business Law Handbook Volume 1 Strategic Information and Basic Laws
Mauritius Business Law Handbook Volume 1 Strategic Information and Basic Laws
Mayotte Business Law Handbook Volume 1 Strategic Information and Basic Laws
Mexico Business Law Handbook Volume 1 Strategic Information and Basic Laws
Micronesia Business Law Handbook Volume 1 Strategic Information and Basic Laws
Moldova Business Law Handbook Volume 1 Strategic Information and Basic Laws

Monaco Business Law Handbook Volume 1 Strategic Information and Basic Laws
Mongolia Business Law Handbook Volume 1 Strategic Information and Basic Laws
Monserrat Business Law Handbook Volume 1 Strategic Information and Basic Laws
Morocco Business Law Handbook Volume 1 Strategic Information and Basic Laws
Mozambique Business Law Handbook Volume 1 Strategic Information and Basic Laws
Myanmar Business Law Handbook Volume 1 Strategic Information and Basic Laws
Namibia Business Law Handbook Volume 1 Strategic Information and Basic Laws
Nauru Business Law Handbook Volume 1 Strategic Information and Basic Laws
Nepal Business Law Handbook Volume 1 Strategic Information and Basic Laws
Netherlands Business Law Handbook Volume 1 Strategic Information and Basic Laws
New Caledonia Business Law Handbook Volume 1 Strategic Information and Basic Laws
New Zealand Business Law Handbook Volume 1 Strategic Information and Basic Laws
Nicaragua Business Law Handbook Volume 1 Strategic Information and Basic Laws
Niger Business Law Handbook Volume 1 Strategic Information and Basic Laws
Nigeria Business Law Handbook Volume 1 Strategic Information and Basic Laws
Niue Business Law Handbook Volume 1 Strategic Information and Basic Laws
Northern Mariana Islands Business Law Handbook Volume 1 Strategic Information and Basic Laws
Norway Business Law Handbook Volume 1 Strategic Information and Basic Laws
Oman Business Law Handbook Volume 1 Strategic Information and Basic Laws
Pakistan Business Law Handbook Volume 1 Strategic Information and Basic Laws
Palau Business Law Handbook Volume 1 Strategic Information and Basic Laws
Palestine (West Bank & Gaza) Business Law Handbook Volume 1 Strategic Information and Basic Laws
Panama Business Law Handbook Volume 1 Strategic Information and Basic Laws
Papua New Guinea Business Law Handbook Volume 1 Strategic Information and Basic Laws
Paraguay Business Law Handbook Volume 1 Strategic Information and Basic Laws
Peru Business Law Handbook Volume 1 Strategic Information and Basic Laws
Philippines Business Law Handbook Volume 1 Strategic Information and Basic Laws
Pitcairn Islands Business Law Handbook Volume 1 Strategic Information and Basic Laws
Poland Business Law Handbook Volume 1 Strategic Information and Basic Laws
Polynesia French Business Law Handbook Volume 1 Strategic Information and Basic Laws
Portugal Business Law Handbook Volume 1 Strategic Information and Basic Laws
Qatar Business Law Handbook Volume 1 Strategic Information and Basic Laws
Romania Business Law Handbook Volume 1 Strategic Information and Basic Laws
Russia Business Law Handbook Volume 1 Strategic Information and Basic Laws
Rwanda Business Law Handbook Volume 1 Strategic Information and Basic Laws
Saint Kitts and Nevis Business Law Handbook Volume 1 Strategic Information and Basic Laws
Saint Lucia Business Law Handbook Volume 1 Strategic Information and Basic Laws
Saint Vincent and The Grenadines Business Law Handbook Volume 1 Strategic Information and Basic Laws
Samoa (American) A Business Law Handbook Volume 1 Strategic Information and Basic Laws
Samoa (Western) Business Law Handbook Volume 1 Strategic Information and Basic Laws
San Marino Business Law Handbook Volume 1 Strategic Information and Basic Laws
Sao Tome and Principe Business Law Handbook Volume 1 Strategic Information and Basic Laws
Saudi Arabia Business Law Handbook Volume 1 Strategic Information and Basic Laws
Scotland Business Law Handbook Volume 1 Strategic Information and Basic Laws
Senegal Business Law Handbook Volume 1 Strategic Information and Basic Laws
Serbia Business Law Handbook Volume 1 Strategic Information and Basic Laws
Seychelles Business Law Handbook Volume 1 Strategic Information and Basic Laws
Sierra Leone Business Law Handbook Volume 1 Strategic Information and Basic Laws
Singapore Business Law Handbook Volume 1 Strategic Information and Basic Laws
Slovakia Business Law Handbook Volume 1 Strategic Information and Basic Laws
Slovenia Business Law Handbook Volume 1 Strategic Information and Basic Laws

Solomon Islands Business Law Handbook Volume 1 Strategic Information and Basic Laws
Somalia Business Law Handbook Volume 1 Strategic Information and Basic Laws
South Africa Business Law Handbook Volume 1 Strategic Information and Basic Laws
Spain Business Law Handbook Volume 1 Strategic Information and Basic Laws
Sri Lanka Business Law Handbook Volume 1 Strategic Information and Basic Laws
St. Helena Business Law Handbook Volume 1 Strategic Information and Basic Laws
St. Pierre & Miquelon Business Law Handbook Volume 1 Strategic Information and Basic Laws
Sudan Business Law Handbook Volume 1 Strategic Information and Basic Laws
Sudan South Business Law Handbook Volume 1 Strategic Information and Basic Laws
Suriname Business Law Handbook Volume 1 Strategic Information and Basic Laws
Swaziland Business Law Handbook Volume 1 Strategic Information and Basic Laws
Sweden Business Law Handbook Volume 1 Strategic Information and Basic Laws
Switzerland Business Law Handbook Volume 1 Strategic Information and Basic Laws
Syria Business Law Handbook Volume 1 Strategic Information and Basic Laws
Taiwan Business Law Handbook Volume 1 Strategic Information and Basic Laws
Tajikistan Business Law Handbook Volume 1 Strategic Information and Basic Laws
Tanzania Business Law Handbook Volume 1 Strategic Information and Basic Laws
Thailand Business Law Handbook Volume 1 Strategic Information and Basic Laws
Togo Business Law Handbook Volume 1 Strategic Information and Basic Laws
Tonga Business Law Handbook Volume 1 Strategic Information and Basic Laws
Trinidad and Tobago Business Law Handbook Volume 1 Strategic Information and Basic Laws
Tunisia Business Law Handbook Volume 1 Strategic Information and Basic Laws
Turkey Business Law Handbook Volume 1 Strategic Information and Basic Laws
Turkmenistan Business Law Handbook Volume 1 Strategic Information and Basic Laws
Turks & Caicos Business Law Handbook Volume 1 Strategic Information and Basic Laws
Tuvalu Business Law Handbook Volume 1 Strategic Information and Basic Laws
Uganda Business Law Handbook Volume 1 Strategic Information and Basic Laws
Ukraine Business Law Handbook Volume 1 Strategic Information and Basic Laws
United Arab Emirates Business Law Handbook Volume 1 Strategic Information and Basic Laws
United Kingdom Business Law Handbook Volume 1 Strategic Information and Basic Laws
United States Business Law Handbook Volume 1 Strategic Information and Basic Laws
Uruguay Business Law Handbook Volume 1 Strategic Information and Basic Laws
Uzbekistan Business Law Handbook Volume 1 Strategic Information and Basic Laws
Vanuatu Business Law Handbook Volume 1 Strategic Information and Basic Laws
Vatican City Business Law Handbook Volume 1 Strategic Information and Basic Laws
Venezuela Business Law Handbook Volume 1 Strategic Information and Basic Laws
Vietnam Business Law Handbook Volume 1 Strategic Information and Basic Laws
Virgin Islands, British Business Law Handbook Volume 1 Strategic Information and Basic Laws
Wake Atoll Business Law Handbook Volume 1 Strategic Information and Basic Laws
Wallis & Futuna Business Law Handbook Volume 1 Strategic Information and Basic Laws
Western Sahara Business Law Handbook Volume 1 Strategic Information and Basic Laws
Yemen Business Law Handbook Volume 1 Strategic Information and Basic Laws
Zambia Business Law Handbook Volume 1 Strategic Information and Basic Laws
Zimbabwe Business Law Handbook Volume 1 Strategic Information and Basic Laws

To order and for additional analytical and marketing information, please contacts
International Business Publications, USA at:
P.O. Box 15343, Washington, DC 20003, USA. Phone: (202) 546-210 Fax: (202) 546-32
E-mail: ibpusa@comcast.net

www.ingramcontent.com/pod-product-compliance
Lightning Source LLC
LaVergne TN
LVHW080032210926
848481LV00011B/3163
* 9 7 8 1 4 3 3 0 8 5 6 3 5 *